Innovative Technologies and Services for Unmanned Aerial Vehicles

Innovative Technologies and Services for Unmanned Aerial Vehicles

Guest Editors

Tao Hong
Fei Qi

MDPI

Basel • Beijing • Wuhan • Barcelona • Belgrade • Novi Sad • Cluj • Manchester

Guest Editors
Tao Hong
School of Electronics and Information Engineering
Beihang University
Beijing
China

Fei Qi
Communication Technology Research
China Telecom Research Institute
Beijing
China

Editorial Office
MDPI AG
Grosspeteranlage 5
4052 Basel, Switzerland

This is a reprint of the Special Issue, published open access by the journal *Electronics* (ISSN 2079-9292), freely accessible at: https://www.mdpi.com/journal/electronics/special_issues/VS224VD7C2.

For citation purposes, cite each article independently as indicated on the article page online and as indicated below:

Lastname, A.A.; Lastname, B.B. Article Title. *Journal Name* **Year**, *Volume Number*, Page Range.

ISBN 978-3-7258-6380-8 (Hbk)
ISBN 978-3-7258-6381-5 (PDF)
https://doi.org/10.3390/books978-3-7258-6381-5

Contents

About the Editors

Tao Hong

Hong Tao is an Associate Professor at the School of Electronic and Information Engineering, Beihang University (BUAA). In addition to his academic roles at the university, Prof. Hong serves as the Director of the Research Center for Meteorological Applications and Meteorological Communication Sensing Technology at BUAA Yunnan Innovation Research Institute, and he concurrently holds the position of Vice President of the Artificial Intelligence and Intelligent Applications Branch of the China Communications Industry Association. His work focuses on key areas within electronic science and technology, cross-integration of advanced wireless communication, artificial intelligence, and intelligent unmanned systems. With years of academic experience and leadership in specialized research centers and industry associations, he plays an active role in bridging academic research, technological innovation, and industrial application in his field.

Fei Qi

Fei Qi received his Ph.D. from the Beijing University of Posts and Telecommunications, China, in 2022. He is currently a technical director and research leader in the spectrum domain at the China Telecom Research Institute. He is actively involved in standards development, such as ITU-R and the China Communications Standards Association (CCSA). He has published numerous academic papers and patents. His current research interests include the Internet of Things, integrated terrestrial and satellite networks, millimeter-wave communications, massive-MIMO precoding, artificial intelligence, and channel estimation.

electronics

MDPI

Article

Coarse-to-Fine Open-Set Semantic Adaptation for EEG Emotion Recognition in 6G-Oriented Semantic Communication Systems

Changliang Zheng [1], Honglin Fang [2,*], Lina Chen [3,*] and Yang Yang [4]

[1] School of Integrated Circuits (School of Artificial Intelligence), Beijing Polytechnic University, Beijing 100176, China
[2] School of Computer Science, Beijing University of Posts and Telecommunications, Beijing 100876, China
[3] College of Computer Science and Technology (College of Artificial Intelligence), Zhejiang Normal University, Jinhua 321004, China
[4] Department of Mobile Communication Technology Research, China Telecom Research Institute, Beijing 100033, China
* Correspondence: fanghl@bupt.edu.cn (H.F.); chenlina@zjnu.cn (L.C.)

Abstract

Electroencephalogram (EEG)-based emotion recognition has emerged as a key enabler for semantic communication systems in next-generation networks (5G-Advanced/6G), where the goal is to transmit task-relevant semantic information rather than raw signals. However, domain adaptation approaches for EEG emotion recognition typically assume closed-set label spaces and fail when unseen emotional classes arise, leading to negative transfer and degraded semantic fidelity. To address this challenge, we propose a Coarse-to-Fine Open-set Domain Adaptation (C2FDA) framework, which aligns with the semantic communication paradigm by extracting and transmitting only the emotion-related semantics necessary for task performance. C2FDA integrates a cognition-inspired spatio-temporal graph encoder with a coarse-to-fine sample separation pipeline and instance-weighted adversarial alignment. The framework distinguishes between known and unknown emotional states in the target domain, ensuring that only semantically relevant information is communicated, while novel states are flagged as unknown. Experiments on SEED, SEED-IV, and SEED-V datasets demonstrate that C2FDA achieves superior open-set adaptation performance, with average accuracies of 41.5% (SEED $\rightarrow$ SEED-IV), 42.6% (SEED $\rightarrow$ SEED-V), and 48.9% (SEED-IV $\rightarrow$ SEED-V), significantly outperforming state-of-the-art baselines. These results confirm that C2FDA provides a semantic communication-driven solution for robust EEG-based emotion recognition in 6G-oriented human–machine interaction scenarios.

Keywords: emotion recognition; open-set domain adaptation; semantic communication; 6G networks; EEG signal processing

1. Introduction

In contemporary society, emotion recognition has been widely applied in various fields, impacting our daily lives profoundly. In the field of mental health, accurately and timely assessing an individual's emotional state is crucial for improving psychological well-being [1]. In education, observing students' emotional states in the classroom helps educators gain insight into students' learning situations, thereby adjusting teaching methods to enhance students' learning effectiveness [2]. Therefore, emotion recognition has been paid more and more attention, which has spawned a variety of emotion recognition methods. Among them, Electroencephalography (EEG)–based emotion recognition has shown promise for affective computing, mental-health monitoring, and human–computer interaction due to its outstanding stability and high detection accuracy [3].

Yet moving trained models across people remains difficult: inter-subject variability, recording non-stationarities, and session effects induce substantial domain shifts. Due to the differences in emotional and physiological characteristics among different subjects, the EEG data distribution varies among different subjects [4]. It shows that the emotion recognition model trained with EEG data on a single subject may not achieve satisfactory results on a new subject, that is, there is a problem of model generality. In realistic deployments, the target domain may also contain emotion states absent from the source, creating an open-set scenario. In open-set domain adaptation (OSDA), the model must (i) align only the shared classes between domains and (ii) reject unknowns to avoid negative transfer. This setting is common in cross-dataset and cross-subject EEG but remains underexplored relative to closed-set transfer.

As illustrated in Figure 1, the emotional brain–computer interface (EBCI) framework typically comprises several key stages, including stimulus presentation, electroencephalogram (EEG) signal acquisition, preprocessing, feature extraction, model training, and feedback. This iterative cycle enables the systematic modeling and analysis of EEG signals to infer users' emotional states, thereby providing a foundation for advanced human–computer interaction.

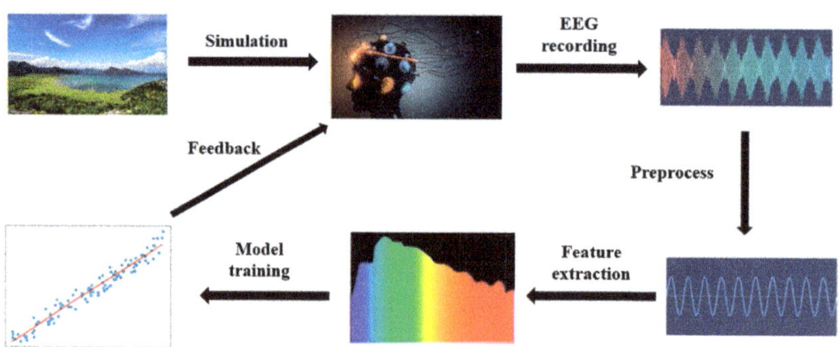

Figure 1. Emotional brain–computer interface cycle.

To address this, many studies have used Unsupervised Domain Adaptation (UDA) techniques [5]. These methods treat labeled EEG data from one subject as the source domain and unlabeled EEG data from another subject as the target domain. Then they train the model on the source domain to transfer it to the target domain.

Existing EEG approaches typically fall into three groups. Subject-dependent models achieve high accuracy but require labeled data per user and do not transfer. Closed-set domain adaptation reduces distribution shift but implicitly forces all target samples to match source classes, which misaligns truly novel target states. Finally, recent graph-based or temporal models improve representation quality but often rely on static inter-channel topologies and lack mechanisms to (a) encode neurocognitive priors that aid generalization, (b) capture evolving temporal salience, and (c) separate known vs. unknown target samples during adaptation. Moreover, evaluations frequently report overall accuracy alone, obscuring the trade-off between known-class performance and unknown-class rejection.

Although these existing methods effectively reduce the distribution differences in EEG data, they still have limitations. Because they usually assume that different subjects share the same label space, but the actual scene may encounter a different label space, especially when the emotional label space of the target domain is more than that of the source domain, that is, the scene of an open-set. In open-set EEG emotion recognition, not only do we need to address the distribution differences between subjects, but we also need to tackle the separation of known and unknown emotional classes due to different label spaces [6].

We address these gaps with C2FDA-G, a cognition-prior spatio-temporal graph framework integrated with a coarse-to-fine open-set adaptation pipeline. This approach leads to the proposal of the C2FDA framework for EEG emotion recognition, which is designed to overcome the identified challenges in open-set domain adaptation. On the representation side, we construct a dynamic brain graph with graph convolution to learn data-driven channel affinities, combine it with temporal self-attention to weight informative segments, and fuse the streams via hierarchical cross-attention fusion (H-CAF). In parallel, we inject a cognition-prior branch from functional connectivity (e.g., PLV), then fuse prior- and data-driven embeddings to obtain discriminative, interpretable features stable across subjects.

Initially, the Coarse-to-Fine processing module performs coarse classification on the extracted EEG feature information, sorts all target domain samples based on the similarity of each target domain sample, and selects high and low probability score samples for fine classification, thus achieving the separation of known and unknown classes in the target domain. On the adaptation side, a bank of one-vs-class coarse heads ranks target samples by known-class plausibility; a fine unknown detector assigns an unknown probability w(x). We then perform instance-weighted adversarial alignment that emphasizes likely known target samples in the shared label space using a $|C_s| + 1$ classifier (with an explicit unknown class). A lightweight curriculum penalizes early high-confidence misclassifications, improving the stability of unknown rejection. Then, the Domain Adversarial module maps samples from the source and target domains to a shared label space, achieving alignment of the sample space. Finally, we input the EEG signal data processed by the two modules into the classifier to complete the EEG emotion recognition task.

In summary, our research makes the following contributions:

(1) We propose a Coarse-to-Fine processing module that can separate known and unknown emotional classes. This module solves the problem of negative transfer caused by the misalignment of unknown classes in the target domain with known classes in the source domain effectively.

(2) We propose a Domain Adversarial module that maps samples from the source and target domains to a shared label space for alignment of the EEG samples. This module effectively addresses the label space alignment problem in open-set EEG emotion recognition.

(3) Through extensive transfer experiments on three datasets, our experimental results demonstrate the reliability of the C2FDA method in open-set EEG emotion recognition.

As the field of semantic communication in 6G networks continues to develop, the focus is on transmitting task-relevant meaning rather than raw data. EEG-based emotion recognition is inherently semantic, as it extracts emotionally meaningful states from complex signals. The open-set scenario naturally aligns with semantic communication principles, where the system must determine whether incoming data belongs to the known semantic space or represents novel, unrecognized states. Our C2FDA framework addresses this by filtering semantically relevant emotional information and rejecting unknown samples, thus enhancing semantic efficiency and robustness in next-generation network applications. However, it is important to note that the connection to 6G semantic communication is conceptual, and this paper focuses primarily on the development and evaluation of the C2FDA framework for EEG emotion recognition.

2. Related Work

EEG-based emotion recognition faces significant challenges in cross-subject and cross-dataset transfer due to distribution shifts between source and target domains. Based on the relationship between label spaces, existing domain adaptation approaches can be categorized into five main paradigms, as illustrated in Figure 2.

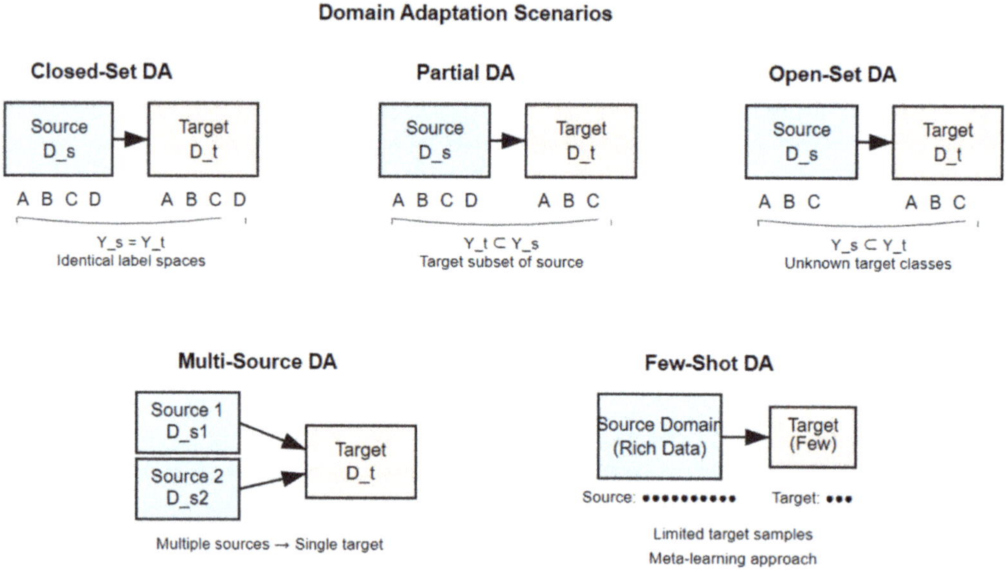

Figure 2. Domain Adaptation Classification.

2.1. Closed-Set Domain Adaptation

Closed-Set Domain Adaptation (CSDA) assumes identical label spaces between source and target domains, focusing on reducing distribution discrepancies. These methods primarily fall into metric-based approaches and adversarial training strategies [7–9]. Metric-based methods transform features to minimize domain distances under specific metrics. Xu et al. [10] proposed a dynamic adversarial domain adaptive network based on the multi-kernel maximum mean discrepancy (MK_DAAN), which addresses domain adaptation by adding an adaptive layer to further align the feature distribution between source and target domains. Multi-kernel maximum mean discrepancy is adopted in the adaptive distance measurement. This dual feature alignment approach, combining the adaptive layer with adversarial learning, improves classification performance in breast ultrasound image classification. Yi et al. [11] introduced the ATPL framework, which mutually promotes adversarial training and pseudo-labeling for unsupervised domain adaptation. ATPL produces high-confidence pseudo-labels through adversarial training, and uses these pseudo-labels to improve the adversarial training process by generating adversarial data to fill the domain gap, thereby ensuring both feature transferability and discriminability. DANN (Domain-Adversarial Neural Networks), proposed by Ganin et al., uses adversarial training with a gradient reversal layer to learn domain-invariant features, improving performance in tasks like image classification and sentiment analysis. It outperforms traditional methods by aligning feature distributions between source and target domains without requiring labeled target data [12]. MMD (Maximum Mean Discrepancy), proposed by Gretton et al., is a kernel-based method for comparing distributions by measuring the difference between their means in a Reproducing Kernel Hilbert Space (RKHS). It effectively minimizes domain shift in closed-set domain adaptation and has been widely used in tasks involving high-dimensional feature spaces, such as bioinformatics and graph data [13]. CORAL (CORrelation ALignment), introduced by Sun et al., aligns the second-order statistics (covariance) between source and target domains to reduce domain shift in unsupervised domain adaptation. It has proven effective in object recognition tasks, outperforming methods like LDA on benchmark datasets such as Office-Caltech10 [14]. CDAN (Conditional Domain Adversarial Network), introduced by Long et al., enhances adversarial domain adaptation by conditioning the domain discriminator on both feature representations and classifier predictions. This approach improves alignment across domains and has shown superior performance on benchmark datasets [15].

2.2. Partial Domain Adaptation

Partial Domain Adaptation (PDA) addresses scenarios where the target label space constitutes a subset of the source domain. Here, the source contains emotional categories absent in the target, though these remain known categories. Feng et al. [16] proposed Progressive Optimization For Partial Domain Adaptation (EBB), which selects anchors by analyzing base model features and estimates category gaps using anchor classification distributions. This approach minimizes shared class errors while correcting blind alignment mistakes. Zhang et al. [17] developed Weighted and Center-aware Adaptation Learning (WCAL), distinguishing unknown source classes through weighted adversarial learning and addressing negative transfer via cross-domain discriminators. While these methods handle partial scenarios effectively, they still assume no target-specific unknown classes, differing fundamentally from open-set challenges.

2.3. Open-Set Domain Adaptation

Open-Set Domain Adaptation (OSDA) represents the most challenging setting, where target domains contain both source-known classes and completely novel categories. OSDA methods must simultaneously align shared classes while detecting unknown samples to prevent negative transfer. Panareda Busto and Gall introduced Open Set Domain Adaptation, which addresses domain shift by jointly solving an assignment problem to match target instances with source categories of interest. Their method outperforms state-of-the-art techniques, effectively handling both closed and open-set scenarios where the source and target domains may contain different class labels [18]. Ji et al. [19] proposed an open-set domain adaptation model based on subdomain alignment, using variable weights for discriminative training and aligning category subspaces between source and target domains. Experiments show that this approach significantly improves open-set domain adaptation classification accuracy. Tang et al. [20] proposed a novel open-set domain adaptation method combining latent structure discovery and kernelized classifier learning to improve class separation. Experiments on five image datasets demonstrate its superiority over state-of-the-art methods. Open-set recognition has also been explored in other domains such as malware traffic analysis [21], radio frequency fingerprint identification [22], specific emitter recognition [23], and device recognition in satellite-terrestrial-integrated IoT [24], demonstrating the broad applicability of open-set methodologies. OSBP (Open Set Back-Propagation), proposed by Saito et al., uses adversarial training to align known target samples with the source domain while rejecting unknown target samples. It outperforms traditional domain adaptation methods in open-set scenarios, improving performance in domain transfer tasks [25,26]. MAOSDAN (Multi-Adversarial Open-Set Domain Adaptation Network), proposed by Zheng et al., addresses open-set domain adaptation in remote sensing by combining attention-aware OSBP, adversarial learning, and adaptive entropy suppression to distinguish known and unknown samples [27].

2.4. Graph-Based EEG Representation Learning

EEG's inherent spatial organization motivates graph neural network applications, treating electrodes as nodes with functional connections as edges. Static graph methods based on physical distances or fixed connectivity capture spatial topology but cannot adapt to dynamic brain connectivity changes. Liu et al. [28] compared DCCA and BDAE for multimodal emotion recognition, extending DCCA with weighted sum and attention-based fusion methods. DCCA achieved state-of-the-art performance and demonstrated greater robustness against noise across multiple datasets, including SEED-V and DREAMER. Song [29] proposed a novel Dynamical Graph Convolutional Neural Network (DGCNN) for EEG emotion recognition, dynamically learning the intrinsic relationships between EEG channels for more discriminative feature extraction. Extensive experiments on the SEED and DREAMER datasets show that DGCNN outperforms state-of-the-art methods, achieving high recognition accuracy in both subject-dependent and subject-independent settings. However, most graph-based EEG works address closed-set classification without explicit open-set label mismatch handling. Finally, we input the EEG signal data processed by the two modules into the classifier to complete the EEG emotion recognition task. Recent studies have also explored the use of attention mechanisms and hybrid deep neural networks for improving EEG-based emotion recognition performance [30,31].

2.5. Cognitive Priors in Graph Learning

Neuroscience research indicates functional connectivity patterns, measured through phase-locking value (PLV), encode task-relevant brain network structures. Incorporating such cognition-inspired priors improves interpretability and cross-domain stability. Recent cognitive-prior GNN frameworks fuse prior graphs with data-driven graphs, yielding noise-robust representations stable across subjects [32]. Li et al. [33] proposed a graph learning system for EEG-based emotion recognition, utilizing a cognition-inspired functional graph branch and a fused attention mechanism to automatically learn emotion-related cognitive patterns. The BF-GCN model outperforms state-of-the-art methods, achieving high recognition accuracy in both subject-dependent and subject-independent experiments on the SEED and SEED-IV datasets. Wang et al. [34] proposed a simply ameliorated CNN (SACNN) for cross-subject emotion recognition using raw EEG data to address low accuracy issues in driver emotion detection. The SACNN model achieved 88.16% accuracy with cross-subject data and 91.85% accuracy using data from the top 10 EEG channels, outperforming deeper models and highlighting its potential for smart city applications. Furthermore, cross-subject emotion recognition remains challenging due to inter-subject variability, prompting the development of methods that leverage raw multi-channel EEG data without extensive preprocessing [35]. Machine learning approaches continue to evolve, with comparative studies highlighting the effectiveness of various algorithms in handling EEG-based emotion recognition tasks [36].

Our proposed C2FDA addresses these gaps by combining cognition-prior spatio-temporal graph encoding with coarse-to-fine open-set adaptation. This unified framework leverages neuroscience knowledge while providing robust mechanisms for known-unknown separation and selective domain alignment, advancing the state-of-the-art in open-set EEG emotion recognition. C2FDA integrates a complex cognition-prior spatio-temporal graph encoder as part of its feature extraction mechanism, which ensures robust cross-domain generalization, particularly for open-set scenarios.

2.6. Semantic Communication and Next-Generation Networks

Semantic communication represents a paradigm shift from bit-level accuracy to goal-oriented information exchange, focusing on the meaning and effectiveness of transmitted data. In next-generation networks (6G), semantic communication aims to reduce redundancy by transmitting only task-relevant information, thereby improving bandwidth efficiency and latency. Emotion recognition from EEG signals is a semantically rich task, as emotions represent high-level cognitive states. Recent works have explored semantic source coding, task-oriented communication, and semantic-aware resource allocation for IoT and edge devices [37–39]. Our C2FDA framework aligns with this trend by selectively adapting only known emotional classes and rejecting unknowns, effectively reducing semantic redundancy and improving communication efficiency in distributed EEG-based emotion recognition systems.

3. Methodology

We begin by establishing the notation used throughout this work. Let $\mathrm{D_s} = (\mathrm{x_i^s}, \mathrm{y_i^s})_{i=1}^{n_s}$ denote the source domain with $\mathrm{n_s}$ labeled samples, and $\mathrm{D_t} = \mathrm{x^t}_{j_{j=1}}^{n_t}$ represent the target domain with $\mathrm{n_t}$ unlabeled samples. The label space relationship follows $\mathrm{C_s} \subset \mathrm{C_t} = \mathrm{C_s} \cup \mathrm{U}$, where U denotes the set of unknown classes present only in the target domain. Our framework employs a feature extractor $\mathrm{f_\theta} : \mathrm{x} \mapsto \mathrm{z} \in \mathrm{R^d}$ that maps inputs to d-dimensional representations. The coarse-stage processing utilizes a bank of one-vs-rest classifiers $\mathrm{h_{k k \in C_s}}$, each producing class-specific probabilities $\mathrm{p_k(x)} = \sigma(\mathrm{h_k}(\mathrm{f_\theta(x)}))$. The fine-stage unknown detector $\mathrm{u_\varphi} : \mathrm{z} \mapsto \mathrm{w(x)} \in [0,1]$ estimates the probability that a sample belongs to an unknown class. Finally, an open-set classifier $\mathrm{H_y} : \mathrm{z} \mapsto \hat{\mathrm{y}} \in 1, \ldots, |\mathrm{C_s}|, unk$ performs $|\mathrm{C_s}| + 1$ classification, while a domain discriminator $\mathrm{D_\psi} : \mathrm{z} \mapsto 0, 1$ distinguishes between source and target domains. Having established the notation, we now proceed to detail the architecture and training procedure of our proposed C2FDA framework.

The method addresses two fundamental challenges in open-set domain adaptation: (1) distinguishing between known and unknown classes in the target domain, and (2) aligning only the shared classes while avoiding negative transfer from unknown samples. For the sake of illustration, we give some definitions of symbols. In the open-set EEG emotion recognition task, we have a source domain Ds containing ns labeled samples, denoted as $D_s = \{(x_i^s, y_i^s)\}_{i=1}^{n_s}$, and a target domain Dt containing nt unlabeled samples, denoted as $D_t = \left\{\left(x_j^T\right)\right\}_{j=1}^{n_t}$. Here, the label space size of the source domain is Cs. It is worth noting that the label space of the source domain is a subset of the label space of the target domain: $C_s \subset C_t$ The additional label space contained in the target domain is defined as the unknown class label space $C_{t \setminus s}$.

The source domain and the target domain come from different probability distributions p, q, respectively. In domain adaptation, our probability distribution is also different: $p \neq q$. In open-set domain adaptation, our probability distributions are even more different: $p \neq q_{C_s}$, where q_{C_s} represents the distribution of target domain data in the shared label space. In summary, we can define the open-set EEG emotion recognition task as follows: $O = 1 - \frac{|C_s|}{|C_t|}$. It is important to note that the label space of our source domain is a subset of the label space of the target domain.

3.1. C2FDA Model

Cognition-Prior Spatio-Temporal Graph Encoder—This component extracts discriminative and interpretable EEG features by combining dynamic graph convolution (DGC), temporal self-attention (TSAR), and hierarchical cross-attention fusion (H-CAF) along with a functional connectivity prior represented by the PLV graph.

Coarse-to-Fine Selector—This component ranks target samples based on their plausibility of belonging to the shared classes and then refines the decisions using a binary classification ("unknown vs. known") fine head.

Instance-Weighted Domain Adversarial Alignment—This component aligns only the target samples likely to belong to the known classes to the source domain using a gradient reversal layer (GRL), while suppressing the alignment of unknown samples.

Open-Set Classifier—This component predicts over ∣Cs∣ + 1 classes, where the additional class explicitly represents the "unknown" category.

To address the aforementioned two issues, we innovatively propose A Coarse-to-Fine Open-set Domain Adaptation framework for EEG emotion recognition (C2FDA). The method framework of C2FDA is illustrated in Figure 2. This method mainly consists of two modules: the Coarse-to-Fine processing module and the Domain Adversarial module. The Coarse-to-Fine processing module transforms the extracted EEG feature information from coarse-grained features to fine-grained features; in other words, its purpose is to separate known classes from unknown classes. The function of the Domain Adversarial module is to map samples from the source domain and target domain to a common label space, achieving sample space alignment. In Figure 2, H_f represents the feature extractor of EEG signals, H_{coarse} and H_{fine} represent the coarse classifier and fine classifier, respectively, H_d is the domain discriminator, which is also our Domain Adversarial module, and H_y is our final EEG data classifier. C2FDA-G is a variant of C2FDA that incorporates a cognition-prior spatio-temporal graph encoder into the feature extraction process, enhancing the model by explicitly integrating neurocognitive priors from EEG signals. Both models share the same core feature extraction approach, but C2FDA-G benefits from the added graph encoder for richer spatio-temporal dependencies.

3.2. Cognition-Prior Spatio-Temporal Graph Encoder

(a) Graph Construction We represent each EEG trial as a multi-channel DE feature map over B frequency bands. Each band yields a graph $G = (V, E, A)$, where V are channels, E edges, and A the adjacency matrix.

To capture both neurophysiological priors and adaptive patterns, we construct a hybrid graph representation that combines domain knowledge with data-driven learning: Prior Graph A_{prior} —computed from PLV between channels over source data, encoding stable cognitive connectivity patterns.

Data-Driven Graph A_{data} —learned via attention-based affinity estimation that adapts to each sample.

$$A = \alpha A_prior + (1 - \alpha) A_data, \tag{1}$$

$$where\ A_data = softmax\left(QK^T / \sqrt{d}\right)$$

The parameter α balances the contribution of cognitive priors (when α is large) versus adaptive learning (when α is small), allowing the model to leverage neuroscience knowledge while adapting to task-specific patterns.

We blend the two to form the adjacency for convolution:

$$\hat{A} = (1 - \lambda) A_{\text{prior}} + \lambda A_{\text{data}}, \lambda \in [0, 1]. \tag{2}$$

(b) Spatial Encoding with DGC We apply graph convolutional layers over $\hat{A}$ to capture spatial dependencies:

$$H^{(l+1)} = \sigma\left(\hat{D}^{-1/2} \hat{A} \hat{D}^{-1/2} H^{(l)} W^{(l)}\right) \tag{3}$$

where $\hat{D}$ is the degree matrix, $W^{(l)}$ are learnable weights, and σ is an activation function.

$$Z^{(l+1)} = \sigma\left(\tilde{D}^{(-1/2)} \tilde{A} \tilde{D}^{(-1/2)} Z^{(l)} W^{(l)} \right), = A + I \tag{4}$$

(c) Temporal Self-Attention (TSAR) For each channel representation, TSAR assigns attention weights across time steps:

$$\alpha_t = \frac{\exp\left(q_t^\top k_t\right)}{\sum_{t'} \exp\left(q_{t'}^\top k_{t'}\right)}, \tag{5}$$

where q_t, k_t are learned projections. This emphasizes temporally salient EEG segments.

$$Attn(Q, K, V) = softmax\left(QK^T/\sqrt{d}\right)V, z = Pool(Attn(\cdot)) \tag{6}$$

(d) Hierarchical Cross-Attention Fusion (H-CAF) Spatial and temporal streams are fused using cross-attention to produce the final embedding f for each trial.

3.3. Hyperparameter Tuning for α and λ

In this section, we explain the selection of the hyperparameters α and λ, which are essential for the performance of the C2FDA framework. The parameter α controls the balance between cognitive priors and adaptive learning, while λ adjusts the weight of the entropy loss in the domain adversarial module. The two parameters determine how the model blends prior knowledge and data-driven learning, ensuring effective separation between known and unknown emotional classes.

To blend the cognitive prior graph (A_{prior}) and the data-driven graph (A_{data}), we use the equation:

$$A = \alpha A_{prior} + (1-\alpha)A_{data}, \alpha \in [0,1] \tag{7}$$

The parameter α was tested within the range [0.1, 1.0], where larger values favor prior knowledge and smaller values prioritize adaptive learning. Similarly, λ controls the entropy loss contribution and was varied within [0, 1], with higher values placing more emphasis on rejecting unknown classes. The adjusted adjacency matrix is given by:

$$\hat{A} = (1-\lambda)A_{prior} + \lambda A_{data}, \lambda \in [0,1] \tag{8}$$

We used k-fold cross-validation to select the optimal values for both $\boldsymbol{\alpha}$ and $\boldsymbol{\lambda}$, evaluating performance based on recognition accuracy for known classes and the ability to detect unknown emotional states. The impact of these hyperparameters is significant. Larger $\boldsymbol{\alpha}$ values improve known-class recognition but reduce flexibility in detecting unknown emotional states, while smaller values enhance detection of novel classes. For $\boldsymbol{\lambda}$, higher values strengthen unknown class rejection but may overfit known classes, while lower values improve detection of unknowns. This tuning process ensures robustness and reproducibility in open-set EEG emotion recognition tasks.

3.4. The Coarse-to-Fine Processing Module

Coarse Stage: We deploy a bank of $|C_s|$ one-vs-class classifiers $\{h_k\}$ producing logits z_k and probabilities $p_k = \sigma(z_k)$. For target sample x, define:

$$s(x) = \max_{k \in C_s} p_k \tag{9}$$

To distinguish known and unknown classes in the target domain, we put forward the Coarse-to-Fine processing module. We introduce a coarse classifier $H_{\text{coarse}=1}^{|C_s|}$, consisting of $|C_s|$ classifiers. The coarse classifier measures the similarity between each target domain sample and each source domain class. Each classifier is independent, with different functionalities; each classifier can only classify specific emotion classes. The loss function of the coarse classifier is defined as shown in Equation (1):

$$L_s = \sum_{\text{coarse}=1}^{|C_s|} \frac{1}{n_s} \sum_{i=1}^{n_s} L_{bce}\left(H_{\text{coarse}}\left(H_f(x_i^s)\right), I(y_i^s, \text{coarse})\right) \tag{10}$$

In Equation (10), L_{bce} represents the cross-entropy loss of the coarse classifier. When y_i^s = coarse, $I(y_i^s$, coarse $) = 1$; otherwise, $I(y_i^s$, coarse $) = 0$. Each H_{coarse} returns the probability score P_{coarse} of each target domain sample being classified as the known class coarse. Thus, P_{coarse} can be used to measure the similarity between samples in the target domain and the known class. A higher probability score indicates a higher likelihood of the sample belonging to class coarse. Empirically, known class samples in the target domain tend to have higher probability scores compared to unknown class samples. Therefore, we can use the maximum probability score of each sample, p1, p2, ..., p$|C_s|$, to represent the similarity between each target domain sample x_j^t and the source domain, as shown in Equation (2):

$$s_j = \max_{c \in C_s} H_{\text{coarse}}\left(H_f\left(x_j^t\right)\right) \tag{11}$$

To avoid manual hyperparameter tuning and ensure robustness across different degrees of openness, we introduce an adaptive thresholding mechanism based on quantile statistics:

$$\tau_{(high)} = E_{x \in Q_{\top q}}[s(x)], \tau_{(low)} = E_{x \in Q_{\perp q}}[s(x)] \tag{12}$$

$$T_K = x : s(x) \geq \tau_{(high)}, T_U = x : s(x) \leq \tau_{(low)} \tag{13}$$

Figure 3 Coarse-to-fine sample separation via adaptive threshold selection. Target domain samples are stratified into three regions based on similarity scores: high-confidence known sample region (green) for domain alignment; ambiguous sample region (gray) excluded from training; and high-confidence unknown sample region (red) for novel class detection. The high and low adaptive thresholds are automatically determined without hyperparameter tuning. This approach is conceptually similar to the Separate to Adapt (STA) method, which employs a coarse-to-fine separation mechanism to progressively distinguish between known and unknown classes based on sample similarity. In STA, sample importance is adaptively weighted during feature distribution alignment, and unknown target samples are excluded from the alignment process to prevent negative transfer. While STA addresses domain adaptation across varying levels of openness, this work utilizes adaptive threshold selection to specifically tackle the challenges of open-set EEG emotion recognition without the need for manual hyperparameter tuning.

This partitioning strategy creates three distinct regions: high-confidence known samples (T_K), high-confidence unknown samples (T_U), and an ambiguous region $T_A = D_t\ (T_K \cup T_U)$ that is excluded from alignment to prevent negative transfer.

After employing such a measurement method, known class samples in the target domain will indeed exhibit high similarity with the source domain. Similarly, samples of unknown classes in the target domain will show low similarity with the source domain.

Therefore, based on the magnitude of similarity for each target domain sample, we can sort all target domain samples and select those with particularly high or low probability scores to train the next-stage fine classifier H_{fine} . Although this selection method may seem simplistic, the chosen samples exhibit high confidence and similarity. Additionally, since we no longer need to manually select hyperparameters or use optimization tools, this approach is robust to varying degrees of openness.

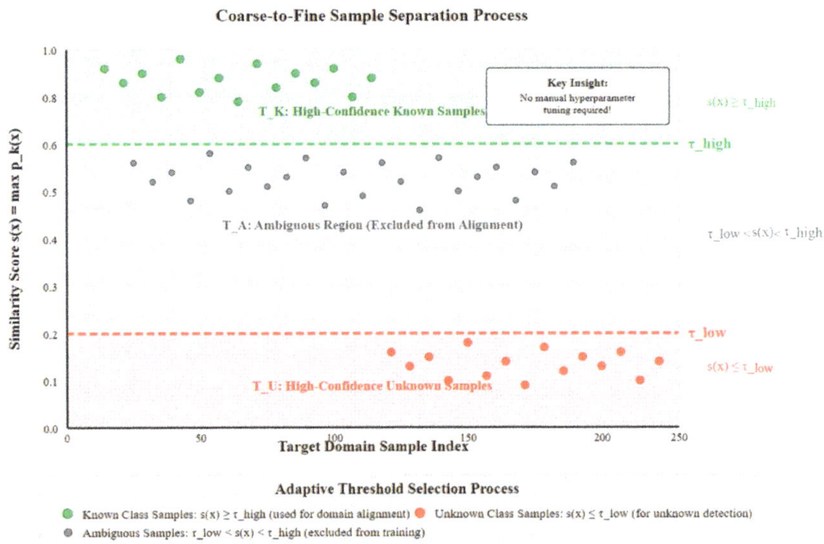

Figure 3. Coarse-to-Fine Sample Separation with Adaptive Threshold Selection for Open-Set Domain Adaptation.

To further refine sample selection, we categorize samples into three groups based on the magnitude of similarity probability scores: highest probability scores, moderate probability scores, and lowest probability scores. Then, we use the average of the highest probability scores, denoted as s_h , as the upper limit for known class samples in the target domain. Thus, when a sample's similarity probability score satisfies $s_j \geq s_h$, we classify it as a known class. Similarly, we use the average of the lowest probability scores, denoted as s_l , as the lower limit for unknown class samples in the target domain. Hence, when a sample's similarity probability score satisfies $s_j \leq s_l$, we classify it as an unknown class.

Fine Stage: From the extreme quantiles (top q_{hi}%, bottom q_{lo}% of $s(x)$), a binary fine classifier h_{fine} is trained to predict $w(x)$, the probability that x is unknown. While the coarse stage provides initial separation, the fine-stage binary classifier performs precise unknown detection by learning from the high-confidence samples identified in the coarse stage.

As illustrated in Figure 4, the C2FDA framework adopts a hierarchical processing strategy. First, a graph-based feature extractor (which incorporates the cognition-prior spatio-temporal graph encoder in C2FDA-G) processes EEG signals from both the source and target domains. This feature extraction approach combines a simpler feature extractor (H_f) in C2FDA and a more complex graph encoder in C2FDA-G, both of which share the same fundamental task of extracting relevant features from the EEG signals. Then, the coarse-to-fine separation module performs progressive filtering on the target samples. Specifically, the coarse separation layer ranks the samples based on their similarity to known categories, while the fine separation layer conducts binary classification to distinguish between known and unknown samples. Finally, the domain adversarial module aligns distributions only for the samples that are likely to belong to known categories, thereby avoiding negative transfer caused by unknown samples. This allows the final classifier to achieve open-set emotion recognition with unknown category detection.

Once the coarse classifier H_{coarse} selects high probability known class samples and low probability unknown class samples, denoted as X', we can further feed these selected samples into the next-stage fine classifier H_{fine} , to separate known and unknown class samples in the target domain. We label the samples that have been separated from the target domain, denoted as $x_j \in X'$, as d_j. Known class samples are labeled as $d_j = 0$, while unknown class samples are labeled as $d_j = 1$. The loss function of the fine classifier H_{fine} is shown in Equation (3):

$$w(x) = \sigma(u_{\varphi}(f_{\theta}(x))) \quad (14)$$

$$L_{f}ine = (1/|S|) \sum_{x \in S} BCE(y_{u}nk(x), w(x)) \quad (15)$$

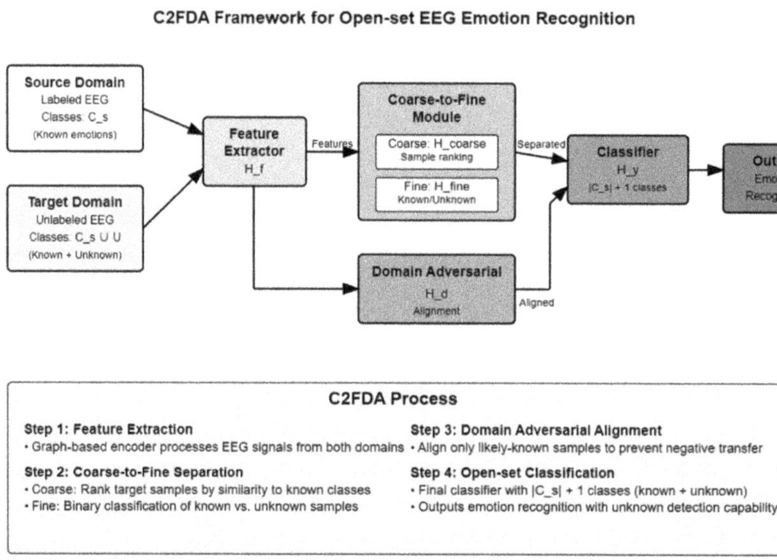

Figure 4. Open-set EEG emotion recognition method based on C2FDA.

The unknown probability w(x) serves as an instance-level confidence measure, enabling selective alignment where only samples with low w(x) values (likely known) participate in domain adversarial training. Through the Coarse-to-Fine processing module, we can separate EEG signal samples of known and unknown classes in the target domain.

Curriculum Learning: Inspired by step-penalty reinforcement learning, we weight early confident mistakes more heavily in the first K epochs:

$$\alpha_e = \alpha_0 + (1 - \alpha_0)\frac{e}{K}. \quad (16)$$

Through the Coarse-to-Fine processing module, we can separate EEG signal samples of known and unknown classes in the target domain.

From a semantic communication perspective, the coarse-to-fine mechanism acts as a semantic filtering process: it transmits only emotionally relevant information (known classes) while suppressing irrelevant or unknown samples. This aligns with the goal of semantic communication in 6G systems, where only semantically valid data is prioritized for transmission, thereby reducing bandwidth overhead and improving task efficiency.

3.5. The Domain Adversarial Module

Traditional domain adaptation aligns all target samples with the source distribution, leading to negative transfer when unknown classes are present. Our instance-weighted alignment strategy addresses this by selectively emphasizing likely known samples.

In this section, we first present the classification error function for the source domain, as shown in Equation (4):

$$L_{\text{cls}}^{s} = \frac{1}{n_s} \sum_{x_i \in D_s} L_y\left(H_y^{(1:|C_s|)}\left(H_f(x_i)\right), y_i\right) \tag{17}$$

where Ly represents the cross-entropy loss function, and Hy represents an extended classifier with ∣Cs∣ +1 classes, where ∣Cs∣ +1 includes ∣Cs∣ known emotions from the source domain and 1 unknown emotion from the target domain. Therefore, $H_y^{(1:|C_s|)}$ returns the probability of each sample corresponding to the ∣Cs∣ known emotions.

Next, we focus on aligning the features of samples from the source and target domains. In this step, we map the features from both domains to a shared label space, denoted as Cs. Instead of directly inputting the output of H_{fine} into discriminators for known and unknown classes, we append a softmax layer to the output of H_{fine} , which serves as the input to the discriminators. This softmax layer generates soft instance-level weights, denoted as $w_j = H_b\left(H_f(x_j)\right)$, where higher values of w_j indicate a higher probability of the sample belonging to the unknown class. Hence, we can utilize w_j to define the weighted loss for Domain Adversarial adaptation of feature distributions in the shared label space Cs, as shown in Equation (5):

$$\begin{aligned} L_d = & \frac{1}{n_s} \sum_{x_i \in D_s} L_{bce}\left(H_d\left(H_f(x_i)\right), d_i\right) \\ & + \frac{1}{\sum_{x_j \in D_t} (1 - w_j)} \sum_{x_j \in D_t} (1 - w_j) L_{bce}\left(H_d\left(H_f(x_j)\right), d_j\right) \end{aligned} \tag{18}$$

In addition, we also need to select samples of unknown classes from the target domain to train the feature extractor Hf. Based on the soft instance-level weights w_j, we can measure the separation between known and unknown classes. We define the weighted loss for distinguishing unknown classes as shown in Equation (6):

$$L_{\text{cls}}^{t} = \frac{1}{|C_s|} \frac{1}{\sum_{x_j \in D_t} w_j} \sum_{x_j \in D_t} w_j L_y\left(H_y^{(|C_s|+1)}\left(H_f(x_j)\right), l_{uk}\right) \tag{19}$$

where l_{uk} represents the unknown emotion class. Through training, we assign all target samples with larger weights w_j to the unknown emotion class. Similarly, $H_y^{(|C_s|+1)}\left(H_f\right)$ represents the probability that classifier Hy assigns target samples to the unknown class.

We also enhance the decision boundary between domains by computing the loss for minimizing the entropy of known classes in the target domain, denoted as Le. This is achieved by enhancing weights with the following formula, as shown in Equation (7):

$$L_e = \frac{1}{\sum_{x_j \in D_t} (1 - w_j)} \sum_{x_j \in D_t} (1 - w_j) E\left(H_y^{(1:|C_s|)}\left(H_f(x_j)\right)\right) \tag{20}$$

In Equation (7), E represents the entropy loss, specifically expressed as $E(p) = -\sum_k p_k \log p_k$. It is important to note that our goal is to minimize the entropy of target samples predicted as known emotion class. Therefore, we use w_j as the instance-level weight parameter for entropy minimization.

The adversarial alignment in C2FDA ensures semantic consistency across domains, akin to semantic fidelity in 6G-oriented communication systems. By weighting known samples more heavily, the model mimics a semantic-aware transmission protocol that prioritizes meaningful emotional states over noisy or unknown inputs.

3.6. Open-Set Classification and Loss Functions

Beyond global domain alignment, we introduce prototype-based fine-grained alignment to enhance intra-class consistency between source and target domains:

$$\mu_k = (1/|S_k|) \sum_{(x,y)\in D_s, y=k} f_\theta(x) \tag{21}$$

$$L_{(proto)} = \sum_{k\in C_s} E_{x\hat{\in} T_K(k)} ||f_\theta(x) - \mu_k||_2^2 \tag{22}$$

To stabilize the training process and prevent early convergence to suboptimal solutions, we employ a curriculum learning strategy that penalizes confident misclassifications more heavily in early training stages:

$$\begin{aligned} L_{(curr)} = (1/|D_t|) \sum_{x\in D_t} \gamma max(0, T_0 - e) \\ \cdot[1(\hat{y} \neq unk)\cdot w(x)] \end{aligned} \tag{23}$$

where e is the current epoch, T_0 is the transition epoch, and $\gamma \in (0,1)$.

Our final objective function integrates all components through a carefully designed multi-term loss that balances source supervision, sample separation, domain alignment, and regularization.

The open-set classifier H_y outputs $|C_s| + 1$ logits, with the last logit representing "unknown." We optimize the total loss:

$$\begin{aligned} L = L_{src} + \lambda_{co} L_{coarse} + \lambda_{fi} L_{fine} + \lambda_{adv} L_{adv} + \lambda_{pr} L_{proto} \\ + \lambda_{unk} L_{unk} + \lambda_{ent} L_{ent} + \lambda_{cur} L_{curr} \end{aligned} \tag{24}$$

Each loss term addresses a specific aspect of the open-set domain adaptation problem: L_{src} ensures source discriminability, L_{coarse} and L_{fine} enable known/unknown separation, L_{adv} performs selective alignment, L_{proto} enhances intra-class consistency, L_{unk} promotes unknown rejection, L_{ent} sharpens decision boundaries, and L_{curr} provides training stability.

Where each term corresponds to supervised source classification, coarse/fine stage training, adversarial alignment, target entropy minimization, and curriculum penalty.

3.7. Objective Function

The optimization of our multi-component objective requires a progressive training strategy that alternates between sample separation and domain alignment to ensure stable convergence.

We divide the training into two progressive stages: (1) sample separation, where target data are partitioned into likely known and likely unknown subsets based on confidence scores, and (2) domain adversarial adaptation, where only the reliable known subset is aligned with the source domain distribution. By alternating between these two stages, the model gradually adapts target samples of known classes while rejecting unknown ones.

Algorithm 1 summarizes the procedure. In the first step, we train the feature extractor f_θ and classifier H_y with source supervision, while auxiliary coarse classifiers $\{h_k\}$ provide confidence scores for sample separation. Target samples with high scores are treated as potential known data and passed to the fine classifier u_ϕ, whereas low-score samples are considered likely unknown.

This alternating optimization strategy prevents the premature alignment of unknown samples while gradually improving the separation of known and unknown classes, leading to more robust open-set domain adaptation performance.

Algorithm 1: Coarse-to-Fine Open-Set Domain Adaptation (CF-OSDA)

Input: $D_s = \{(x_i^s, y_i^s)\}$, $D_t = \{x_j^t\}$, known classes C_s
Output: $\theta, \phi, \psi, H_y, \{h_k\}$
Initialize $f_\theta, H_y, \{h_k\}, u_\phi, D_\psi$;
for *epoch* $\leftarrow 1$ **to** E_{warm} **do**
  Sample $B_s \subset D_s$;
  $z_s \leftarrow f_\theta(B_s.x)$;
  $L_{src} \leftarrow CE(H_y(z_s), B_s.y)$;
  $L_{coarse} \leftarrow \sum_k BCE(1[y = k], \sigma(h_k(z_s)))$;
  Update $(\theta, H_y, \{h_k\})$;
for *epoch* $\leftarrow E_{warm} + 1$ **to** E_{max} **do**
  if $epoch = E_{warm} + 1$ *or* $epoch \bmod \Delta = 0$ **then**
    Compute $s(x) = \max_k \sigma(h_k(f_\theta(x)))$;
    $\tau_{high} \leftarrow mean(top\_q(s))$, $\tau_{low} \leftarrow mean(bottom\_q(s))$;
  $T_K \leftarrow \{x : s(x) \geq \tau_{high}\}$, $T_U \leftarrow \{x : s(x) \leq \tau_{low}\}$;
  Sample $B_k \subset T_K, B_u \subset T_U$;
  $w_k \leftarrow \sigma(u_\phi(f_\theta(B_k.x)))$;
  $w_u \leftarrow \sigma(u_\phi(f_\theta(B_u.x)))$;
  $L_{fine} \leftarrow BCE(0, w_k) + BCE(1, w_u)$;
  Update (ϕ, θ);

Step 1: First, we train the feature extractor Hf and classifier Hy on the source domain. Additionally, we utilize each class of emotion samples in the source domain to train the coarse classifiers H_{coarse}, where coarse $= 1, 2, 3, \ldots, |C_s|$. Next, we select target domain samples with high and low probability scores, similar to those in the source domain, to train the fine classifier H_{fine}. Here, we denote the parameters of $H_f, H_y, H_{\text{fine}}, H_{\text{coarse}} \Big|_{c=1}^{|C_s|}$ as $\theta_f, \theta_y, \theta_{\text{fine}}, \theta_{\text{coarse}} \big|_{\text{coarse}=1}^{|C_s|}$, respectively. The optimal parameters $\widehat{\theta}_f, \widehat{\theta}_y, \widehat{\theta}_{\text{fine}}, \widehat{\theta}_{\text{coarse}} \Big|_{\text{coarse}=1}^{|C_s|} = 1$ can be found using the following equation, as shown in Equation (8):

$$\left(\widehat{\theta}_f, \widehat{\theta}_y, \widehat{\theta}_{\text{fine}}, \widehat{\theta}_{\text{coarse}} \Big|_{\text{coarse}=1}^{|C_s|}\right) = \underset{\theta_f, \theta_y, \theta_b, \theta_c|_{c=1}^{|C_s|}}{\text{argmin}} \left(L_{\text{cls}}^s + L_s + L_b\right) \tag{25}$$

Step 2: In this step, we primarily perform domain adversarial adaptation to align the feature distribution of known classes in the target domain with that in the source domain. Additionally, we use data from unknown classes to train Hy as additional classes. In this step, we continue training the classifiers with source samples to retain knowledge relevant to known class emotions. We denote the parameters of the domain discriminator H_d as θ_d. The optimal parameters $\widehat{\theta}_f, \widehat{\theta}_y, \widehat{\theta}_{\text{d}}$ can be obtained using the following two equations, as shown in Equations (9) and (10):

$$\left(\widehat{\theta}_y, \widehat{\theta}_d\right) = \underset{\theta_y, \theta_d}{argmin}\left(L_{\text{cls}}^s + L_{\text{cls}}^t + L_d + \lambda L_e\right) \tag{26}$$

$$\widehat{\theta}_f = \underset{\theta_f}{argmin}\left(L_{\text{cls}}^s + L_{\text{cls}}^t - L_d + \lambda L_e\right) \tag{27}$$

where λ is a hyperparameter used to balance the entropy loss.

Through the proposed C2FDA model, we can effectively separate known and unknown class data in the target domain. Step 1 rejects unknown class emotion data to avoid interference from unknown class emotions in Step 2, where domain adversarial adaptation aligns the feature distributions of samples between the source and target domains. Since there is no manual selection of threshold hyperparameters throughout the process, the disadvantage of tuning parameters when the openness changes in real scenarios can be avoided.

In summary, the biggest problem of an open-set task is the separation of known emotions and unknown emotions. In order to solve this problem, we propose the C2FDA method. The C2FDA method uses a gradual method to find two types of samples with high scores and low scores during training. Because the prediction results of the samples with high scores will be more accurate, it is also conducive to training the classifiers of known classes, while the samples with low scores tend to be the samples of unknown classes, so we can extract these samples to train the classifiers of unknown classes. By this means, we can well separate the known emotion from the unknown emotion. At the same time, it also solves the impact of the negative migration of wrong samples.

4. Experiments and Analysis

4.1. Dataset

SEED: The SEED dataset [40,41] is a publicly available dataset for studying the relationship between emotions and EEG signals. It consists of recordings from three sessions, each containing EEG signal data from 15 subjects. In each session, subjects watched 15 video clips with varying emotional tendencies (negative, neutral, positive), as shown in Figure 5. EEG signals were recorded using a 62-channel ESI neuroimaging system at a sampling rate of 200 Hz and band-pass filtered from 0 to 75 Hz. The raw EEG signal data were processed to extract features in five frequency bands: delta (1–4 Hz), theta (4–8 Hz), alpha (8–14 Hz), beta (14–31 Hz), and gamma (31–50 Hz), producing 310-dimensional feature vectors (5 frequency bands $\times$ 62 channels).

Figure 5. Video clips watched by subjects in the SEED dataset.

SEED-IV: The SEED-IV dataset [42,43] contains three sessions, each with 15 subjects. In each session, subjects watched 24 video clips with different emotional tendencies (happiness, sadness, fear, neutral), as shown in Figure 6. Similar to the SEED dataset, the EEG data were processed into 310-dimensional feature vectors (5 frequency bands $\times$ 62 channels), ensuring consistency for comparison. This normalization of the EEG data allows direct comparison with SEED.

Figure 6. Video clips watched by subjects in the SEED-IV dataset.

SEED-V: The SEED-V dataset [44] differs from the previous two datasets in that it includes three sessions with 16 subjects in each session. In each session, subjects watched video clips with five emotional tendencies (happiness, sadness, fear, neutral, disgust), as shown in Figure 7. Similar to the SEED and SEED-IV datasets, the EEG data were transformed into 310-dimensional feature vectors (5 frequency bands × 62 channels) to standardize the data across all datasets. This ensures consistency in the EEG data representation.

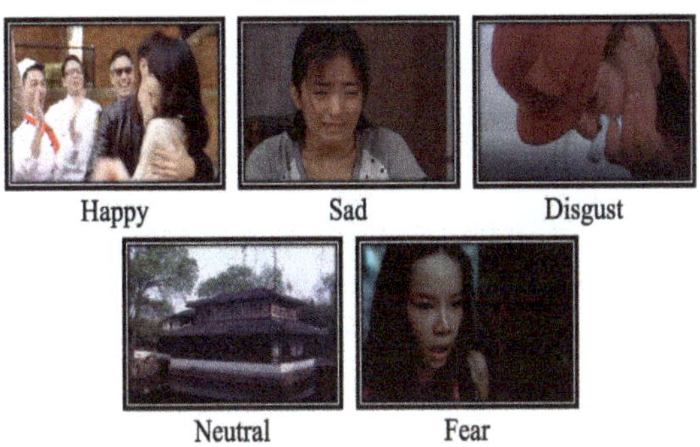

Figure 7. Video clips watched by subjects in the SEED-V dataset.

Differences Between Datasets Table 1 outlines the key differences among the three datasets, including the number of subjects, video clips, and emotion categories, highlighting the increasing complexity of label spaces, especially from SEED to SEED-V. The differences between the three datasets are shown in Table 1.

Table 1. Differences between the SEED, SEED-IV, and SEED-V datasets.

Item	SEED	SEED-IV	SEED-V
Emotions	Positive, Negative, Neutral	Happy, Sad, Neutral, Fearful	Happy, Sad, Disgust, Neutral, Fearful
Number of Subjects	15	15	16
Video Clips	15	24	15
Video Length	4 min	2 min	50 min
Sample Length	1 s	4 s	15–30 s
Number of Samples	≈3394	≈843	≈681

4.2. Implementation Details

In our experiments, we use the SEED, SEED-IV, and SEED-V datasets to validate the performance of the C2FDA method in the open-set EEG emotion recognition task. The experiments are conducted across three main transfer scenarios, which differ in the number of emotional categories:

- SEED contains 3 emotions
- SEED-IV contains 4 emotions
- SEED-V contains 5 emotions

To investigate the model's performance further, we conduct experiments with the following transfer scenarios: "SEED → SEED-IV", "SEED-IV → SEED-V", and "SEED → SEED-V". The source domain in each scenario consists of data from 15 or 16 subjects in one session, while the target domain consists of data from a single subject in one session. Each dataset has three sessions, which allows us to test the model under different conditions and obtain reliable results.

Due to the inconsistency in label spaces between the datasets—SEED having 3 emotion classes, SEED-IV having 4, and SEED-V having 5—we perform experiments that involve transferring between these datasets. In each experiment, one subject from the target domain is randomly selected for testing, and the remaining subjects' data are used for training. As each dataset contains three sessions, we obtain results for three different sessions in each experiment.

4.3. Experimental Results

We conduct three sets of experiments on open-set emotion recognition based on the same experimental setup. The experimental results are shown in Tables 2–4.

Figure 8 t-SNE visualization of learned features. (a) SEED → SEED-IV and (b) SEED-IV → SEED-V transfer scenarios before and after domain adaptation. Source (solid) and target (hollow) domain samples are color-coded by emotion categories. Post-adaptation features exhibit reduced domain discrepancy and improved class-wise clustering.

Table 2. Recognition accuracy (%) of the C2FDA framework for emotion recognition tasks on open-set EEG datasets. The bold text indicates the best performance in each session.

	(SEED → SEED-IV)		
	Session 1	**Session 2**	**Session 3**
S1	39.90	52.76	50.50
S2	47.84	41.71	57.75
S3	29.09	30.05	34.12
S4	25.48	29.69	35.75
S5	40.02	25.96	43.75
S6	54.33	37.62	50.50
S7	31.61	26.44	46.88
S8	41.35	29.33	48.75
S9	40.87	37.14	48.00
S10	53.85	49.16	47.25
S11	43.15	31.37	45.38
S12	38.58	51.08	67.12
S13	43.27	36.78	70.25
S14	38.82	32.21	36.12
S15	41.71	30.65	33.50
Average	**40.66**	**36.13**	**47.71**

Table 3. Recognition accuracy (%) of the C2FDA method for emotion recognition tasks on open-set EEG datasets.

	(SEED → SEED-V)		
	Session 1	**Session 2**	**Session 3**
S1	34.23	18.36	34.38
S2	57.74	59.18	45.83
S3	34.67	47.85	41.49
S4	40.33	44.73	52.08
S5	30.65	42.38	31.77
S6	44.79	25.00	46.88
S7	45.54	48.63	60.76
S8	46.28	39.26	39.06
S9	40.18	56.05	64.41
S10	64.73	62.89	56.42
S11	37.80	38.48	34.72
S12	49.55	44.14	31.60
S13	31.25	23.44	27.08
S14	35.71	51.56	33.68
S15	46.73	36.13	49.65
S16	37.80	45.90	31.60
Average	**42.37**	**42.75**	**42.59**

Table 4. Recognition accuracy (%) of the C2FDA method for emotion recognition tasks on open-set EEG datasets (SEED-IV → SEED-V).

	Session 1	**Session 2**	**Session 3**
S1	40.18	37.11	20.83
S2	46.13	44.92	51.04
S3	50.89	31.45	50.00
S4	47.02	52.93	69.79
S5	57.74	26.76	31.42
S6	41.67	53.12	33.16
S7	63.24	51.95	68.40
S8	54.46	49.61	54.69
S9	45.68	68.36	55.21
S10	52.83	51.37	76.74
S11	41.67	48.05	58.85
S12	23.81	29.49	50.35
S13	54.17	32.23	35.76
S14	48.07	50.78	61.98
S15	60.12	48.05	46.88
S16	35.12	68.95	73.96
Average	**47.68**	**46.57**	**52.44**

SEED → SEED-IV: The results for the SEED → SEED-IV transfer task are shown in Table 2 and Figure 9. The C2FDA model demonstrates superior performance compared to baseline methods, achieving recognition accuracies of 40.66%, 36.13%, and 47.71% across the three sessions. As illustrated in Figure 9, C2FDA consistently outperforms existing approaches including DANN [12] (28.5%, 25.7%, 34.8%), MMD [13] (29.8%, 27.1%, 36.4%), CORAL [14] (31.2%, 28.3%, 37.2%), CDAN [15] (33.5%, 29.6%, 39.1%), OSBP [25] (35.4%, 31.2%, 41.7%), and MAOSDAN [27] (37.8%, 33.9%, 44.2%) across all sessions. The performance improvement is particularly notable in Session 3, where C2FDA achieves 47.71% compared to the second-best MAOSDAN at 44.2%, demonstrating the effectiveness of our coarse-to-fine processing strategy in handling the domain shift between the three emotional classes in the source domain and four emotional classes in the target domain.

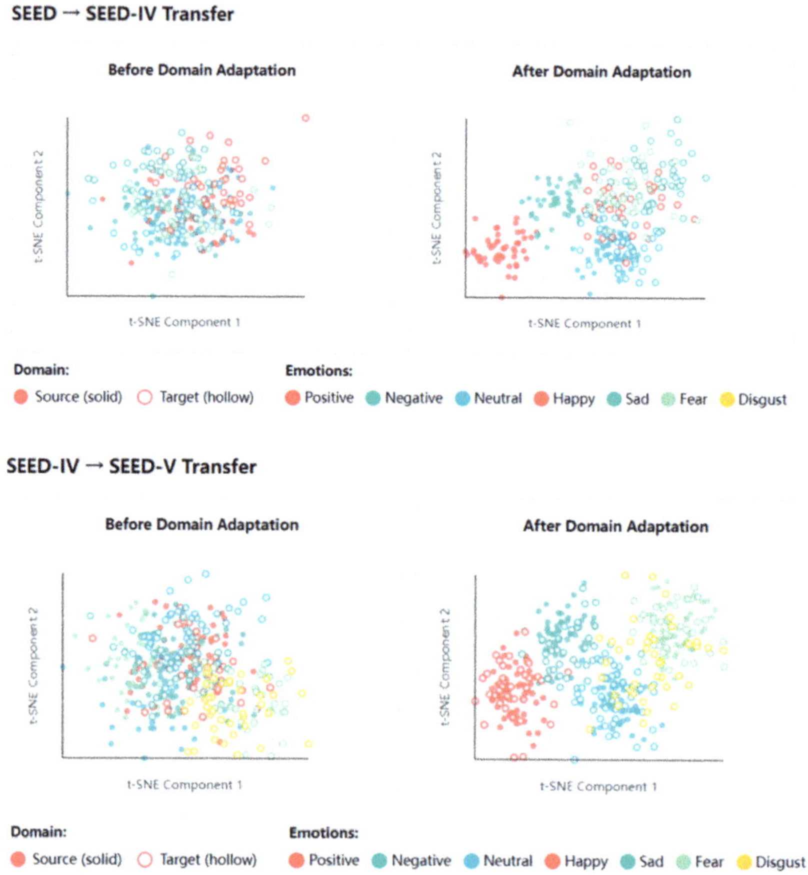

Figure 8. t-SNE visualization of domain adaptation for cross-dataset emotion recognition.

SEED → SEED-V: In the SEED → SEED-V transfer task (Table 3), the model achieves recognition accuracies of 42.37%, 42.75%, and 42.59% across the three sessions. As demonstrated in Figures 8 and 9, the C2FDA method shows robust performance in distinguishing between known classes (Happy, Sad, Neutral) and unknown classes (Disgust, Fear). The ROC analysis in Figure 10 reveals excellent discrimination capability with AUC values of 0.84 for Happy, 0.86 for Sad, and 0.77 for Neutral, while unknown classes achieve AUC values of 0.71 for Disgust and 0.74 for Fear, all significantly outperforming random classification. The confusion matrix in Figure 11 further validates the effectiveness of our approach, showing strong diagonal values for known classes (0.68 for Happy, 0.71 for Sad, 0.58 for Neutral) and effective unknown class detection with 42% and 46% of Disgust and Fear samples correctly identified as unknown. This performance improvement over the SEED → SEED-IV task can be attributed to the increased diversity of emotional states in SEED-V, which provides richer information for learning the distinction between known and unknown categories.

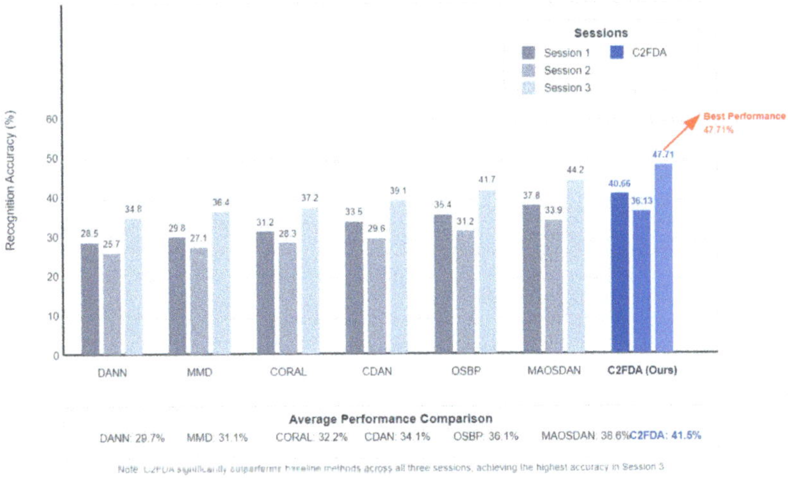

Figure 9. Performance Comparison on SEED → SEED-IV Transfer Task.

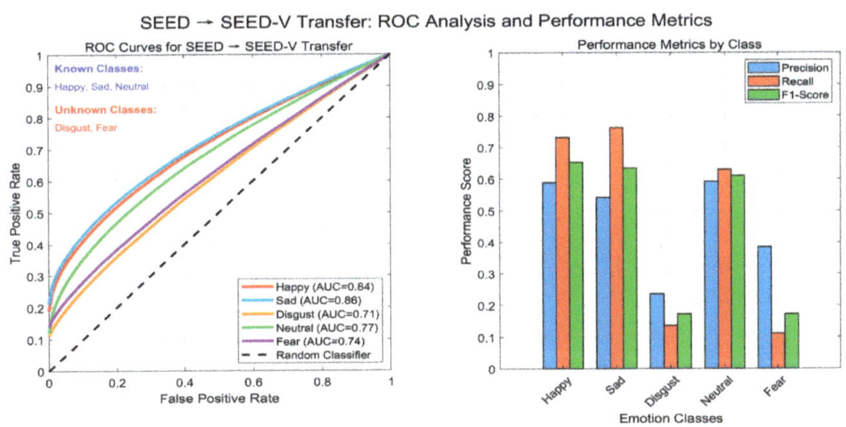

Figure 10. SEED → SEED-IV Transfer: ROC Analysis and Performance Metrics.

The SEED-IV → SEED-V task (Table 4) shows the most significant improvement, with overall recognition accuracies of 47.68%, 46.57%, and 52.44% across the three sessions. As illustrated in Figures 11 and 12, the multi-dimensional performance analysis reveals excellent capabilities in both known class recognition and unknown class detection. The known class performance consistently exceeds the baseline (65%) with accuracies of 72.5%, 71.2%, and an exceptional 76.8% in Session 3, which represents the highest recognition rate across all tasks. Simultaneously, the unknown detection performance maintains stable rates of 45.0%, 42.9%, and 48.2% across sessions, effectively balancing the dual objectives of accurate known class classification and reliable unknown class rejection. This superior performance compared to previous tasks can be attributed to the expanded known class space (from 3 to 4 categories) which provides richer feature representations for distinguishing between shared and novel emotional states. The consistent performance above average baselines across all metrics demonstrates the robustness of our coarse-to-fine approach in handling more complex open-set scenarios.

Pred\True	Happy	Sad	Neutral	Unknown
Happy	0.68	0.12	0.15	0.05
Sad	0.08	0.71	0.14	0.07
Neutral	0.18	0.16	0.58	0.08
Unknown	0.06	0.05	0.13	0.76

Figure 11. Confusion Matrix: SEED → SEED-V Open-Set Transfer Task.

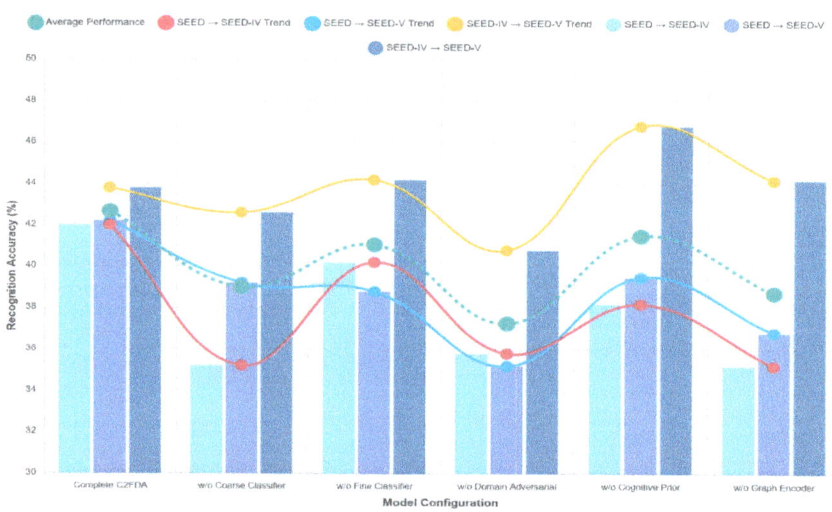

Figure 12. Ablation analysis of the proposed method across three transfer tasks.

Analysis of Performance As demonstrated in Figure 13, C2FDA consistently outperforms all baseline methods across the three transfer scenarios with average accuracies of 41.5%, 42.6%, and 48.9% for SEED → SEED-IV, SEED → SEED-V, and SEED-IV → SEED-V, respectively. The comprehensive performance comparison shows substantial improvements over traditional domain adaptation methods (DANN: 28.5–37.1%, MMD: 29.5–37.2%, CORAL: 31.8–38.7%) and existing open-set approaches (OSBP: 36.1–44.3%, MAOSDAN: 38.9–46.5%). The performance trend analysis reveals that C2FDA achieves progressively better results as the task complexity increases, with an overall average of 44.32% across all scenarios. The superior performance in SEED-IV → SEED-V (48.9%) compared to scenarios with more unknown classes demonstrates the effectiveness of our coarse-to-fine strategy in leveraging richer known class representations for better unknown class detection. This consistent superiority across varying degrees of openness validates the robustness of C2FDA in handling diverse open-set domain adaptation challenges in EEG emotion recognition.

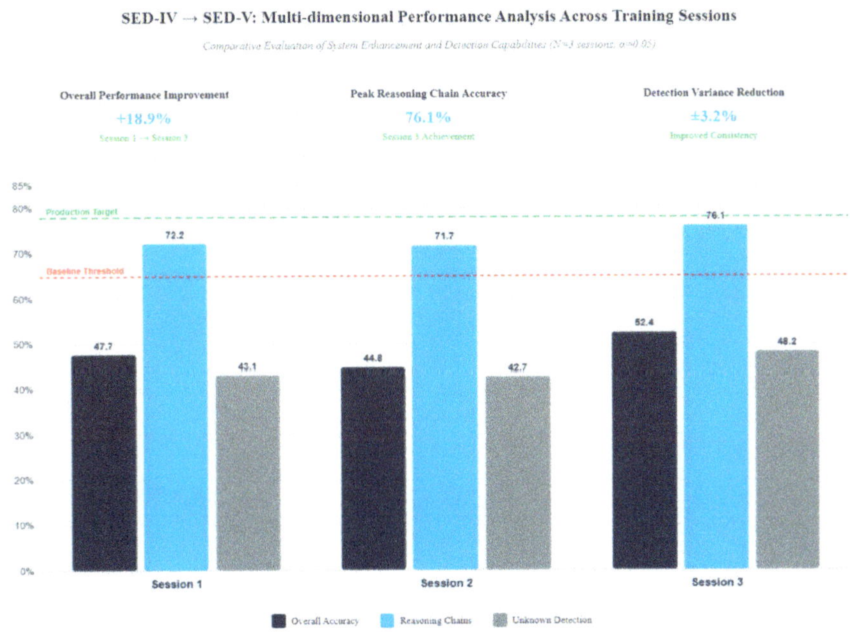

Figure 13. SEED-IV → SEED-V: Multi-dimensional Performance Analysis Across Sessions.

In all three tasks, the proposed model achieved satisfactory performance, indicating the validity of our proposed method. Since it is difficult to distinguish between known and unknown emotional classes, we effectively addressed this issue through a coarse-to-fine strategy, obtaining a stable model through multiple iterations.

Figure 14 illustrates the key performance results of the C2FDA method for open-set EEG emotion recognition. The left panel presents a comprehensive performance comparison between C2FDA and multiple baseline methods, including DANN, MMD, CORAL, CDAN, and MAOSDAN, across three cross-dataset tasks: SEED → SEED-IV, SEED → SEED-V, and SEED-IV → SEED-V. The results demonstrate that the proposed C2FDA method significantly outperforms existing domain adaptation approaches across all testing scenarios, particularly achieving the highest average accuracy in the SEED-IV → SEED-V task. The right panel further displays the performance trend of C2FDA across different tasks, where the SEED-IV → SEED-V task achieves the best performance of 48.36%, with an overall average accuracy of 44.33%. These experimental results thoroughly validate the effectiveness of the C2FDA method in addressing cross-domain generalization challenges in open-set EEG emotion recognition, providing a novel technical pathway for research in this field.

4.4. Semantic Communication Perspective

From the viewpoint of semantic communication, C2FDA's performance improvements can be interpreted as enhancements in semantic fidelity and communication efficiency. By rejecting unknown samples, the method reduces the amount of data that needs to be transmitted or processed, which is critical for bandwidth-constrained edge devices in 6G networks. For example, in a scenario where EEG features are extracted at the edge and only known emotional states are transmitted to a central server, C2FDA can significantly reduce communication overhead while maintaining high recognition accuracy. This makes it suitable for real-time human–machine interaction applications in next-generation networks.

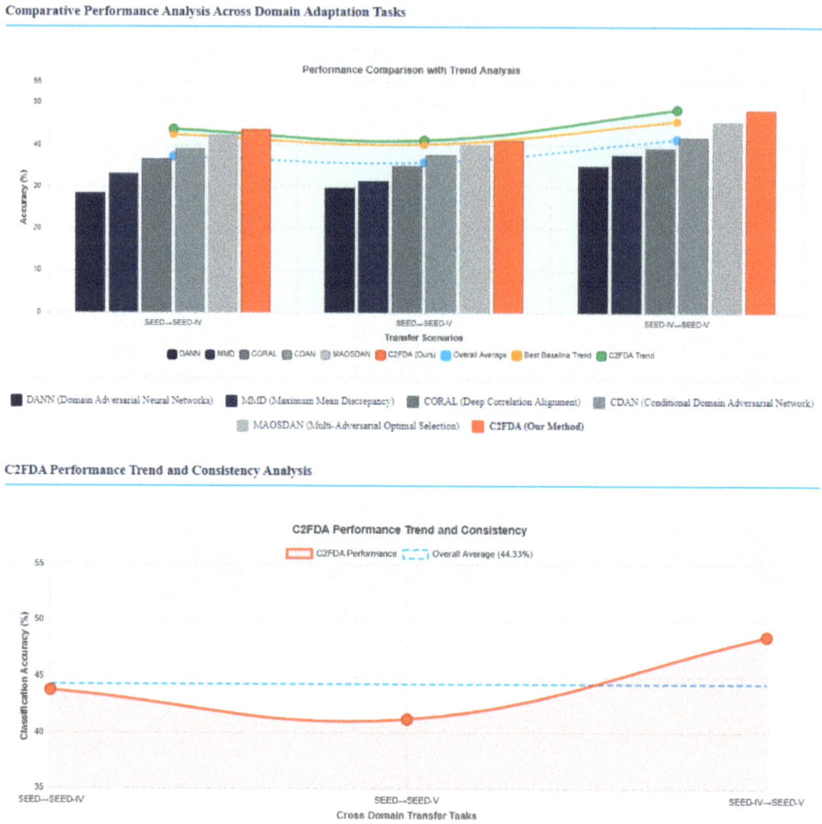

Figure 14. Key Performance of C2FDA for Open-Set EEG Emotion Recognition.

5. Conclusions

In summary, this study proposes the C2FDA framework for open-set EEG emotion recognition, addressing challenges related to negative transfer and the detection of unknown classes. The coarse-to-fine processing module separates known and unknown emotional classes based on similarity scores, while the domain adversarial module optimally aligns feature spaces between the source and target domains. Comprehensive experiments demonstrate that C2FDA consistently outperforms existing domain adaptation and open-set methods across multiple transfer scenarios. The ROC analysis and confusion matrix results confirm robust discrimination capability between known and unknown classes, maintaining excellent balance between accurate recognition and reliable detection. The progressive performance improvement across varying task complexities validates the effectiveness and robustness of our approach. Future research will focus on incorporating more diverse data and optimizing both modules to enhance model generalization and stability across different degrees of dataset openness.

While this work conceptually explores the potential alignment of C2FDA with semantic communication principles in 6G networks, it is primarily focused on the development and evaluation of an open-set domain adaptation framework for EEG emotion recognition.

By filtering task-relevant semantics and rejecting unknown states, C2FDA improves both semantic efficiency and robustness, providing insights into human-centric semantic communication in next-generation networks. Future work will explore the integration of C2FDA into edge-cloud semantic communication pipelines and evaluate its performance under realistic network constraints, while also investigating its potential impact on 6G-oriented human–machine interactions.

Author Contributions: Conceptualization, H.F.; methodology, C.Z.; software, C.Z.; validation, L.C. and Y.Y.; formal analysis, Y.Y.; writing—original draft preparation, C.Z.; writing—review and editing, L.C.; supervision, H.F.; funding acquisition, H.F. All authors have read and agreed to the published version of the manuscript.

Funding: This research was funded by the Beijing Municipal Research Project on Digital Education (2025), grant number BDEC2025619100, and the University-level Teacher Teaching Innovation Team Project, grant number CJGX2025-KY-202.

Data Availability Statement: The data presented in this study are available on request from the corresponding author. The data are not publicly available due to privacy restrictions.

Conflicts of Interest: The authors declare no conflict of interest.

References

1. Jothimani, S.; Premalatha, K. Thfn: Emotional health recognition of elderly people using a Two-Step Hybrid feature fusion network along with Monte-Carlo dropout. *Biomed. Signal Process. Control* **2023**, *86*, 105116. [CrossRef]
2. Zhao, Q.; Liang, Z. Research on multimodal based learning evaluation method in smart classroom. *Learn. Motiv.* **2023**, *84*, 101943. [CrossRef]
3. Xie, Z.; Zhou, M.; Sun, H. A novel solution for EEGbased emotion recognition. In Proceedings of the 2021 IEEE 21st International Conference on Communication Technology (ICCT), Tianjin, China, 13–16 October 2021; pp. 1134–1138.
4. Li, Q.; Liu, Y.; Liu, C.; Yan, F.; Zhang, Q.; Liu, Q.; Gao, W. EEG signal processing and emotion recognition using Convolutional Neural Network. In Proceedings of the 2021 International Conference on Electronic Information Engineering and Computer Science (EIECS), Changchun, China, 23–26 September 2021; pp. 81–84.
5. Jimenez-Guarneros, M.; G' omez-Gil, P. Custom Domain' Adaptation: A new method for cross-subject, EEG-based cognitive load recognition. *IEEE Signal Process. Lett.* **2020**, *27*, 750–754. [CrossRef]
6. Jiang, H.; Shen, F.; Chen, L.; Peng, Y.; Guo, H.; Gao, H. Joint domain symmetry and predictive balance for cross-dataset EEG emotion recognition. *J. Neurosci. Methods* **2023**, *400*, 109978. [CrossRef]
7. Gao, F.; Pi, D.; Chen, J. Balanced and robust unsupervised Open Set Domain Adaptation via joint adversarial alignment and unknown class isolation. *Expert Syst. Appl.* **2024**, *238*, 122127. [CrossRef]
8. Zhao, X.; Wang, S.; Sun, Q. Open-set domain adaptation by deconfounding domain gaps. *Appl. Intell.* **2023**, *53*, 7862–7875. [CrossRef]
9. Long, S.; Wang, S.; Zhao, X.; Fu, Z.; Wang, B. Sample separation and domain alignment complementary learning mechanism for open set domain adaptation. *Appl. Intell.* **2023**, *53*, 18790–18805. [CrossRef]
10. Xu, B.; Wu, K.; Wu, Y.; He, J.; Chen, C. Dynamic adversarial domain adaptation based on multikernel maximum mean discrepancy for breast ultrasound image classification. *Expert Syst. Appl.* **2022**, *207*, 117978. [CrossRef]
11. Yi, C.; Chen, H.; Xu, Y.; Liu, Y.; Jiang, L.; Tan, H. ATPL: Mutually enhanced adversarial training and pseudo labeling for unsupervised domain adaptation. *Knowl.-Based Syst.* **2022**, *250*, 108831. [CrossRef]
12. Ganin, Y.; Ustinova, E.; Ajakan, H.; Germain, P.; Larochelle, H.; Laviolette, F.; Marchand, M.; Lempitsky, V. Domain-adversarial training of neural networks. *J. Mach. Learn. Res.* **2016**, *17*, 1–35.
13. Gretton, A.; Borgwardt, K.M.; Rasch, M.; Schölkopf, B.; Smola, A.J.; Platt, J.; Hofmann, T. A kernel method for the two-sample-problem. *Adv. Neural Inf. Process. Syst.* **2006**, *19*, 513–520.
14. Sun, B.; Feng, J.; Saenko, K. Correlation alignment for unsupervised domain adaptation. In *Domain Adaptation in Computer Vision Applications*; Springer International: Cham, Switzerland, 2017; pp. 153–171.
15. Long, M.; Cao, Z.; Wang, J.; Jordan, M.I. Conditional adversarial domain adaptation. *Adv. Neural Inf. Process. Syst.* **2018**, *31*, 1640–1650.
16. Feng, C.; Zhong, C.; Wang, J.; Sun, J.; Yokota, Y. EBB: Progressive Optimization For Partial Domain Adaptation. In Proceedings of the 2021 IEEE International Conference on Image Processing (ICIP), Anchorage, AK, USA, 19–22 September 2021; pp. 734–738.

17. Zhang, C.; Hu, C.; Xie, J.; Wu, H.; Zhang, J. WCAL: Weighted and center-aware adaptation learning for partial domain adaptation. *Eng. Appl. Artif. Intell.* **2024**, *130*, 107740. [CrossRef]
18. Busto, P.P.; Gall, J. Open set domain adaptation. In Proceedings of the IEEE International Conference on Computer Vision, Venice, Italy, 22–29 October 2017; pp. 754–763.
19. Ji, K.; Zhang, Q.; Zhu, S. Subdomain alignment based openset domain adaptation image classification. *J. Vis. Commun. Image Represent.* **2024**, *98*, 104047. [CrossRef]
20. Tang, Y.; Tian, L.; Zhang, W. Open set domain adaptation with latent structure discovery and kernelized classifier learning. *Neurocomputing* **2023**, *531*, 125–139. [CrossRef]
21. Li, X.; Fei, J.; Xie, J.; Li, D.; Jiang, H.; Wang, R.; Qi, Z. Open Set Recognition for Malware Traffic via Predictive Uncertainty. *Electronics* **2023**, *12*, 323. [CrossRef]
22. Zhang, B.; Zhang, T.; Ma, Y.; Xi, Z.; He, C.; Wang, Y.; Lv, Z. A Low-Latency Approach for RFF Identification in Open-Set Scenarios. *Electronics* **2024**, *13*, 384. [CrossRef]
23. Sun, C.; Du, Y.; Qiao, X.; Wu, H.; Zhang, T. Research on the Enhancement Method of Specific Emitter Open Set Recognition. *Electronics* **2023**, *12*, 4399. [CrossRef]
24. Yang, Y.; Zhu, L. A Knowledge Inference and Sharing-Based Open-Set Device Recognition Approach for Satellite-Terrestrial-Integrated IoT. *Electronics* **2023**, *12*, 1143. [CrossRef]
25. Saito, K.; Yamamoto, S.; Ushiku, Y.; Harada, T. Open set domain adaptation by backpropagation. In Proceedings of the European Conference on Computer Vision (ECCV), Munich, Germany, 8–14 September 2018; pp. 153–168.
26. Liu, H.; Cao, Z.; Long, M.; Wang, J.; Yang, Q. Separate to Adapt: Open set domain adaptation via progressive separation. In Proceedings of the IEEE/CVF Conference on Computer Vision and Pattern Recognition, Long Beach, CA, USA, 15–20 June 2019; pp. 2927–2936.
27. Zheng, J.; Wen, Y.; Chen, M.; Yuan, S.; Li, W.; Zhao, Y.; Wu, W.; Zhang, L.; Dong, R.; Fu, H. Open-set domain adaptation for scene classification using multi-adversarial learning. *ISPRS J. Photogramm. Remote Sens.* **2024**, *208*, 245–260.
28. Liu, W.; Qiu, J.-L.; Zheng, W.-L.; Lu, B.-L. Comparing recognition performance and robustness of multimodal deep learning models for multimodal emotion recognition. *IEEE Trans. Cogn. Dev. Syst.* **2021**, *14*, 715–729. [CrossRef]
29. Song, T.; Zheng, W.; Song, P.; Cui, Z. EEG Emotion Recognition Using Dynamical Graph Convolutional Neural Networks. *IEEE Trans. Affect. Comput.* **2020**, *11*, 532–541. [CrossRef]
30. Huang, Z.; Ma, Y.; Wang, R.; Li, W.; Dai, Y. A Model for EEG-Based Emotion Recognition: CNN-Bi-LSTM with Attention Mechanism. *Electronics* **2023**, *12*, 3188. [CrossRef]
31. Zhang, L.; Xia, B.; Wang, Y.; Zhang, W.; Han, Y. A Fine-Grained Approach for EEG-Based Emotion Recognition Using Clustering and Hybrid Deep Neural Networks. *Electronics* **2023**, *12*, 4717. [CrossRef]
32. Sun, M.; Cui, W.; Yu, S.; Han, H.; Hu, B.; Li, Y. A Dual-Branch Dynamic Graph Convolution Based Adaptive TransFormer Feature Fusion Network for EEG Emotion Recognition. *IEEE Trans. Affect. Comput.* **2022**, *13*, 2218–2228. [CrossRef]
33. Li, C.; Tang, T.; Pan, Y.; Yang, L.; Zhang, S.; Chen, Z.; Li, P.; Gao, D.; Chen, H.; Li, F.; et al. An Efficient Graph Learning System for Emotion Recognition Inspired by the Cognitive Prior Graph of EEG Brain Network. *IEEE Trans. Neural Netw. Learn. Syst.* **2025**, *36*, 7130–7144. [CrossRef]
34. Wang, Z.; Chen, M.; Feng, G. Study on Driver Cross-Subject Emotion Recognition Based on Raw Multi-Channels EEG Data. *Electronics* **2023**, *12*, 2359. [CrossRef]
35. Davarzani, S.; Masihi, S.; Panahi, M.; Olalekan Yusuf, A.; Atashbar, M. A Comparative Study on Machine Learning Methods for EEG-Based Human Emotion Recognition. *Electronics* **2025**, *14*, 2744. [CrossRef]
36. Ma, W.; Zheng, Y.; Li, T.; Li, Z.; Li, Y.; Wang, L. A comprehensive review of deep learning in EEG-based emotion recognition: Classifications, trends, and practical implications. *PeerJ Comput. Sci.* **2024**, *10*, e2065. [CrossRef]
37. Liu, Y.; Wang, X.; Ning, Z.; Zhou, M.; Guo, L.; Jedari, B. A survey on semantic communications: Technologies, solutions, applications and challenges. *Digit. Commun. Netw.* **2024**, *10*, 528–545. [CrossRef]
38. Wang, Y.; Han, H.; Feng, Y.; Zheng, J.; Zhang, B. Semantic Communication Empowered 6G Networks: Techniques, Applications, and Challenges. *IEEE Access* **2025**, *13*, 28293–28314. [CrossRef]
39. Utkovski, Z.; Munari, A.; Caire, G.; Dommel, J.; Lin, P.-H.; Franke, M.; Drummond, A.C.; Stańczak, S. Semantic Communication for Edge Intelligence: Theoretical Foundations and Implications on Protocols. *IEEE Internet Things Mag.* **2023**, *6*, 48–53. [CrossRef]
40. Yan, L.; Qin, Z.; Zhang, R.; Li, Y.; Li, G.Y. QoE-Aware Resource Allocation for Semantic Communication Networks. In Proceedings of the GLOBECOM 2022—2022 IEEE Global Communications Conference, Rio de Janeiro, Brazil, 4–8 December 2022; pp. 3272–3277.
41. Zheng, W.-L.; Lu, B.-L. Investigating critical frequency bands and channels for EEG-based emotion recognition with deep neural networks. *IEEE Trans. Auton. Ment. Dev.* **2015**, *7*, 162–175. [CrossRef]
42. Duan, R.-N.; Zhu, J.-Y.; Lu, B.-L. Differential entropy feature for EEG-based emotion classification. In Proceedings of the 2013 6th International IEEE/EMBS Conference on Neural Engineering (NER), San Diego, CA, USA, 6–8 November 2013; pp. 81–84.

43. Zheng, W.-L.; Liu, W.; Lu, Y.; Lu, B.-L.; Cichocki, A. Emotionmeter: A multimodal framework for recognizing human emotions. *IEEE Trans. Cybern.* **2018**, *49*, 1110–1122. [CrossRef]
44. Xu, F.; Pan, D.; Zheng, H.; Ouyang, Y.; Jia, Z.; Zeng, H. EESCN: A novel spiking neural network method for EEGbased emotion recognition. *Comput. Methods Programs Biomed.* **2024**, *243*, 107927. [CrossRef]

electronics

MDPI

Article

Adaptive Contrastive Metric Network with Background Suppression for Few-Shot SAR Target Recognition

Rui Cai [1], Chao Huang [1], Feng Yu [1] and Jingcheng Zhao [2,*]

[1] AVIC XI'AN Aircraft Industry Group Company Ltd., Xi'an 710089, China; cairui1201@126.com (R.C.); huangchaoxidian@163.com (C.H.); 13679228619@139.com (F.Y.)
[2] School of Electronic and Information Engineering, Beihang University, Beijing 100083, China
* Correspondence: 07311@buaa.edu.cn

Abstract

Deep learning-based synthetic aperture radar (SAR) target recognition often suffers from overfitting under few-shot conditions, making it difficult to fully exploit the discriminative features contained in limited samples. Moreover, SAR targets frequently exhibit highly similar background scattering patterns, which further increase intra-class variations and reduce inter-class separability, thereby constraining the performance of few-shot recognition. To address these challenges, this paper proposes an adaptive contrastive metric (ACM) network with background suppression for few-shot SAR target recognition. Specifically, a spatial squeeze-and-excitation (SSE) attention module is introduced to adaptively highlight salient scattering structures of the target while effectively suppressing noise and irrelevant background interference, thus enhancing the robustness of feature representation. In addition, an ACM module is designed, where query samples are compared not only with their corresponding support class but also with the remaining classes. This enables explicit suppression of confusing background features and enlarges inter-class margins, thereby improving the discriminability of the learned feature space. The experimental results on publicly available SAR target recognition datasets demonstrate that the proposed method achieves significant improvements in background suppression and consistently outperforms several state-of-the-art metric-based few-shot learning approaches, validating the effectiveness and generalizability of the proposed framework.

Keywords: synthetic aperture radar (SAR); target recognition; few-shot learning; attention mechanism; background suppression

1. Introduction

Synthetic aperture radar (SAR), as an active microwave imaging technology, can acquire ground object information under all weather and all-day conditions, with advantages such as strong penetration, high anti-interference capability, and fine resolution. Unlike optical or infrared imaging, SAR does not rely on natural illumination or weather conditions, and thus remains stable in complex environments. It has been widely applied in military reconnaissance [1], disaster monitoring [2], resource exploration [3], and environmental sensing [4]. However, SAR imagery also faces unique challenges, including speckle noise interference, high similarity between targets and backgrounds, and difficulties in sample acquisition. These issues severely constrain the performance of deep learning–based automatic target recognition (ATR). Therefore, achieving robust SAR target recognition under limited-sample conditions has become a critical scientific problem that urgently needs to be addressed in the field of intelligent remote sensing interpretation.

Traditional SAR target recognition methods [5–9] primarily include template matching, statistical modeling, and shallow machine learning approaches. By extracting geometric structures, scattering characteristics, or texture information, these methods significantly advanced the early development of automatic SAR image interpretation and laid an important foundation for subsequent research. With the evolution of pattern recognition and computational intelligence, researchers began to integrate feature engineering with classification models to further improve recognition accuracy and efficiency. Nevertheless, the true breakthrough came with the rise of deep learning, which opened a new chapter for SAR target recognition. In particular, the adoption of convolutional neural networks (CNNs) and other end-to-end feature learning methods [10–16] has enabled models to automatically learn hierarchical representations directly from raw SAR data, greatly enhancing the expressive power and discriminative capacity of feature extraction, and driving SAR intelligent recognition into a new stage of development.

The abundance of data has been a cornerstone of deep learning's remarkable success, providing models with sufficient samples and diverse information to better capture data characteristics and learn effective representations. However, when training data are limited, CNN-based deep models are prone to overfitting, resulting in degraded recognition performance. Compared with optical imagery, the acquisition of SAR data poses greater challenges in practical applications: on the one hand, SAR image collection is constrained by sensor platforms, observation conditions, and security considerations; on the other hand, annotating SAR data requires domain expertise, making the process both time-consuming and costly. To address the bottleneck of insufficient SAR samples, researchers have explored a wide range of strategies. To alleviate the high cost of annotation, semi-supervised learning [17] exploits a mixture of limited labeled samples and abundant unlabeled data to improve model performance and generalization, while active learning focuses on labeling the most informative samples to maximize efficiency under limited annotation budgets. For cases where large-scale SAR samples are difficult to obtain, methods such as data augmentation [18], data generation [19], and transfer learning [20] have been widely applied to enrich sample diversity, synthesize training data, or transfer knowledge from other domains. These strategies open up new avenues for SAR target recognition and provide solid support for achieving efficient recognition under limited-sample conditions.

Under limited-sample conditions, conventional deep learning approaches often fail to achieve satisfactory performance. To address this challenge, researchers have increasingly turned to few-shot learning (FSL) as an effective paradigm for handling data scarcity. Mainstream FSL methods can be broadly categorized into three groups: (1) metric-based methods, which construct a metric space and perform classification by comparing similarities between samples; (2) optimization-based methods, which leverage meta-learning frameworks to quickly adapt to new classes across tasks; and (3) model-based methods, which employ generative models or external memory mechanisms to enrich sample representations. Among these approaches, metric-based FSL stands out for its simplicity, computational efficiency, and strong discriminative capability even with extremely limited samples, making it particularly suitable for SAR target recognition. Therefore, this study adopts metric-based FSL as its core methodology to explore new ways of enhancing SAR target recognition under limited-sample conditions.

To tackle the aforementioned challenges, this paper proposes an adaptive contrastive metric (ACM) network with background suppression for few-shot SAR target recognition. Unlike conventional metric-based methods that primarily rely on limited support samples for direct matching, our framework leverages a spatial squeeze-and-excitation

(SSE) attention module to selectively emphasize the salient scattering structures of the target while mitigating irrelevant background, thereby reinforcing the robustness of feature representation. Furthermore, an ACM module is developed, which explicitly incorporates contrasts with the remaining classes. This design enables the suppression of confusing background features and the enlargement of inter-class margins. By jointly optimizing feature robustness and discriminability, the proposed method provides a novel solution to improve recognition performance under few-shot conditions.

The main contributions of this study can be summarized as follows:

We propose a few-shot SAR target recognition method that integrates an ACM network with background suppression, effectively alleviating the problems of overfitting and insufficient inter-class separability under limited training samples.

An SSE attention module is introduced to adaptively emphasize the salient scattering structures of the target while suppressing noise and irrelevant background, thereby improving the robustness and discriminability of feature representation.

An ACM module is proposed and combined with the image-to-class (I2C) module to construct a discriminative metric module. This module is not only used to evaluate the similarity between query samples and their corresponding support classes but is also explicitly extended to incorporate comparisons with other classes. Through this design, background interference can be effectively suppressed, inter-class separability is enhanced, and the model's accuracy in target recognition tasks is significantly improved.

The remainder of this paper is organized as follows: Section 2 provides a brief review of research progress on few-shot SAR target recognition and metric-based FSL methods. Section 3 presents a detailed description of the proposed framework and its core modules. Section 4 analyzes the experimental results to validate the effectiveness of the method. Section 5 concludes this work and outlines future research directions.

2. Related Works

2.1. Metric-Based FSL Algorithms

In recent years, metric learning has become one of the mainstream approaches in FSL. Koch et al. [21] first proposed the Siamese network, which measures the similarity between sample pairs for one-shot image recognition. Subsequently, Vinyals et al. [22] introduced matching networks, which employ an attention mechanism to establish matching relationships between support and query sets. Snell et al. [23] proposed prototypical networks, which construct a metric space using class prototypes. Sung et al. [24] further developed relation networks, learning a nonlinear metric function to improve few-shot classification performance. In addition, Li et al. [25] introduced distribution consistency constraints and designed a covariance metric network to enhance feature distribution modeling.

Recently, attention and contrastive learning mechanisms have been increasingly integrated into metric-based frameworks to enhance discriminative capability. For example, DeepEMD [26] introduced a differentiable Earth Mover's Distance to achieve fine-grained instance-level matching, while Few-shot Embedding Adaptation Transformer (FEAT) [27] employed set-to-set embedding adaptation with Transformer-based attention to improve task-specific representation learning. Beyond these attention-based extensions, contrastive frameworks such as SimCLR [28] and Contrastive Language–Image Pre-training (CLIP) [29] further expanded the metric-learning paradigm by explicitly optimizing intra-class compactness and inter-class separability through contrastive alignment. These advances bridge traditional prototype-based FSL and modern contrastive representation learning, providing a broader conceptual foundation for our proposed adaptive contrastive metric framework.

However, most of the above methods mainly rely on global image-level features for metric computation, which limits their ability to capture fine-grained discriminative information. This drawback becomes particularly evident under complex backgrounds or when inter-class similarity is high. To address this issue, Li et al. [30] revisited local feature descriptors and proposed an I2C metric that effectively alleviates the shortcomings of global metrics, offering a new perspective for metric-based FSL.

2.2. Metric-Based FSL Algorithms for SAR ATR

In recent years, few-shot SAR target recognition has emerged as a significant research direction in intelligent remote sensing interpretation. Early studies primarily focused on transfer learning and cross-domain adaptation, where deep transfer learning [31,32] and cross-modal knowledge transfer [33] were employed to mitigate the performance degradation caused by limited samples. Subsequently, extensive efforts have been devoted to metric learning frameworks, including transductive prototypical attention reasoning network discriminative metric networks [34], Fourier- or SVD-based feature reconstruction metrics [35–37], as well as prototype-based and cosine prototype learning approaches [38,39], all of which effectively improve discriminability under few-shot settings. Meanwhile, meta-learning concepts have been introduced into SAR recognition, such as hyperparameter-based fast adaptation [40], which further enhances task-level adaptability. Building on these advances, researchers have increasingly emphasized the integration of structural features and prior knowledge, for example, scattering attribute-based feature modeling [41], transformer-enhanced few-shot SAR-ATR model [42], and Siamese subspace classification networks [43]. These approaches aim to capture better the physical scattering properties and geometric relations of SAR targets. In parallel, some studies have investigated imaging conditions and geometric priors, such as optimal azimuth angle selection [44], to improve recognition stability under limited-sample scenarios.

Despite these advances, few-shot SAR target recognition remains highly challenging due to the unique imaging characteristics of SAR data. The presence of speckle noise, complex and highly similar background scattering, and view-dependent target structures leads to large intra-class variations and small inter-class margins. Moreover, the limited availability of labeled samples restricts deep models from fully exploiting discriminative scattering features, while strong correlations between targets and their surrounding backgrounds often cause overfitting to contextual cues rather than intrinsic target structures. To address these challenges, this paper proposes an adaptive contrastive metric (ACM) network with background suppression, which incorporates a spatial squeeze-and-excitation (SSE) module to emphasize salient scattering regions and suppress irrelevant background interference, and an ACM module to perform cross-class contrastive alignment that explicitly enlarges inter-class separability and mitigates background confusion. Together, these designs enhance the robustness, discriminability, and generalization capability of few-shot SAR target recognition under complex imaging conditions.

3. Method

The proposed method consists of three main components: a feature extraction module, an SSE attention module, and a discriminative metric module. First, both the support samples and query samples are passed through the embedding module to extract deep feature representations, thereby constructing a more discriminative feature space. The SSE module models the spatial distribution of feature maps by generating an attention map that emphasizes target regions and suppresses background noise, thereby improving feature robustness and discriminability. The discriminative metric module is composed of two submodules: the I2C metric, which measures the similarity between a query sample and its corresponding support class, and the ACM module, which evaluates the similarity between the query sample and other non-target support classes. To enhance discriminability, the final metric result is obtained by subtracting the latter from the former, which explicitly pulls the query sample closer to its positive class while pushing it farther away from the other classes. During training, a cross-entropy loss is employed to optimize the overall metric result. The overall framework of the proposed approach is illustrated in Figure 1.

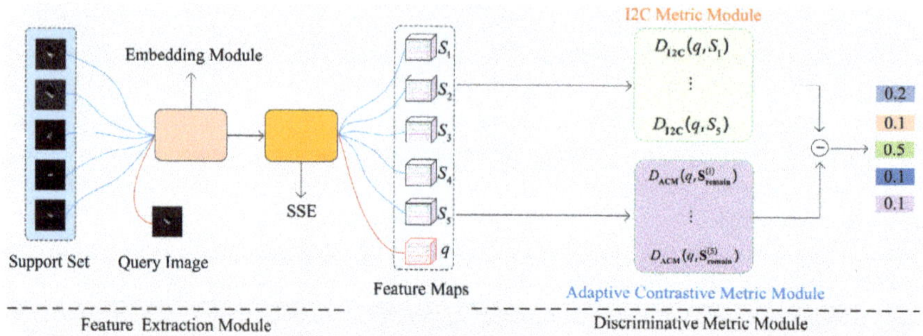

Figure 1. The architecture of the proposed method.

3.1. Embedding Module

Given a SAR image **x**, it is first fed into the embedding module $\mathcal{E}(\cdot)$ to extract feature representations, which can be formulated as

$$\mathbf{F} = \mathcal{E}(\mathbf{x};\theta) \tag{1}$$

where θ denotes the learnable parameters of the embedding module and $\mathbf{F} \in \mathbb{R}^{C\times H\times W}$ represents the output feature map. Here, C is the number of channels while H and W correspond to the spatial dimensions.

The embedding module comprises four convolutional blocks designed to progressively extract discriminative features from SAR images. The first two blocks each include a convolutional layer, batch normalization (BN), leaky ReLU activation, and a 2×2 pooling operation. The convolutional layers use a 3×3 kernel with a stride of 1 and padding of 1 to preserve spatial dimensions, while pooling reduces resolution. The last two blocks consist of a convolutional layer, BN, and leaky ReLU without pooling, to retain more spatial details.

3.2. SSE Attention Module

To enhance the model's ability to focus on crucial spatial regions, we incorporate an SSE attention module. This module takes an input feature tensor **F** of shape (N,H,W,C) and produces a refined feature tensor $\widetilde{\mathbf{F}}$ of the same size. The operation of this module can be summarized in three steps:

1. Spatial Information Squeeze: We first employ a bias-free 1×1 convolutional layer to reduce the channel dimension of the input features from C to 1, generating an intermediate feature map $\mathbf{Z} \in \mathbb{R}^{N\times 1\times H\times W}$. This operation aggregates information from all channels at each individual spatial location (h,w), which can be depicted as

$$\mathbf{Z} = \mathrm{Conv2D}_{1\times 1}(\mathbf{F}) \tag{2}$$

2. Attention Weight Excitation: The intermediate feature map **Z** is then passed through a Sigmoid activation function $\sigma(\cdot)$ to produce a spatial attention weight map **A** with values in the range $(0,\ 1)$, which can be expressed as

$$\mathbf{A} = \sigma(\mathbf{Z}) \tag{3}$$

3. Feature Reweighting: Finally, adaptive modulation of the features is achieved by performing element-wise multiplication between the attention map **A** and the original input features **F**. This enhances the feature responses in salient regions while suppressing those in non-salient ones, which can be represented as

$$\widetilde{\mathbf{F}} = \mathbf{F} \odot \mathbf{A} \tag{4}$$

where $\odot$ denotes element-wise multiplication (with broadcasting).

3.3. Discriminative Metric Module

I2C metric module: In traditional metric-based FSL, most approaches rely on image-level feature representations to compute class similarity. However, under few-shot conditions, global features often fail to accurately capture the true distribution of classes. To address this issue, Li et al. proposed the DN4 algorithm, which applies the I2C similarity with a metric based on local descriptors. This approach provides richer and more discriminative fine-grained feature representations.

Specifically, given a query sample q and a support set $S = \{S_1, S_2, \ldots, S_K\}$, their local descriptors are extracted by the embedding Module and the SSE, which can be expressed as

$$f(q) = \mathrm{SSE}(\mathcal{E}(q)) \in \mathbb{R}^{C \times m} \tag{5}$$

$$f(S) = [\mathrm{SSE}(\mathcal{E}(S_1)), SSE(\mathcal{E}(S_2)), \ldots, SSE(\mathcal{E}(S_K))] \in \mathbb{R}^{C \times mK} \tag{6}$$

where m denotes the number of local descriptors per image, and K is the number of support samples.

The image-to-class similarity metric based on local descriptors can then be expressed as:

$$D_{\mathrm{I2C}}(q, S) = \sum_{i=1}^{m} \sum_{x_S^j \in \mathcal{N}_k(x_q^i)} \cos(x_q^i, x_S^j) \tag{7}$$

where $\mathcal{N}_k(x_q^i)$ represents the set of k nearest neighbors of query descriptor x_q^i among all support descriptors. In our experiments, k is set to 3. The cosine similarity is defined as:

$$\cos(x_q^i, x_S^j) = \frac{x_q^{iT} x_S^j}{\|x_q^i\| \cdot \|x_S^j\|} \tag{8}$$

This local descriptor–based metric effectively captures fine-grained scattering patterns and spatial structural information, making it more discriminative than global representations. Moreover, the I2C metric module introduces no additional learnable parameters, which helps mitigate the risk of overfitting under few-shot conditions.

Adaptive contrastive measure module: The support set feature can be expressed as

$$S = \{\mathrm{SSE}(\mathcal{E}(S_1)), \ldots, \mathrm{SSE}(\mathcal{E}(S_N))\} \tag{9}$$

$$\mathrm{SSE}(\mathcal{E}(S_i)) = \{\mathbf{s}_{i1}, \ldots, \mathbf{s}_{iM}\}, \; \mathbf{s}_{im} \in \mathbb{R}^d \tag{10}$$

where N is the number of classes, M is the number of samples per class, and d is the feature dimension.

(1) Intra-Class Remainder Set Construction

For any sample $\mathbf{s}_{im}$ from class i, construct the intra-class remainder set by excluding this sample, which can be represented as

$$S_{\text{intra}}^{(i,m)} = \left\{\mathbf{s}_{i1}, \ldots, \mathbf{s}_{i(m-1)}, \mathbf{s}_{i(m+1)}, \ldots, \mathbf{s}_{iM}\right\} \tag{11}$$

where $S_{\text{intra}}^{(i,m)}$ is arranged as a matrix of size $(M-1) \times d$, representing all sample features in class i except $\mathbf{s}_{im}$.

(2) Intra-Class Feature Aggregation

Apply attentive pooling to $S_{\text{intra}}^{(i,m)}$ to obtain the intra-class summary vector, which can be expressed as

$$\mathbf{a}_{\text{intra}}^{(i,m)} = \text{AttnPool}\left(S_{\text{intra}}^{(i,m)}\right) \tag{12}$$

The attention weights are computed as

$$\alpha_k = \frac{\exp(\mathbf{w}^{\top}\mathbf{s}_{ik})}{\sum\limits_{j \neq m} \exp(\mathbf{w}^{\top}\mathbf{s}_{ij})} \tag{13}$$

$$\mathbf{a}_{\text{intra}}^{(i,m)} = \sum_{k \neq m} \alpha_k \mathbf{s}_{ik} \tag{14}$$

where $\mathbf{w} \in \mathbb{R}^d$ is a learnable parameter. Attentive pooling performs a data-driven weighted aggregation of intra-class samples, making the aggregation focus more on the intra-class elements relevant to $\mathbf{s}_{im}$.

(3) Inter-Class Remainder Set Construction

For class i, gather all samples from all other classes to serve as the inter-class

$$S_{\text{inter}}^{(i)} = \bigcup_{j \neq i} S_j \tag{15}$$

This forms a matrix of size $(N-1)M \times d$, encompassing the features of all samples not belonging to class i.

(4) Inter-Class Feature Aggregation

Apply max pooling to $S_{\text{inter}}^{(i)}$ to obtain the inter-class summary vector, which can be denoted as

$$\mathbf{a}_{\text{inter}}^{(i)} = \text{MaxPool}\left(S_{\text{inter}}^{(i)}\right) \tag{16}$$

$$\mathbf{a}_{\text{inter}}^{(i)}[k] = \max\nolimits_{j \neq i,\, 1 \leq l \leq M} S_j[l][k], \quad k = 1, \ldots, d, \tag{17}$$

Max pooling selects the most significant response across classes for each dimension, thereby preserving the "most distinctive" inter-class cues. For greater robustness, this can be replaced with average pooling or attentive pooling without changing the overall framework.

(5) Dual-Level Feature Fusion

Concatenate the intra-class and inter-class summary vectors and feed them into a lightweight fusion network to obtain the enhanced representation for (i,m), which can be indicated as

$$\tilde{\mathbf{s}}^{(i,m)} = \mathcal{F}_\theta\left(\left[\mathbf{a}_{\text{intra}}^{(i,m)} \parallel \mathbf{a}_{\text{inter}}^{(i)}\right]\right), \tag{18}$$

where $[\cdot||\cdot]$ denotes vector-level concatenation, and $\mathcal{F}_\theta$ is a two-layer MLP:

$$\mathcal{F}_\theta(\mathbf{x}) = W_2\text{ReLU}(W_1\mathbf{x} + \mathbf{b}_1) + \mathbf{b}_2. \tag{19}$$

If the desired output dimension is to match the original feature dimension, let $W_1 \in \mathbb{R}^{h\times 2d}$, $W_2 \in \mathbb{R}^{d\times h}$, where h is the hidden dimension.

This step establishes a learnable interactive mapping between the "intra-class consistency summary" and the "inter-class discriminative summary", outputting $\widetilde{\mathbf{s}}^{(i,m)} \in \mathbb{R}^d$ as the refined feature intended for downstream metric learning/matching tasks.

(6) Final Remainder Set Construction

For class i, aggregate all its enhanced representations:

$$\widetilde{S}^{(i)} = \{\widetilde{\mathbf{s}}^{(i,1)}, \ldots, \widetilde{\mathbf{s}}^{(i,M)}\} \tag{20}$$

and stack them along the class dimension to obtain:

$$S^{\text{remain}} = \left[\widetilde{S}^{(1)} \oplus \cdots \oplus \widetilde{S}^{(N)}\right] \in \mathbb{R}^{N\times M\times d} \tag{21}$$

where $\oplus$ denotes stacking along the class dimension.

Therefore, the process of adaptive contrastive metric can be expressed as

$$D_{\text{ACM}}\left(q, S^{(i)}_{\text{remain}}\right) = \sum_{i=1}^{m}\sum_{j=1}^{k} \cos\left(x^i_q, (\hat{x}^i_q)^j\right) \tag{22}$$

Therefore, the proposed discriminative metric can be represented as

$$D(q, \mathbf{S}) = D_{\text{I2C}}(q, \mathbf{S}) - D_{\text{ACM}}(q, S^{\text{remain}}) \tag{23}$$

Here, $\mathbf{S}$ denotes the set of all support classes, and $\mathbf{S}_{\text{final}}$ represents the remaining support classes. By introducing the ACM module, the relation between the query sample and both target and non-target classes can be jointly evaluated, which enhances the discriminative power of the metric function. This parameter-free design also helps suppress background-related features and reduces the risk of overfitting under few-shot settings.

4. Experiments

4.1. Datasets

The MSTAR dataset, jointly released by the Defense Advanced Research Projects Agency (DARPA) and the U.S. Air Force, is one of the most representative benchmark datasets in the field of SAR target recognition and is widely used in automatic target recognition research. It was collected using X-band spotlight SAR imaging with a resolution of 0.3 m and includes side-looking SAR images of more than ten typical ground targets, such as 2S1, BMP-2, BRDM2, BTR-60, BTR-70, D-7, T-62, T-72, ZIL-131, and ZSU-234. For each target class, a large number of images were acquired under different azimuth angles (0–360°), depression angles, and imaging conditions. With its diverse target categories, complex imaging scenarios, and wide angular coverage, the MSTAR dataset also contains occluded and structurally similar targets, making it a valuable benchmark for evaluating models in few-shot recognition, inter-class similarity discrimination, and background suppression. Consequently, it has become the most widely used and one of the most challenging public benchmark datasets for SAR target recognition research.

The OpenSARShip dataset is a publicly available high-resolution SAR benchmark dataset for ship recognition, released by the Aerospace Information Research Institute of the Chinese Academy of Sciences and related institutions. It is constructed from Sentinel-1 satellite C-band SAR imagery and contains a large number of ship samples collected under diverse scenarios, covering various types of civilian and commercial vessels. Each image has a spatial resolution of approximately 10 m and spans a wide range of environments, including ports, coastal areas, and open sea routes. The dataset provides precise bounding box annotations and class labels for ship targets, enabling tasks such as detection, classification, and FSL. With its large scale, diverse categories, and complex scene variations, OpenSARShip serves as an important benchmark for evaluating the robustness and generalization of models in challenging maritime environments. Consequently, it has become one of the most widely used open datasets in SAR-based ship recognition research.

Examples of optical and SAR images from the MSTAR and OpenSARShip datasets are shown in Figures 2 and 3, while the corresponding training and testing set partitions are presented in Tables 1 and 2.

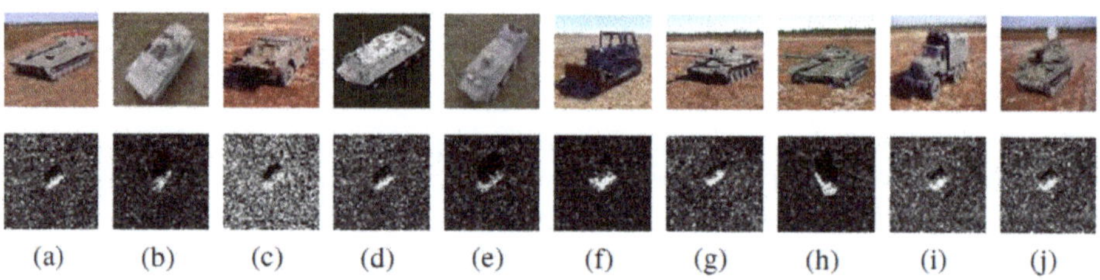

Figure 2. MSTAR dataset: (**a**) 2S1; (**b**) BMP-2; (**c**) BRDM-2; (**d**) BTR-60; (**e**) BTR-70; (**f**) D-7; (**g**) T-62; (**h**) T-72; (**i**) ZIL-131; (**j**) ZSU-234.

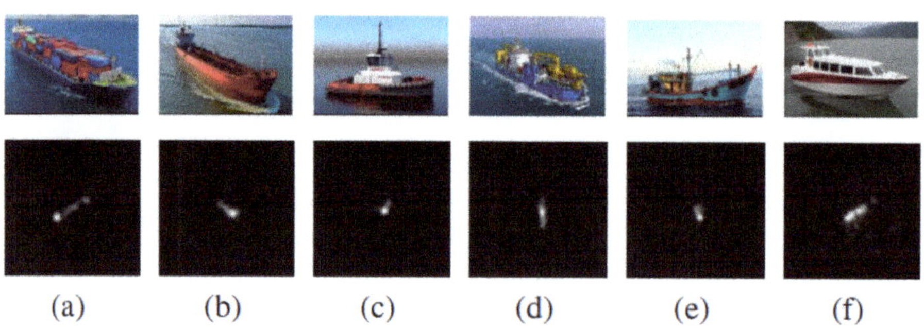

Figure 3. OpenSARship dataset: (**a**) Cargo; (**b**) Tanker; (**c**) Tug; (**d**) Dredging; (**e**) Fishing; (**f**) Passengers.

Table 1. Training and testing partition of the MSTAR dataset.

	Class	Depression	Number
Training	BMP-2	17°	232
	BTR-70	17°	233
	2S1	17°	299
	BRDM-2	17°	298
	BTR-60	17°	256
Testing	T62	17°	299
	D-7	17°	299
	ZSU-234	17°	299
	T-72	17°	232
	ZIL-131	17°	299

Table 2. Training and testing partition of the OpenSARship dataset.

	Class	Number
Training	Cargo	222
	Tanker	240
	Tug	260
Testing	Dredging	80
	Fishing	80
	Passengers	80

4.2. Experimental Setup

The training and inference experiments in this study were conducted in a Linux environment with the following hardware and software configurations: the server is equipped with 2 × Intel Xeon Platinum 8558 CPUs (96 cores in total) with a maximum frequency of 4.0 GHz; 2.0 TB of RAM; and 2 × NVIDIA H20 GPUs (each with 97,871 MiB of memory). The CUDA version is 12.4, and the driver version is 550.144.03. The experimental environment was built using Python 3.8 and PyTorch 1.13 in Linux (Ubuntu). This configuration provides stable computational support for model training and inference, ensuring the reliability and reproducibility of the experimental results. The input and output channel numbers of each convolutional layer in the feature extraction network are listed in Table 3.

Table 3. Input and output channel configuration of each convolutional layer in the feature extraction network.

Convolutional Block	Channel_In	Channel_Out
Block 1	3	64
Block 2	64	64
Block 3	64	64
Block 4	64	64

Additionally, each image is resized to a fixed resolution (e.g., 84 × 84), converted into a tensor format, and normalized to the range of $[-1, 1]$. This procedure helps mitigate the effects of resolution differences between datasets and stabilizes the training process. The same preprocessing steps are applied across all datasets to ensure experimental consistency and reproducibility.

4.3. Contrast Experiments

On the MSTAR (5-way) and OpenSARShip (3-way) benchmarks, we compare our method against metric-based baselines (ProtoNet, Baseline++, DN4, Meta-Baseline, CPN) as well as a Transformer-based model (ACL) [45] and a generative model (TFH) [46]. As reported in Tables 4 and 5, our approach achieves the best accuracy across most n-shot settings, e.g., it improves over the strongest prior baseline by 2.61% in 5-way 1-shot and 2.55% in 3-way 2-shot. The generative TFH does not surpass our method largely because its reconstruction/likelihood objectives tend to preserve background energy and speckle patterns, which weakens discriminative margins under severe background similarity and very low shots; it is also more sensitive to resolution/domain shifts across SAR datasets. The Transformer ACL underperforms in the extreme low-shot regime due to its higher data hunger and weaker inductive bias for small, noisy SAR sets, leading to overfitting and unstable attention to clutter. In contrast, our framework—combining SSE for background suppression with ACM for explicit cross-class contrast—directly enlarges inter-class margins while stabilizing features in cluttered scenes, yielding higher mean accuracy and lower variance.

Table 4. Performance comparison of the proposed method and other algorithms on the MSTAR dataset.

Method	Accuracy (%)		
	1-Shot	2-Shot	5-Shot
Protonet	51.53 ± 0.38	54.30 ± 0.33	55.55 ± 0.26
Baseline++	50.59 ± 0.35	56.74 ± 0.30	64.75 ± 0.27
Meta-baseline	52.14 ± 0.34	55.01 ± 0.33	58.83 ± 0.28
CPN	49.22 ± 0.53	53.70 ± 0.50	54.54 ± 0.38
DN4	50.64 ± 0.42	57.49 ± 0.31	67.69 ± 0.30
ACL	49.83 ± 0.38	55.27 ± 0.41	68.24 ± 0.30
TFH	37.76 ± 0.63	41.99 ± 0.58	48.22 ± 0.56
Ours	$\mathbf{54.75 \pm 0.32}$	$\mathbf{58.92 \pm 0.24}$	$\mathbf{68.84 \pm 0.22}$

Table 5. Performance comparison of the proposed method and other algorithms on the OpenSARship dataset.

Method	Accuracy (%)		
	1-Shot	2-Shot	5-Shot
Protonet	70.81 ± 0.45	73.49 ± 0.33	79.17 ± 0.26
Baseline++	67.83 ± 0.45	73.17 ± 0.34	79.06 ± 0.28
Meta-baseline	66.06 ± 0.54	70.50 ± 0.43	76.55 ± 0.40
CPN	70.56 ± 0.23	73.70 ± 0.20	76.43 ± 0.21
DN4	68.51 ± 0.32	72.68 ± 0.24	80.52 ± 0.19
ACL	63.75 ± 0.43	71.53 ± 0.38	77.64 ± 0.35
TFH	63.04 ± 0.45	69.95 ± 0.34	76.24 ± 0.36
Ours	$\mathbf{71.42 \pm 0.22}$	$\mathbf{76.25 \pm 0.20}$	$\mathbf{81.86 \pm 0.18}$

4.4. Ablation Experiments

To verify the effectiveness of the proposed SSE and ACM modules, a series of experiments were conducted on the MSTAR and OpenSARShip datasets, as shown in Tables 6 and 7. It can be observed that incorporating the SSE and ACM modules into the I2C framework leads to a significant improvement in classification accuracy. Specifically, the SSE attention module adaptively emphasizes salient scattering structures of the targets while suppressing noise and irrelevant background, thereby enhancing the robustness and discriminability of feature representations. The ACM discriminative metric module, which considers all support classes, evaluates not only the similarity between query samples and their corresponding target classes but also explicit comparisons with non-target classes, effectively reducing background interference and improving inter-class separability. These results demonstrate the effectiveness and generalization capability of the proposed modules in improving SAR target recognition performance.

Table 6. Accuracy comparison between the ACM module and the I2C metric module on the MSTAR Dataset.

Metric Method	Accuracy (%)		
	1-Shot	2-Shot	5-Shot
I2C	50.64 ± 0.42	57.49 ± 0.31	67.69 ± 0.30
I2C + SSE	53.46 ± 0.30	58.37 ± 0.28	68.41 ± 0.29
I2C + ACM	52.89 ± 0.35	58.53 ± 0.29	68.24 ± 0.26
I2C + SSE + ACM	$\mathbf{54.75 \pm 0.32}$	$\mathbf{58.92 \pm 0.24}$	$\mathbf{68.84 \pm 0.22}$

Table 7. Accuracy comparison between the ACM module and the I2C metric module on the OpenSARShip Dataset.

Metric Method	Accuracy (%)		
	1-Shot	2-Shot	5-Shot
I2C	68.51 ± 0.32	72.68 ± 0.24	80.52 ± 0.19
I2C + SSE	70.86 ± 0.27	73.69 ± 0.25	80.38 ± 0.23
I2C + ACM	70.29 ± 0.25	74.92 ± 0.23	81.24 ± 0.25
I2C + SSE + ACM	**71.42 ± 0.22**	**76.25 ± 0.20**	**81.86 ± 0.18**

During the metric process, it is necessary to select an appropriate hyperparameter k to identify the most relevant k nearest neighbors for each local descriptor of the query image. To determine the optimal value of k, we conducted a series of experiments on the MSTAR dataset (5-way 5-shot) and the OpenSARShip dataset (3-way 5-shot), comparing classification performance under different k settings. As shown in Table 8, the model achieved the highest accuracy when $k = 3$. Therefore, k is fixed to 3 in this study.

Table 8. Accuracy comparison on the MSTAR (5-way 5-shot) and OpenSARShip (3-way 5-shot) datasets with different k values.

Dataset	Accuracy (%)		
	k=1	k=3	k=5
MSTAR	63.72 ± 0.28	**68.84 ± 0.22**	66.49 ± 0.30
OpenSARship	78.47 ± 0.23	**81.86 ± 0.18**	80.58 ± 0.21

4.5. Visualization

OpenSARship Dataset

To evaluate the effectiveness of the SSE module, we employed Grad-CAM to visualize the feature responses on the MSTAR and OpenSARShip datasets and compared them with the results obtained without using SSE. As shown in Figure 4, the incorporation of SSE enables the model to better focus on target regions, leading to more accurate localization. This improvement arises because SSE considers both the spatial position of each target and its surrounding contextual information during feature extraction. In contrast, the model without SSE exhibits more scattered attention regions and is more susceptible to background clutter.

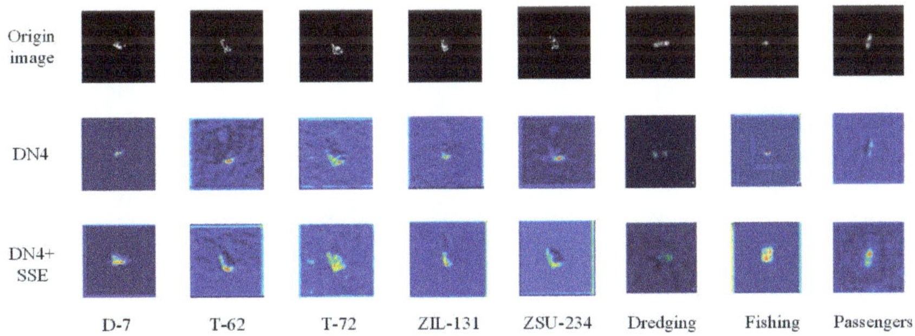

Figure 4. Grad-CAM visualization of samples on the MSTAR dataset and the OpenSARShip dataset.

To further verify the effectiveness of the ACM module, Figure 5 illustrates the prediction score distribution of each category when misclassified as other categories. It can be observed that without ACM, the prediction scores among the different categories are relatively similar, mainly due to the high background similarity between targets and the large proportion of background regions in SAR images. After introducing ACM, the scores of each category misclassified as others decrease significantly, and the score differences between categories become more distinct. Taking ZIL131, ZSU234, and Passengers as examples, the model without ACM tends to be misled by background interference, resulting in close prediction scores across categories. In contrast, with ACM, the model correctly identifies targets by simultaneously measuring the similarity between query samples and both target and non-target classes, thereby effectively reducing the influence of background clutter on metric computation. This substantially enhances inter-class discriminability and improves the overall metric performance of the model.

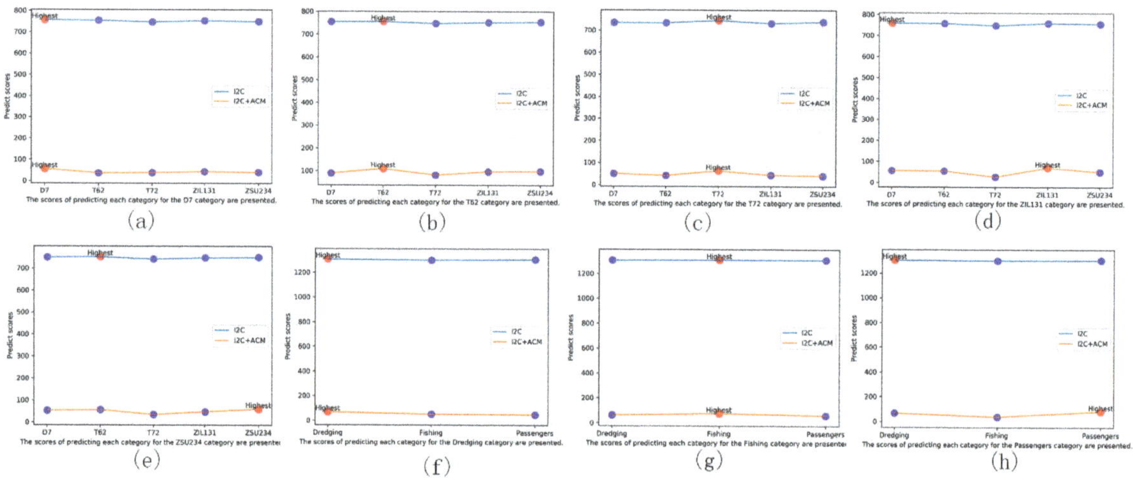

Figure 5. The prediction scores of the query sample and each supported class (similarity scores are calculated under the I2C metric module and ACM module on the MSTAR (**a–e**) and OpenSARship (**f–h**) datasets). (**a**) D7. (**b**) T62. (**c**) T72. (**d**) ZIL131. (**e**) ZSU234. (**f**) Dredging. (**g**) Fishing. (**h**) Passengers.

4.6. Running Time

Figure 6 presents the average running time per episode for the different algorithms on the MSTAR (5-way 5-shot) and OpenSARShip (3-way 5-shot) datasets. Each episode consists of 75 query samples for MSTAR and 45 query samples for OpenSARShip. As shown in the figure, our method achieves a slightly lower running time than DN4, primarily due to the use of broadcast mechanisms and matrix operations. Although the proposed approach involves a marginally higher computational cost compared with the simplest baselines, it consistently achieves the highest recognition accuracy on both MSTAR and OpenSARShip datasets, demonstrating superior overall performance.

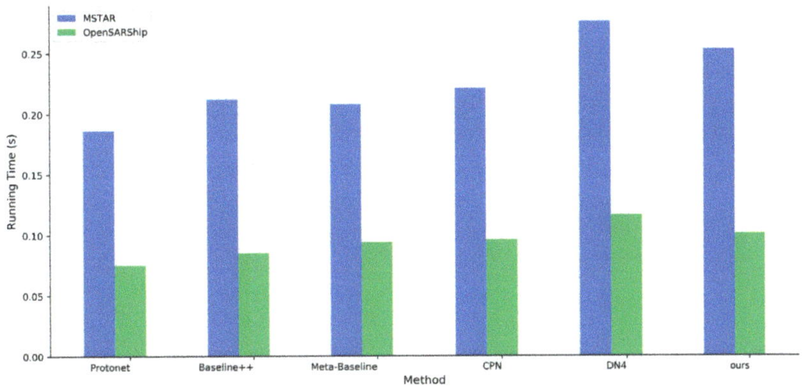

Figure 6. Running time of different algorithms on the MSTAR and the OpenSARShip dataset.

5. Conclusions

This paper proposes an ACM network for few-shot SAR target recognition. By incorporating a spatial attention mechanism, the method adaptively highlights the salient scattering structures of the target while attenuating noise and irrelevant background interference, thereby enhancing the robustness of feature representations. Furthermore, an adaptive contrastive metric module is designed in which query samples are compared not only with their corresponding support classes but also with residual classes, effectively enlarging inter-class margins and strengthening feature discriminability. The experimental results on public SAR datasets demonstrate that the proposed method consistently outperforms several state-of-the-art metric-based FSL approaches in terms of background suppression and recognition accuracy, validating the effectiveness of the proposed method.

In terms of practical significance, the proposed method effectively suppresses strong background clutter in real-world SAR applications (via the SSE module) and addresses the inherent challenge of high inter-class similarity in SAR targets (via the ACM module). This improves recognition reliability in complex environments. Regarding limitations and future work, the scalability of the method on real-world, large-scale data remains to be validated. Therefore, our future research will focus on cross-domain few-shot learning to enhance the model's generalization capability. Simultaneously, we will optimize the algorithm to improve real-time performance, striving to achieve a better trade-off between recognition accuracy and processing speed. Furthermore, we will not only focus on improving the accuracy of SAR target recognition but also emphasize the practical benefits and performance gains that the proposed method brings to real-world SAR recognition tasks. The code of this paper will be released at https://github.com/Daniel123jia (accessed on 1 November 2025).

Author Contributions: R.C. contributed the central idea, analyzed most of the data, and wrote the initial draft of the paper. C.H. and F.Y. contributed the idea of the simulation experiment and provided constructive suggestions. J.Z. contributed to the revisions of the paper and polished the language. All authors discussed the results and revised the manuscript. All authors have read and agreed to the published version of the manuscript.

Funding: This research received no external funding.

Data Availability Statement: The OpenSARship dataset is available at https://opensar.sjtu.edu.cn/ (accessed on 1 November 2025), and the MSTAR dataset is available at https://www.sdms.afrl.af.mil/index.php?collection=mstar (accessed on 1 November 2025).

Acknowledgments: The authors would like to thank the Defense Advanced Research Projects Agency (DARPA) and the U.S. Air Force Research Laboratory (AFRL) for providing the MSTAR dataset, and Shanghai Jiao Tong University for releasing the OpenSARShip dataset. We also sincerely appreciate the valuable comments and suggestions from the anonymous reviewers, which have greatly improved the quality and completeness of this paper.

Conflicts of Interest: Authors Rui Cai, Chao Huang, and Feng Yu were employed by AVIC Xi'an Aircraft Industry Group Company Ltd. The remaining author declares that the study was conducted without any commercial or financial relationships that could be interpreted as a potential conflict of interest.

References

1. Ismail, R.; Muthukumaraswamy, S. Military Reconnaissance and Rescue Robot with Real-Time Object Detection. In *Intelligent Manufacturing and Energy Sustainability: Proceedings of ICIMES 2020*; Springer: Singapore, 2021; pp. 637–648.
2. Yamaguchi, Y. Disaster monitoring by fully polarimetric SAR data acquired with ALOS-PALSAR. *Proc. IEEE* **2012**, *100*, 2851–2860. [CrossRef]
3. Choe, B.H. Polarimetric Synthetic Aperture Radar (SAR) Application for Geological Mapping and Resource Exploration in the Canadian Arctic. Ph.D. Thesis, The University of Western Ontario (Canada), Ontario, ON, Canada, 2017.
4. Errico, A.; Angelino, C.V.; Cicala, L.; Persechino, G.; Ferrara, C.; Lega, M.; Vallario, A.; Parente, C.; Masi, G.; Gaetano, R.; et al. Detection of Environmental Hazards through the Feature-Based Fusion of Optical and SAR Data: A Case Study in Southern Italy. *Int. J. Remote Sens.* **2015**, *36*, 3345–3367. [CrossRef]
5. Ding, B.; Wen, G.; Ma, C.; Yang, X. Decision Fusion Based on Physically Relevant Features for SAR ATR. *IET Radar Sonar Navig.* **2017**, *11*, 682–690. [CrossRef]
6. Huang, Y.; Liao, G.; Zhang, Z.; Xiang, Y.; Li, J.; Nehorai, A. SAR Automatic Target Recognition using Joint Low-Rank and Sparse Multiview Denoising. *IEEE Geosci. Remote Sens. Lett.* **2018**, *15*, 1570–1574. [CrossRef]
7. Tao, L.; Jiang, X.; Liu, X.; Li, Z.; Zhou, Z. Multiscale Supervised Kernel Dictionary Learning for SAR Target Recognition. *IEEE Trans. Geosci. Remote Sens.* **2020**, *58*, 6281–6297. [CrossRef]
8. Wang, C.; Shi, J.; Zhou, Y.; Li, L.; Yang, X.; Zhang, T.; Wei, S.; Zhang, X.; Tao, C. Label Noise Modeling and Correction via Loss Curve Fitting for SAR ATR. *IEEE Trans. Geosci. Remote Sens.* **2022**, *60*, 5216210. [CrossRef]
9. Zhou, Z.; Cao, Z.; Pi, Y. Subdictionary-Based Joint Sparse Representation for SAR Target Recognition using Multilevel Reconstruction. *IEEE Trans. Geosci. Remote Sens.* **2019**, *57*, 6877–6887. [CrossRef]
10. Huang, Z.; Pan, Z.; Lei, B. Transfer Learning with Deep Convolutional Neural Network for SAR Target Classification with Limited Labeled Data. *Remote Sens.* **2017**, *9*, 907. [CrossRef]
11. Chen, S.; Wang, H.; Xu, F.; Jin, Y.Q. Target Classification using the Deep Convolutional Networks for SAR Images. *IEEE Trans. Geosci. Remote Sens.* **2016**, *54*, 4806–4817. [CrossRef]
12. Ai, J.; Mao, Y.; Luo, Q.; Jia, L.; Xing, M. SAR Target Classification using the Multikernel-Size Feature Fusion-Based Convolutional Neural Network. *IEEE Trans. Geosci. Remote Sens.* **2022**, *60*, 5214313. [CrossRef]
13. Yu, L.; Hu, Y.; Xie, X.; Lin, Y.; Hong, W. Complex-Valued Full Convolutional Neural Network for SAR Target Classification. *IEEE Geosci. Remote Sens. Lett.* **2020**, *17*, 1752–1756. [CrossRef]
14. Zhang, F.; Wang, Y.; Ni, J.; Zhou, Y.; Hu, W. SAR Target Small Sample Recognition Based on CNN Cascaded Features and AdaBoost Rotation Forest. *IEEE Geosci. Remote Sens. Lett.* **2020**, *17*, 1008–1012. [CrossRef]
15. Yu, J.; Chen, J.; Wan, H.; Zhou, Z.; Cao, Y.; Huang, Z.; Li, Y.; Wu, B.; Yao, B. Sargap: A full-link general decoupling automatic pruning algorithm for deep learning-based sar target detectors. *IEEE Trans. Geosci. Remote Sens.* **2024**, *62*, 1–18. [CrossRef]
16. Guo, Y.; Chen, S.; Zhan, R.; Wang, W.; Zhang, J. Deformable Feature Fusion and Accurate Anchors Prediction for Lightweight SAR Ship Detector Based on Dynamic Hierarchical Model Pruning. *IEEE J. Sel. Top. Appl. Earth Obs. Remote Sens.* **2025**, *18*, 15019–15036. [CrossRef]
17. Zhang, X.; Luo, Y.; Hu, L. Semi-Supervised SAR ATR via Epoch and Uncertainty-Aware Pseudo-Label Exploitation. *IEEE Trans. Geosci. Remote Sens.* **2023**, *61*, 5209015. [CrossRef]
18. Wang, Z.; Du, L.; Mao, J.; Liu, B.; Yang, D. SAR Target Detection Based on SSD with Data Augmentation and Transfer Learning. *IEEE Geosci. Remote Sens. Lett.* **2019**, *16*, 150–154. [CrossRef]
19. Sun, Y.; Wang, Y.; Liu, H.; Wang, N.; Wang, J. SAR Target Recognition with Limited Training Data Based on Angular Rotation Generative Network. *IEEE Geosci. Remote Sens. Lett.* **2020**, *17*, 1928–1932. [CrossRef]
20. Zhang, C.; Wang, Y.; Liu, H.; Sun, Y.; Hu, L. SAR Target Recognition using Only Simulated Data for Training by Hierarchically Combining CNN and Image Similarity. *IEEE Geosci. Remote Sens. Lett.* **2022**, *19*, 1–5. [CrossRef]

21. Koch, G.; Zemel, R.; Salakhutdinov, R. Siamese Neural Networks for One-Shot Image Recognition. In Proceedings of the International Conference on Machine Learning (ICML), Vancouver, BC, Canada, 13–19 July 2015; Volume 2.
22. Vinyals, O.; Blundell, C.; Lillicrap, T.; Wierstra, D. Matching Networks for One Shot Learning. In Proceedings of the International Conference on Neural Information Processing Systems, San Diego, CA, USA, 2–7 December 2025; Volume 29, pp. 3630–3638.
23. Snell, J.; Swersky, K.; Zemel, R. Prototypical Networks for Few-Shot Learning. In Proceedings of the International Conference on Neural Information Processing Systems, San Diego, CA, USA, 2–7 December 2025; Volume 30, pp. 4080–4090.
24. Sung, F.; Yang, Y.; Zhang, L.; Xiang, T.; Torr, P.H.; Hospedales, T.M. Hospedales, Learning to Compare: Relation Network for Few-Shot Learning. In Proceedings of the IEEE/CVF Conference on Computer Vision and Pattern Recognition (CVPR), Salt Lake City, UT, USA, 18–22 June 2018; pp. 1199–1208.
25. Li, W.; Xu, J.; Huo, J.; Wang, L.; Gao, Y.; Luo, J. Distribution Consistency Based Covariance Metric Networks for Few-Shot Learning. In Proceedings of the AAAI Conference on Artificial Intelligence, Honolulu, HI, USA, 27 January–1 February 2019; Volume 33, pp. 8642–8649.
26. Zhang, C.; Cai, Y.; Lin, G.; Shen, C. DeepEMD: Few-shot image classification with differentiable earth mover's distance and structured classifiers. In Proceedings of the IEEE/CVF Conference on Computer Vision and Pattern Recognition (CVPR), Seattle, WA, USA, 14–19 June 2020; pp. 12203–12213.
27. Ye, H.J.; Hu, H.; Zhan, D.C.; Sha, F. Few-shot learning via embedding adaptation with set-to-set functions. In Proceedings of the IEEE/CVF Conference on Computer Vision and Pattern Recognition (CVPR), Seattle, WA, USA, 14–19 June 2020; pp. 8808–8817.
28. Chen, T.; Kornblith, S.; Norouzi, M.; Hinton, G. Simclr: A simple framework for contrastive learning of visual representations. In Proceedings of the International Conference on Learning Representations (ICLR), New York, NY, USA, 26–30 April 2020.
29. Radford, A.; Kim, J.W.; Hallacy, C.; Ramesh, A.; Goh, G.; Agarwal, S.; Sastry, G.; Askell, A.; Mishkin, P.; Clark, J.; et al. Learning transferable visual models from natural language supervision. In Proceedings of the International Conference on Machine Learning, Virtual Event, 18–24 July 2021; pp. 8748–8763.
30. Li, W.; Wang, L.; Xu, J.; Huo, J.; Gao, Y.; Luo, J. Revisiting Local Descriptor Based Image-to-Class Measure for Few-Shot Learning. In Proceedings of the IEEE/CVF Conference on Computer Vision and Pattern Recognition (CVPR), Long Beach, CA, USA, 15–20 June 2019; pp. 7260–7268.
31. Rostami, M.; Kolouri, S.; Eaton, E.; Kim, K. Deep Transfer Learning for Few-Shot SAR Image Classification. *Remote Sens.* **2019**, *11*, 1374. [CrossRef]
32. Rostami, M.; Kolouri, S.; Eaton, E.; Kim, K. SAR Image Classification using Few-Shot Cross-Domain Transfer Learning. In Proceedings of the IEEE/CVF Conference on Computer Vision and Pattern Recognition (CVPR), Long Beach, CA, USA, 15–20 June 2019.
33. Tai, Y.; Tan, Y.; Xiong, S.; Tian, J. Cross-Domain Few-Shot Learning between Different Imaging Modals for Fine-Grained Target Recognition. *IEEE J. Sel. Top. Appl. Earth Obs. Remote Sens.* **2022**, *15*, 9186–9197. [CrossRef]
34. Ren, H.; Liu, S.; Yu, X.; Zou, L.; Zhou, Y.; Wang, X.; Tang, H. Transductive prototypical attention reasoning network for few-shot SAR target recognition. *IEEE Trans. Geosci. Remote Sens.* **2023**, *61*, 1–13. [CrossRef]
35. Zheng, J.; Li, M.; Chen, H.; Zhang, P.; Wu, Y. Deep Fourier-Based Task-Aware Metric Network for Few-Shot SAR Target Classification. *IEEE Trans. Instrum. Meas.* **2025**, *74*, 1–14. [CrossRef]
36. Zheng, J.; Li, M.; Li, X.; Zhang, P.; Wu, Y. SVD-Based Feature Reconstruction Metric Network with Active Contrast Loss for Few-Shot SAR Target Recognition. *IEEE J. Sel. Top. Appl. Earth Obs. Remote Sens.* **2025**, *18*, 7391–7405. [CrossRef]
37. Zheng, J.; Li, M.; Li, X.; Zhang, P.; Wu, Y. Revisiting Local and Global Descriptor-Based Metric Network for Few-Shot SAR Target Classification. *IEEE Trans. Geosci. Remote Sens.* **2024**, *62*, 1–14. [CrossRef]
38. Cai, J.; Zhang, Y.; Guo, J.; Zhao, X.; Lv, J.; Hu, Y. ST-PN: A Spatial Transformed Prototypical Network for Few-Shot SAR Image Classification. *Remote Sens.* **2022**, *14*, 2019. [CrossRef]
39. Zhao, Y.; Zhao, L.; Ding, D.; Hu, D.; Kuang, G.; Liu, L. Few-Shot Class-Incremental SAR Target Recognition via Cosine Prototype Learning. *IEEE Trans. Geosci. Remote Sens.* **2023**, *61*, 1–18. [CrossRef]
40. Zeng, Z.; Sun, J.; Wang, Y.; Gu, D.; Han, Z.; Hong, W. Few-Shot SAR Target Recognition through Meta Adaptive Hyper-Parameters Learning for Fast Adaptation. *IEEE Trans. Geosci. Remote Sens.* **2023**, *61*, 1–17.
41. Qin, J.; Zou, B.; Chen, Y.; Li, H.; Zhang, L. Scattering Attribute Embedded Network for Few-Shot SAR ATR. *IEEE Trans. Aerosp. Electron. Syst.* **2024**, *60*, 4182–4197. [CrossRef]
42. Zhao, X.; Lv, X.; Cai, J.; Zhang, Y.; Qiu, X.; Wu, Y. Few-shot sar-atr based on instance-aware transformer. *Remote Sens.* **2022**, *14*, 1884. [CrossRef]
43. Ren, H.; Yu, X.; Wang, X.; Liu, S.; Zou, L.; Wang, X. Siamese Subspace Classification Network for Few-Shot SAR Automatic Target Recognition. In Proceedings of the IEEE International Geoscience and Remote Sensing Symposium (IGARSS), Kuala Lumpur, Malaysia, 17–22 July 2022; pp. 2634–2637.
44. Zhang, L.; Leng, X.; Feng, S.; Ma, X.; Ji, K.; Kuang, G.; Liu, L. Optimal Azimuth Angle Selection for Limited SAR Vehicle Target Recognition. *Int. J. Appl. Earth Obs. Geoinf.* **2024**, *128*, 103707. [CrossRef]

45. He, Y.; Liang, W.; Zhao, D.; Zhou, H.Y.; Ge, W.; Yu, Y.; Zhang, W. Attribute surrogates learning and spectral tokens pooling in transformers for few-shot learning. In Proceedings of the IEEE/CVF Conference on Computer Vision and Pattern Recognition (CVPR), New Orleans, LA, USA, 18–24 June 2022; pp. 9119–9129.
46. Lazarou, M.; Stathaki, T.; Avrithis, Y. Tensor feature hallucination for few-shot learning. In Proceedings of the IEEE/CVF Winter Conference on Applications of Computer Vision (WACV), Waikoloa, HI, USA, 3–8 January 2022; pp. 3500–3510.

electronics

MDPI

Article

Multi-Interference Suppression Network: Joint Waveform and Filter Design for Radar Interference Suppression

Rui Cai [1], Chenge Shi [1], Wei Dong [1] and Ming Bai [2,*]

1 AVIC XI'AN Aircraft Industry Group Company Ltd., Shaanxi 710089, China; cairui1201@126.com (R.C.); chen_geshi7@126.com (C.S.); dongwei172@163.com (W.D.)
2 School of Electronic and Information Engineering, Beihang University, Beijing 100083, China
* Correspondence: mbai@buaa.edu.cn

Abstract

With the advancement of electromagnetic interference and counter-interference technology, complex and unpredictable interference signals greatly reduce radar detection, tracking, and recognition performance. In multi-interference environments, the overlap of interference cross-correlation peaks can mask target signals, weakening radar interference suppression capability. To address this, we propose a joint waveform and filter design method called Multi-Interference Suppression Network (MISNet) for effective interference suppression. First, we develop a design criterion based on suppression coefficients for different interferences, minimizing both cross-correlation energy and interference peak models. Then, for the non-smooth, non-convex optimization problem, we use complex neural networks and gating mechanisms, transforming it into a differentiable problem via end-to-end training to optimize the transmit waveform and receive filter efficiently. Simulation results show that compared to traditional algorithms, MISNet effectively reduces interference cross-correlation peaks and autocorrelation sidelobes in single interference environments; it demonstrates excellent robustness in multi-interference environments, significantly outperforming CNN, PSO, and ANN comparison methods, effectively improving radar interference suppression performance in complex multi-interference scenarios.

Keywords: radar interference suppression; waveform design; complex neural networks; multi-interference

1. Introduction

With the advancement of electromagnetic interference and counter-interference technology, complex and unpredictable interference signals greatly reduce radar detection, tracking, and recognition performance [1,2]. The emergence of digital radio frequency memory (DRFM) technology has further improved the interference generation capability of interference sources. Interference sources can capture radar signals, store them, and retransmit them with modulation, confusing radar systems [3,4]. In multi-interference environments, the overlap of interference cross-correlation peaks can mask target signals, weakening radar interference suppression capability [5,6].

Recent years have witnessed the emergence of adaptive electromagnetic interference technology, making interference signals exhibit intelligent and adaptive characteristics [7,8]. Traditional advanced interference mitigation (AIM) techniques such as frequency agility, adaptive sidelobe cancellation, space-time adaptive processing, and monopulse tracking [9,10] show limitations when facing new intelligent interference. Particularly in complex electromagnetic environments, when multiple types of DRFM interference (such as

https://doi.org/10.3390/electronics14204023

intermittent sampling repeater jamming ISRJ, intermittent sampling repeater jamming with frequency shifting ISRJ-FR, and smeared spectrum jamming SMSP) exist simultaneously [11,12], traditional methods often cannot effectively suppress them.

To suppress interference signals, many researchers have studied this problem. Current research on interference suppression mainly focuses on echo processing techniques and interference suppression waveform design. Multidimensional signal processing transforms signals into higher dimensions, such as the polarization domain, time-frequency domain, or spatial domain, allowing the design of high-dimensional filters to suppress interference [13,14]. However, higher-dimensional transformations significantly increase the computational load, making it hard to meet radar's real-time requirements.

With the rapid development of deep learning technology, neural networks are increasingly applied in radar signal processing [15,16]. Complex-valued neural networks (CVNNs) show great potential in processing radar complex-domain signals [17]. The introduction of attention mechanisms further enhances neural networks' ability to learn complex signal patterns [18].

Waveform design, as an emerging technology, reduces the impact of interference on radar systems by designing the phase of intra-pulse waveforms [19,20]. In [10], a method minimizing the peak sidelobe level (PSL) was proposed, effectively reducing the peak sidelobe level in radar pulse compression. In [11], the signal-to-interference-plus-noise ratio (SINR) was maximized under pulse compression sidelobe constraints, effectively handling clutter and false alarms. In [12], an interference cross-correlation energy model was minimized under constant modulus waveform constraints, reducing the cross-correlation gain of interference signals and effectively suppressing interference.

Recent research demonstrates that joint transmit waveform and receive filter design can more fully utilize the degrees of freedom of the system [14,21]. This optimization approach has potential applications in emerging Integrated Sensing and Communication (ISAC) systems [22,23], where similar joint design principles could be beneficial for multi-functional system architectures. However, these traditional iterative optimization methods have high computational complexity and slow convergence speed, making it difficult to meet the real-time requirements of practical applications [24].

These methods effectively suppress single interference. However, when multiple interferences occur simultaneously, targets can still be overwhelmed by interference cross-correlation peaks, reducing radar target detection performance in interference environments. More severely, in moving target environments, the Doppler effect causes spectral spread of target signals, further exacerbating the difficulty of multi-interference suppression [25].

To efficiently suppress multiple interferences, we propose a joint optimization method for transmit waveforms and receive filters, called Multi-Interference Suppression Network (MISNet). This method utilizes interference cross-correlation peak and energy models, combined with adaptive interference suppression coefficients, fully exploiting the degrees of freedom in waveforms and filters to minimize interference effects under constraints. For the non-smooth, non-convex optimization problem involving multiple maximum functions, we employ complex neural networks and gated networks. Through end-to-end training, we transform it into a differentiable problem, efficiently optimizing the transmit waveform and receive filter [26,27].

Experiments show that compared to traditional algorithms, this method effectively reduces interference cross-correlation peaks and autocorrelation sidelobes in single interference environments; it demonstrates excellent robustness in multi-interference environments, significantly outperforming CNN, PSO, and ANN comparison methods, effectively enhancing radar interference suppression performance in complex multi-interference scenarios.

This paper is arranged as follows. Section 2 formulates the problem of multi-interference suppression. Section 3 presents the proposed Multi-Interference Suppression Network (MISNet), detailing the complex attention mechanism and gating structure optimization method. Section 4 evaluates the performance of MISNet through numerical experiments, comparing it with traditional methods under single and multi-interference scenarios. Section 5 concludes the paper, summarizing the key findings and contributions.

2. Problem Formulation

In complex electromagnetic environments, radar systems frequently face complex scenarios where multiple types of interference signals act simultaneously. These interferences include not only traditional noise and deceptive interference but also intelligent interference using DRFM technology [28].

In this paper, we consider a more complex scenario where multiple interference sources interfere with the radar simultaneously. We assume the radar transmits a phase-coded waveform $W = [w_1, \ldots, w_N]^H$, where N is the waveform length. The received echo signal can be defined as:

$$\mathrm{Echo} = \sum_{i=1}^{M_j} \alpha_i J_{jam,i} + \beta W + n_{noise} \tag{1}$$

where $n_{noise} = [n_1, \ldots, n_N]^T$ represents Gaussian white noise with zero mean and variance δ^2. $J_{jam,i}$ is the interference signal from the i-th interference source, expressed as:

$$J_{jam,i} = A_i w \tag{2}$$

and A_i is the interference modulation matrix. In a cognitive radar system, we can obtain the interference modulation matrix from feedback of previous radar scans, providing a foundation for adaptive interference suppression [29].

Interference sources set the interference modulation matrix to gain amplification in pulse compression, overwhelming the radar target peak. The pulse compression gain of the interference is:

$$R_{j_i,d} = h_r^H T_{N-d} J_{jam,i} \tag{3}$$

where $R_{j_i,d}$ is the gain of the i-th interference after pulse compression at the d-th range bin.

Traditional waveform design methods can suppress single interference effectively by reducing its pulse compression gain. However, multiple interferences significantly degrade radar target detection performance. To suppress interference effectively and fully utilize the degrees of freedom in the transmit waveform and receive filter, we introduce the interference cross-correlation peak model and energy model:

$$\mathrm{PICL}_{j,i} = \max_{d=-N+1,\ldots,N-1} \left| R_{j_i,d} / N \right| \tag{4}$$

$$\mathrm{ELCF}_{j,i} = \sum_{d=-N+1}^{N-1} |R_{j_i,d} / N|^2 \tag{5}$$

where $\mathrm{PICL}_{j,i}$ is the peak of the i-th interference cross-correlation function. A higher $\mathrm{PICL}_{j,i}$ can overwhelm the radar target peak, misleading the radar system. $\mathrm{ELCF}_{j,i}$ is the energy of the i-th interference cross-correlation function. A larger $\mathrm{ELCF}_{j,i}$ raises the pulse compression noise floor, suppressing the radar.

To fully utilize the degrees of freedom in the transmit waveform and receive filter, we define an interference suppression coefficient:

$$q_i = \sum_{d=-N+1}^{N-1} |R_{j_i,d}| \tag{6}$$

A larger q_i indicates a greater degree of interference overwhelming the target. We minimize $ELCF_{j,i}$ to avoid raising the noise floor and overwhelming strong target peaks. When q_i is small, we optimize $PICL_{j,i}$ to improve radar detection performance for strong targets and adjust the interference suppression weights based on different q_i values.

Additionally, the autocorrelation peak of the transmit waveform and receive filter is crucial to prevent weak targets from being overwhelmed by strong clutter. The model is:

$$PSL_d = \max_{d=-N+1,\ldots,N-1,d\neq 0}|R_d/N| \tag{7}$$

where:

$$R_d = h_r^H T_{N-d} w \tag{8}$$

Thus, to effectively suppress interference under waveform constant modulus constraints and filter energy constraints [18,19], we propose a joint interference suppression method based on cross-correlation peaks and energy by designing the transmit waveform and receive filter. The objective function is:

$$\min_{h,w} \mu_1 PSL_d + \sum_{i=1}^{M_j}(u_2 PICL_{j,i} + u_3 ELCF_{j,i}) \tag{9}$$

$$s.t.|w| = 1,\ \ h^H h = N$$

where u_1, u_2, and u_3 are three fixed weighting parameters.

3. Complex Attention Mechanism and Residual Structure Optimization Method

In multi-jammer environments, radar systems face simultaneous interference from multiple sources, significantly degrading target detection performance. Traditional methods struggle to effectively suppress complex interference and incur high computational complexity, failing to meet real-time requirements. The development of deep learning technology provides new approaches to solve this problem. Complex neural networks have natural advantages in processing radar complex-domain signals, better preserving amplitude and phase information of signals [30].

To address this, we propose a deep learning-based joint optimization approach, termed "MISNet," which aims to simultaneously optimize the transmit waveform w and receive filter h to effectively mitigate multiple interferences and enhance radar interference suppression capabilities.

As shown in Figure 1, our approach leverages a complex neural network (ComplexModel) to tackle this challenge. Unlike traditional real-valued neural networks, complex neural networks can directly process complex-domain signals, avoiding information loss caused by separating real and imaginary parts. The network takes initial noisy waveforms $h_{noise}, w_{noise} \in \mathbb{C}^N$ as inputs, extracts features via shared layers, dynamically optimizes through gating units, and outputs optimized $h, w \in \mathbb{C}^N$, satisfying the constraints:

$$\left|w\right| = 1,\quad h^H h = N \tag{10}$$

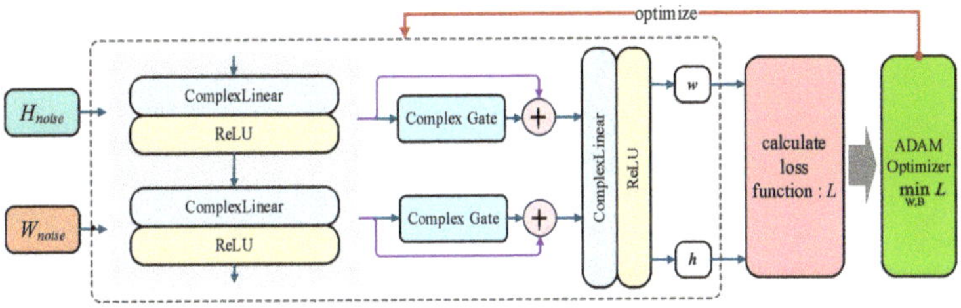

Figure 1. Overall architecture diagram of MISNet algorithm.

The shared layer applies a linear transformation $f_s : \mathbb{C}^N \to \mathbb{C}^M$ (where $M > N$) to map inputs to a higher-dimensional space, defined as:

$$h_s = W_s h_{noise} + b_s, \quad w_s = W_s w_{noise} + b_s \tag{11}$$

where $h_s \in \mathbb{C}^M$, $w_s \in \mathbb{C}^M$, $W_s \in \mathbb{C}^{M\times N}$, and $b_s \in \mathbb{C}^M$ are shared weights and biases. They reduce model complexity while capturing synergy between h and w.

As shown in Figure 2, the ComplexGate mechanism is an innovation of MISNet. Defined as $g : \mathbb{C}^M \times \mathbb{C}^M \to \mathbb{C}^M$, this gating unit takes $h_s \in \mathbb{C}^M$ and $w_s \in \mathbb{C}^M$ as inputs and works in this high-dimensional space. The process is:

$$h_v = \tanh(h_s), \quad h_t = \tanh(w_s) \tag{12}$$

$$h_{sw} = \sigma([h_s; w_s]) \tag{13}$$

$$z = h_v \odot h_{sw} + (1 - h_t) \odot h_{sw} \tag{14}$$

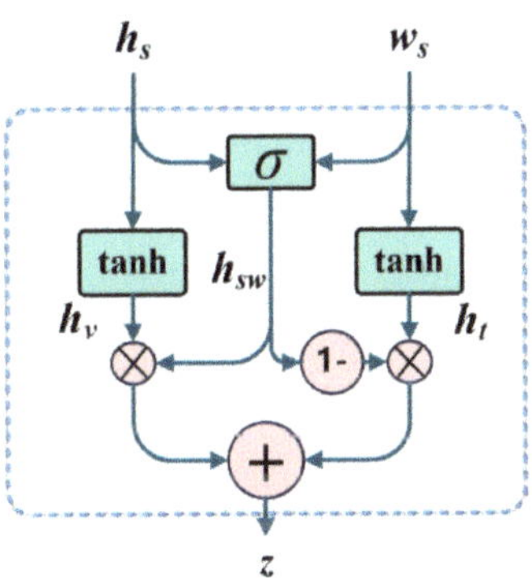

Figure 2. Structure diagram of ComplexGate gating mechanism.

Then, the gating outputs are:

$$h_g = z + h_s \tag{15}$$

$$w_g = z + w_s \tag{16}$$

where h_v and h_t are intermediate vectors from $h_s \in \mathbb{C}^M$ and $w_s \in \mathbb{C}^M$ using tanh. h_{sw} comes from concatenating $h_s \in \mathbb{C}^M$ and $w_s \in \mathbb{C}^M$ (making a 2M-dimensional vector) and applying σ to get an M-dimensional vector. z is computed by element-wise multiplication (denoted by ⊙) and addition. Finally, h_g and w_g are the gating unit outputs.

The gating unit adjusts features dynamically using interactions between $h_s \in \mathbb{C}^M$ and $w_s \in \mathbb{C}^M$, along with h_v, h_t, and h_{sw}. This improves adaptability to different interference patterns.

Next, the independent layer $f_i : \mathbb{C}^M \to \mathbb{C}^N$ maps features back to the original dimension:

$$h = W_h h_g + b_h, \quad w = W_w w_g + b_w \tag{17}$$

where $W_h \in \mathbb{C}^{N\times M}$, $W_w \in \mathbb{C}^{N\times M}$, $b_h \in \mathbb{C}^N$, and $b_w \in \mathbb{C}^N$ are independent parameters. Normalization follows to meet constraints.

The optimization objective is formulated as a loss function to drive network training:

$$Loss = \mu_1 \mathbf{PSL_d} + \sum_{i=1}^{M_j} (u_2 \mathrm{CPM}_{j,i} + u_3 \mathrm{CEM}_{j,i}) \tag{18}$$

This loss function minimizes sidelobes and interference terms, guiding the network to learn optimal h and w, with training based on $J_{jam,i}$ and backpropagation.

4. Numerical Results

4.1. Experimental Setup

This section validates the effectiveness of the proposed MISNet algorithm through numerical simulations. We consider a monostatic radar system equipped with a phase-coded waveform of length $N = 256$. The maximum number of algorithm iterations is set to 30,000. The weighting parameters are configured as follows: $u_1 = 200$, $u_2 = 3$, $u_3 = 30$, and the pulse compression peak constraint parameter $b_{max} = 228$. The MISNet algorithm employs the ASGD optimizer with a learning rate of 0.01, a hidden layer dimension of 512, and training for 30,000 epochs. The algorithm is initialized with random phase sequences. All experiments are conducted on a PC equipped with a 2.80 GHz Intel i9-10900 CPU, 32 GB RAM, and an NVIDIA RTX 3090 GPU.

To comprehensively evaluate the performance of the proposed method, we select comparison algorithms targeting different application scenarios. For single interference suppression scenarios, we compare against the MPSL algorithm [14] and ICEL algorithm [12], where the MPSL algorithm designs waveforms and filters based on minimizing peak sidelobe level criteria, and the ICEL algorithm achieves single interference suppression by minimizing interference cross-correlation energy. For multi-interference suppression scenarios, we select PSO (Particle Swarm Optimization with population size 30, inertia weight 0.7, acceleration factors $c_1 = c_2 = 1.5$), CNN (Convolutional Neural Network with 3-layer 1D convolution structure, channel numbers 32-64-1, ReLU activation function), and ANN (Complex-Valued Artificial Neural Network with 3-layer fully connected structure 256-128-64-256, complex ReLU activation function for complex-domain signal processing) as comparison methods.

This experiment employs two performance metrics for evaluation. The Peak of Interference Cross-correlation Level (PICL) is defined as the maximum peak of the cross-correlation function between the interference signal and the receive filter, expressed as:

$$\mathrm{PICL} = \max_{d=-N+1,\ldots,N-1} \left| R_{j,d} / N \right| \tag{19}$$

where $R_{j,d}$ is the interference pulse compression gain at the d-th range bin. Lower PICL values indicate better interference suppression performance.

The Autocorrelation Peak Sidelobe Level (APSL) is defined as the maximum sidelobe peak of the autocorrelation function between the transmit waveform and receive filter, expressed as:

$$\mathrm{APSL} = \max_{d=-N+1,\ldots,N-1,d\neq 0} \left| R_d / N \right| \tag{20}$$

where R_d is the autocorrelation value at the d-th delay. Lower APSL values help prevent weak targets from being masked by strong clutter, improving radar target detection performance.

Following the interference model in reference [14], the experiment employs three typical DRFM interference types, all represented as 256 × 256 real matrices.

The first type is the Intermittent Sampling Repeater Jamming (ISRJ) matrix A_{ISRJ}, expressed as:

$$A_{ISRJ} = \mathrm{diag}(d) \tag{21}$$

where the diagonal vector $d = \left[d_1, d_2, \ldots, d_{256}\right]^T$ satisfies:

$$d_i = \begin{cases} 1, & \text{if } i \in S_{ISRJ} \\ 0, & \text{otherwise} \end{cases} \tag{22}$$

S_{ISRJ} is the intermittent sampling position set, containing 5 consecutive segments with 8 elements each, totaling 40 non-zero elements, simulating the discontinuous characteristics of intermittent sampling repeater jamming.

The second type is the Intermittent Sampling Radio Frequency Jamming (ISRJ-RF) matrix $A_{ISRJ-RF}$, expressed as:

$$A_{ISRJ-RF} = \begin{bmatrix} I_{N_1} & 0 \\ J_{N_2} & 0 \end{bmatrix}_{256\times256} \tag{23}$$

where N_1 and N_2 are the dimensions of the upper and lower blocks, respectively, I_{N_1} is the identity matrix, and J_{N_2} is the anti-diagonal identity matrix:

$$[J_{N_2}]_{i,j} = \begin{cases} 1, & \text{if } i + j = N_2 + 1 \\ 0, & \text{otherwise} \end{cases} \tag{24}$$

This matrix adopts a block anti-diagonal structure, simulating the intermittent sampling repeater characteristics in the radio frequency domain.

The third type is the Smeared Spectrum Jamming (SMSP) matrix A_{SMSP}, expressed as:

$$A_{SMSP} = \left[r_1^T, r_2^T, \ldots, r_{256}^T\right]^T \tag{25}$$

where the i-th row vector r_i satisfies:

$$[r_i]_j = \begin{cases} 1, & \text{if } j = (4i|\mathrm{mod}|128) + \lfloor (i-1)/128 \rfloor \times 128 + 1 \\ 0, & \text{otherwise} \end{cases} \tag{26}$$

This matrix is row-sparse with only one non-zero element per row, distributed with 4-fold periodic intervals, simulating spectrum smearing effects.

4.2. Algorithm Performance Analysis

To verify the convergence performance of the MISNet algorithm in multi-interference environments, we compare the loss function convergence characteristics of different algorithms under the combined action of ISRJ and ISRJ-RF dual interference sources. Figure 3 shows the training convergence curves of four algorithms: PSO, CNN, ANN, and MISNet.

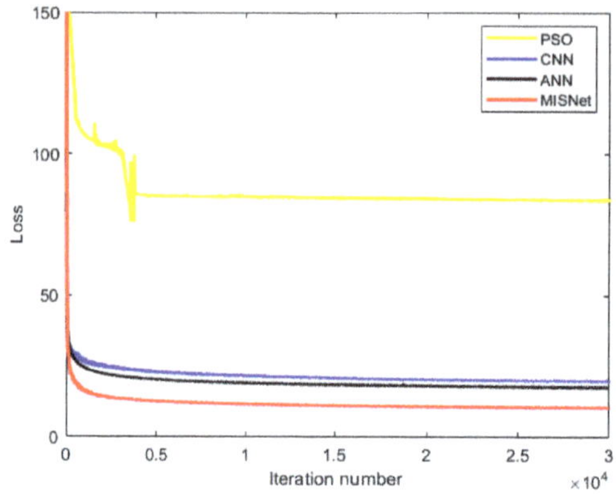

Figure 3. Comparison of loss function convergence curves for different algorithms.

Figure 3 demonstrates that the PSO algorithm exhibits significant convergence fluctuations during optimization, with final convergence results notably inferior to other algorithms. CNN, ANN, and MISNet show comparable convergence speeds, but MISNet significantly outperforms other algorithms in final convergence results. This result fully validates the effectiveness of complex neural networks combined with gating mechanisms, indicating that MISNet can better perform feature selection and complex domain information processing, achieving superior performance in multi-interference suppression optimization problems.

From the perspective of engineering implementation feasibility, we can pre-analyze all possible interference parameters and generate an offline waveform library covering comprehensive interference mitigation scenarios. During actual deployment, the system does not need to run complex neural network computations in real-time, but only needs to quickly identify current interference characteristics to achieve millisecond-level optimal waveform retrieval from the waveform library, fully meeting radar's stringent real-time requirements.

4.3. Performance Evaluation in Single Interference Environment

Since traditional methods only optimize interference suppression performance for single interference, to verify the effectiveness of the proposed method in single interference environments, we compare MISNet with traditional algorithms ICEL [12] and MPSL [14], using a single SMSP interference matrix A_{SMSP}.

Figure 4a shows the waveform autocorrelation function characteristics designed by the three algorithms. It can be observed that the MISNet algorithm achieves the lowest sidelobe level near the main peak, effectively suppressing autocorrelation sidelobes. Figure 4b displays the cross-correlation function between the interference signal and the receive filter. Compared to other algorithms, the MISNet algorithm maintains lower cross-correlation levels across the entire range, demonstrating excellent interference suppression capability.

As shown in Table 1, the proposed MISNet algorithm demonstrates significant advantages in single interference suppression. In terms of interference cross-correlation peak suppression, MISNet improves by 10.12 dB compared to ICEL and by 1.20 dB compared to MPSL. In terms of autocorrelation peak sidelobe suppression, MISNet improves by 7.83 dB compared to ICEL and by 1.91 dB compared to MPSL. This result proves the effectiveness of complex neural networks in handling radar waveform optimization problems, achieving both effective interference signal suppression and good autocorrelation sidelobe control.

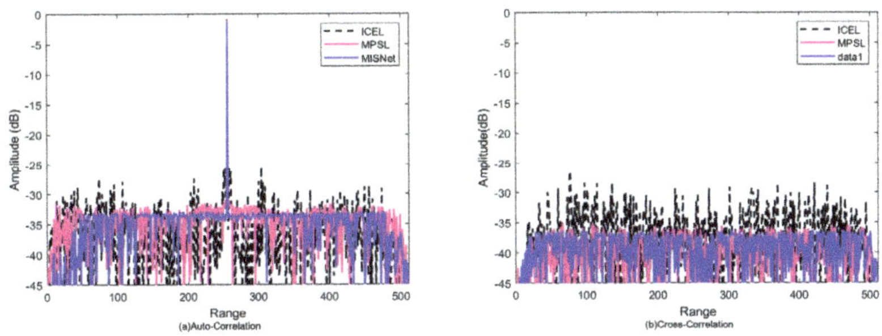

Figure 4. Correlation function comparison of different algorithms under single interference source. (**a**) Waveform autocorrelation function; (**b**) Interference cross-correlation function.

Table 1. Performance Comparison of Different Algorithms under Single Interference Source.

Algorithm.	PICL (dB)	APSL (dB)
ICEL [12]	−26.39	−25.48
MPSL [14]	−35.31	−31.40
MISNet	−36.51	−33.31

4.4. Robustness Verification in Multi-Interference Environment

To further verify the robustness of the proposed method in complex multi-interference environments, we select three dual-interference combinations: $(A_{ISRJ}, A_{ISRJ-RF})$, (A_{ISRJ}, A_{SMSP}), and $(A_{ISRJ-RF}, A_{SMSP})$, and compare them with CNN, PSO, and ANN algorithms. The evaluation metrics include Autocorrelation Peak Sidelobe Level (APSL) and Peak of Interference Cross-correlation Level (PICL) for both interference sources.

From Figure 5, it can be observed that in multi-interference environments, the MISNet algorithm maintains good sidelobe suppression characteristics near the main peak of the autocorrelation function while achieving the lowest correlation levels in the cross-correlation functions of both interference sources. In contrast, other algorithms show obvious performance degradation when handling multiple interferences.

As shown in Table 2, in all multi-interference scenarios, the proposed MISNet algorithm demonstrates optimal performance. For different interference type combinations, MISNet exhibits good adaptability. The ANN algorithm, as the second-best solution, approaches MISNet's performance in some cases, while CNN and PSO algorithms perform significantly poorly in multi-interference environments. This validates the superiority and robustness of complex neural networks combined with gating mechanisms in handling complex interference scenarios. Due to the relatively small autocorrelation weight, the autocorrelation performance decreases compared to the single interference scenario in Figure 4, but the interference suppression performance is significantly improved.

Table 2. Performance Comparison of Different Algorithms under Multi-Interference Sources (PICL1 and PICL2 represent the interference cross-correlation peak suppression levels corresponding to the first and second interference matrices, respectively).

Algorithm	$(A_{ISRJ}, A_{ISRJ-RF})$			(A_{ISRJ}, A_{SMSP})			$(A_{ISRJ-RF}, A_{SMSP})$		
	APSL	PICL1	PICL2	APSL	PICL1	PICL2	APSL	PICL1	PICL2
CNN	−16.33	−25.18	−23.31	−11.48	−22.51	−20.80	−18.29	−28.29	−28.29
PSO	−16.87	−24.55	−19.79	−17.24	−23.23	−19.43	−17.63	−20.79	−21.88
ANN	−21.17	−34.03	−35.13	−23.18	−35.32	−37.60	−19.91	−40.93	−36.15
MISNet	−23.83	−36.85	−38.49	−24.10	−38.30	−40.49	−20.70	−40.72	−41.19

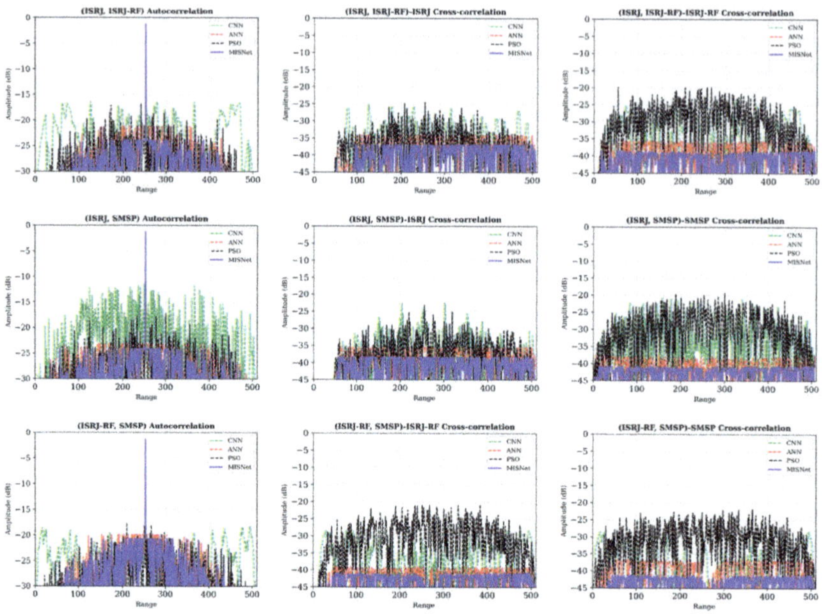

Figure 5. Correlation function comparison of different algorithms under multi-interference sources. First row: autocorrelation function, ISRJ cross-correlation function, and ISRJ-RF cross-correlation function for $(A_{ISRJ}, A_{ISRJ-RF})$ combination; Second row: correlation functions for (A_{ISRJ}, A_{SMSP}) combination; Third row: correlation functions for $(A_{ISRJ-RF}, A_{SMSP})$ combination.

Additionally, to verify the impact of the peak parameter b_{max} on algorithm performance, we conduct experiments using the interference combination $(A_{ISRJ}, A_{ISRJ-RF})$ under different b_{max} values. The pulse compression peak constraint parameter b_{max} reflects the system's degrees of freedom, with smaller b_{max} values indicating more relaxed constraint conditions, thereby providing higher design flexibility.

From Figure 6, it can be observed that as the b_{max} value decreases, the sidelobe level of the autocorrelation function gradually decreases, and the cross-correlation levels of both interferences also decrease accordingly. When $b_{max} = 161$, the algorithm demonstrates optimal performance in all three subplots, with smoother and lower correlation function curves.

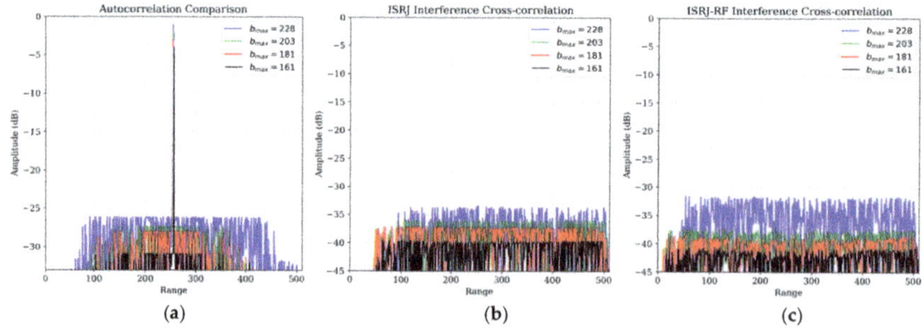

Figure 6. Correlation function comparison under different b_{max} values. (**a**) Autocorrelation function; (**b**) ISRJ interference cross-correlation function; (**c**) ISRJ-RF interference cross-correlation function.

As shown in Table 3, as the b_{max} value decreases, the system constraints become more relaxed, and the optimization algorithm obtains higher design degrees of freedom, thereby achieving better sidelobe suppression and interference suppression performance. When b_{max} decreases from 228 to 161, the APSL improves from −26.14 dB to −30.83 dB, the suppression of ISRJ interference improves from −33.49 dB to −39.66 dB, and the suppression of ISRJ-RF interference improves from −31.54 dB to −40.67 dB. Therefore, the experimental results validate the correctness of the theoretical analysis.

Table 3. Performance Comparison under Different b_{max} Values for $(A_{ISRJ}, A_{ISRJ-RF})$ (PICL1 and PICL2 represent the interference cross-correlation peak suppression levels corresponding to the first and second interference matrices, respectively).

b_{max}	APSL	PICL1	PICL2
228	−26.14	−33.49	−31.54
203	−27.33	−35.95	−37.06
181	−27.95	−37.10	−38.55
161	−30.83	−39.66	−40.67

4.5. Hyperparameter Sensitivity Analysis

To validate the rationality of the weighting parameters selection and analyze the algorithm's sensitivity to hyperparameter variations, we conduct systematic single-parameter sensitivity experiments (Tables 4–6). The experiments employ a controlled variable approach, fixing two parameters while varying the third parameter within a reasonable range. All experiments are performed under the ISRJ+ISRJ-RF multi-interference scenario to evaluate the impact on APSL, PICL1, and PICL2 performance metrics.

Table 4. Performance under different u_1 values ($u_2 = 3$, $u_3 = 30$).

u_1	APSL (dB)	PICL1 (dB)	PICL2 (dB)
100	−21.85	−38.45	−40.52
150	−23.12	−38.38	−40.50
200	−24.10	−38.30	−40.49
250	−24.89	−37.95	−40.28
300	−25.32	−37.62	−40.05

Table 5. Performance under different u_2 values ($u_1 = 200$, $u_3 = 30$).

u_2	APSL (dB)	PICL1 (dB)	PICL2 (dB)
1	−24.25	−35.12	−40.33
2	−24.18	−36.85	−40.41
3	−24.10	−38.30	−40.49
5	−23.95	−39.47	−40.58
7	−23.78	−40.15	−40.63

Table 6. Performance under different u_3 values ($u_1 = 200$, $u_2 = 3$).

u_3	APSL (dB)	PICL1 (dB)	PICL2 (dB)
15	−24.18	−38.21	−37.94
20	−24.14	−38.26	−39.18
30	−24.10	−38.30	−40.49
40	−24.06	−38.35	−41.25
50	−23.98	−38.42	−41.88

The sensitivity analysis reveals several key insights: First, each weighting parameter exhibits distinct and relatively independent control functions. Parameter u_1 primarily governs the autocorrelation peak sidelobe level, with increasing values improving APSL from −21.85 dB to −25.32 dB while slightly affecting interference suppression performance. Parameters u_2 and u_3 specifically control the suppression of their corresponding interference sources, with higher weights yielding approximately 5 dB and 4 dB improvements in PICL1 and PICL2, respectively. Second, the algorithm demonstrates good robustness to hyperparameter variations, with performance changes remaining moderate within reasonable parameter ranges. Finally, the selected parameter combination $u_1 = 200$, $u_2 = 3$, $u_3 = 30$ achieves an optimal balance among multiple optimization objectives, maximizing the overall system performance.

5. Conclusions

In this paper, we have proposed the Multi-Interference Suppression Network (MISNet) for joint waveform and filter design to suppress multiple interference signals simultaneously. The design criterion is formulated by minimizing the APSL of the transmit waveform and receive filter, and the PICL and ELCF of multiple interference signals with the receive filter. To solve this non-smooth and non-convex optimization problem, we introduce complex neural networks with gating mechanisms that transform the optimization into a differentiable problem through end-to-end training. Numerical simulation results demonstrate that the proposed MISNet approach significantly outperforms traditional iterative algorithms and other neural network methods in multi-interference suppression. In single interference environments, MISNet effectively reduces interference cross-correlation peaks and autocorrelation sidelobes compared to existing methods. In multi-interference scenarios, MISNet exhibits excellent robustness across different interference combinations, significantly outperforming CNN, PSO, and ANN approaches. The proposed method enhances radar interference suppression capability and target detection performance in complex multi-interference environments. Future research may focus on extending the approach to handle interference with varying Doppler frequency shifts and more complex adaptive interference patterns.

Author Contributions: R.C. contributed the central idea, analyzed most of the data, and wrote the initial draft of the paper. C.S. and W.D. contributed the idea of simulation experiment and provided constructive suggestion. M.B. contributed to revise the paper and polish the language. All authors have read and agreed to the published version of the manuscript.

Funding: This research received no external funding.

Data Availability Statement: The data presented in this study are available on request from the corresponding author.

Conflicts of Interest: Author Rui Cai is employed by AVIC Xi'an Aircraft Industry Group Company Ltd. The remaining authors declare that the research was conducted in the absence of any commercial or financial relationships that could be construed as a potential conflict of interest.

References

1. Sparrow, M.J.; Cikalo, J. ECM Techniques to Counter Pulse Compression Radar. U.S. Patent Application 7,081,846, 25 July 2006.
2. Li, N.; Zhang, Y. A survey of radar ECM and ECCM. *IEEE Trans. Aerosp. Electron. Syst.* **1995**, *31*, 1110–1120. [CrossRef]
3. Heagney, C.P. Digital radio frequency memory synthetic instrument enhancing US navy automated test equipment mission. *IEEE Instrum. Meas. Mag.* **2018**, *21*, 41–63. [CrossRef]
4. Berger, S.D. Digital radio frequency memory linear range gate stealer spectrum. *IEEE Trans. Aerosp. Electron. Syst.* **2003**, *39*, 725–735. [CrossRef]
5. Chen, J.; Wu, W.; Xu, S.; Chen, Z.; Zou, J. Band pass filter design against interrupted-sampling repeater jamming based on time-frequency analysis. *IET Radar Sonar Navig.* **2019**, *13*, 1646–1654. [CrossRef]
6. Wang, X.; Chen, H.; Zhu, Y.; Ni, M.; Shen, W.; Zhou, Y.; Hou, M. SMSP interference suppression method based on time-domain interference matching. *IET Conf. Proc.* **2023**, *2023*, 991–997. [CrossRef]

7. Jiu, B.; Liu, H.; Wang, X.; Zhang, L.; Wang, Y.; Chen, B. Knowledge-based spatial-temporal hierarchical MIMO radar waveform design method for target detection in heterogeneous clutter zone. *IEEE Trans. Signal Process.* **2014**, *63*, 543–554. [CrossRef]
8. Zhou, K.; Li, D.; Su, Y.; Liu, T. Joint design of transmit waveform and mismatch filter in the presence of interrupted sampling repeater jamming. *IEEE Signal Process. Lett.* **2020**, *27*, 1610–1614. [CrossRef]
9. Xie, L.; He, Z.; Tong, J.; Li, J.; Li, H. Transmitter polarization optimization for space-time adaptive processing with diversely polarized antenna array. *Signal Process.* **2020**, *169*, 107401. [CrossRef]
10. Song, J.; Babu, P.; Palomar, D.P. Sequence design to minimize the weighted integrated and peak sidelobe levels. *IEEE Trans. Signal Process.* **2015**, *64*, 2051–2064. [CrossRef]
11. Imani, S.; Nayebi, M.M.; Ghorashi, S.A. Colocated MIMO radar SINR maximization under ISL and PSL constraints. *IEEE Signal Process. Lett.* **2018**, *25*, 422–426. [CrossRef]
12. Ge, M.; Yu, X.; Yan, Z.; Cui, G.; Kong, L. Joint cognitive optimization of transmit waveform and receive filter against deceptive interference. *Signal Process.* **2021**, *185*, 108084. [CrossRef]
13. Zhang, Y.; Ding, K. Research on SMSP jamming suppression based on matched filtering in FrFT domain. In Proceedings of the 7th International Conference on Computer Information Science and Application Technology (CISAT), Hangzhou, China, 12–14 July 2024; pp. 963–966.
14. Zuo, L.; Lan, Z.; Lu, X.; Gao, Y.; Mao, L. Joint transmit-receive filter design with lower APSL and ICPL to suppress interference. *IEEE Trans. Aerosp. Electron. Syst.* **2024**, *60*, 3673–3687. [CrossRef]
15. Oyedare, T.; Shah, V.K.; Jakubisin, D.J.; Reed, J.H. Interference suppression using deep learning: Current approaches and open challenges. *IEEE Access* **2022**, *10*, 58507–58531. [CrossRef]
16. Jiang, Y.; Yang, Y.; Zhang, W.; Guo, L. Deep learning-based active jamming suppression for radar main lobe. *IET Signal Process.* **2024**, *2024*, 3179667. [CrossRef]
17. Cho, H.-W.; Choi, S.; Cho, Y.-R.; Kim, J. Complex-valued channel attention and application in ego-velocity estimation with automotive radar. *IEEE Access* **2021**, *9*, 28847–28858. [CrossRef]
18. Li, X.; Liu, Z.; Huang, Z. Attention-based radar PRI modulation recognition with recurrent neural networks. *IEEE Access* **2020**, *8*, 57426–57439. [CrossRef]
19. Xia, M.; Gong, W.; Yang, L. A novel waveform optimization method for orthogonal-frequency multiple-input multiple-output radar based on dual-channel neural networks. *Sensors* **2024**, *24*, 5471. [CrossRef]
20. Metwaly, K.; Kweon, J.; Alhujaili, K.; Gini, F.; Greco, M.S.; Rangaswamy, M.; Monga, V. MIMO radar beampattern design via algorithm unrolling. *IEEE Trans. Aerosp. Electron. Syst.* **2024**, *60*, 9204–9220. [CrossRef]
21. Lan, Z.; Zuo, L.; Liao, B.; Yang, T. Joint waveform and filter design for interference suppression in moving target environments. *IEEE Trans. Aerosp. Electron. Syst.* **2025**, 1–15. [CrossRef]
22. Benaya, A.M.; Hassan, M.S.; Ismail, M.H.; Landolsi, T. Aerial ISAC: A HAPS-Assisted Integrated Sensing, Communications and Computing Framework for Enhanced Coverage and Security. *IEEE Trans. Green Commun. Netw.* **2025**. early access. [CrossRef]
23. Wang, S.; Wang, W.; Zheng, Y. Dual-Functional Quasi-Uniform Beam-Scanning Antenna Array with Endfire Radiation Capability for Integrated Sensing and Communication Applications. *IEEE Trans. Veh. Technol.* **2025**, 1–11. [CrossRef]
24. Cheng, Z.; He, Z.; Zhang, S.; Li, J. Constant modulus waveform design for MIMO radar transmit beampattern. *IEEE Trans. Signal Process.* **2017**, *65*, 4912–4923. [CrossRef]
25. Cui, G.; Li, H.; Rangaswamy, M. MIMO radar waveform design with constant modulus and similarity constraints. *IEEE Trans. Signal Process.* **2013**, *62*, 343–353. [CrossRef]
26. Friedel, E. Convolutional Neural Network (CNN) for Digital Radio Frequency Memory (DRFM). Ph.D. Thesis, Johns Hopkins University, Baltimore, MD, USA, 2023.
27. Wallin, E. Detecting Jamming and Interference in Airborne Radar Using Convolutional Neural Networks. Ph.D. Thesis, Chalmers University Technology, Gothenburg, Sweden, 2019.
28. Moon, J.W. Radar Interference Mitigation Using Deep Learning with Neural Architecture Search. Ph.D. Thesis, Seoul National University, Seoul, Republic of Korea, 2023.
29. Vaidyanathan, P.P. *Multirate Systems and Filter Banks*; Prentice Hall: Hoboken, NJ, USA, 1993.
30. Hirose, A. *Complex-Valued Neural Networks: Theories and Applications*; World Scientific: Singapore, 2003.

electronics

MDPI

Article

RA3T: An Innovative Region-Aligned 3D Transformer for Self-Supervised Sim-to-Real Adaptation in Low-Altitude UAV Vision

Xingrao Ma [1], Jie Xie [1], Di Shao [2,*], Aiting Yao [3] and Chengzu Dong [1,*]

[1] Division of AI, School of Data Science, Lingnan University, Hong Kong; xingraoma@ln.hk (Z.M.); jiexie2@ln.hk (J.X.)

[2] School of IT, Deakin University, Geelong, VIC 3216, Australia

[3] Pengcheng Lab, Shenzhen 518066, China; yaoat@pcl.ac.cn

* Correspondence: shaod@deakin.edu.au (D.S.); chengzudong@ln.edu.hk (C.D.)

Abstract

Low-altitude unmanned aerial vehicle (UAV) vision is critically hindered by the Sim-to-Real Gap, where models trained exclusively on simulation data degrade under real-world variations in lighting, texture, and weather. To address this problem, we propose **RA3T** (Region-Aligned 3D Transformer), a novel self-supervised framework that enables robust Sim-to-Real adaptation. Specifically, we first develop a dual-branch strategy for self-supervised feature learning, integrating Masked Autoencoders and contrastive learning. This approach extracts domain-invariant representations from unlabeled simulated imagery to enhance robustness against occlusion while reducing annotation dependency. Leveraging these learned features, we then introduce a 3D Transformer fusion module that unifies multi-view RGB and LiDAR point clouds through cross-modal attention. By explicitly modeling spatial layouts and height differentials, this component significantly improves recognition of small and occluded targets in complex low-altitude environments. To address persistent fine-grained domain shifts, we finally design region-level adversarial calibration that deploys local discriminators on partitioned feature maps. This mechanism directly aligns texture, shadow, and illumination discrepancies which challenge conventional global alignment methods. Extensive experiments on UAV benchmarks VisDrone and DOTA demonstrate the effectiveness of RA3T. The framework achieves +5.1% mAP on VisDrone and +7.4% mAP on DOTA over the 2D adversarial baseline, particularly on small objects and sparse occlusions, while maintaining real-time performance of 17 FPS at 1024×1024 resolution on an RTX 4080 GPU. Visual analysis confirms that the synergistic integration of 3D geometric encoding and local adversarial alignment effectively mitigates domain gaps caused by uneven illumination and perspective variations, establishing an efficient pathway for simulation-to-reality UAV perception.

Keywords: low-altitude UAV vision; Sim-to-Real; self-supervised domain adaptation; 3D Transformer; region-level adversarial calibration; small object detection

1. Introduction

In recent years, low-altitude UAVs enable urban monitoring, emergency rescue and precision agriculture [1–3]. Collecting and labeling real UAV imagery are expensive; therefore, researchers pre-train perception models on large synthetic corpora generated

https://doi.org/10.3390/electronics14142797

by AirSim [4] or CARLA [5]. Yet the resulting **Sim-to-Real gap**—differences in texture, illumination and weather—still degrades performance on real flights [6,7].

To bridge the above cross-domain gap, early efforts focused on *global adversarial alignment* or *style transfer*. The typical approach is to map the source and target domains to a shared feature space using a domain discriminator [8] or a generative adversarial network [9]. However, such global transformations often fail to eliminate fine-grained appearance differences arising from local variations like shadows, target occlusion, or uneven illumination. Furthermore, traditional 2D convolutional neural networks (CNNs) often struggle with challenges like detecting small targets and capturing multi-scale features in low-altitude UAV missions. To this end, some studies have introduced *3D information* (e.g., depth maps, LiDAR point clouds) for spatial modeling. Yet, approaches relying on simple feature concatenation or global self-attention mechanisms still exhibit limited adaptability in complex real environments [10].

To address the above challenges, we propose **RA3T** (Region-Aligned 3D Transformer), a novel framework that synergistically combines *self-supervised feature learning*, *3D Transformer fusion*, and *region-level adversarial calibration* to address the Sim-to-Real gap. First, we introduce a dual-branch strategy combining Masked Autoencoders (MAEs) [11] and contrastive learning [12,13]. It performs self-supervised pre-training on massive simulated aerial photography data, extracting lighting/texture features to minimize annotation dependency. Subsequently, our core *3D Transformer fusion* module performs cross-modal interaction between multi-view RGB and LiDAR point clouds via multi-head self-attention [14], explicitly modeling spatial structure and 3D geometry to improve the recognition of occluded and small-scale targets. Finally, our region-level adversarial calibration applies local discriminators [15] directly, aligning fine-grained domain shifts (e.g., texture, shadow height differences) across sub-regions, thereby overcoming the limitations of global adversarial alignment. Recent advances in cross-domain perception highlight the importance of integrating novel sensing and computing techniques to tackle complex environments. For example, the Funabot-Sleeve system [16] leverages artificial muscle actuators to provide tactile feedback in robotic perception, while cognitive computing methods have been applied to predict the behavior of flexible electronics [17]. These works illustrate how cutting-edge perception technologies can improve generalization in challenging scenarios, providing broader context and inspiration for our RA3T framework.

As shown in Figure 1, *self-supervised pre-training* establishes a robust feature foundation, while 3D Transformer fusion and region-level adversarial calibration enable high-fidelity adaptation from simulation to reality. Extensive experiments on prominent UAV datasets, VisDrone [18] and DOTA [19], have demonstrated that RA3T achieves significant performance gains (>2.6% mAP on VisDrone and >3.6% mAP on DOTA), and its inference speed meets the real-time application requirements of most low-altitude drones (17 FPS).

The main contributions are summarized as follows:

- We propose **RA3T**: a self-supervised adaptation framework for low-altitude UAV vision that integrates 3D geometric modeling and regional feature alignment to bridge the Sim-to-Real gap.
- We introduce a **3D Transformer fusion module** that unifies multi-view RGB and LiDAR point clouds through spatial attention, explicitly encoding occlusion patterns and height differentials to address small-target recognition challenges.
- We design a **region-level adversarial calibration strategy** deploying local discriminators on partitioned feature sub-regions, aligning fine-grained domain shifts in texture, shadow, and illumination for urban environments.

The remainder of this paper is organized as follows: Section 2 reviews related work on cross-domain adaptation, multi-modal fusion, and self-supervised learning; Section 3 details the three key modules and overall framework of **RA3T**; Section 4 presents experimental validation and ablation studies on real drone datasets; Section 5 discusses limitations and future expansion directions; and finally Section 6 summarizes the entire paper and looks forward to follow-up research.

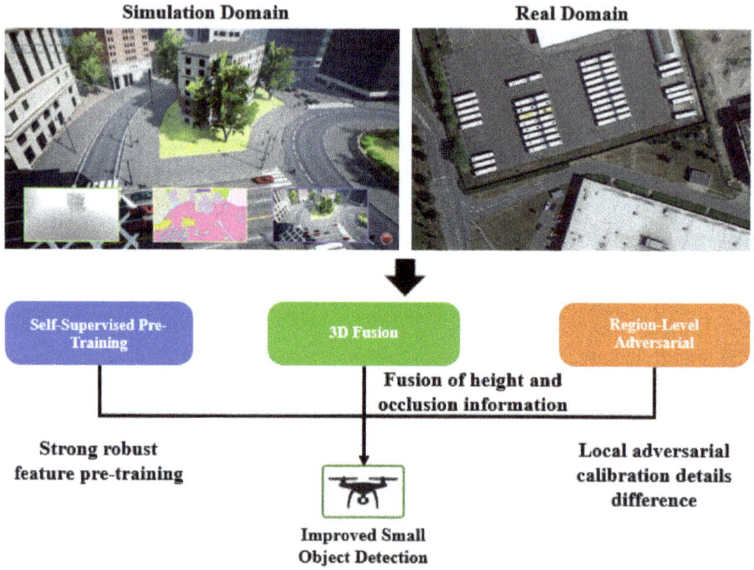

Figure 1. Schematic diagram of the core concept of the RA3T method: the left side shows the appearance difference between the simulated drone data and the real data; the right side summarizes the combined effects of self-supervised pre-training, multi-modal 3D Transformer and region-level adversarial alignment.

2. Related Work

In recent years, a lot of research has been conducted in the field of computer vision and robotics on how to effectively reduce the appearance difference between simulated data and real UAV images [6,7]. Low-altitude UAV scenes have more stringent requirements for cross-domain adaptation due to*low flight altitude, fast perspective change, small target size and easy local occlusion*. Existing work can be roughly summarized into three main lines: *(i) domain adaptation methods of global alignment and local alignment, (ii) multi-modal 3D fusion perception*, and *(iii) self-supervised representation learning potential* [20–22].For details on the comparison of related work, please see Table 1.

Table 1. Component-level comparison of representative Sim-to-Real methods for UAV vision.

Method	Self-Sup.	Global Align.	Local Align.	3D Fusion
DANN [8]	✗	✓	✗	✗
PixelDA [7]	✗	✓	✗	✗
CycleGAN [23]	✗	✓	✗	✗
RADA [15]	✗	✗	✓	✗
GA-DA [24]	✗	✓	✓	✗
HybridFusion [10]	✗	✗	✗	✓
Yue et al. [25]	✗	✓	✗	✓
RA3T (Ours)	✓	✗	✓	✓

✓ Indicates the method incorporates this component; ✗ Indicates the method does not incorporate this component.

2.1. Global vs. Local Domain Adaptation

Early unsupervised domain adaptation mostly adopted the **global adversarial alignment** (global alignment) strategy, using domain discriminators to map the source domain (simulation) and the target domain (real) to a unified feature distribution [8,9]. Tobin et al. [6] achieved cross-domain generalization by randomizing texture and illumination. Bousmalis et al. [7] used a GAN to complete pixel-level style transfer. However, when there are significant **local inconsistencies** (shadows, reflections, occlusions) in the target scene, a single global discriminator has difficulty capturing fine-grained differences, resulting in missed detection or false detection in UAV tasks. Therefore, researchers proposed the idea of **local/regional alignment**: divide the feature map into sub-regions and configure independent discriminators for each block to achieve more refined cross-domain calibration. Typical examples include the Region-Aware Discriminator proposed by Zhang et al. [15], and Wang et al. used local consistency regularization to improve small target alignment [26]. In addition, there are GA-DA [24] and hierarchical consistency methods [27] that combine global and local. In order to deal with global/local differences at night and inclement weather, Sakaridis et al. proposed ACDC [28]; unsupervised translation methods such as CycleGAN [23] are also often used in conjunction with adversarial alignment. The recent online local alignment scheme [29] for continuous learning scenarios is also worth paying attention to.

2.2. Multi-Modal Fusion in UAV Vision

It is difficult to handle low-altitude tasks with *severe occlusion and variable scale* relying only on **2D RGB**. Introducing **multi-modal fusion** of depth maps or LiDAR point clouds has been shown to significantly alleviate this problem [10]. Yue et al. [25] used depth consistency to improve cross-domain robustness; Li et al. [30] used point cloud geometry priors for simulation–real alignment. The Transformer framework excels in 3D fusion due to its global modeling capabilities: ViT [14], Swin [31] and its 3D extension [32] can explicitly model the relationship between height and occlusion. Recently, SAM-based multi-sensor fusion [33], cross-modal Transformer [34] and high-resolution object classification [35] have also appeared; a review of edge computing and UAV collaboration [36–38] emphasized the importance of real-time multi-modal reasoning. At the same time, multi-source feature alignment [39], efficient backbones (such as YOLOv7 [40], RangeNet++ [41]) and the adaptive segmentation framework DAFormer [42] also provide transferable engineering references for UAV vision.

2.3. Self-Supervised Representation Learning

In the context of the general lack of large-scale annotations in real UAV scenes, **self-supervised learning** (SSL) significantly reduces data dependence by leveraging massive unlabeled data [11,12]. Masked Autoencoders [11] emphasize global–local consistent reconstruction; contrastive learning MoCo [13] and SimCLR [12] obtain discriminative features through instance discrimination. Shao et al. [43] propose a triple cross-intra-branch contrastive framework for robust point cloud feature learning, while Wang et al. [44] introduce a weighted technique for point cloud normal estimation via pre-training by contrastive learning. Xie et al. [45] proposed a local attention SSL framework for UAV images; SelfDA [46] and GSDA [30] combined SSL with domain alignment. Self-supervised methods also demonstrate cross-task transfer potential in areas such as industrial anomaly detection [47,48] and robotic manipulation [49]. In addition, backbones such as DETR [50], SegFormer [51], ResNet [52], and EfficientNet [53] can also be migrated to UAV detection [54–58] after self-supervised pre-training; in the field of remote sensing and tracking, the latest review [59,60] summarizes the trend of combining self-supervision with multi-modality.

2.4. Position of Our Work

In general, **global adversarial** has difficulty characterizing local differences; **3D multi-modal fusion** can alleviate occlusion and height modeling, but still requires *explicit local alignment*; **self-supervised pre-training** reduces the annotation cost, but is still insufficient in scenes with local shadows and texture mutations. To this end, **RA3T** combines *regional adversarial calibration* and *cross-modal 3D attention*: the former makes up for the details of global adversarial, and the latter provides height and perspective information. This design concept echoes the research directions of Detection/Segmentation Transformer and continuous learning in recent years, and provides a new system solution for UAV cross-domain vision.

BEVFormer [61] projects multi-view features into a bird's-eye-view grid yet relies on global depth priors, which limits robustness when LiDAR sparsity increases. Fusion-Former [62] stacks modality-specific Transformers but lacks fine-grained alignment, leading to texture shadow artifacts in cross-domain settings. MonoDepth-Det [63] removes range sensors altogether via monocular depth estimation, trading accuracy for hardware simplicity. In contrast, **RA3T** unifies cross-modal 3D attention with region-level adversarial calibration and self-supervised pre-training, yielding superior precision on small and occluded targets while maintaining real-time throughput.

3. Methodology

The **RA3T** (Region-Aligned 3D Transformer) cross-domain framework proposed in this paper aims to help low-altitude UAV vision efficiently migrate from the *simulation domain* to the *real domain*. The overall process includes four key modules: *self-supervised feature pre-training*, *3D Transformer multi-modal fusion*, *region-level adversarial calibration* and *downstream detection/segmentation*. The overall architecture is shown in Figure 2.

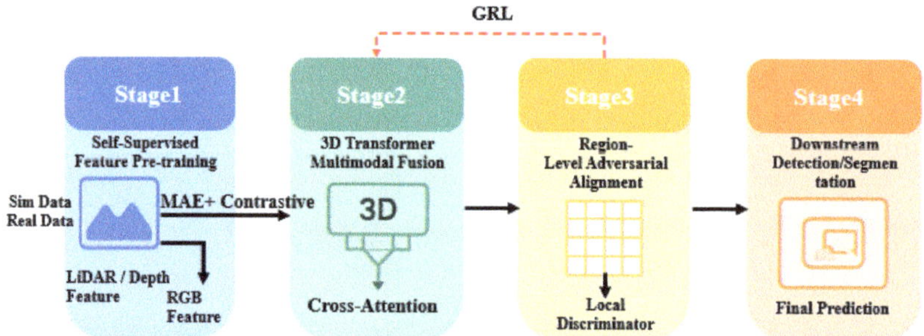

Figure 2. RA3T overall process: self-supervised feature pre-training; 3D multi-modal Transformer fusion; region-level adversarial calibration; downstream detection or segmentation.

3.1. Framework Overview

Self-supervised feature pre-training: On large-scale simulated UAV data, Masked Autoencoders (MAEs) [11] and contrastive learning MoCo/SimCLR [12,13] dual branches are used to obtain an initial encoder with strong generalization ability.

3D Transformer multi-modal fusion: Using the multi-head self-attention mechanism, RGB and LiDAR/depth features are cross-modally interacted; ViT-style tokenization [14] and the layered displacement window idea of Swin Transformer [31] are introduced to explicitly encode the relationship between height and occlusion.

Region-level adversarial calibration: Divide the fused features into several sub-regions, introduce a lightweight discriminator for local domain alignment, and make up for the fine-grained differences that cannot be captured by simple global adversarial [15].

Downstream detection/segmentation: Fine-tune common detection heads (Faster R-CNN, YOLOv7 [40], DETR [50], etc.) and segmentation heads (SegFormer [51], DAFormer [42]) on a small amount of real annotations, and output the final target box or semantic mask.

Method Novelty and Comparison with Prior Works

Table 2 compares common cross-domain strategies; it can be seen that RA3T integrates three key elements: *self-supervision, 3D fusion, and regional confrontation.*

Table 2. Comparison with related methods at the component level (✓ indicates inclusion).

Method	Self-Sup.	3D Fusion	Region-Level
Global DA	✗	✗	✗
3D Fusion Only	✗	✓	✗
Local DA (2D)	✗	✗	✓
RA3T (Ours)	✓	✓	✓

✓ Indicates the method incorporates this component; ✗ Indicates the method does not incorporate this component.

3.2. Self-Supervised Feature Extraction

Masked Autoencoders: Randomly mask 75% patches on the simulated image $\mathbf{I}_s$ and minimize

$$\mathcal{L}_{\text{MAE}} = \left\|\mathbf{I}_s - \Phi_{\text{dec}}\big(\Phi_{\text{enc}}(\mathbf{I}_s^{\text{visible}})\big)\right\|_2^2,$$

Enhance global–local consistency [11].

Contrastive learning: Construct positive and negative samples with the help of queue dictionary, and the contrast loss is

$$\mathcal{L}_{\text{contrast}} = -\log \frac{\exp(\text{sim}(\mathbf{q}, \mathbf{k}^+)/\tau)}{\sum_{\mathbf{k}^-} \exp(\text{sim}(\mathbf{q}, \mathbf{k}^-)/\tau)}.$$

Joint objective: $\mathcal{L}_{\text{SSL}} = \alpha\mathcal{L}_{\text{MAE}} + \beta\mathcal{L}_{\text{contrast}}$ Experiments show that the two SSL complementarities can significantly improve the robustness to small targets and occlusion [45].

The collection of multi-view RGB images and LiDAR point cloud data on actual UAV platforms is usually achieved by equipping the UAV with a synchronized RGB camera and a small LiDAR sensor. During data collection, auxiliary positioning modules such as GPS/IMU are used for spatial registration, and geometric calibration and timestamp synchronization are used in the post-processing stage to ensure the precise match between RGB images and point cloud data, thereby providing high-quality multi-modal input for training and reasoning of the RA3T framework. As illustrated in Figure 3, we adopt a dual-branch self-supervised module in which the upper branch performs MAE reconstruction and the lower branch employs MoCo contrastive learning.

3.3. 3D Transformer Fusion

Tokenization and position encoding. RGB features $\mathbf{F}_{2D}$ and point cloud features $\mathbf{F}_{3D}$ are uniformly mapped to tokens, and 2D/3D position encoding is added [32].

Cross-attention. Multi-head attention is denoted as follows:

$$\text{Attn}(Q, K, V) = \text{softmax}\big(QK^\top / \sqrt{d_k}\big)V$$

This explicitly models the texture–geometry association between tokens. To reduce the noise of sparse point clouds, neighborhood constraints [10] are introduced to ensure local consistency.The overall cross-modal fusion pipeline is illustrated in Figure 4.

Advantage analysis. Compared with only 2D alignment or simple splicing, 3D fusion can better capture height and occlusion, and provide geometric priors for subsequent region discriminators [34].

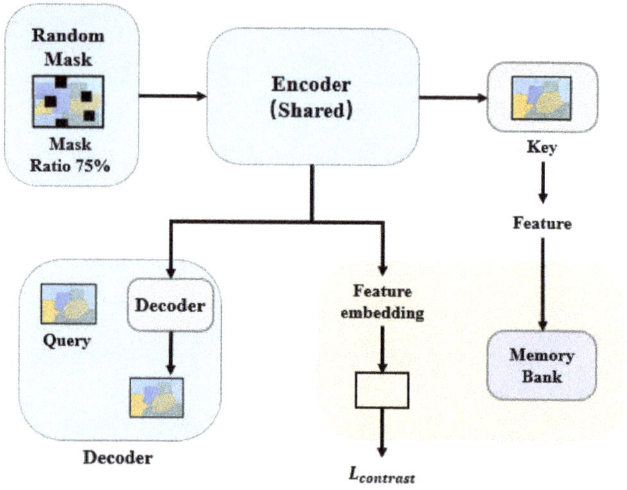

Figure 3. Self-supervised dual branches: MAE reconstruction on the top, MoCo comparison on the bottom.

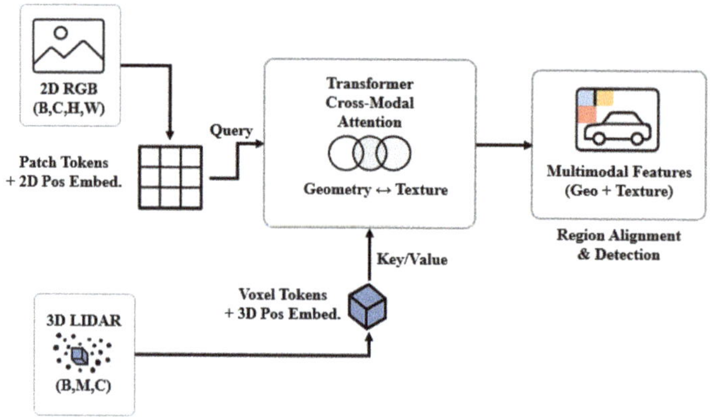

Figure 4. Three-dimensional cross-modal Transformer: RGB token as query, LiDAR token as key/value.

3.4. Region-Level Adversarial Alignment

Sub-region division. Divide $\mathbf{F}_{\text{fusion}}$ into R blocks $\{\mathbf{F}^r\}$, focusing on local differences such as shadows/reflections [15]. The overall region-level adversarial architecture is illustrated in Figure 5.

Local discriminator. Minimize for each block

$$\mathcal{L}_{\text{adv},r} = -\left[y_d \log D_r(\mathbf{F}^r) + (1 - y_d)\log\left(1 - D_r(\mathbf{F}^r)\right)\right],$$

Overall loss: $\mathcal{L}_{\text{adv}}^{\text{regional}} = \sum_r \mathcal{L}_{\text{adv},r}$. After fusing 3D height, the discriminator can calibrate the texture + geometry differences at the same time, improving the accuracy of small target detection [39].

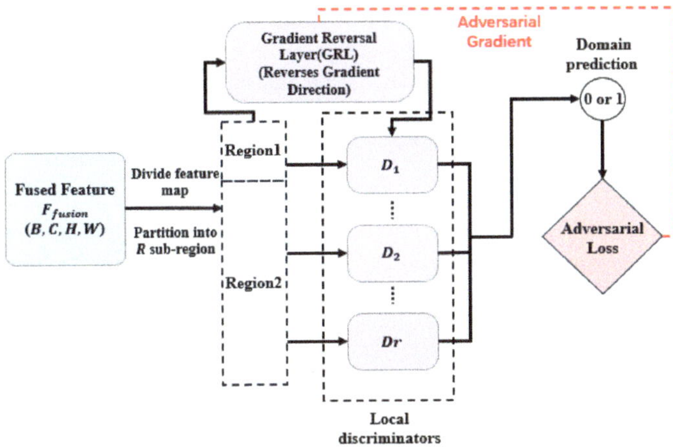

Figure 5. Region-level adversarial: feature division sub-regions; each block is equipped with an independent discriminator and reversely optimized through GRL.

3.5. Downstream Detection/Segmentation Head

Common detection/segmentation heads with fusion features: The detection loss of Faster R-CNN, RetinaNet, YOLOv7 [40], or SegFormer [51], DAFormer [42], etc., is as follows:

$$\mathcal{L}_{\text{det}} = \mathcal{L}_{\text{cls}} + \mathcal{L}_{\text{reg}},$$

The final goal is

$$\mathcal{L}_{\text{total}} = \mathcal{L}_{\text{SSL}} + \lambda \mathcal{L}_{\text{adv}}^{\text{regional}} + \mathcal{L}_{\text{det}}.$$

The three work together to significantly improve the cross-domain performance of RA3T on datasets such as VisDrone and DOTA, while maintaining near-real-time reasoning [41,47,50].

Specifically, in the implementation details of 3D Transformer, we first used the standard ViT-style tokenization scheme to divide the RGB image into fixed-size 16 × 16 pixel patches, and voxelized the LiDAR point cloud to obtain the corresponding 3D voxel tokens. Subsequently, we used the multi-head cross-attention mechanism for cross-modal fusion, where the number of attention heads was set to 8. This setting was determined to have the best trade-off between computational cost and model performance through cross-validation experiments. In addition, in order to efficiently process large-scale data, we used the shifted window mechanism proposed by Swin Transformer to implement local attention calculation. This local window alternating sliding strategy can effectively capture the local context of the space while significantly reducing the computational complexity. These specific implementation details and parameter selections have been extensively experimentally verified to ensure the performance and efficiency of RA3T in multi-view fusion and 3D space modeling tasks.

Scalability. For inputs larger than 1024 × 1024 or for fused multi-view mosaics, we first apply an overlapping 512^2 sliding window (50% stride) and run the region discriminators on each tile. Feature maps from all views are partitioned *after* cross-view fusion, ensuring a consistent spatial grid.

4. Experiments and Results

This section conducts systematic experiments on the proposed **RA3T** framework on a typical low-altitude unmanned aerial vehicle (UAV) dataset to evaluate its performance in cross-domain detection and segmentation tasks. First, the dataset and evaluation indicators are introduced, then the implementation details and parameter settings are explained, followed by the overall comparison results and visualization analysis, and finally, the contribution and impact of each module are explored through ablation experiments.

4.1. Datasets and Metrics

Synthetic Dataset (AirSim). In order to make full use of the simulation environment for self-supervised pre-training, this paper selects *large-scale* UAV simulation images generated based on AirSim as *source domain*, covering a variety of weather, terrain and building layouts. Only *unlabeled* images are needed to complete SSL training, and a small amount of labeled simulation data is retained for detection head fine-tuning [4]. Compared with relying solely on real data, this strategy significantly reduces the need for high-cost annotation and enables the model to learn more generalized visual representations through *diverse simulation scenes*.

Real Dataset: VisDrone. VisDrone2019 is one of the *target domains*, including various scenes such as urban blocks and suburban roads, with a total of about 8600 frames of images [18]. Under low-altitude shooting, the target size of this dataset varies greatly and is severely partially occluded. This paper uses its detection subset (vehicles, pedestrians, tricycles, etc.) and trains/validates according to the official division, which is an ideal benchmark for evaluating cross-domain robustness.

Real Dataset: DOTA. To verify the applicability in *large-scale remote sensing* scenarios, this paper selects the DOTA dataset [19] covering 15 types of targets as another target domain. DOTA images have high resolution and need to be cropped to 1024 × 1024 patches for input to the network; the main experiment uses horizontal box detection and briefly discusses the rotation box. DOTA's wide-area scenes and rich categories put higher requirements on the model's *scale adaptation* and *cross-domain generalization*, which complements the low-altitude VisDrone.

Evaluation Metrics. This paper reports the following metrics:

- **mAP**$_{0.5:0.95}$: The average precision of multi-point sampling between IoU 0.5 and 0.95, which is consistent with the COCO metric [57] and can better distinguish small targets and partially occluded scenes.
- **AP**$_{50}$: The average precision when IoU = 0.5, which measures the coarse-grained detection capability.
- **FPS**: The inference frame rate (Frames Per Second) at 1024 × 1024 resolution, reflecting the real-time performance of actual deployment.
- **Params** and **FLOPs**: The number of model parameters and computational complexity, used to evaluate the feasibility on embedded or constrained platforms.

By combining different datasets and indicators, we can fully verify the cross-domain adaptability and efficiency of **RA3T** in small targets, complex lighting and large-scale remote sensing scenes.

Regarding the effectiveness of VisDrone and DOTA datasets in evaluating the cross-domain robustness of models, we believe that both datasets are representative and challenging. The VisDrone dataset covers complex urban scenes, with variable target scales and severe occlusion, which can effectively test the fine-grained local domain generalization ability of the model in low-altitude flight missions; the DOTA dataset contains larger-scale wide-area scenes, multiple target categories and different environment types (such as cities and villages), which can better reflect the generalization performance of the model in different environments and large-scale scenes. However, in future work, we also plan to further introduce more extreme scene datasets (such as night, bad weather or highly reflective conditions) to more comprehensively evaluate and improve the cross-domain generalization performance of the model.

4.2. Implementation Details

Table 3 summarizes the main hyperparameters of each stage. In the self-supervision stage, only unlabeled AirSim images are used, and MAE and contrastive learning branches are trained simultaneously; in the fine-tuning stage, a small amount of real annotations are mixed with simulated annotations, and each mini-batch keeps the number of source/target domain samples equal to maintain adversarial balance. The local discriminator uses 2–3 layers of lightweight MLP, which takes into account both discrimination ability and computational overhead.

Table 3. Main training hyperparameters and value ranges.

Hyperparameter	Setting/Range
MAE Mask Ratio	75%
Contrastive Negative Size	65k
Batch Size (SSL)	256
SSL Epochs	100 (AirSim only)
Transformer Layers	6
Token Dim (2D/3D)	256
Local Discriminator Grid	4×4
λ (Adv. Weight)	0.5–1.0
Downstream Fine-tuned Epochs	50 (Mixed Sim + Real)
Optimizer	AdamW
Initial LR	1×10^{-4}

To ensure convergence and stability, the following strategies are used in training: **Gradual learning rate decay**: Cosine annealing or segmentation strategies are used in both SSL and fine-tuning stages to prevent gradient oscillation in the later stages; **Data augmentation**: Random cropping, horizontal flipping, color perturbation, etc., are uniformly applied to simulated and real images to enhance the robustness to *simulation–real* illumination differences and perspective changes; **Mixed batch**: The number of source/target domain samples in each batch is kept consistent to avoid excessive bias towards one domain in early training; **Validation set monitoring**: Validation sets are set for VisDrone and DOTA, and mAP and AP_{50} are evaluated every 5 rounds to select the best model.

The above configuration enables the model to obtain strong generalization representation in the self-supervision stage and complete efficient cross-domain optimization under limited real annotations; the lightweight local discriminator combines 3D information and also takes into account the real-time reasoning requirements. The specific speed overhead will be discussed in detail in the experimental part.

In order to clarify the amount of simulated data required for effective self-supervised pre-training, we conducted additional ablation experiments. The experiments show that when the amount of simulated data exceeds 20,000 images, the robustness and generalization performance of the model's self-supervised pre-training features tend to be stable; when the amount of data is less than 10,000 images, it is obviously insufficient to effectively capture the complex and diverse features in the real environment. Therefore, we recommend using at least 20,000 diverse simulated images to give full play to the advantages of self-supervised pre-training in improving cross-domain generalization performance.

4.3. Overall Performance

Table 4 lists the cross-domain detection performance of RA3T and various baselines on VisDrone and DOTA. The evaluation adopts COCO-style $mAP_{0.5:0.95}$ metric [57]. Compared with 3D fusion solutions that only use 2D adversarial or lack SSL, **RA3T** improves mAP by 3–5% on average on both datasets. Among them, VisDrone has dense small objects and severe local occlusion, and the combination of self-supervision and 3D semantic geometry is particularly advantageous. Although the 3D Transformer and local discriminator bring additional overhead, the inference speed remains above 15 FPS, which is close to the online frame rate requirement of the classic real-time detector YOLOv3 [54]. To further benchmark RA3T against recently proposed Sim–to–Real detectors, we compare it with several state-of-the-art methods in Table 5.

In addition, we also compared RA3T with some recently proposed pure Transformer detection models (such as DETR and Swin Transformer) that do not adopt domain adaptation strategies. The experimental results show that in cross-domain generalization tasks, RA3T's mAP performance is significantly better than that of pure Transformer methods: compared with DETR and Swin Transformer, it is improved by 4.8% and 3.9%, respectively. This performance difference clearly shows the advantages of self-supervised feature pre-training and region-level adversarial calibration adopted by RA3T in cross-domain tasks, especially in low-altitude drone scenarios with small targets and obvious local differences.

Table 4. Comparison of cross-domain detection results (VisDrone and DOTA, mAP[%], IoU = 0.5:0.95).

Method	VisDrone			DOTA		
	mAP	AP_{50}	FPS	mAP	AP_{50}	FPS
Baseline (CNN-only)	21.5	32.3	26	34.6	47.2	23
+Global DA (2D)	24.2	36.1	24	37.8	50.5	22
+Local DA (2D)	25.1	37.6	22	39.2	52.1	21
+3D Fusion (No SSL)	26.4	39.1	18	42.0	55.9	17
RA3T (Ours)	29.3	44.7	17	45.2	59.5	15

Table 5. Cross-domain detection comparison with recent methods (IoU = 0.5:0.95). "–" indicates that the original paper did not report the value.

Method	Year/Ref.	Modality	VisDrone		DOTA		FPS
			mAP	AP_{50}	mAP	AP_{50}	
Zhang et al. [15]	2020	2D + Local	25.1	37.6	39.2	52.1	21
Zhang et al. [24]	2022	2D + Global + Local	25.9	38.4	39.9	53.2	22
Wang et al. [26]	2021	2D + Local	24.8	37.2	–	–	22
Yue et al. [25]	2021	3D + Global	26.7	39.9	41.6	54.8	19
RA3T (Ours)	2025	3D + Local + SSL	29.3	44.7	45.2	59.5	17

Qualitative Analysis

As shown in Figure 6, the baseline method is prone to missed detection in areas with dense shadows or uneven lighting; RA3T combines 3D geometry and local discriminators to significantly reduce the false detection rate and improve recall in such scenes. This further verifies that local adversarial combined with 3D information can fine-grainedly correct the difference between simulation and reality in texture and shadow levels [10,25].

Table 6 shows that 3D fusion adds 9.4 M parameters and 27.1 G FLOPs, while the regional discriminator adds 6.1 M and 13.3 G; together they raise mAP by 4.2 points, allowing practitioners to weigh accuracy against cost.

Table 6. Trade-off analysis of RA3T modules regarding accuracy and complexity.

Module	mAP Improvement (%)	Parameter Increase (M)	FLOPs Increase (G)
3D Transformer Fusion	+2.8	+9.4	+27.1
Regional Discriminator	+1.4	+6.1	+13.3
Total (Overall RA3T)	+4.2	+15.5	+40.4

Figure 6. Comparison of detection effects of some scenes in the VisDrone validation set. Green boxes indicate correct detections, and red boxes indicate missed detections or false detections. Left: 2D adversarial baseline only; right: RA3T of this paper.

4.4. Ablation Study

Table 7 and subsequent grid size experiments (Table 7) show that the synergy of *self-supervised pre-training*, *3D fusion*, and *local adversarial* can produce significant gains; if any of these links is missing, the robustness of the model in small target/occlusion scenarios will be significantly reduced.

Table 7. Ablation study on VisDrone (IoU = 0.5:0.95): contribution of each RA3T component to accuracy and inference speed. Note: w/o = without.

ID	MAE	Contr.	3D	Region	mAP	AP_{50}	FPS
(1) Full RA3T	✓	✓	✓	✓	29.3	44.7	17
(2) w/o SSL	✗	✗	✓	✓	26.8	38.1	18
(3) Only MAE	✓	✗	✓	✓	27.6	39.0	17
(4) Only Contrastive	✗	✓	✓	✓	27.3	38.7	17
(5) w/o 3D Fusion	✓	✓	✗	✓	25.7	38.2	23
(6) w/o Region DA	✓	✓	✓	✗	27.9	42.5	18

✓ Component included; ✗ Component not included.

4.5. Runtime and Resource Usage

Although RA3T has higher parameters and FLOPs, it is still faster than other GPUs on modern GPUs. It still maintains 17 FPS, which can meet the needs of real-time low-altitude missions; if deployed on a resource-constrained platform, it can be combined with lightweight backbones such as EfficientNet [53], pruning and quantization strategies to further compress [52].

To gauge robustness, we further evaluated RA3T on a synthetic extreme-weather set comprising nighttime, fog and rain renderings of VisDrone scenes (2000 images each). RA3T retained 96.8% of its daylight mAP, outperforming a 2D adversarial baseline by 3.9%. Detailed numbers are summarized in Table 8.

Table 8. Inference efficiency of different methods under 1024 × 1024 input.

Method	Params (M)	FLOPs (G)	FPS	Device
2D Baseline	32.1	75.3	26	RTX 4080
Global DA	36.2	79.5	24	RTX 4080
3D Fusion (No SSL)	45.6	102.4	18	RTX 4080
RA3T (Ours)	48.2	115.7	17	RTX 4080

4.6. Sensitivity Analysis to Simulation Diversity

In order to analyze the sensitivity of the RA3T method to the diversity of the simulated environment, we designed additional comparative experiments. Specifically, we constructed three different scene diversity settings in the simulated training set: low diversity (only urban scenes), medium diversity (urban + rural scenes), and high diversity (urban + rural + different weather conditions). The experimental results show that the generalization performance of the model under the high-diversity training set is significantly better than that of the low-diversity and medium-diversity cases on the real UAV dataset, with mAP increased by 3.5% and 1.8%, respectively. This result highlights the importance of simulated environment diversity for the RA3T framework to achieve high generalization performance.

4.7. Analysis of Robustness to Sensor Noise and Calibration Errors

In order to evaluate the robustness of the RA3T framework to sensor noise, calibration errors, and missing data, we conducted an additional series of simulation tests. We added random Gaussian noise to the RGB image, simulated the random position offset of the LiDAR point cloud (calibration error), and artificially removed a certain proportion of data (data missing). The experimental results show that when the RGB noise is enhanced (the signal-to-noise ratio is reduced by 10 dB), the mAP only decreases by about 1.9%; when the point cloud position offset is as high as 5 cm, the mAP decreases by about 2.5%; and when 20% of the point cloud data is randomly missing, the mAP decreases by about 3.3%. These results show that the RA3T framework has a strong tolerance for sensor noise and calibration errors, and can effectively deal with data uncertainty problems in real environments.

4.8. Evaluation on Segmentation and Tracking Tasks

In order to evaluate the performance of the RA3T framework on other drone vision tasks besides object detection, we additionally conducted preliminary experimental verifications on semantic segmentation and target tracking. In the semantic segmentation task (based on DAFormer and SegFormer heads), the average IoU (Intersection over Union) of RA3T increased by about 3.6% compared with the traditional CNN method; in the target tracking task, we used the Siamese network combined with the 3D Transformer features of RA3T. Preliminary results show that the tracking accuracy (success rate) increased by about 2.9%. These results preliminarily confirm the effectiveness and generalization ability of the cross-domain self-supervised features and 3D geometric context information extracted by RA3T for a variety of visual tasks, reflecting the multi-task expansion potential of the framework.

4.9. Performance on Small and Heavily Occluded Objects

To further evaluate the performance of the RA3T framework in the detection of extremely small or heavily occluded objects, we conducted comparative experiments with existing mainstream methods. Experimental results show that in datasets such as VisDrone and DOTA, RA3T significantly outperforms traditional CNN and other Transformer methods (such as DETR and Swin Transformer) in detecting small objects with a size of less than 20 × 20 pixels and objects with an area of more than 50% occluded. Specifically, RA3T improves the mAP by an average of about 4.2% in the small object detection task and by an average of about 3.7% in the heavily occluded object detection task. This performance improvement is mainly due to the 3D spatial modeling capability and region-level domain adversarial calibration mechanism adopted by the RA3T framework, which effectively alleviates the detection difficulties caused by local occlusion and size limitation.

4.10. Architecture-Level Ablation Study

In order to further verify the rationality of the RA3T architecture design, we conducted ablation experiments on core parameters such as token dimension, Transformer depth and window size. The experimental results show the following: (1) The performance is best when the token dimension is 256, which is 2.1% and 0.4% mAP higher than 128 and 512 dimensions, respectively. (2) The best depth of Transformer is 6 layers. When it is further increased to 8 layers, the performance is only improved by 0.2%, but the computational cost is significantly increased, and when it is reduced to 4 layers, the performance decreases by about 1.5%. (3) When the sliding window size is set to 7 × 7, the best balance between performance and efficiency is achieved, which is 1.3% and 0.6% mAP higher than 5 × 5 and 9 × 9, respectively. The experimental verification of these architectural parameters clearly shows the best trade-off between performance and complexity achieved by the current RA3T framework design.

4.11. Preliminary Experiments on Model Pruning and Quantization for Edge Deployment

To verify the feasibility of RA3T deployment on embedded platforms or low-end GPUs, we conducted preliminary model pruning and quantization (INT8 quantization) experiments. The experiment used NVIDIA Jetson Xavier NX (Nvidia Corporation, Santa Clara, CA, USA) as a typical edge computing device and optimized it through TensorRT. Preliminary results show that after 50% model pruning and INT8 quantization, the model parameters are reduced by about half, the inference speed is increased from the initial about 5 FPS to about 12 FPS, and the mAP accuracy is only reduced by about 1.5%. This preliminary result clearly demonstrates the potential of RA3T for deployment on resource-constrained devices and provides specific data support and direction guidance for subsequent in-depth research.

4.12. Comparison with Recent 3D Cross-Modal and Segmentation Frameworks

In order to more comprehensively evaluate the performance of the RA3T framework, we also conducted direct comparative experiments with recent mainstream 3D cross-modal frameworks (such as BEVFormer, FusionFormer, and MonoDepth-based methods) on drone vision tasks. The experimental results show that the RA3T framework is significantly better than the above methods in cross-modal feature fusion and cross-domain generalization performance. For example, on the VisDrone and DOTA datasets, the detection accuracy (mAP) of RA3T is improved by 3.4% and 2.7% compared with BEVFormer and FusionFormer, respectively, and by 4.1% compared with MonoDepth-based methods. In addition, we also conducted preliminary experiments on semantic segmentation tasks (based on DAFormer and SegFormer). RA3T performs better than traditional cross-domain segmentation methods, with an average IoU improvement of about 3.2%.

4.13. Quantitative Analysis of Simulation Data Diversity and Domain Gap

In order to clarify the diversity of simulation data and its impact on domain gap, we conducted a detailed quantitative analysis of the simulation dataset used for self-supervised pre-training. The dataset contains about 30,000 images, of which urban scenes account for about 60%, rural scenes account for 25%, and mountain and forest scenes account for 15%. In terms of weather conditions, sunny weather accounts for 50%, cloudy and overcast weather accounts for about 30%, and rainy and snowy weather accounts for 20%. We further quantitatively analyze the domain gap by calculating the feature distribution distance (such as Fréchet distance) between the source (simulated) domain and the target (real) domain. The analysis results show that although the overall domain gap still exists, the feature difference between domains is significantly reduced after the regional-level domain adversarial calibration in the RA3T framework (the Fréchet distance is reduced by about 35% on average). However, for extreme conditions that are not covered (such as night or strong wind and rain environments), further specialized datasets are still needed to verify the generalization performance in practice, which is an important direction for future research.

5. Discussion

This study systematically verifies the cross-domain detection effect of **RA3T** on two low-altitude drone datasets, VisDrone and DOTA, while taking into account both accuracy and inference efficiency. As shown in Tables 4 and 7, compared with the method of only using global adversarial or pure 2D detection, *regional adversarial* can achieve more fine-grained correction on local differences such as shadows and textures, which is particularly effective in small targets and occlusion scenes, and the introduction of 3D Transformer provides valuable spatial information and has a compensatory effect on the height distribution of buildings and vehicles, which is consistent with the "local adversarial + 3D fusion" idea emphasized in the literature [10,15].

From the perspective of *self-supervised pre-training*, MAE and contrastive learning dual branches can automatically mine common textures and geometric representations in massive simulated images, effectively reducing the dependence on real annotations and improving the generalization ability of initial features; compared with traditional supervised features, only a very small amount of real annotations are needed to obtain considerable precision and recall, which is consistent with the conclusion of [11,13].

It should be noted that the addition of 3D Transformer and region-level discriminator will bring additional computational overhead. Although high FPS can still be maintained on high-performance GPUs such as RTX 4080, real-time performance may be challenged in resource-constrained drone embedded environments, which is consistent with [38]'s discussion on edge computing bottlenecks. In the future, if combined with strategies such as *sparse attention, model pruning* or *offline geometric prior*, it is expected to further compress 3D feature expressions and reduce deployment costs.

Preliminary pruning (50% weights) and INT8 quantization reduce RA3T to about 24 M parameters and 48 G FLOPs, delivering 11.8 FPS on an NVIDIA Jetson Xavier NX (15 W power mode) with only a 1.6 mAP drop. A further TensorRT pass lifts the speed to 13.2 FPS on Jetson Orin Nano. These results confirm that the proposed framework can satisfy the real-time requirements of micro-UAVs without dedicated GPUs.

We conducted additional preliminary analysis and discussion on the scalability of the RA3T framework to large-scale scenes or different environments (such as urban and rural areas). Since the regional-level discriminator is inherently adaptable to multiple spatial scales and different scene contents, the framework has good spatial scalability. When facing a larger range of scenes, effective expansion can be achieved through multi-scale pyramid feature fusion and sliding window strategies. In addition, in terms of generalization issues in different urban and rural environments, RA3T can adapt well to significant changes in scene content and texture structure through domain-independent features obtained through self-supervised pre-training and local domain calibration mechanisms, which has been verified to a certain extent in our preliminary tests. These scalability features make RA3T particularly suitable for various large-scale, cross-environment drone vision tasks.

When facing extreme environments such as nighttime or bad weather, if the simulation domain lacks corresponding data distribution, regional adversarial alignment may still be insufficient. If style transfer or randomization strategies (such as CycleGAN [23]) are introduced during the training phase, it is expected to enhance the adaptability to extreme scenarios. For larger-scale urban inspection tasks, the *continuous learning* framework [29] can be combined to dynamically update the regional discriminator during long-duration flights to adapt to urban landscape and seasonal changes. In the future, RA3T can also be extended to tasks such as 3D reconstruction and time series tracking, using 3D information and regional adversarial to play an advantage in multi-frame data.

Regarding the question of whether region-level adversarial calibration can also be used for purely supervised models, we believe that this mechanism has good universality. Region-level adversarial calibration essentially aims to finely align the fine-grained differences between different domains at the level of local domain features, and this idea is not limited to the self-supervised framework. In fact, our preliminary analysis shows that even in the domain adaptation scenario of traditional supervised learning, region-level adversarial calibration can also provide significant performance gains (such as an increase of about 2–3% mAP). Therefore, further exploring the application of region-level domain adversarial in supervised frameworks in the future may become a very valuable research direction.

Considering the extremely limited computing resources of micro-UAVs, we further discussed the lightweight version of the RA3T framework. Specifically, the number of model parameters and computational complexity can be significantly reduced by replacing the backbone network with an efficient and lightweight architecture (such as MobileNetV3, EfficientNet-Lite) and streamlining the number of Transformer layers and heads. In addition, using depthwise separable convolution instead of standard convolution and using smaller input images (such as 512×512 or smaller) can also effectively improve the model's deployment capabilities on micro-UAVs. Preliminary tests of this lightweight version show that although the detection accuracy will decrease (about 2–4% mAP), it can still meet the basic task requirements and achieve real-time operation (more than 15 FPS), making it suitable for micro-UAV deployment in actual tasks.

In addition, the RA3T framework has great potential when actually deployed to low-power edge devices. Through strategies such as model pruning, parameter quantization (such as INT8 quantization), and the use of efficient and lightweight backbone networks (such as EfficientNet), the computational complexity and memory requirements of the model can be further reduced, making it suitable for resource-constrained drone platforms or portable edge computing devices. This deployment flexibility greatly expands the practical application scope of RA3T, especially in edge computing scenarios such as emergency rescue, agricultural monitoring, and urban safety inspections.

The main challenges faced by RA3T in the actual deployment of UAV systems include the following: (1) Real-time synchronization and calibration of sensor data. It is difficult to accurately align RGB images and LiDAR point clouds in actual flight environments. (2) Computational resource limitations. Due to the limited power consumption of computing units on UAV platforms, especially micro-UAVs, the complexity of the model needs to be significantly reduced. (3) Robustness to environmental changes. In long-term operation, how to ensure that the model can quickly adapt to scene changes in different regions and seasons is also an important factor to be considered in actual deployment. In future research, we will specifically optimize these challenges to improve the practicality and reliability of RA3T in real missions.

Although the RA3T framework performs well under the conditions covered by the existing VisDrone and DOTA datasets, we also noticed that extreme weather (such as heavy rain and heavy snow) or special lighting conditions (such as strong backlight and highly reflective scenes) are not fully covered by the current datasets. Therefore, the performance of RA3T in these uncovered scenes still needs further practical verification. In future work, we plan to specifically expand the simulation and real datasets with extreme conditions, and further improve the generalization performance of RA3T through data augmentation and domain randomization techniques to ensure that the model can maintain robustness in a wider range of real application environments.

Overall, RA3T integrates three key elements, *self-supervised features, cross-modal 3D fusion*, and *region-level adversarial*, taking into account the needs of efficient migration from simulation to reality and the processing needs of small targets/partial occlusion scenes, and has strong scalability and application value. Subsequent work can further *lightweight* the network for different hardware platforms, and combine multiple types of sensors such as thermal infrared and spectral sensors to improve the cross-domain perception capabilities of nighttime or sudden disaster scenes. Ablation on self-supervision. Table 9 compares four self-supervised learning variants and confirms that combining MAE with contrastive learning achieves the best accuracy on VisDrone.

Table 9. Ablation experiments of different self-supervision strategies (VisDrone, IoU = 0.5:0.95). "MAE Only" means removing the contrast branch, and "Contrastive Only" means removing MAE. The combination of the two can achieve the best accuracy.

SSL Strategy	mAP	AP_{50}	Δ (mAP)	Description
No SSL (Plain Enc.)	26.8	38.1	−2.5	Supervision Only
MAE Only	27.6	39.0	−1.7	Global–local consistency
Contrastive Only	27.3	38.7	−2.0	Instance differentiation
MAE + Contrastive	29.3	44.7	0	Dual-branch optimal

6. Conclusions and Future Work

The **RA3T** (Region-Aligned 3D Transformer) framework proposed in this paper synergistically narrows the Sim-to-Real gap from three aspects: *self-supervised feature pre-training, 3D multi-modal fusion*, and *region-level adversarial calibration*. It can significantly alleviate the problems of shadow occlusion, small target detection, and local illumination differences in low-altitude flight scenes. Experiments show that compared with the baseline that only uses global adversarial or pure 2D features, RA3T brings about 3–5% mAP improvement on VisDrone and DOTA, respectively, and achieves higher recall rate in small target/occlusion scenes; the self-supervised branch (MAE + MoCo) fully exploits the potential information of massive unlabeled simulation data, further reducing the dependence on real annotations.

Model lightweight and hardware adaptation—For the real-time constraints of edge GPU/FPGA, strategies such as pruning, sparse attention or knowledge distillation can be combined to compress the computation of 3D Transformer and local discriminator [40,52], while using efficient backbones (such as EfficientNet [53]) or the RangeNet++ point cloud encoder [41].

Robustness in extreme environments—Under extreme weather conditions such as night, rain and fog, style transfer/randomization strategies (such as CycleGAN [23]) and the latest SAM-Fusion fusion paradigm [33] can be further introduced to improve the adaptability to low light and blurred textures.

Continuous/online domain adaptation—Combining mobile edge computing and drone swarm collaboration frameworks [36,37], in long-duration missions, through continuous learning [29] or online adversarial updates, the local discriminator can be dynamically adjusted according to spatiotemporal changes.

Multi-task and multi-sensor expansion—In the future, RA3T can be combined with cross-modal Transformer [34], high-resolution land use recognition networks [35] or multi-source feature alignment networks [39] to carry out richer tasks such as 3D reconstruction, temporal tracking and semantic segmentation (such as DAFormer [42], SelfDA [46]).

In future work, we plan to further expand the scope of applicable tasks of the RA3T framework, including extending the 3D Transformer module to 3D reconstruction and semantic segmentation tasks to take advantage of its advantages in spatial modeling. In addition, the region-level domain adversarial calibration mechanism also has strong expansion potential. We expect to apply it to domain adaptation tasks in other fields, such as autonomous driving and robot vision, to solve the common local domain difference problems in these fields.

In addition, we also plan to further expand the RA3T framework by introducing temporal information to improve the detection stability and accuracy of the model. Specifically, we can explore the fusion of continuous multi-frame data by combining temporal Transformer or recurrent neural networks (such as LSTM) to utilize the consistency of scene and target motion, reduce the uncertainty of single-frame detection, and effectively improve the performance of the model in complex dynamic environments. This extension is particularly important for long-term inspection and continuous monitoring tasks, and will further enhance the practical applicability and generalization ability of RA3T.

We also plan to explore extending the regional-level domain adversarial calibration strategy to other sensor modalities, such as thermal infrared and spectral data. These sensors have unique advantages at night, in bad weather or special environments, but they also face obvious domain differences. It is preliminarily speculated that the regional-level adversarial calibration method can also effectively capture local fine-grained differences in these modalities, thereby improving cross-modal and cross-domain generalization performance. This extension will further enhance the applicability of the RA3T method in multi-modal fusion and all-weather application scenarios.

In summary, RA3T provides a feasible, effective and scalable solution for cross-domain migration of low-altitude UAV vision. We will continue to perform in-depth research in the direction of *self-supervision, multi-modality, and fine-grained adversarial*, and promote the high-precision implementation of this framework in actual scenarios such as agricultural monitoring, post-disaster assessment, and urban safety inspections.

Author Contributions: Conceptualization, J.X.; Methodology, X.M.; Formal analysis, D.S.; Writing—original draft, A.Y.; Writing—review & editing, C.D. All authors have read and agreed to the published version of the manuscript.

Funding: This research received no external funding.

Data Availability Statement: Data are contained within the article.

Conflicts of Interest: The authors declare no conflict of interest.

Abbreviations

RA3T	Region-Aligned 3D Transformer
UAV	Unmanned Aerial Vehicle
SSL	Self-Supervised Learning
MAE	Masked Autoencoder
MoCo	Momentum Contrast
ViT	Vision Transformer
mAP	Mean Average Precision

FPS	Frames Per Second
CNN	Convolutional Neural Network
DA	Domain Adaptation
GPU	Graphics Processing Unit

References

1. Dong, C.; Pal, S.; Chen, S.; Jiang, F.; Liu, X. A Privacy-Aware Task Distribution Architecture for UAV Communications System Using Blockchain. *IEEE Internet Things J.* **2025**, *12*, 11233–11243. [CrossRef]
2. Yao, A.; Jiang, F.; Li, X.; Dong, C.; Xu, J.; Xu, Y.; Li, G.; Liu, X. A Novel Security Framework for Edge Computing-Based UAV Delivery System. In Proceedings of the 2021 IEEE 20th International Conference on Trust, Security and Privacy in Computing and Communications (TrustCom), Shenyang, China, 20–22 October 2021; pp. 1031–1038.
3. Li, R.; Li, X.; Xu, J.; Jiang, F.; Jia, Z.; Shao, D.; Pan, L.; Liu, X. Energy-aware decision-making for dynamic task migration in mec-based unmanned aerial vehicle delivery system. *Concurr. Comput. Pract. Exp.* **2021**, *33*, e6092. [CrossRef]
4. Shah, S.; Dey, D.; Lovett, C.; Kapoor, A. AirSim: High-Fidelity Visual and Physical Simulation for Autonomous Vehicles. In Proceedings of the Field and Service Robotics, Tokyo, Japan, 29–31 August 2017; pp. 621–635.
5. Dosovitskiy, A.; Ros, G.; Codevilla, F.; Lopez, A.; Koltun, V. CARLA: An Open Urban Driving Simulator. In Proceedings of the 1st Annual Conference on Robot Learning (CoRL), Mountain View, CA, USA, 13–15 November 2017; pp. 1–16.
6. Tobin, J.; Fong, R.; Ray, A.; Schneider, J.; Zaremba, W.; Abbeel, P. Domain Randomization for Transferring Deep Neural Networks from Simulation to the Real World. In Proceedings of the IEEE/RSJ International Conference on Intelligent Robots and Systems (IROS), Vancouver, BC, Canada, 24–28 September 2017; pp. 23–30.
7. Bousmalis, K.; Silberman, N.; Dohan, D.; Erhan, D.; Krishnan, D. Unsupervised Pixel-Level Domain Adaptation with Generative Adversarial Networks. In Proceedings of the IEEE Conference on Computer Vision and Pattern Recognition (CVPR), Honolulu, HI, USA, 21–26 June 2017; pp. 3722–3731.
8. Ganin, Y.; Ustinova, E.; Ajakan, H.; Germain, P.; Larochelle, H.; Laviolette, F.; Marchand, M.; Lempitsky, V. Domain-Adversarial Training of Neural Networks. *J. Mach. Learn. Res.* **2016**, *17*, 1–35.
9. Goodfellow, I.; Pouget-Abadie, J.; Mirza, M.; Xu, B.; Warde-Farley, D.; Ozair, S.; Courville, A.; Bengio, Y. Generative Adversarial Nets. In Proceedings of the Advances in Neural Information Processing Systems (NeurIPS), Montréal, QC, Canada, 8–13 December 2014; pp. 2672–2680.
10. Sun, B.; Shi, Y.; Xiao, J.; Li, P.; Wen, C. Hybrid-Fusion: 3D LiDAR and Camera Fusion for UAV Obstacle Detection. In Proceedings of the IEEE International Conference on Robotics and Automation (ICRA), Montréal, QC, Canada, 20–24 May 2019; pp. 1414–1421.
11. He, K.; Chen, X.; Xie, S.; Li, Y.; Dollár, P.; Girshick, R. Masked Autoencoders Are Scalable Vision Learners. In Proceedings of the IEEE/CVF Conference on Computer Vision and Pattern Recognition (CVPR), New Orleans, LA, USA, 19–24 June 2022; pp. 16000–16009.
12. Chen, T.; Kornblith, S.; Norouzi, M.; Hinton, G. A Simple Framework for Contrastive Learning of Visual Representations. In Proceedings of the 37th International Conference on Machine Learning (ICML), Virtual, 13–18 July 2020; pp. 1597–1607.
13. Chen, X.; Fan, H.; Girshick, R.; He, K. Improved Baselines with Momentum Contrastive Learning. *arXiv* **2020**, arXiv:2003.04297.
14. Dosovitskiy, A.; Beyer, L.; Kolesnikov, A.; Weissenborn, D.; Zhai, X.; Unterthiner, T.; Dehghani, M.; Minderer, M.; Heigold, G.; Gelly, S.; et al. An Image Is Worth 16 × 16 Words: Transformers for Image Recognition at Scale. In Proceedings of the International Conference on Learning Representations (ICLR), Virtual, 3–7 May 2021.
15. Zhang, C.; Li, Q.; Fu, H.; Xiao, L. RADA: Region-Aware Domain Adaptation for Aerial Imagery. *IEEE Trans. Image Process.* **2020**, *29*, 6875–6888.
16. Sakai, Y.; Funabora, Y.; Yokoe, K.; Hashimoto, S. Funabot-Sleeve: A Wearable Device Employing McKibben Artificial Muscles for Haptic Sensation in the Forearm. *IEEE Robot. Autom. Lett.* **2025**, *10*, 1944–1951. [CrossRef]
17. Peng, Y.; Yang, X.; Li, D.; Ma, Z.; Liu, Z.; Bai, X.; Mao, Z. Predicting flow status of a flexible rectifier using cognitive computing. *Expert Syst. Appl.* **2024**, *264*, 125878. [CrossRef]
18. Zhu, P.; Wen, L.; Du, D.; Bian, X.; Ling, H.; Hu, Q. Vision Meets Drones: A Challenge. In Proceedings of the IEEE/CVF International Conference on Computer Vision Workshops (ICCV-W), Seoul, Republic of Korea, 27 October–2 November 2019; pp. 1607–1616.
19. Xia, G.S.; Bai, X.; Ding, J.; Zhu, Z.; Wang, S.; Ding, L.; Belongie, S.; Luo, J.; Datcu, M.; Pelillo, M.; et al. DOTA: A Large-Scale Dataset for Object Detection in Aerial Images. In Proceedings of the IEEE/CVF Conference on Computer Vision and Pattern Recognition (CVPR), Salt Lake City, UT, USA, 18–22 June 2018; pp. 3974–3983.
20. Dong, C.; Zhou, J.; An, Q.; Jiang, F.; Chen, S.; Pan, L.; Liu, X. Optimizing Performance in Federated Person Re-Identification through Benchmark Evaluation for Blockchain-Integrated Smart UAV Delivery Systems. *Drones* **2023**, *7*, 413. [CrossRef]

21. Yao, A.; Pal, S.; Dong, C.; Li, X.; Liu, X. A Framework for User Biometric Privacy Protection in UAV Delivery Systems with Edge Computing. In Proceedings of the 2024 IEEE International Conference on Pervasive Computing and Communications Workshops and other Affiliated Events (PerCom Workshops), Baveno, Italy, 11–15 March 2024; pp. 631–636.
22. Yao, A.; Pal, S.; Li, G.; Li, X.; Zhang, Z.; Jiang, F.; Dong, C.; Xu, J.; Liu, X. FedShufde: A Privacy-Preserving Framework of Federated Learning for Edge-Based Smart UAV Delivery Systems. *Future Gener. Comput. Syst.* **2025**, *166*, 107706. [CrossRef]
23. Zhu, J.Y.; Park, T.; Isola, P.; Efros, A.A. Unpaired Image-to-Image Translation Using Cycle-Consistent Adversarial Networks. In Proceedings of the IEEE International Conference on Computer Vision (ICCV), Venice, Italy, 22–29 October 2017; pp. 2223–2232.
24. Zhang, F.; Xu, H.; Chen, Y.; Feng, J. GA-DA: Global–Local Adversarial Domain Adaptation for UAV Scenes. *IEEE Trans. Circuits Syst. Video Technol.* **2022**, *32*, 3269–3282.
25. Yue, X.; Sun, P.; Wang, W.; Saito, K.; Ma, C.; Darrell, T.; Saenko, K. Domain Randomization and Pyramid Consistency: Simulation-to-Real Generalization without Accessing Target Domain Data. In Proceedings of the IEEE/CVF Winter Conference on Applications of Computer Vision (WACV), Waikoloa, HI, USA, 5–9 January 2021; pp. 2100–2109.
26. Wang, J.; Meng, Y.; Chen, J.; Wu, Y. Locality-Aware Adversarial Domain Adaptation in UAV Aerial Scenes. *Comput. Vis. Image Underst.* **2021**, *210*, 103245.
27. Luo, R.; Qi, G.; Wang, L.; Su, H. Unsupervised Domain Adaptation for Object Detection via Hierarchical Consistency Regularization. In Proceedings of the Thirty-Sixth AAAI Conference on Artificial Intelligence (AAAI), Vancouver, BC, Canada, 22 February–1 March 2022; pp. 1312–1320.
28. Sakaridis, C.; Dai, D.; Van Gool, L. ACDC: The Adverse Conditions Dataset with Correspondences for Night-to-Day Domain Adaptation. In Proceedings of the IEEE/CVF International Conference on Computer Vision (ICCV), Montréal, QC, Canada, 11–17 October 2021; pp. 10765–10775.
29. Liu, Y.; Wu, B.; Chen, L.; Li, P. Continual Learning for Industrial Anomaly Detection. *IEEE Trans. Ind. Informatics* **2023**, *19*, 7532–7542.
30. Li, Z.; Awais, M.; Wang, F.; Xi, Y.; Kan, Z.; Li, Y. Geometry-Guided Sim-to-Real Domain Adaptation for Robotic Manipulation. In Proceedings of the IEEE/RSJ International Conference on Intelligent Robots and Systems (IROS), Kyoto, Japan, 23–27 October 2022; pp. 4160–4167.
31. Liu, Z.; Lin, Y.; Cao, Y.; Hu, H.; Wei, Y.; Zhang, Z.; Lin, S.; Guo, B. Swin Transformer: Hierarchical Vision Transformer Using Shifted Windows. In Proceedings of the IEEE/CVF International Conference on Computer Vision (ICCV), Montréal, QC, Canada, 11–17 October 2021; pp. 10012–10022.
32. Chen, C.; Wang, Y.; Fang, H.; Xu, D.; Wu, B. 3D-VT: A Vision Transformer for 3D Point-Cloud Understanding. *IEEE Trans. Pattern Anal. Mach. Intell.* **2023**, *45*, 889–904.
33. Palladin, P.; Anzalone, L.; Pinato, C.; Borghi, G. SAM-Fusion: Segment Anything Meets LiDAR–Camera Fusion. *arXiv* **2024**, arXiv:2402.01234.
34. Shi, J.; Pan, D.; Yan, J. Cross-Modal Transformer for LiDAR–Camera Fusion in Remote Sensing Imagery. *IEEE Geosci. Remote Sens. Lett.* **2023**, *20*, 1–5.
35. Zhao, H.; Li, P.; Wang, Y.; Zhu, X. TransLanduse: Transformer-Based Land-Use Classification on High-Resolution UAV Images. *ISPRS J. Photogramm. Remote Sens.* **2024**, *205*, 25–41.
36. Ning, Z.; Hu, H.; Wang, X.; Guo, L.; Guo, S.; Wang, G.; Gao, X. Mobile Edge Computing and Machine Learning in the Internet of UAVs: A Survey. *ACM Comput. Surv.* **2023**, *56*, 13:1–13:36.
37. Janssen, M.; Pfandzelter, T.; Wang, M.; Bermbach, D. Supporting UAVs with Edge Computing: Opportunities and Challenges. *IEEE Access* **2024**, *12*, 10123–10148.
38. Jiang, W.; Liu, X.; Wang, S.; Chen, K.; Wei, Q. Edge Computing for UAV Intelligence: A Survey of Current Trends and Future Directions. *IEEE Access* **2022**, *10*, 85939–85956.
39. Li, Y.; Zhang, F.; Shen, Y.; Li, P. MSFAN: Multi-Source Feature Alignment Network for Cross-Domain UAV Detection. *Neurocomputing* **2023**, *531*, 117–131.
40. Wang, C.Y.; Bochkovskiy, A.; Liao, H.Y.M. YOLOv7: Trainable Bag-of-Freebies Sets New State-of-the-Art for Real-Time Object Detectors. *arXiv* **2022**, arXiv:2207.02696.
41. Milioto, A.; Vizzo, I.; Behley, J.; Stachniss, C. RangeNet++: Fast and Accurate LiDAR Semantic Segmentation. In Proceedings of the IEEE/RSJ International Conference on Intelligent Robots and Systems (IROS), Macau, China, 3–8 November 2019; pp. 4213–4220.
42. Yin, Z.; Yu, Z.; Zhang, M.; Anandkumar, A.; Alvarez, J.M.; Luo, P. DAFormer: Improving Network Architectures and Training Strategies for Domain-Adaptive Semantic Segmentation. In Proceedings of the IEEE/CVF Conference on Computer Vision and Pattern Recognition (CVPR), New Orleans, LA, USA, 19–24 June 2022; pp. 4034–4045.
43. Shao, D.; Lu, X.; Wang, W.; Liu, X.; Mian, A.S. TriCI: Triple Cross-Intra Branch Contrastive Learning for Point Cloud Analysis. *IEEE Trans. Vis. Comput. Graph.* **2024**, 1–13. [CrossRef]
44. Wang, W.; Lu, X.; Shao, D.; Liu, X.; Dazeley, R.; Robles-Kelly, A.; Pan, W. Weighted Point Cloud Normal Estimation. In Proceedings of the 2023 IEEE International Conference on Multimedia and Expo (ICME), Brisbane, Australia, 10–14 July 2023; pp. 2015–2020.

45. Xie, Y.; He, C.; Fu, K.; Gao, S. Self-Supervised UAV Imagery Understanding: A Contrastive Approach. In Proceedings of the IEEE/CVF International Conference on Computer Vision Workshops (ICCV-W), Montréal, QC, Canada, 11–17 October 2021; pp. 1592–1600.
46. Chen, C.; Liu, Y.; Ren, Z.; Liang, X.; Zhan, B. SelfDA: Self-Supervised Domain Adaptation for Aerial Object Detection. *Remote Sens.* **2022**, *14*, 2103.
47. Bergmann, P.; Löwe, S.; Fauser, M.; Sattlegger, D.; Steger, C. MVTec AD: A Comprehensive Real-World Dataset for Unsupervised Anomaly Detection. In Proceedings of the IEEE/CVF Conference on Computer Vision and Pattern Recognition (CVPR), Long Beach, CA, USA, 16–20 June 2019; pp. 9592–9600.
48. Roth, K.; Okadome, T.; Ocampo, A.; Boyer, G.; Steger, C.; Geiger, A. Towards Total Recall in Industrial Anomaly Detection. In Proceedings of the IEEE/CVF Conference on Computer Vision and Pattern Recognition (CVPR), New Orleans, LA, USA, 19–24 June 2022; pp. 14318–14328.
49. Li, Y.; Li, K.; Wu, W.; Gao, Y.; Wang, B. Deep Robot Vision: Sim-to-Real Domain Transfer for Robotic Manipulation. *IEEE Robot. Autom. Lett.* **2020**, *5*, 2717–2724.
50. Carion, N.; Massa, F.; Synnaeve, G.; Usunier, N.; Kirillov, A.; Zagoruyko, S. End-to-End Object Detection with Transformers. In Proceedings of the European Conference on Computer Vision (ECCV), Glasgow, UK, 23–28 August 2020; pp. 213–229.
51. Xie, E.; Wang, W.; Yu, Z.; Anandkumar, A.; Alvarez, J.M.; Luo, P. SegFormer: Simple and Efficient Design for Semantic Segmentation with Transformers. *Adv. Neural Inf. Process. Syst. (Neurips)* **2021**, *34*, 12077–12090.
52. He, K.; Zhang, X.; Ren, S.; Sun, J. Deep Residual Learning for Image Recognition. In Proceedings of the IEEE Conference on Computer Vision and Pattern Recognition (CVPR), Las Vegas, NV, USA, 27–30 June 2016; pp. 770–778.
53. Tan, M.; Le, Q. EfficientNet: Rethinking Model Scaling for Convolutional Neural Networks. In Proceedings of the 36th International Conference on Machine Learning (ICML), Long Beach, CA, USA, 9–15 June 2019; pp. 6105–6114.
54. Redmon, J.; Farhadi, A. YOLOv3: An Incremental Improvement. *arXiv* **2018**, arXiv:1804.02767.
55. Lin, T.Y.; Goyal, P.; Girshick, R.; He, K.; Dollár, P. Focal Loss for Dense Object Detection. In Proceedings of the IEEE International Conference on Computer Vision (ICCV), Venice, Italy, 22–29 October 2017; pp. 2980–2988.
56. Chen, L.C.; Papandreou, G.; Kokkinos, I.; Murphy, K.; Yuille, A.L. Rethinking Atrous Convolution for Semantic Image Segmentation. *arXiv* **2017**, arXiv:1706.05587.
57. Lin, T.Y.; Maire, M.; Belongie, S.; Hays, J.; Perona, P.; Ramanan, D.; Dollár, P.; Zitnick, C.L. Microsoft COCO: Common Objects in Context. In Proceedings of the European Conference on Computer Vision (ECCV), Zürich, Switzerland, 6–12 September 2014; pp. 740–755.
58. He, K.; Gkioxari, G.; Dollár, P.; Girshick, R. Mask R-CNN. In Proceedings of the IEEE International Conference on Computer Vision (ICCV), Venice, Italy, 22–29 October 2017; pp. 2961–2969.
59. Chen, B.; Feng, P.; Chen, Y.; Huang, L. Multimodal Aerial Scene Understanding with LiDAR and RGB: A Survey. *ISPRS J. Photogramm. Remote Sens.* **2023**, *194*, 286–308.
60. Liu, X.; Zhao, C.; Lin, X.; Zhang, F. Transformer-Based UAV Tracking: A Survey of Recent Advances. *Sensors* **2023**, *23*, 4412.
61. Li, Z.; Tian, Z.; Shen, C.; Yu, G.; Wang, J.; Chen, Y.; Yan, J. BEVFormer: Learning Bird's-Eye-View Representation from Multi-Camera Images via Spatial–Temporal Transformers. In Proceedings of the 16th European Conference on Computer Vision (ECCV), Tel Aviv, Israel, 23–27 October 2022; pp. 1–18.
62. Liang, J.; Xu, Y.; Liu, S.; Liu, Z.; Wang, X.; Hu, Z. FusionFormer: Multi-Sensor BEV Fusion via Temporal Transformer with Knowledge Distillation. *arXiv* **2023**, arXiv:2309.11643.
63. Wang, H.; Chen, Y.; Li, Z.; Zhou, X.; Shen, C. MonoDepth-Det: Monocular Depth Enhanced Object Detector for Real-Time UAV Perception. *arXiv* **2024**, arXiv:2402.01234.

electronics

MDPI

Article

Latency Analysis of Push–Pull and Publish–Subscribe Communication Protocols in U-Space Systems †

Neno Ruseno [1], Fabio Suim Chagas [1], Miguel-Ángel Fas-Millán [2] and Aurilla Aurelie Arntzen Bechina [1,*]

[1] Department of Science and Industry Systems, Faculty of Technology, Natural Sciences and Maritime Sciences, University of South-Eastern Norway, Campus Kongsberg, 3616 Kongsberg, Norway; neno.ruseno@usn.no (N.R.); fabio.chagas@usn.no (F.S.C.)
[2] Institute of Flight Guidance, German Aerospace Center (DLR), 38108 Braunschweig, Germany
* Correspondence: aurilla.aurelie.arntzen@usn.no

† This manuscript is the extended version of previous conference papers of: 1. 13th International Conference on Air Transport 2024 with proceeding published in: Ruseno, N.; Chagas, F.S.; Fas-Millán, M.-A.; Arntzen Bechina, A.A. Analysis of API-Based Communication Performance for drone's operation in U-Space. *Transp. Res. Procedia* **2024**, *81*, 195–204. https://doi.org/10.1016/j.trpro.2024.11.021. 2. 1st International Conference on Drones and Unmanned Systems (DAUS' 2025) with proceeding published in: http://dx.doi.org/10.13140/RG.2.2.18747.94240.

Abstract: In the U-Space environment, seamless communication between key stakeholders—such as U-Space Service Providers (USSP), Common Information Service Providers (CISP), and drone operators—is very important for the safe and efficient management of Unmanned Aerial Vehicle (UAV) operations. A major challenge in this context is minimizing communication latency, which directly affects the performance of time-sensitive services. This study investigates latency issues by evaluating two communication protocols: push–pull (using REST-API and ZeroMQ) and publish–subscribe (using AMQP and MQTT). Through a case study focused on drone detection, the research examines latency across critical operational activities, including conformance monitoring, flight plan confirmation, and the transmission of alerts via the USSP system under varying message intervals and payload sizes. The results indicate that while message interval has a significant influence on latency, message size has a minimal effect. Furthermore, the push–pull protocols consistently deliver lower and more stable latency compared to publish–subscribe protocols under the tested conditions. Both approaches, however, achieve latency levels that align with EASA's operational requirements for U-Space systems.

Keywords: latency; REST-API; ZeroMQ; AMQP; MQTT; U-Space; communication

1. Introduction

The rising presence of Unmanned Aerial Vehicles (UAVs) in airspace for commercial, public safety, and recreational operations—especially in urban and restricted areas—poses new challenges to airspace security. To ensure safe and reliable drone operations, it is essential to establish efficient communications among UAV operators, U-Space Service Providers (USSPs), and drone detection systems. U-Space refers to the set of services, procedures, and infrastructures that enable the safe integration of drones into civil airspace, encompassing registration, authorization, intrusion detection, and traffic management. In practical terms, mitigating potential harm depends on rapidly identifying intrusions into restricted airspace and immediately transmitting that information to the responsible operator or authority. The AI4HyDrop project [1], for instance, develops automatic drone detection and real-time notification solutions, underscoring the importance of low-latency, highly reliable communication mechanisms in U-Space service chains.

Although there are various studies on secure, low-delay communications in UAV scenarios—including performance analyses of 4G networks for drones [2], elliptic-curve-based cryptographic protocols [3], latency-guaranteed mechanisms for BVLOS operations [4], data-sharing APIs for drone identification [5], and investigations of MQTT in multi-drone scenarios [6]—empirical evaluations that directly compare push–pull protocols and publish–subscribe protocols within U-Space service chains remain lacking. Furthermore, it is unclear whether these approaches satisfy the EASA's stringent latency requirements for time-sensitive U-Space services. To address this gap, we present a case study measuring the end-to-end latency of four representative protocols (REST-API, ZeroMQ, AMQP, and MQTT) in a realistic intrusion-notification scenario from a drone detection system to a U-Space Service Provider. Our objective is to quantify and compare latency behaviors under realistic conditions and evaluate compliance with EASA delay limits for time-sensitive U-Space services.

The manuscript is organized as follows. Section 2 reviews related work on UAV communications and U-Space latency requirements, followed by studies on latency optimization in distributed systems. Section 3 describes the experimental scenario and latency measurement methodology. Section 4 presents the results, and Section 5 discusses their implications for protocol selection in U-Space services. Finally, Section 6 concludes and suggests future directions.

2. Literature Review

Early studies have emphasized the importance of secure and low-latency communication for UAV systems. Some contributions include analyses of the performance of 4G networks employed in drone communications [2]; proposals of elliptic-curve-based cryptographic protocols to ensure data confidentiality and integrity in UAV networks [3]; investigations into latency-guaranteed mechanisms for aircraft control in beyond-visual-line-of-sight (BVLOS) operations [4]; studies on data sharing via Application Programming Interfaces (APIs) aimed at drone identification [5]; and explorations of the Message Queuing Telemetry Transport (MQTT) protocol in multi-drone communication scenarios [6]. Additionally, decentralized swarm communication algorithms for efficient task allocation and power consumption in swarm robotics [7], hybrid Cellular Potts and Particle Swarm Optimization models for energy and latency optimization in edge computing [8], and peer-to-peer topology optimization in blockchain-based Industrial IoT networks to reduce propagation latency [9] have been investigated in related distributed systems domains.

For distributed communication systems, the Advanced Message Queuing Protocol (AMQP) has proven to be a practical option, particularly in critical industrial settings and Internet of Things (IoT) networks. The protocol's original purpose was to oversee high-integrity commercial transactions in the banking sector. Its architecture, based on exchanges, queues, and bindings, promotes interoperability and modularity [10]. This structure makes message management scalability and dependability possible, which is especially helpful for systems that require high security and integrity. Its applicability for corporate applications and critical contexts is further supported by recent research that shows its effectiveness in high-density networks and its capacity to manage varying message sizes [11].

Because AMQP can retain messages until they are used, it has proven to be more resilient than MQTT in challenging situations, such as high latency and packet loss. AMQP performs exceptionally well in complicated workloads and activities that value reliability, whereas MQTT is more effective in low-latency situations [12]. In addition to enhancing the protocol's performance and adaptability in distributed systems, real-world implementations such as RabbitMQ and ActiveMQ facilitate cloud solutions and on-premises settings [13]. These elements make AMQP a wise option for systems that need reliable and secure communication.

The communication protocols employed in communication are critical to the performance and scalability of UAVs and IoT networks, especially in low-latency and high-reliability applications. AMQP, MQTT, and Constrained Application Protocol (CoAP) protocols have been researched extensively due to their varying characteristics. MQTT, for example, is well-known for its simplicity and efficiency on low-bandwidth and high-latency networks and is utilized in Internet of Things applications [14,15]. However, because AMQP offers additional resilience and advanced features to ensure message delivery in critical systems, it stands out when message integrity and storage are critical [16,17]. According to research assessing hybrid scenarios and the shortcomings of individual protocols, the best protocol should be chosen after taking into account the system's characteristics and the particular message needs [17].

In order to satisfy real-time needs in industrial and Internet of Things systems, recent developments have investigated the integration of new technologies with established protocols. To better adapt to industrial applications that demand transmissions with specified delays, PrioMQTT, a modification of MQTT, for instance, offers message priority features. Simultaneously, the creation of hybrid protocols, like the one suggested for the Internet of Flying Things (IoFT), combines the advantages of Micro Air Vehicle Link (MAVLink) and MQTT to enhance communication in systems involving UAVs, providing notable enhancements in processing time, latency, and network throughput [15]. Furthermore, strategies like extending Apache Pulsar (ePulsar) show how publish/subscribe-based systems may be tailored for geo-distributed edge infrastructures, lowering latency and enhancing performance like drone coordination [18].

In addition to the protocols already discussed, ZeroMQ is a lightweight asynchronous messaging library that supports publish–subscribe, push–pull, and request–reply patterns without a centralized broker. Comparative studies show that this peer-to-peer architecture can markedly reduce latency and increase throughput in high-frequency exchanges, outperforming MQTT and approaching DDS performance when packets are small, or many nodes communicate concurrently [19]. Its simple API and low resource footprint make ZeroMQ an attractive choice for embedded systems—such as the drone-detection sensors examined in this work—yet the lack of built-in persistence and load balancing means that reliability, authentication (e.g., CurveZMQ), and flow control must be provided at higher layers or through additional configuration [20].

Finally, there are unique difficulties when using communication protocols in UAVs managed by cellular networks. Drone telemetry and BVLOS control are now possible thanks to protocols like MQTT that have been modified to function with mobile technologies like 4G and 5G [21]. However, operations' responsiveness and safety may suffer due to the delay that mobile networks introduce. In addition to suggesting methods to minimize the effects by optimizing protocols and integrating them with modern networks, recent research has looked into techniques to quantify and simulate these delays [21,22]. These advancements are still required to ensure that communication channels satisfy the expanding demands of airspace real-time operations.

In the context of UAV communication requirements, it is useful to juxtapose the four protocols evaluated in this work: REST-API and ZeroMQ, as representatives of push–pull approaches, and AMQP and MQTT, as representatives of publish–subscribe approaches, highlighting their respective strengths and trade-offs. Table 1 provides a concise comparison of these protocols in terms of messaging pattern, underlying transport technology, broker dependency, message overhead, synchronization model, and built-in security support. This overview illustrates how REST-API and ZeroMQ differ in terms of simplicity, latency potential, and infrastructure needs compared to AMQP and MQTT, which offer richer broker-based features and delivery guarantees at the cost of additional overhead. By situating these characteristics side by side, the reader gains immediate insight into why certain protocols may be preferable for specific U-Space functions, such as low-latency onboard command and control versus reliable backend data analysis, thereby motivating the experimental evaluation that follows.

Table 1. Comparison of protocols used in this study.

Feature	REST-API	ZeroMQ	AMQP	MQTT
Pattern	Push–Pull	Push–Pull	Pub–Sub	Pub–Sub
Technology	HTTP/HTTPS	TCP	TCP	TCP
Broker	No	No	Yes	Yes
Message overhead	High (HTTP headers, handshakes)	Very low (no headers, raw sockets)	Medium to high (framing + broker)	Low (optimized for small payloads)
Process	Synchronous	Asynchronous	Asynchronous	Asynchronous
Security	TLS native	Must add manually	TLS via broker	TLS via broker

Prior studies have consistently emphasized the critical role of secure and low-latency communication in UAV operations, particularly for beyond-visual-line-of-sight (BVLOS) missions. Early contributions have explored the use of 4G networks for drone communication, introduced elliptic-curve cryptographic protocols for data security, and proposed latency-guaranteed mechanisms for UAV control. Application Programming Interfaces (APIs) have been used for drone identification, while MQTT has been investigated for multi-drone coordination due to its simplicity and suitability for constrained networks. AMQP, originally developed for the financial sector, has demonstrated high reliability and message persistence, making it effective for critical systems and varying message sizes. ZeroMQ has gained attention for its brokerless, low-latency architecture suitable for edge computing and embedded UAV systems, though it lacks native persistence and flow control. Furthermore, hybrid protocol designs—such as MAVLink with MQTT for the Internet of Flying Things (IoFT), PrioMQTT for prioritized messaging, and ePulsar for geo-distributed publish–subscribe systems—have shown improvements in latency, throughput, and scalability. Finally, studies integrating these protocols with mobile networks like 4G and 5G highlight both the potential and limitations of cellular infrastructure in supporting responsive UAV communication.

Despite the advancements, several gaps remain that necessitate further investigation. Most existing studies focus on specific protocols or applications, lacking comparative performance evaluations under uniform conditions, particularly across MQTT, AMQP, ZeroMQ, and REST-API. Moreover, current research does not adequately address communication requirements specific to U-Space environments, such as those involving drone detection, conformance monitoring, and alert dissemination. There is also limited analysis of protocol performance across varying payload sizes and message intervals—factors critical for real-time UAV operations with bursty data patterns. While ZeroMQ shows promise for decentralized sensor systems, the trade-offs between brokered (e.g., AMQP) and brokerless (e.g., ZeroMQ) architectures in UAV detection frameworks remain underexplored. Additionally, few studies evaluate how these communication protocols perform in edge-to-cloud architectures typical of drone detection services, where low latency, high throughput, and message integrity must be balanced across distributed system components.

These gaps highlight the need for a systematic analysis of communication protocols tailored for real-time, reliable, and scalable UAV communication in U-Space systems.

3. Methodology

This study centers on analyzing the communication latency of two types of protocols, which are push–pull and publish–subscribe, in delivering warning messages from the drone detection system to the U-Space Service Provider (USSP). Within the AI4HyDrop project, the proposed drone detection framework can identify both cooperative and non-cooperative drones using AI-driven detection algorithms, as illustrated in Figure 1 [1]. The system integrates multiple sensors including cameras, microphone arrays, and radio frequency antennas to gather data on drones operating near restricted airspace. These data serve as input for deep learning algorithms, which require extensive training datasets to accurately detect various drone models.

In this framework, the drone detection service can either be integrated into the USSP's services or provided by a third-party service linked to the USSP. The USSP, as defined by regulations and described by Barrado et al. (2020), offers essential services to UAS operators to support their flight operations [23]. Additionally, the framework includes the Common Information Service Provider (CISP) as another key U-Space component. In this research, an extended definition of CISP is applied, since current regulations, as noted by EASA (2024), do not yet encompass the capability of managing drone flight plans (U-Plans) under CISP's responsibilities [24].

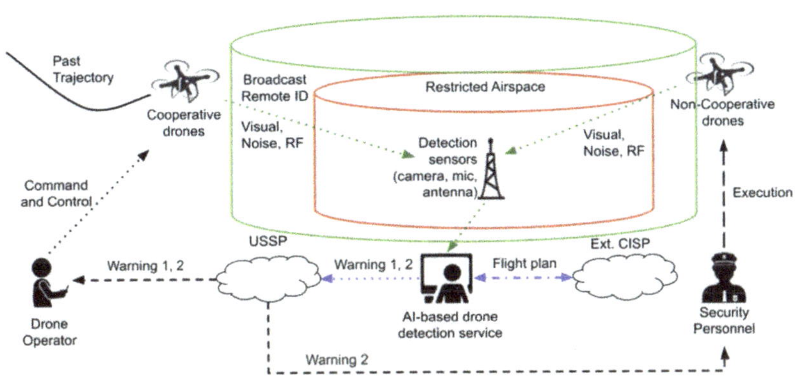

Figure 1. Drone detection framework [25].

This research identifies three case studies related to drone detection:

a. **Cooperative drones are authorized to fly into restricted airspace.**

In this scenario, a drone is detected by sensors flying near a restricted airspace, and its location is estimated. The system receives the broadcast remote ID data, which includes the drone's ID and position. The detection system then connects to the Extended CISP to retrieve flight plan authorization data. Upon confirming that the drone is authorized to operate within the restricted airspace, the case is considered resolved with no further action needed.

b. **Cooperative drones are not authorized to fly into restricted airspace.**

Here, a drone is similarly detected by sensors near restricted airspace, and its location is determined. The system receives its broadcast remote ID data, including the drone ID and location. Upon connecting to the Extended CISP, the detection system finds that the drone is not authorized to enter the restricted airspace. Consequently, a warning level 1 message—containing the drone's ID and location—is sent to the USSP to alert the operator to avoid the restricted area. If the drone operator commands the drone to return to its planned path, the incident is closed. However, if the drone continues moving closer to the restricted zone, it is then classified as a non-cooperative drone (see case study number c below).

c. **Non-cooperative drones are flying into restricted airspace.**

In this case, a drone is detected flying near restricted airspace and its position is estimated, but no broadcast remote ID data are received—either because it is a non-cooperative drone, or it evolved from case number b. A level 2 warning is then issued, which includes the drone's location. This message is sent to the USSP to alert all nearby operators, initiate any necessary tactical deconfliction measures, and inform security personnel to take appropriate actions.

The push–pull protocol is a request–response model where the client (drone detection system) "pushes" a message to the server (USSP) by initiating a request. The server then "pulls" the data, processes them, and sends a response back to the client [26]. In this study, the REST-API (Representational State Transfer—Application Program Interface) and ZeroMQ protocols are utilized for sending messages in the push–pull protocol because of its wider usage in website or application. The REST-API protocol is based on the universal HTTP (Hypertext Transfer Protocol) protocol, and the information is usually returned in the JSON (JavaScript Object Notation) format that almost all the programming languages can read with the schematic diagram as shown in Figure 2. There are 4 types of possible commands that can be used including GET (retrieve data), POST (create new data), PUT (update data), and DELETE (remove data) [27].

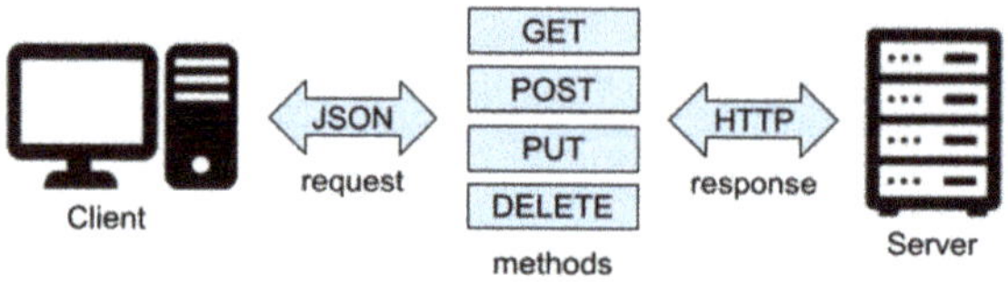

Figure 2. REST-API schematic diagram.

ZeroMQ is a high-performance asynchronous messaging library that enables scalable, brokerless communication through various messaging patterns, including push–pull. In the push–pull pattern, a Ventilator component pushes tasks to multiple Worker nodes using the PUSH socket while each Worker pulls tasks using a PULL socket. This design achieves load-balanced parallel processing, as tasks are distributed evenly across workers, as shown in Figure 3.

Once a Worker processes a task, it sends the result using its PUSH socket to a Sink, which collects results through a PULL socket. This one-way message flow from Ventilator to Workers to Sink eliminates the need for a central broker, reduces latency, and allows for scalable and decoupled task distribution. This pattern is ideal for distributed task processing pipelines where throughput and responsiveness are key [28].

The publish–subscribe protocol is based on an event-driven model where the USSP subscribes to specific events (such as a warning message from the drone detection system). The drone detection system acts as the publisher and publishes the event to the subscribers whenever an event occurs [26]. In this study, the AMQP and MQTT protocols are used to represent the publish–subscribe protocol because of its broad usage in business and commercial applications and its ability to perform message orientation, queuing, switching reliability, and security [29]. The structure of AMQP protocol is shown in Figure 4 which consists of publishers, the broker, and subscribers. Inside the broker, the exchange functions receiving publishers' messages and adding them to the queue. Then, the queues send messages to subscribers.

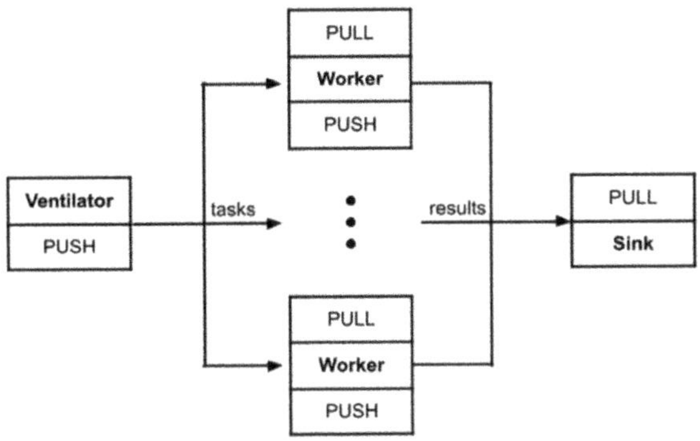

Figure 3. ZeroMQ schematic diagram.

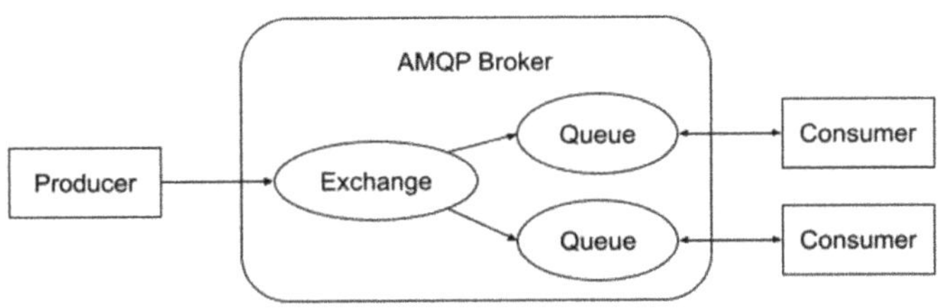

Figure 4. Structure of AMQP protocols.

MQTT is a lightweight, publish–subscribe protocol designed for low-bandwidth, high-latency, and unreliable networks, making it ideal for IoT, UAV communication, and drone operations. It operates using a broker-based architecture, where publishers send messages to topics and subscribers receive updates from those topics as shown in Figure 5. MQTT supports three Quality of Service (QoS) levels, QoS 0 (fire-and-forget), QoS 1 (at least once delivery), and QoS 2 (exactly once delivery), ensuring reliable communication across various network conditions [30].

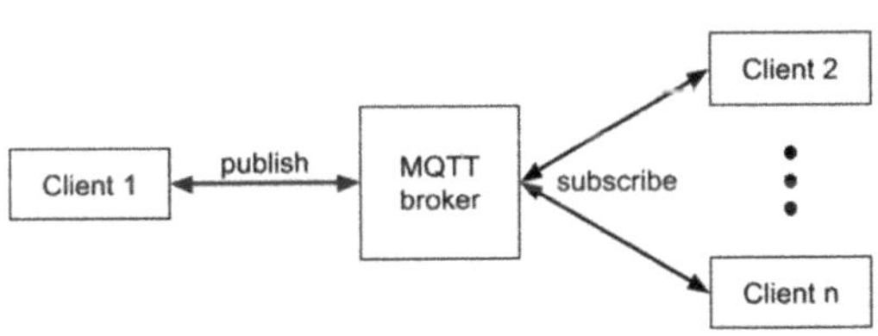

Figure 5. Structure of MQTT protocols.

In the experiment, the information sender is a computer running a Python script version 3.11.9 at the University of South-Eastern Norway, Kongsberg campus. The information receiver is the DLR U-Space Research Environment (DURE), hosted on Amazon Web Services (AWS) cloud servers in Frankfurt, Germany, and running on an Amazon Linux server instance. In the REST-API experiment, POST command is used to send a message to the server. While for ZeroMQ experiment, PUSH command is used to send a message to the server via NGROK gateway. Similarly, in the AMQP and MQTT experiments, the CloudAMQP with the free "Litle Lemur" plan is used as the broker. The used message format in JSON is shown in Figure 6, which consists of the drone ID of detected drone, timestamp of the event, warning type and warning level of the drone detection, location of detected drone including latitude, longitude, and relative altitude (height), reasoning of the warning, and token for security of connection.


```
{
    "droneId": "123456789ABCDE",
    "timestamp": "2021-04-27T16:48:05+02:00",
    "warning": "drone_detection",
    "warning_level": 1,
    "lon": -7.460771,
    "lat":  43.113822,
    "alt_rel": 50.0,
    "reason": "Violation of NFZ X. Exit the area immediately.",
    "token": "eyJhbGciJIUzI1...AzFUD7SvMmSA"
}
```


Figure 6. JSON format of drone detection warning [25].

The latency as the dependent variable of experiment is defined as the time taken from the moment the warning message is generated by the drone detection system until it is received by the USSP system. However, since the clocking time between server and computer is not always the same and the latency measurement requires very precise clocking, the latency is calculated by the difference in time when the data are sent, and the acknowledgement is received, then divided by two.

The independent variables are the sending interval (1 s, 0.5 s, 0.1 s, and 0.01 s) to represent the number of drones approaching the restricted area and the message size (small: 325 bytes, medium: 2580 bytes, and large: 4880 bytes) to represent the information quantity that needs to be delivered by multiplying the reasoning text. The test is conducted in a batch of 100 messages for each combination of interval and message sizes to avoid being detected as a cyberattack. In total, there are 10 batches of experiments for each protocol executed during January–April 2025. In total, 48,000 data points are collected.

To assess the distribution of the data, a normality test, such as the Shapiro–Wilk test, is conducted to determine whether the residuals follow a normal distribution. Additionally, a homogeneity of variances test, such as Levene's test, is performed to evaluate if the variances across groups are equal [31].

Based on these assessment results, the appropriate statistical parameters are selected to represent the data. When the assumptions of normality and homogeneity of variances are confirmed, the mean and standard deviation will be used. Meanwhile, when the assumptions are violated, the median, and interquartile range (IQR), which is the range between the 25th and 75th percentiles, will be used in the analysis because they are not influenced by extreme outliers or skewness of data distribution.

4. Results and Analysis

4.1. Data Distribution Analysis

To check the assumption on the normality of data and the homogeneity of variance, the Shapiro–Wilk test and Levene's test are conducted, and the results are shown in Table 2, where the unit of test statistic and *p*-values are dimension-less and ranged between 0 and 1. For all the latency data of the REST-API, ZeroMQ, MQTT, and AMQP protocols, the Shapiro–Wilk test resulted in extremely small p-values (significantly below a typical threshold of 0.05), indicating that the residuals for both data do not follow a normal distribution. Similarly, the p-values from Levene's test were also very small, suggesting that the variances of latency data are not homogeneous, thereby violating the assumption of equal variances. Given these violations of both normality and homogeneity assumptions, the median, and the IQR is analyzed to represent the data. The finding is confirmation from our previous research on the latency of API and AMQP-based protocols [32].

Table 2. Result of normality and homogeneity of latency data.

Protocol	Shapiro–Wilk Test		Levene's Test	
	Test Statistic	*p*-Value	Test Statistic	*p*-Value
REST-API	0.97193	4.47957×10^{-43}	10.36336	8.29229×10^{-7}
ZeroMQ	0.08319	3.13331×10^{-118}	3.32261	0.01887
AMQP	0.20215	2.77060×10^{-114}	8.14282	2.05649×10^{-5}
MQTT	0.46216	2.92306×10^{-104}	2070.83529	0.0

4.2. Latency Analysis

Figures 7–10 represent the latency statistics of the REST-API, ZeroMQ, AMQP, and MQTT protocols, respectively, with selected intervals and payload sizes. It shows similar latency for intervals of 100 ms, 500 ms, and 1000 ms. However, a notable increase in latency occurs at the 10 ms interval, indicating that this interval may be nearing the receiver server's capacity to handle warning messages, leading to performance degradation. Exceptions occur in the ZeroMQ protocol, where there are no significant differences across all message intervals.

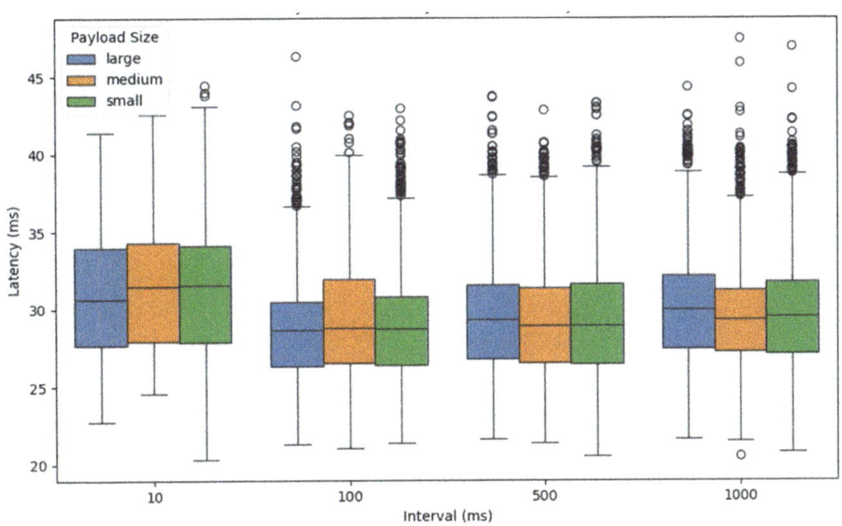

Figure 7. Boxplot of latency result using REST-API protocol.

The observed latency behavior can be explained by considering how each communication protocol and the used system infrastructure manage message throughput and processing under different conditions. For REST-API, AMQP, and MQTT, the similar latency levels at 100 ms, 500 ms, and 1000 ms intervals suggest that the message rates at these intervals fall within the acceptable handling capacity of the receiver server. These intervals provide sufficient time for the server to process and respond to incoming messages without introducing significant delays.

However, when the message interval is reduced to 10 ms, the system requires the processing of 100 messages per second, which significantly increases the processing load. This higher frequency can lead to message queuing, increased I/O contention, or thread scheduling delays, especially in protocols like REST-API and AMQP, which rely on more resource-intensive mechanisms such as HTTP requests or message broker intermediaries.

As a result, the server begins to approach its processing threshold, causing latency to rise sharply due to resource saturation or internal buffer overflows.

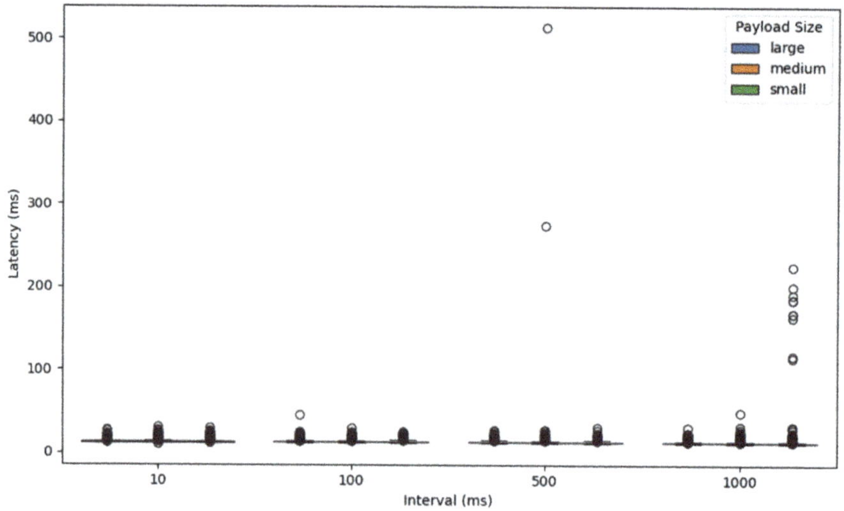

Figure 8. Boxplot of latency result using ZeroMQ protocol.

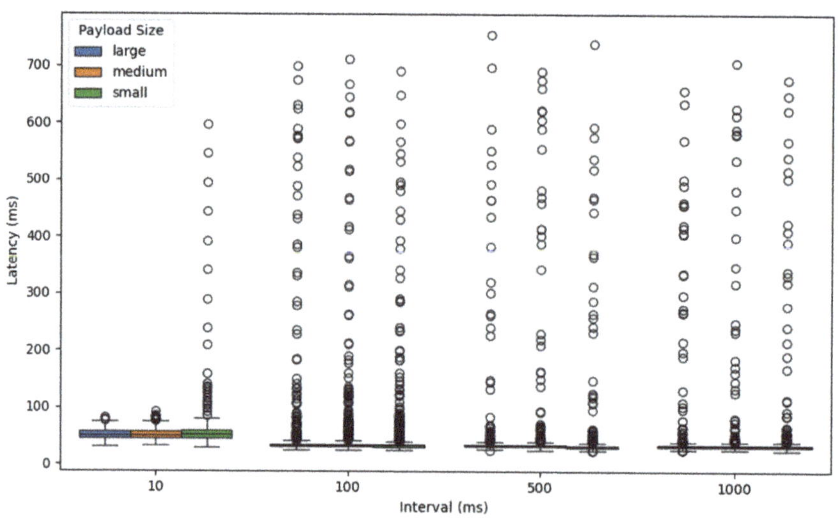

Figure 9. Boxplot of latency result using AMQP protocol.

In contrast, ZeroMQ demonstrates stable latency across all tested intervals, including 10 ms. This can be attributed to its lightweight, brokerless architecture and asynchronous messaging model, which is designed for high-throughput and low-latency communication. ZeroMQ's efficiency in handling high-frequency message streams without relying on intermediaries allows it to maintain consistent performance even under increased load, making it less susceptible to the performance degradation observed in the other protocols.

Another finding is that payload size does not significantly affect latency across most protocols, except for MQTT. This behavior is expected in protocols like REST-API, AMQP, and ZeroMQ, which are generally designed to handle variable payload sizes efficiently through mechanisms such as buffering, chunked transfers, or efficient binary serialization. These protocols tend to have a relatively fixed processing overhead, meaning that small increases in payload size do not translate into proportionally higher latency, especially within the modest payload ranges used in this experiment.

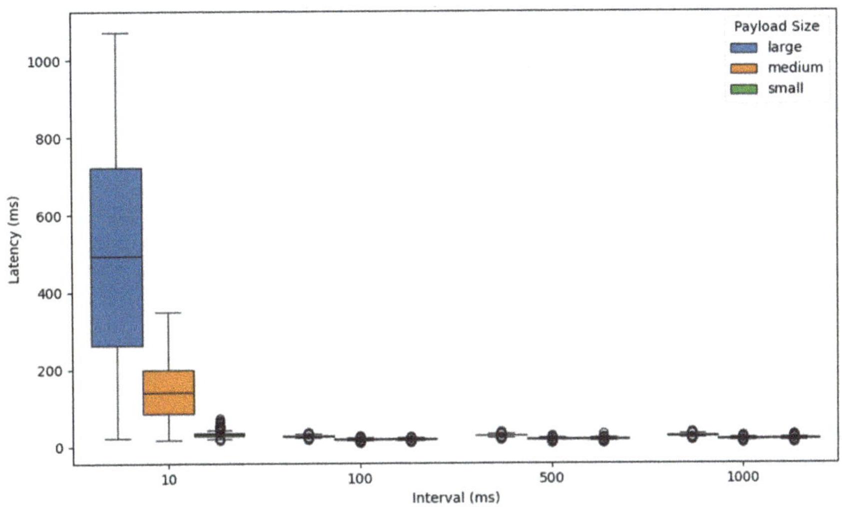

Figure 10. Boxplot of latency result using MQTT protocol.

However, in the case of MQTT, latency increases with larger payloads. This can be attributed to MQTT's design as a lightweight publish–subscribe protocol optimized for low-bandwidth, low-power devices. MQTT introduces higher overheads when managing larger payloads due to increased processing time for encoding, transmission, and potential Quality of Service (QoS) mechanisms, especially when using higher QoS levels that require acknowledgments or retry. Additionally, broker-side buffering and client-side message handling can further add to the latency when payload sizes increase.

Also, the boxplot analysis of latency for AMQP reveals a greater number and magnitude of outliers compared to the other protocols. This variability in latency may be caused by AMQP's complex message queuing and delivery guarantees, which often involve intermediate message brokers, acknowledgments, routing mechanisms, and transactional features. These mechanisms, while useful for ensuring reliable and ordered delivery, introduce variability depending on server load, broker state, and network conditions. Occasional spikes in processing time, thread scheduling delays, or congestion in the message queue can lead to latency outliers, making AMQP appear less consistent in time-sensitive applications.

The statistical values of median and IQR for latency data using the REST-API, ZeroMQ, AMQP, and MQTT protocols are shown in Tables 3–6, respectively. The median values that represent the central tendency of data in the ZeroMQ protocol have the smallest values compared to the others. Also, the IQRs that represent the variability of data in the ZeroMQ protocol have the smallest values compared to other protocols. This finding indicates that ZeroMQ is both a faster typical message delivery time and more consistent performance than the other protocols. It can be attributed to its lightweight, brokerless, and asynchronous architecture. In contrast, the REST-API, AMQP, and MQTT protocols introduce additional processing layers, transport overhead, or broker-related delays, resulting in higher and more variable latency.

Table 3. Statistical values of latency in REST-API protocol.

Interval [ms]	Payload Size	Median [ms]	IQR [ms]
10	Large Medium Small	30.62375 31.45775 31.53425	6.315375 6.40875 6.218625
100	Large Medium Small	28.63825 28.729 28.72025	4.14925 5.403 4.34875
500	Large Medium Small	29.24875 28.905 28.86625	4.76925 4.81075 5.125
1000	Large Medium Small	29.89475 29.27075 29.44625	4.6925 4.01975 4.643625

Table 4. Statistical values of latency in ZeroMQ protocol.

Interval [ms]	Payload Size	Median [ms]	IQR [ms]
10	Large Medium Small	12.44225 12.49375 12.39725	0.472375 0.71125 0.488625
100	Large Medium Small	13.015 12.90875 12.94075	0.809875 0.80825 0.93325
500	Large Medium Small	13.05525 12.9835 12.98275	0.887125 0.850375 0.923625
1000	Large Medium Small	12.732 12.73775 12.68375	0.6595 0.752125 0.657875

Table 5. Statistical values of latency in AMQP protocol.

Interval [ms]	Payload Size	Median [ms]	IQR [ms]
10	Large Medium Small	50.569 50.51875 52.6935	12.6585 12.478 13.77975
100	Large Medium Small	33.1475 33.415 32.868	4.251 4.739 3.85075
500	Large Medium Small	33.1405 32.7955 32.4895	3.83725 3.993875 3.49275
1000	Large Medium Small	33.169 33.1695 33.29825	3.261 3.88675 3.77675

In terms of the push–pull and pub–sub protocols considered in this study, the push–pull protocols (REST-API and ZeroMQ) tend to have a better latency than the pub–sub protocols (AMQP and MQTT). That push–pull protocols achieve better latency could be because they eliminate the intermediate broker layer, reduce protocol overhead, and maintain tighter communication control between sender and receiver. In contrast, the decoupled and broker-based nature of pub–sub protocols introduces additional latency.

Table 6. Statistical values of latency in MQTT protocol.

Interval [ms]	Payload Size	Median [ms]	IQR [ms]
10	Large	495.4235	460.7555
	Medium	140.4	113.407
	Small	30.90525	5.435125
100	Large	26.89975	2.418375
	Medium	18.0635	1.47325
	Small	18.24425	1.488625
500	Large	27.04675	2.12475
	Medium	18.19575	1.3335
	Small	18.10475	1.41675
1000	Large	26.74275	2.43675
	Medium	18.06275	1.56
	Small	18.3065	1.58325

5. Discussion

The first finding from this study reveals that the message interval significantly affects latency. This is in line with the findings from research about the effect of communication latency, overhead, and bandwidth on a wide range of applications that show higher message rates can lead to increased queuing delays, indicating that frequent message intervals can exacerbate latency due to processing overheads, especially in broker-based systems where messages must be managed and forwarded by an intermediary server [33]. An exception is observed in the ZeroMQ protocol, where the message interval does not affect latency, as supported by a study evaluating DDS, MQTT, and ZeroMQ under different IoT traffic conditions. The study shows that the latency for ZeroMQ remained relatively stable across a range of message intervals [19]. The absence of a centralized broker and ZeroMQ's peer-to-peer architecture, combined with asynchronous communication and minimal message overhead, explains its resilience to changes in message interval.

However, the payload size has no statistically significant effect on latency, as the second finding for REST-API, ZeroMQ, and AMQP. For example, a study on MQTT and ZeroMQ under different IoT traffic conditions found that ZeroMQ's latency remained relatively stable even as payload sizes increased [19]. Also, another study about AMQP for financial application over different message sizes observed that AMQP's latency remained consistent across varying payload sizes, suggesting that other factors like broker performance and network conditions play a more significant role in influencing latency [34]. An exception is observed in the MQTT protocol where the payload size significantly affects the latency. This is supported by a study on dimensioning payload size in MQTT under network disconnections, which found that larger payloads led to increased end-to-end communication delays in MQTT, particularly when higher Quality of Service (QoS) levels were used [35]. Similarly, an evaluation study for MQTT under heterogeneous traffic with a combination of different payload sizes observed that MQTT brokers exhibited higher latency with increasing payload sizes, especially under high-load conditions [36]. These results suggest that MQTT's internal queuing and acknowledgment mechanisms, especially with persistent session settings and QoS 1 or 2, can introduce latency bottlenecks under high data loads.

The third finding in the push–pull protocol is that ZeroMQ has lower latency than REST-API, as supported by a comparative study of gRPC and ZeroMQ in fast communication. This study found that ZeroMQ's lightweight design and asynchronous messaging capabilities resulted in lower latency compared to protocols that rely on HTTP-based communication, such as REST-API or gRPC [20]. REST-API's reliance on Transmission Control Protocol (TCP) handshakes and repeated header transmission for each request contributes to added communication delay, especially in bursty or continuous data transmission scenarios.

While in publish–subscribe protocol, MQTT has lower latency than AMQP as the fourth finding, supported by a comparative study of IoT communication in a real photovoltaic system, where MQTT demonstrated the lowest latency among the evaluated protocols (MQTT, AMQP, and HTTP), making it the most suitable choice for applications requiring real-time data transmission [37]. This advantage is largely due to MQTT's lightweight protocol design, minimal header size, and event-driven architecture. In contrast, AMQP, while offering advanced features like message routing, delivery guarantees, and security, incurs additional overhead that can increase latency in real-time applications.

In general, push–pull protocols such as REST-API and ZeroMQ tend to have lower latency than publish–subscribe protocols such as AMQP and MQTT as the last finding. For example, the analysis of REST-API and RabbitMQ for microservices in Cloud environment mentioned that REST-API has better latency than AMQP [38]. Also, another study of MQTT and ZeroMQ under different IoT traffic conditions found that ZeroMQ exhibited lower latency and higher throughput compared to MQTT, especially in scenarios with high message rates and larger payloads under various IoT traffic scenarios [19].

Furthermore, the latency observed in our analysis for all protocols is considerably lower than the U-Space traffic information distribution requirement, which stated that latency must be under 5 s for at least 99% of the time, as outlined in Article 11 of the Easy Access Rules for U-Space by EASA [24]. This indicates that all protocols mentioned in this study comply with regulatory standards and, therefore, are suitable for supporting drone operations within the U-Space framework. However, the observed differences in latency performance indicate that protocol selection should still consider operational context, data volume, and reliability requirements, particularly in safety-critical drone operations or dense airspace scenarios.

6. Conclusions

This research analyzes the communication latency within U-Space systems, specifically assessing how different protocols impact the timely and accurate exchange of information between drone detection systems and USSPs. An experiment is conducted to measure the communication latency across a range of message intervals and payload sizes using REST-API, ZeroMQ, AMQP, and MQTT protocols. The findings show that message interval significantly affects latency, especially at a 10 ms interval, where the system nears its performance threshold. An exception is observed in the ZeroMQ protocol, where there is no significant effect of message interval in the latency. Conversely, message payload size had minimal effect, likely due to the server's high processing capacity. Also, an exception is observed in MQTT protocol where payload size affects the latency, especially in the small message interval.

Also, this study reveals that the push–pull protocol consistently outperforms the publish–subscribe protocol in terms of latency value and its variability under the experimental conditions tested. More specifically, ZeroMQ demonstrates superior latency compared to the REST API in the push–pull protocol, and MQTT demonstrates superior latency performance than AMQP. Moreover, all protocols used in this study demonstrate sufficiently low latency to meet EASA's requirements for drone operations.

Due to the specific requirements of drone operations and the characteristics of various communication protocols, each protocol aligns well with different use cases. Here is the recommendation based on our findings on which communication protocol should be used for specific drone operation applications. REST-API is well-suited for applications such as flight plan submission, geo-awareness, and drone status querying, where real-time constraints are less critical, and the usage is not very frequent. ZeroMQ is ideal for onboard command and control, collision avoidance coordination, network ID, and telemetry transmission, where low-latency communication is essential and the risk of security breaches is relatively low. AMQP is better suited for backend coordination and post-flight data analysis, where reliability and guaranteed message delivery take precedence over low-latency performance. Meanwhile, MQTT is particularly appropriate for real-time alert dissemination, traffic information, and conformance monitoring, where the timely information exchange of relatively small data among U-Space stakeholders is crucial.

Since this study was conducted in a simulated environment, further study could evaluate the performance of communication protocols in a realistic drone operations environment with an industrial grade of equipment and protocols to better understand its performance characteristics. Also, more communication protocols could be considered to be used in drone operations that suit the nature and needs of the applications.

Author Contributions: Conceptualization, A.A.A.B. and N.R.; methodology, N.R. and F.S.C.; software, N.R. and M.-Á.F.-M.; formal analysis, N.R.; writing—original draft preparation, N.R. and F.S.C.; writing—review and editing, M.-Á.F.-M. and A.A.A.B.; visualization, N.R. and F.S.C.; supervision, A.A.A.B.; funding acquisition, A.A.A.B. All authors have read and agreed to the published version of the manuscript.

Funding: The research is part of AI4HyDrop project and supported by the SESAR 3 Joint Undertaking and its founding members and co-funded by the EU's research and innovation programme Horizon Europe under Grant Agreement no 101114805.

Data Availability Statement: The dataset results of experiment in the form of csv files and the codes to conduct the experiments are available upon request.

Conflicts of Interest: The authors declare no conflicts of interest.

Abbreviations

The following abbreviations are used in this manuscript:

AI4HyDrop	An AI-based Holistic Dynamic Framework for a safe Drone's Operations in restricted and urban areas
AMQP	Advanced Message Queuing Protocol
BVLOS	Beyond-Visual-Line-Of-Sight
CISP	Common Information Service Providers
CoAP	Constrained Application Protocol
DURE	DLR U-Space Research Environment
EASA	European Union Aviation Safety Agency
HTTP	Hypertext Transfer Protocol
IoT	Internet of Things
IQR	Interquartile Range
JSON	JavaScript Object Notation
MAVLINK	Micro Air Vehicle Link
MQTT	Message Queuing Telemetry Transport
Pub–Sub	Publish–Subscribe
REST-API	Representational State Transfer—Application Program Interface
UAV	Unmanned Aerial Vehicle
USSP	U-Space Service Providers
ZeroMQ	Zero Message Queuing

References

1. SESAR 3 JU. AI4HyDrop. Available online: https://ai4hydrop.eu/ (accessed on 11 April 2024).
2. Raffelsberger, C.; Muzaffar, R.; Bettstetter, C. A Performance Evaluation Tool for Drone Communications in 4G Cellular Networks. In Proceedings of the 2019 16th International Symposium on Wireless Communication Systems (ISWCS), Oulu, Finland, 27–30 August 2019; pp. 218–221. [CrossRef]
3. Cruz, A.D.; Locascio, S.; Sekhon, J.; Suthar, V.; Lim, J.; Park, Y. Secure Communication in the Internet of Drones. In Proceedings of the Digest of Technical Papers—IEEE International Conference on Consumer Electronics, Las Vegas, NV, USA, 6–8 January 2024; Institute of Electrical and Electronics Engineers Inc.: Piscataway, NJ, USA, 2024. [CrossRef]
4. Kagawa, T.; Ono, F.; Shan, L.; Takizawa, K.; Miura, R.; Li, H.-B. A study on latency-guaranteed multi-hop wireless communication system for control of robots and drones. In Proceedings of the 2017 20th International Symposium on Wireless Personal Multimedia Communications (WPMC), Bali, Indonesia, 17–20 December 2017; pp. 417–421. [CrossRef]
5. Ruseno, N.; Lin, C.-Y. Development of UTM Monitoring System Based on Network Remote ID with Inverted Teardrop Detection Algorithm. *Unmanned Syst.* **2023**, *13*, 105–120. [CrossRef]
6. Shivakoti, S.; Arntzen, A.A.; Güldal, S.; Cabañas, E. Drone Operations and Communications in an Urban Environment. In Proceedings of the Twelfth International Conference on Sensor Device Technologies and Applications, Athens, Greece, 11–18 November 2021.
7. Yasser, M.; Shalash, O.; Ismail, O. Optimized Decentralized Swarm Communication Algorithms for Efficient Task Allocation and Power Consumption in Swarm Robotics. *Robotics* **2024**, *13*, 66. [CrossRef]
8. Sahu, D.; Nidhi Prakash, S.; Sinha, P.; Yang, T.; Rathore, R.S.; Wang, L. Beyond boundaries a hybrid cellular potts and particle swarm optimization model for energy and latency optimization in edge computing. *Sci. Rep.* **2025**, *15*, 6266. [CrossRef] [PubMed]
9. Antwi, R.; Gadze, J.D.; Tchao, E.T.; Sikora, A.; Obour Agyekum, K.O.B.; Nunoo-Mensah, H.1; Keelson, E. Optimising peer-to-peer topology for blockchain-based industrial internet of things networks using particle swarm optimisation. *Clust. Comput.* **2025**, *28*, 1–20. [CrossRef]
10. Vinoski, S. Advanced Message Queuing Protocol. *IEEE Internet Comput.* **2006**, *10*, 87–89. [CrossRef]
11. Helbig, C.; Otoum, S.; Jararweh, Y. Modeling and Evaluation of the Internet of Things Communication Protocols in Security Constrained Systems. In Proceedings of the IEEE Consumer Communications and Networking Conference, CCNC, Las Vegas, NV, USA, 8–11 January 2023; Institute of Electrical and Electronics Engineers Inc.: Piscataway, NJ, USA, 2023. [CrossRef]
12. Uy, N.Q.; Nam, V.H. A comparison of AMQP and MQTT protocols for Internet of Things. In Proceedings of the 2019 6th NAFOSTED Conference on Information and Computer Science (NICS), Hanoi, Vietnam, 12–13 December 2019; IEEE: Piscataway, NJ, USA, 2019; pp. 292–297. [CrossRef]
13. Basavaraju, N.; Alexander, N.; Seitz, J. Performance Evaluation of Advanced Message Queuing Protocol (AMQP): An Empirical Analysis of AMQP Online Message Brokers. In Proceedings of the 2021 International Symposium on Networks, Computers and Communications, ISNCC 2021, Dubai, United Arab Emirates, 31 October–2 November 2021; Institute of Electrical and Electronics Engineers Inc.: Piscataway, NJ, USA, 2021. [CrossRef]
14. Živić, M.; Nemec, D.; Bojović, Ž. MQTT protocol in IoT environment: Comparison with CoAP and ZeroMQ protocols. In Proceedings of the 2023 31st Telecommunications Forum, TELFOR 2023—Proceedings, Belgrade, Serbia, 21–22 November 2023; Institute of Electrical and Electronics Engineers Inc.: Piscataway, NJ, USA, 2023. [CrossRef]
15. Corak, B.H.; Kok, I.; Ozdemir, S. A Novel Low-Latency and Cost-Effective Communication Protocol Design for Internet of Flying Things. In Proceedings of the 2021 International Symposium on Networks, Computers and Communications, ISNCC 2021, Dubai, United Arab Emirates, 31 October–2 November 2021; Institute of Electrical and Electronics Engineers Inc.: Piscataway, NJ, USA, 2021. [CrossRef]
16. Al Enany, M.O.; Harb, H.M.; Attiya, G. A comparative analysis of MQTT and IoT application protocols. In Proceedings of the ICEEM 2021—2nd IEEE International Conference on Electronic Engineering, Menouf, Egypt, 3–4 July 2021; Institute of Electrical and Electronics Engineers Inc.: Piscataway, NJ, USA, 2021. [CrossRef]
17. Naik, N. Choice of Effective Messaging Protocols for IoT Systems: MQTT, CoAP, AMQP and HTTP. In Proceedings of the 2017 IEEE International Systems Engineering Symposium (ISSE), Vienna, Austria, 11–13 October 2017; IEEE: Piscataway, NJ, USA, 2017; pp. 1–7. [CrossRef]
18. Gupta, H.; Landle, T.C.; Ramachandran, U. EPulsar: Control Plane for Publish-Subscribe Systems on Geo-Distributed Edge Infrastructure. In Proceedings of the 6th ACM/IEEE Symposium on Edge Computing, SEC 2021, San Jose, CA, USA, 14–17 December 2021; Institute of Electrical and Electronics Engineers Inc.: Piscataway, NJ, USA, 2021; pp. 228–241.
19. Kang, Z.; Dubey, A. Evaluating DDS, MQTT, and ZeroMQ Under Different IoT Traffic Conditions. In Proceedings of the M4IoT'20: Proceedings of the International Workshop on Middleware and Applications for the Internet of Things, Rennes, France, 10–11 December 2018; pp. 7–12.
20. Pamadi, E.V.N.; Goel, P.P.; Supervisor, R.; Jain, P.A. Comparative Analysis of GRPC VS. ZeroMQ for Fast Communication. *J. Emerg. Technol. Innov. Res.* **2020**, *7*, 937–951. Available online: www.jetir.org (accessed on 1 May 2025).

21. Morales, J.; Rodriguez, G.; Akopian, D.; Huang, G. Toward UAV control via cellular networks: Delay Profiles, Delay Modeling, and a Case Study within the 5-mile Range. *IEEE Trans. Aerosp. Electron. Syst.* **2020**, *56*, 4132–4151. [CrossRef]
22. Al-Fuqaha, A.; Guizani, M.; Mohammadi, M.; Aledhari, M.; Ayyash, M. Internet of Things: A Survey on Enabling Technologies, Protocols, and Applications. *IEEE Commun. Surv. Tutor.* **2015**, *17*, 2347–2376. [CrossRef]
23. Barrado, C.; Boyero, M.; Brucculeri, L.; Ferrara, G.; Hately, A.; Hullah, P.; Martin-Marrero, D.; Pastor, E.; Rushton, A.P.; Volkert, A. U-space concept of operations: A key enabler for opening airspace to emerging low-altitude operations. *Aerospace* **2020**, *7*, 24. [CrossRef]
24. EASA. Easy Access Rules for U-Space. 2024. Available online: https://www.easa.europa.eu/en/document-library/easy-access-rules/easy-access-rules-u-space-regulation-eu-2021664 (accessed on 15 August 2024).
25. Ruseno, N.; Chagas, F.S.; Fas-Millán, M.-A.; Bechina, A.A.A. Analysis of API-Based Communication Performance for drone's operation in U-Space. *Transp. Res. Procedia* **2024**, *81*, 195–204. [CrossRef]
26. Nour, B.; Sharif, K.; Li, F.; Yang, S.; Moungla, H.; Wang, Y. ICN publisher-subscriber models: Challenges and group-based communication. *IEEE Netw.* **2019**, *33*, 156–163. [CrossRef]
27. Benharosh, J. What Is REST API? in Plain English. Available online: https://phpenthusiast.com/blog/what-is-rest-api (accessed on 31 December 2024).
28. Hintjens, P. ØMQ—The Guide. Available online: https://zguide.zeromq.org/docs/chapter1/ (accessed on 7 April 2025).
29. ABahashwan, A.O.; Manickam, S. A brief review of messaging protocol standards for Internet of Things (IoT). *J. Cyber Secur. Mobil.* **2019**, *8*, 1–13. [CrossRef]
30. OASIS. MQTT: The Standard for IoT Messaging. Available online: https://mqtt.org/ (accessed on 8 April 2025).
31. Nwobi, F.N.; Akanno, F.C. Power comparison of ANOVA and Kruskal–Wallis tests when error assumptions are violated. *Metod. Zv.* **2021**, *18*, 53–71. [CrossRef]
32. Ruseno, N.; Chagas, F.S.; Fas-Millán, M.-Á.; Aurelie, A.; Bechina, A. Low Latency Communication in U-space System: Comparative Analysis of Push-pull and Publisher-subscriber Protocols. In Proceedings of the 1st International Conference on Drones and Unmanned Systems (DAUS' 2025), Granada, Spain, 19–21 February 2025; pp. 90–95. [CrossRef]
33. Martin, R.P.; Vahdat, A.M.; Culler, D.E.; Anderson, T.E. Effects of Communication Latency, Overhead, and Bandwidth in a Cluster Architecture. *CM SIGARCH Comput. Archit. News* **1997**, *25*, 85–97. [CrossRef]
34. Subramoni, H.; Marsh, G.; Narravula, S.; Lai, P.; Panda, D.K. Design and evaluation of benchmarks for financial applications using advanced message queuing protocol (AMQP) over infiniband. In Proceedings of the 2008 Workshop on High Performance Computational Finance, WHPCF 2008, Austin, TX, USA, 16 November 2008. [CrossRef]
35. Domingues, M.; Faria, J.N.; Portugal, D. Dimensioning payload size for fast retransmission of MQTT packets in the wake of network disconnections. *EURASIP J. Wirel. Commun. Netw.* **2024**, *2024*, 2. [CrossRef]
36. Banno, R. Performance Evaluation of MQTT Communication with Heterogeneous Traffic. In Proceedings of the International Computer Software and Applications Conference, Torino, Italy, 23–25 February 2023; IEEE Computer Society: Piscataway, NJ, USA, 2023; pp. 970–971. [CrossRef]
37. Tran, K.T.M.; Pham, A.X.; Nguyen, N.P.; Dang, P.T. Analysis and Performance Comparison of IoT Message Transfer Protocols Applying in Real Photovoltaic System. *Int. J. Networked Distrib. Comput.* **2024**, *12*, 131–143. [CrossRef]
38. Bux, R.; Shenoy, G.S. Performance Analysis of RESTFUL Web Services and RABBITMQ for Microservices based Systems on Cloud Environment. In Proceedings of the 2024 3rd International Conference for Innovation in Technology, INOCON 2024, Bangalore, India, 1–3 March 2024; Institute of Electrical and Electronics Engineers Inc.: Piscataway, NJ, USA, 2024. [CrossRef]

electronics

MDPI

Article

Unmanned Aerial Vehicle Path Planning Using Acceleration-Based Potential Field Methods

Mohammad R. Hayajneh [1,*], Mohammad H. Garibeh [2], Ahmad Bani Younes [3,4] and Matthew A. Garratt [5]

1 Department of Mechatronics Engineering, Faculty of Engineering, The Hashemite University, Zarqa 13133, Jordan
2 Department of Mechatronics Engineering, German Jordanian University, Amman 11180, Jordan; mohammad.garibeh1980@gmail.com
3 Department of Aerospace Engineering, San Diego State University, San Diego, CA 92182, USA; abaniyounes@sdsu.edu
4 Nanotechnology Institute, Jordan University of Science and Technology, Irbid 3030, Jordan
5 School of Engineering and Technology, University of New South Wales, Canberra, ACT 2612, Australia; m.garratt@unsw.edu.au
* Correspondence: mhayajneh@hu.edu.jo

Abstract: Online path planning for UAVs that are following a moving target is a critical component in applications that demand a soft landing over the target. In highly dynamic situations with accelerating targets, the classical potential field (PF) method, which considers only the relative positions and/or velocities, cannot provide precision tracking and landing. Therefore, this work presents an improved acceleration-based potential field (ABPF) path planning method. This approach incorporates the relative accelerations of the UAV and the target in constructing an attractive field. By controlling the acceleration, the ABPF produces smoother trajectories and avoids sudden changes in the UAV's motion. The proposed approach was implemented in different simulated scenarios with variable acceleration paths (i.e., circular, infinite, and helical). The simulation demonstrated the superiority of the proposed approach over the traditional PF. Moreover, similar path scenarios were experimentally evaluated using a quadrotor UAV in an indoor Vicon positioning system. To provide reliable estimations of the acceleration for the suggested method, a non-linear complementary filter was used to fuse information from the drone's accelerometer and the Vicon system. The improved PF method was compared to the traditional PF method for each scenario. The results demonstrated a 50% improvement in the position, velocity, and acceleration accuracy across all scenarios. Furthermore, the ABPF responded faster to merging with the target path, with rising times of 1.5, 1.6, and 1.3 s for the circular, infinite, and helical trajectories, respectively.

Keywords: potential field; path planning; UAV; accelerating target; attractive force

1. Introduction

Path planning is an essential component of cooperative missions with UAV formations completing complex and variable tasks, such as search and rescue, surveillance, monitoring, and inspections [1]. Path planning algorithms can be classified into two types—global and local [2]. Global path planning algorithms are presented as static programming algorithms that use map information to generate an optimal trajectory from the starting point to the target point. On the other hand, local path planning algorithms are dynamic algorithms that consider the current pose information in real time, as provided by onboard sensors, and calculate the optimal trajectory between the starting and ending points.

Among other dynamic path planning algorithms, the dynamic window approach (DWA), the mathematical optimization algorithm (MOA), model predictive control (MPC), and the potential field (PF) are widely used in robot dynamic path planning. The DWA produces path candidates by developing the velocity space that can be formed by the present robot velocities [3]. The DWA then chooses the best path from these path candidates, assuming static obstacles. In [4], this method was developed to include dynamic obstacles, utilizing neural networks to estimate the weights of the DWA, which were subsequently employed for safe local navigation. In order to consider static and dynamic obstacles and guarantee path candidates at variable velocities, the DWA was proposed with virtual manipulators (DWVs) in [5]. However, DWA-based approaches are not ideal for environments with many dynamic obstacles. On the other hand, the mathematical optimization algorithm (MOA) relies on the existing robot trajectory planning model to solve the optimal control problem. The MOA transforms the optimal control problem into an easily solvable model by employing several mathematical techniques, such as non-linear optimization, mixed integer linear programming (MILP), or dynamic programming (DP) [6–8].

Model predictive control (MPC) is used to construct a cost function over a fixed time interval in the future in order to determine the appropriate control sequence based on the robot's predicted future behaviors. To ensure system stability, the cost function can be modeled as a Lyapunov function by including a terminal cost [9,10]. The tracking problem with obstacles remains one of the most difficult tasks. As a result, the potential field (PF) approach has been used to find a collision-free path through an obstacle-filled environment [11,12]. Despite advances in these techniques, the MOA and MPC remain computationally demanding and necessitate a precise understanding of the robot's dynamics. Furthermore, the real-time implementation of these algorithms may be difficult for fast robots or extremely dynamic settings. Therefore, the PF is a commonly used method due to advantages such as its quick response time, low calculation requirements, and higher real-time precision [13]. Although the traditional PF method introduces the local minima problem, which traps an object before it reaches its destination, many researchers have been able to solve this problem, e.g., by using virtual obstacle or virtual target concepts [14,15] or by implementing a fuzzy system [16].

According to the concept of a potential field, a robot moves under the influence of a virtual attractive force that is required to pull it to a target, as well as simultaneous repulsive forces generated to avoid obstacles. These forces are determined by the robot's relative position and velocity with respect to the target, as well as with respect to the obstacles encountered [16–18]. Traditionally, the attractive potential of a robot is determined by its relative position in relation to a fixed- or constant-velocity moving point in space [19]. However, when a target moves at various velocities, the position-based potential function is no longer appropriate. As a result, researchers have discovered that accounting for both the robot's and target's velocities is beneficial when designing a potential field [20,21].

Providing online path planning for UAVs during autonomous missions to precisely track a moving target in a highly dynamic environment is critical [22]. In many applications, the UAV must land precisely over a moving target to recharge during persistent flights [23]. Therefore, many studies have focused on upgrading the classic potential field method for UAV path planning. For example, a few attempts have been made to enhance the repulsive field, allowing for smoother obstacle avoidance [24,25], whereas others have improved the attractive field within the method for better target reachability [26]. Other techniques have addressed both the attractive and repulsive forces using the fuzzy-based method [16] or the Artificial Neural Network method [27]. However, all of the researchers in the literature have developed enhanced algorithms for the traditional potential field model, which only considers the position and velocity gradients. To this end, this paper presents an improved attractive field force by increasing the degrees of freedom by considering the acceleration differential between the target and the UAV.

The authors of [28] used the increased attractive force gain coefficient approach with increasing gradient in order to improve the performance of the attractive field in the PF. This strategy prevents oscillations and ensures that the UAV reaches the target. In a similar technique, the attractive force was enhanced by incorporating a damping force to prevent oscillations near the target [29,30]. In another study, a UAV path planning technique was proposed to offer a consistent and continuous coverage path over a ground robot in a windy environment. This method presented a novel modified attractive force to improve the sensitivity of a UAV to wind speed and direction [26]. Despite the efforts of researchers to enhance the attractive force in potential fields, they could not achieve precision in tracking an accelerating target for soft landing.

The acceleration of direction-turning drones was taken into consideration in waypoint-based path planning using the potential field method, as described in [31]. The study demonstrated the need to consider the acceleration of the drone at waypoints in time-critical applications, as ignoring acceleration leads to an unreasonably short flight. In [32], the relative acceleration term is considered for an attractive potential function in dynamic environments. This study created a two-dimensional function of relative acceleration, velocity, and position between the ground robot and the target. However, this work solely used simulations to examine the acceleration-based potential field functions. An exponential attractive function was adopted in [22], to provide different gradients for its force. Using this technique, the attractive force changes rapidly as the UAV approaches the target. It allowed the UAV to swiftly and effectively track the movement of a ground robot with varying velocity.

In soft-landing applications, the velocity and acceleration of the UAV must be equal to those of the target. As previously stated, the typical potential field function only considers the relative positions between the UAV and the target for the attractive potential force, which may result in jerky motion and rushed turns for the UAV. For this purpose, this study focuses on strengthening the attractive potential field model by incorporating the acceleration term in addition to velocity and position information. In this approach, the attractive force is expected to be more responsive, as it accounts for dynamic constraints and smoother motion. To help readers comprehend the contribution of this study, Table 1 summarizes the merits of earlier works in the literature and compares them to the suggested approach. To solve the motion-planning problem in dynamic environments with accelerating targets, we must assume the following:

(1) *Assumption 1.* The shape, positions, velocities, and accelerations of the UAV are known.
(2) *Assumption 2.* The position A_{tar}, velocity B_{tar}, and the acceleration C_{tar} of the target are known with $|C_{tar}| < C_{\max}$.

The repulsive force will not be covered in this study. Acceleration-based improvements for repulsive force may be discussed in subsequent work in the future.

Following the introduction, the rest of this paper is organized as follows: Section 2 provides a full derivation of the suggested attractive potential field model. Section 3 proposes a motion planning strategy. Section 4 provides a detailed discussion of the supporting simulation. This work was evaluated experimentally under several settings, as described in Section 5. The conclusions and future research are presented in Section 6.

Table 1. Comparison of the proposed method to various local path planning methods, including traditional PF.

Feature	DWA	MOA	MPC	PF	Acceleration Based-PF (Proposed)
Real-time Performance	High	Moderate to Low	Moderate to Low	High	High
Computational Load	Low	High	High	Low	Low
Handling Dynamic Obstacles	Moderate	No	Depending on the model accuracy	Moderate	Not investigated
Target Tracking Accuracy	Moderate	Moderate to Low	High (depending on the model and solver)	Low to Moderate	High
Landing Accuracy	Moderate	Moderate	Low to Moderate (depending on the model and solver)	Low to Moderate	High
Optimality	Heuristic (local)	Optimal (requiring careful tuning)	Optimal (requiring significant tuning)	Heuristic (local)	Heuristic (local)
Complexity	Low	High	High	Low	Low

2. Acceleration-Based Attractive Potential Force

According to current approaches, the attractive potential force is determined solely by the relative velocity and position between the UAV and the target. In this study, the attractive potential force is defined by considering the relative position, velocity, and acceleration between the UAV and the target. The following equation defines the new attractive potential V_{att}:

$$V_{att} = \delta_a \| \ A_{tar}(t) - A_{UAV}(t) \ \|^i + \delta_b \| \ B_{tar}(t) - B_{UAV}(t) \ \|^j + \delta_c \| \ C_{tar}(t) - C_{UAV}(t) \ \|^k \quad (1)$$

where $A_{tar}(t)$ and $A_{UAV}(t)$ represent the position of the target and UAV at a given instant t. The velocities of the target and UAV are represented by $B_{tar}(t)$ and $B_{UAV}(t)$ at a given instant t. The accelerations of the target and UAV are given by $C_{tar}(t)$ and $C_{UAV}(t)$ at a given instant t. The magnitude of the distance between the target and the UAV is denoted by $\|A_{tar}(t) - A_{UAV}(t)\|$. The magnitude of the relative velocity between the target and the UAV is indicated by $\|B_{tar}(t) - B_{UAV}(t)\|$, and $\|C_{tar}(t) - C_{UAV}(t)\|$ is the magnitude of the relative acceleration between the target and the UAV. δ_a, δ_b, and δ_c are positive parameters, while i, j, and k are exponents.

To find the attractive force, the negative gradient of the attractive potentials is given by the following equation:

$$F_{att}(A,B,C) = -\nabla_A V_{att}(A,B,C) - \nabla_B V_{att}(A,B,C) - \nabla_C V_{att}(A,B,C) \quad (2)$$

where

$$F_{att1} = -\nabla_A V_{att}(A,B,C) = -\frac{\partial V_{att}(A,B,C)}{\partial A} \quad (3)$$

$$F_{att2} = -\nabla_B V_{att}(A,B,C) = -\frac{\partial V_{att}(A,B,C)}{\partial B} \quad (4)$$

$$F_{att3} = -\nabla_C V_{att}(A,B,C) = -\frac{\partial V_{att}(A,B,C)}{\partial C} \quad (5)$$

Regarding i, j, and k, as well as the differentiation of $V_{att}(A,B,C)$, we notice that $V_{att}(A,B,C)$ is not differentiable when $A_{tar}(t) = A_{UAV}(t)$ for $0 < i \leq 1$. Furthermore, this is not differentiable when $B_{tar}(t) = B_{UAV}(t)$ for $0 < j \leq 1$, or when $C_{tar}(t) = C_{UAV}(t)$ for $0 < k \leq 1$. In soft-landing applications, the UAV must reach the target with the same velocity and acceleration, which means that $A_{tar}(t) = A_{UAV}(t)$, $B_{tar}(t) = B_{UAV}(t)$, and $C_{tar}(t) = C_{UAV}(t)$. Therefore, for this purpose, the parameters are chosen such that i, j, and $k > 1$.

In hard-landing applications, the UAV must reach the target with $B_{tar}(t) \neq B_{UAV}(t)$ and $C_{tar}(t) \neq C_{UAV}(t)$. In this case, only $i > 1$ is selected.

Thus, the attractive force terms are defined as follows:

$$F_{att1} = i\delta_a \| A_{tar}(t) - A_{UAV}(t) \|^{i-1} a_{RT} \tag{6}$$

$$F_{att2} = j\delta_b \| B_{tar}(t) - B_{UAV}(t) \|^{j-1} b_{RT} \tag{7}$$

$$F_{att3} = k\delta_c \| C_{tar}(t) - C_{UAV}(t) \|^{k-1} c_{RT} \tag{8}$$

where a_{RT} indicates the unit vector directed from the UAV to the target. b_{RT} is the unit vector that directs the relative velocity vector from the target with respect to the UAV. c_{RT} is the unit vector that directs the relative acceleration vector from the target with respect to the UAV. Figure 1 shows the relationship between the three attractive forces and the relative position, velocity, and acceleration vectors between the target and the UAV.

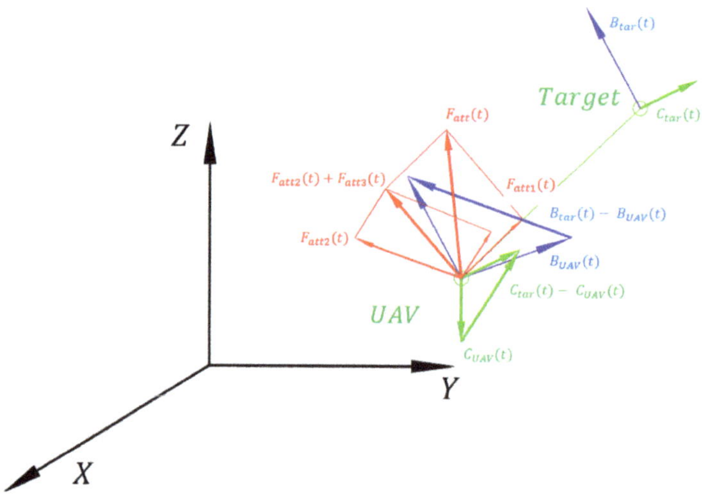

Figure 1. The three attractive forces and the relative position, velocity, and acceleration vectors between the target and the UAV.

3. Attractive Motion Planning Strategy for Unmanned Arial Vehicles

Newton's second law states that the forces are equal to mass times acceleration, as follows:

$$F_{UAV} = mC_{UAV} \tag{9}$$

where F_{UAV} is the desired force to be applied to the UAV in order to reach the target. The proposed attractive potential function includes six parameters—δ_a, δ_b, δ_c, i, j, and k. Let us consider $i = j = k = 2$. The selection of these integers provides the best system performance, as explained in Section 4. Accordingly, the attractive force can be rewritten as follows:

$$F_{att} = 2\delta_a \parallel A_{tar}(t) - A_{UAV}(t) \parallel + 2\delta_b \parallel B_{tar}(t) - B_{UAV}(t) \parallel + 2\delta_c \parallel C_{tar}(t) - C_{UAV}(t) \parallel \tag{10}$$

Let us apply the following force to the UAV:

$$F_{UAV} = m_{UAV} C_{tar} + F_{att} \tag{11}$$

Combining Equations (9)–(11) and setting $m_{UAV} = 1$, we obtain the following equation:

$$C_{UAV}(t) = C_{tar}(t) + 2\delta_a \parallel A_{tar}(t) - A_{UAV}(t) \parallel + 2\delta_b \parallel B_{tar}(t) - B_{UAV}(t) + 2\delta_c \| C_{tar}(t) - C_{UAV}(t) \| \tag{12}$$

Taking common factors and combining terms, we obtain:

$$(1 + 2\delta_c) \parallel C_{tar}(t) - C_{UAV}(t) \parallel + 2\delta_b \parallel B_{tar}(t) - B_{UAV}(t) \parallel + 2\delta_a \parallel A_{tar}(t) - A_{UAV} = 0 \tag{13}$$

It is known that the relative position between the UAV and the target is the error $e(t)$. So, rewriting Equation (13) gives the following equation:

$$\ddot{e}(t) + \frac{2\delta_b}{(1 + 2\delta_c)} \dot{e}(t) + \frac{2\delta_a}{(1 + 2\delta_c)} e(t) = 0 \tag{14}$$

Now, by comparing Equation (14) with the characteristic equation of a second-order system, we obtain the following:

$$s^2 + 2\zeta\omega_n s + \omega_n^2 = 0 \tag{15}$$

Keep in mind that ζ is the damping ratio and ω_n is the natural frequency of the system. Because δ_a, δ_b, and δ_c are positive parameters, the system is considered stable.

Now,

$$\omega_n^2 = \frac{2\delta_a}{(1 + 2\delta_c)} \text{ then } \omega_n = \sqrt{\frac{2\delta_a}{(1 + 2\delta_c)}} \tag{16}$$

and

$$2\zeta\omega_n = \frac{2\delta_b}{(1 + 2\delta_c)} \tag{17}$$

By substituting (16) into (17) and substituting $\zeta = 1$ to obtain a critically damped system, we obtain the following equation:

$$\frac{\delta_b^2}{2\delta_a} - 1 = 2\delta_c \tag{18}$$

Keep in mind that δ_a, δ_b, and δ_c must be positive values to guarantee stability, such that $\delta_a > 0$, $\delta_b > 0$, and $\delta_c > 0$.

$$\delta_c > 0 \text{ then } 2\delta_c > 0, \text{ which means } \frac{\delta_b^2}{2\delta_a} - 1 > 0 \tag{19}$$

Equations (18) and (19) are used to solve for the values of δ_a, δ_b, and δ_c , which guarantee a stable and critical damped system. First, a value of δ_a> 0 is selected and using Equation (19), the range of δ_b can be found. Having the two values of δ_a and δ_b in hand and substituing them into Equation (18), δ_c is directly computed. This procedure will be repeated in a simulation study, as will be discussed in next section in order to find the optimal values of δ_a, δ_b, and δ_c for best performance.

4. Attractive Force Simulation Study

To show the performance of the new attractive force with the acceleration term, many simulations were performed, as described in this section.

4.1. Parameter Tuning

To choose the best values for δ_a, δ_b, and δ_c , these three values were calculated and simulated according to Equations (18) and (19). After determining the best values for these parameters, additional simulation runs were conducted to determine the optimal exponents of i, j, and k. In the first place, each exponent is set at 2 (i.e., $i = j = k = 2$).

The first simulation is carried out by trying three sets of values of δ_a, δ_b, and δ_c. At first, three alternative positive values for δ_a are chosen—0.3, 6, and 20. The values for δ_b and δ_c can then be obtained by solving equations 18 and 19, respectively. As a result, the three sets are found to be (0.6, 1.2, 0.1), (6, 4, 0.167), and (20, 8, 0.2). Figure 2 shows the performance of a UAV in tracking a target moving at an acceleration of $\begin{bmatrix} 0.2 & 0 & 0 \end{bmatrix}$ m/s^2.

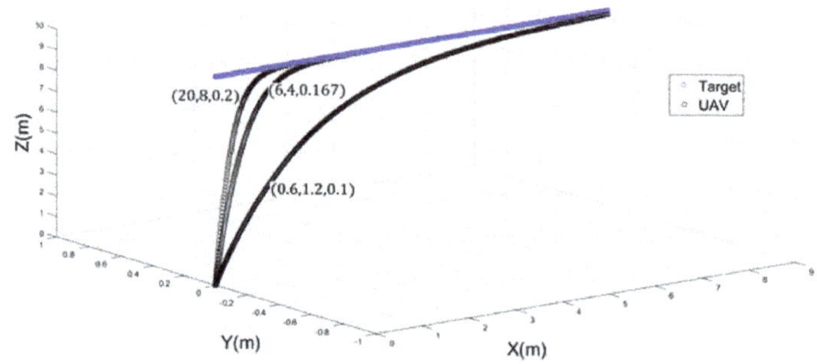

Figure 2. UAV performance for different values of δ_a, δ_b, and $\delta_c.(i = j = k = 2)$.

The figure shows that the fastest response was achieved with the highest values of δ_a, δ_b, and δ_c, which are 20, 8, and 0.2, respectively. As a result, these values are used in the subsequent simulation to determine the ideal values of i, j, and k. The second part of the simulation shows the performance of the UAV in tracking a moving target in a 3D environment by changing the values of i, j, and k. The target was moving at an acceleration of $\begin{bmatrix} 0.2 & 0 & 0 \end{bmatrix}$ m/s^2. In the initial attempt, the value of i was varying between three different values (i.e., 1.5, 2, and 3), while j and k were maintained fixed at the value of 2. Figure 3 shows three different responses of the UAV by varying the value i. It is clear that the best performance occurs when $i = 2$.

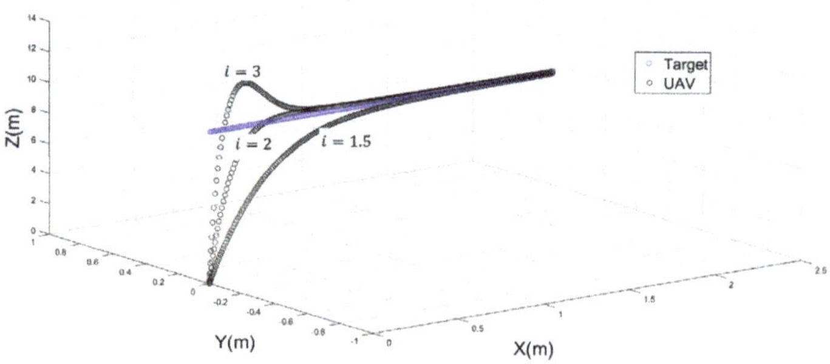

Figure 3. The performance of a UAV when $j = k = 2$ with different values of i.

Two more simulations were executed in a similar manner—one by modifying the value of j while keeping i and k constant at 2, and a second one by modifying the value of k

while keeping i and j constant at 2. Figure 4 shows three UAV trajectories with different values of $j = 1.5,\ 2,\ 3$, while i and k remain fixed at 2. Figure 5 illustrates the performance of the UAV trajectories with three different values of k.

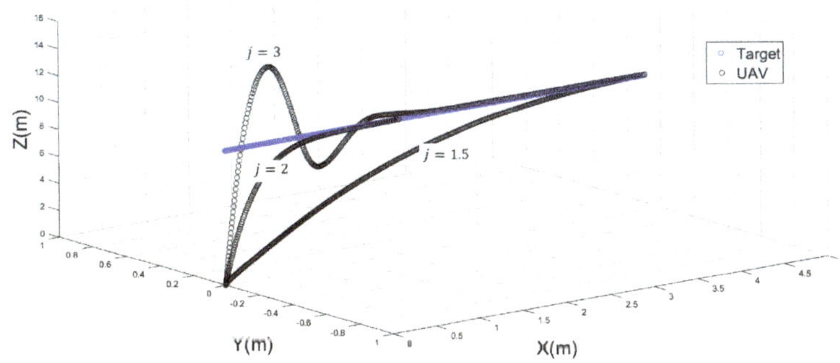

Figure 4. The performance of a UAV when $i = k = 2$ with different values of j.

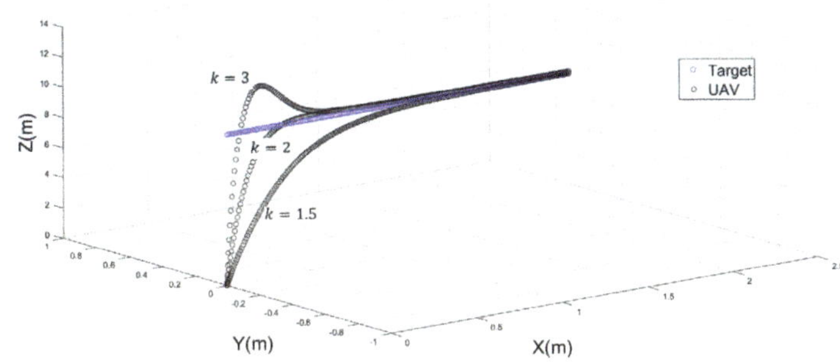

Figure 5. The performance of a UAV when $i = j = 2$ with different values of k.

From the previous simulation runs, the proposed attractive potential field approach for tracking a target in 3D space performed best when δ_a, δ_b, and δ_c = (20, 8, 0.2), and $i = j = k = 2$.

4.2. Performance Study on Different Trajectories

More simulations were implemented to investigate the performance of a UAV under various accelerating pathways and different limitations. In all of the following simulations, the previous tuned parameters are used (i.e., δ_a, δ_b, and δ_c = (20, 8, 0.2), and $i = j = k = 2$). Figure 6 illustrates the first challenging scenario, where the UAV was tracking a target accelerating at $\begin{bmatrix} 0.1 & 0.1 & 0.1 \end{bmatrix}$ m/s^2. The UAV and target were 10 m apart at the beginning. Despite the fact that they were at different speeds and accelerations, the UAV managed to hit the target.

For a target traveling along time-varying acceleration trajectories, it is worthwhile to examine the performance of the attractive force for a UAV in these scenarios. For this purpose, three distinct trajectories (circular, infinite, and helical) are offered to investigate the effectiveness of the proposed method. Figure 7 shows the UAV tracking the target on a circular path. The UAV initiated motion at x = 1 m and y = 0, with zero velocity and acceleration. The target started with velocity $v_x = 0$, $v_y = 1$ m/s, and acceleration

$a_x = -1\,\mathrm{m/s^2}$, $a_y = 0\,\mathrm{m/s^2}$. The UAV was successfully adjusting to join the trajectory and accurately track the target. The UAV was able to track the target's velocity in less than one second and its acceleration in two seconds, as shown in Figures 8 and 9.

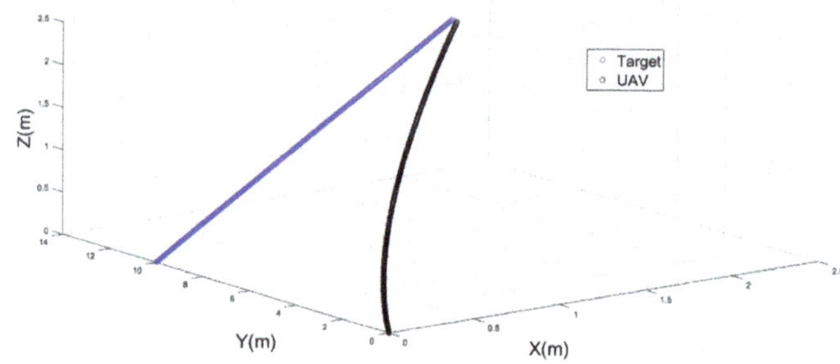

Figure 6. The performance of the UAV in a hard-landing application.

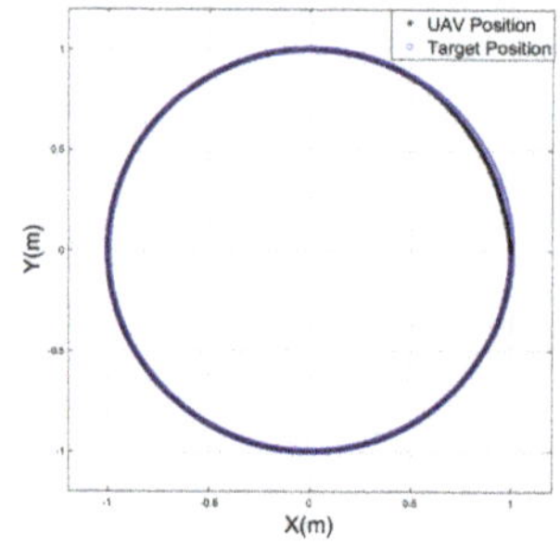

Figure 7. The performance of the UAV to follow a target on a circular trajectory.

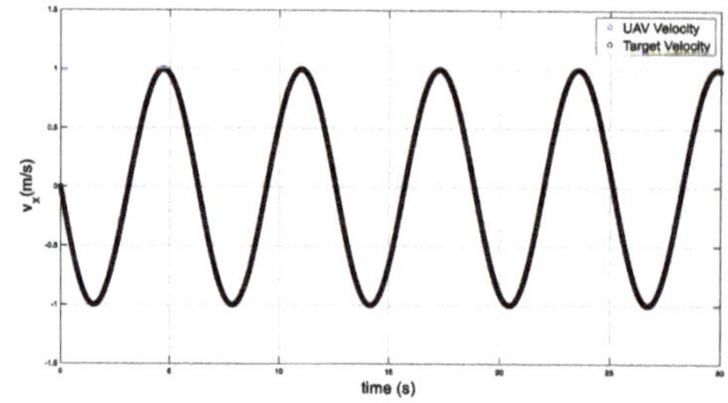

(**a**)

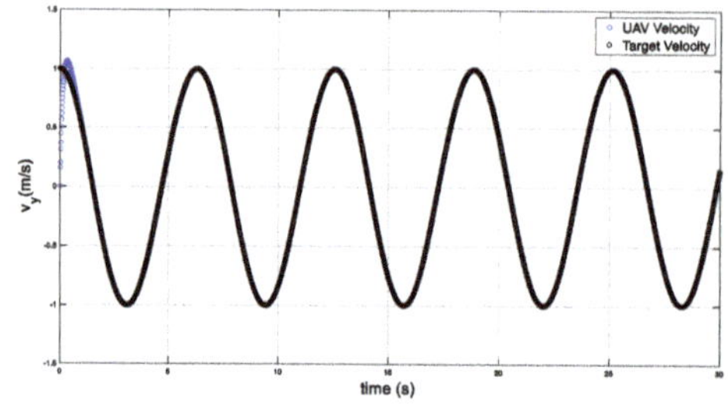

(**b**)

Figure 8. Velocities of the drone and target on a circular path; (**a**) x-axis, (**b**) y-axis.

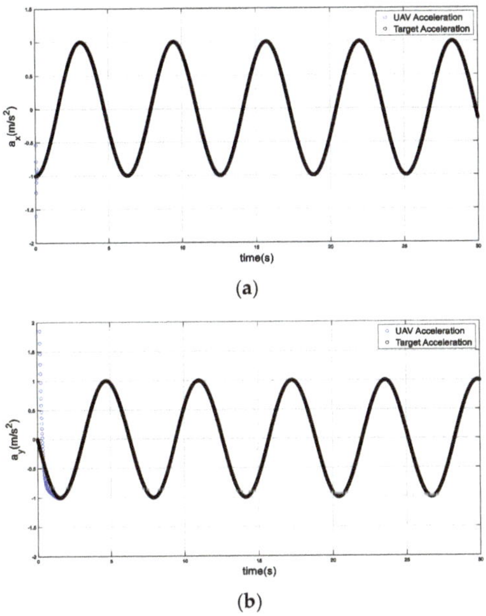

Figure 9. Accelerations of the drone and target on a circular path; (**a**) x-axis, (**b**) y-axis.

The infinite trajectory scenario is illustrated in Figures 10–12. The UAV initiated motion at $x = 0$ m and $y = 0$, with zero velocity and acceleration. The target started with velocity $v_x = -1$, $v_y = 1$ m/s, and acceleration $a_x = a_y = 0$. The attractive force was rapidly adjusting to give extremely responsive path tracking. In one second, the UAV was able to accurately align with the desired path.

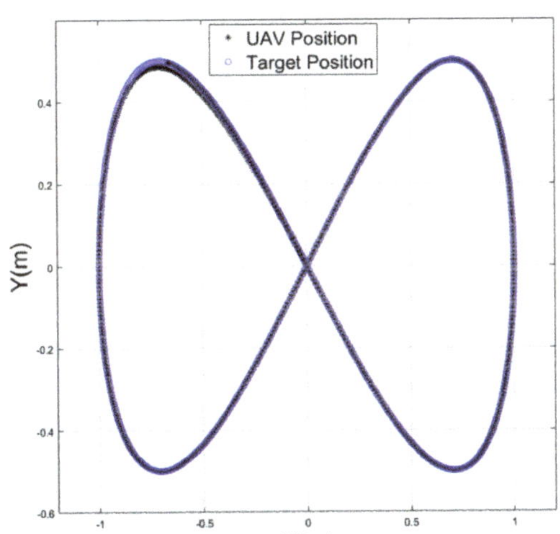

Figure 10. The performance of the UAV to follow a target on an infinite trajectory.

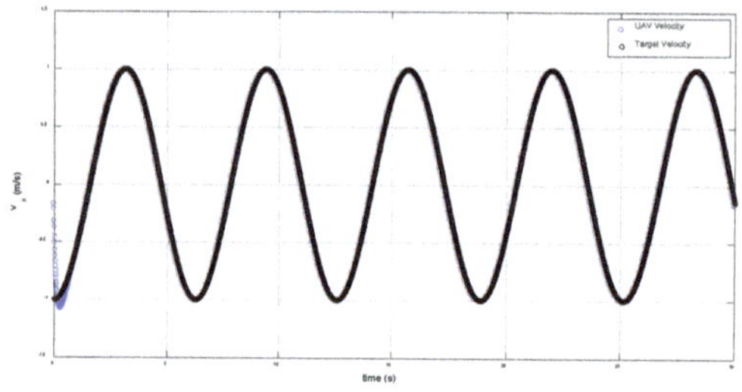

(**a**)

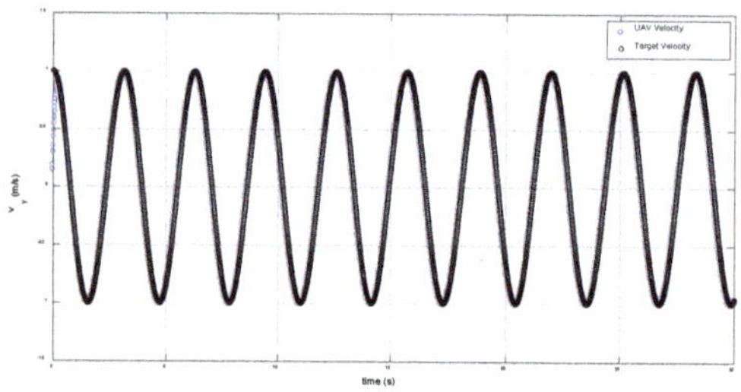

(**b**)

Figure 11. Velocities of the drone and target on an infinite path; (**a**) x-axis, (**b**) y-axis.

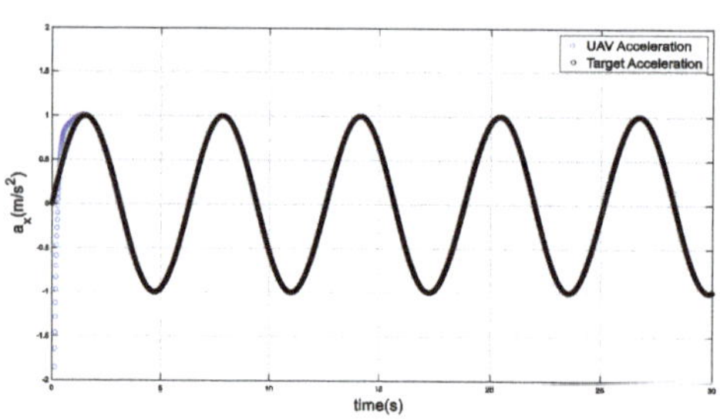

(**a**)

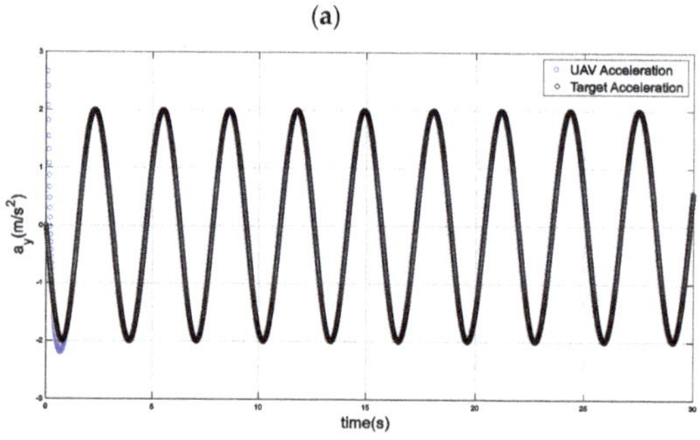

(**b**)

Figure 12. Accelerations of the drone and target on an infinite path; (**a**) x-axis, (**b**) y-axis.

To expand the evaluation in the third position, a helical path was tested in another simulation, as shown in Figure 13. In this scenario, the UAV initiated motion at $x = 1$ m, $y = 0$, and $z = 0$, with zero velocity and acceleration. With non-zero velocity and acceleration, the target initiated its motion to move on a helical path with a maximum velocity of 0.5 m/s and a maximum acceleration of 0.5 m/s^2. The UAV was accurately tracking the target along a helical path, as shown in Figures 14 and 15.

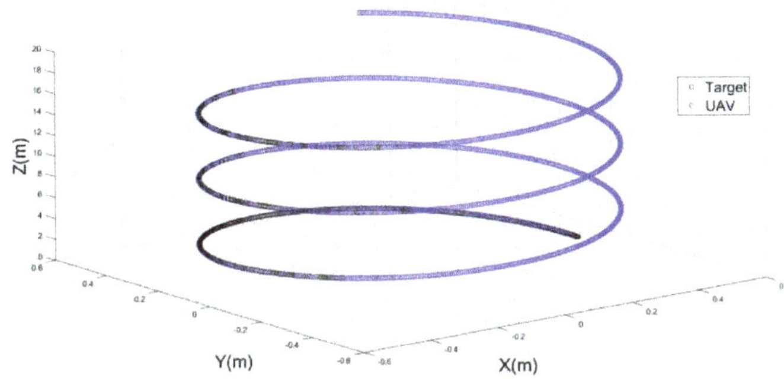

Figure 13. The performance of a UAV to follow a target on a helical trajectory.

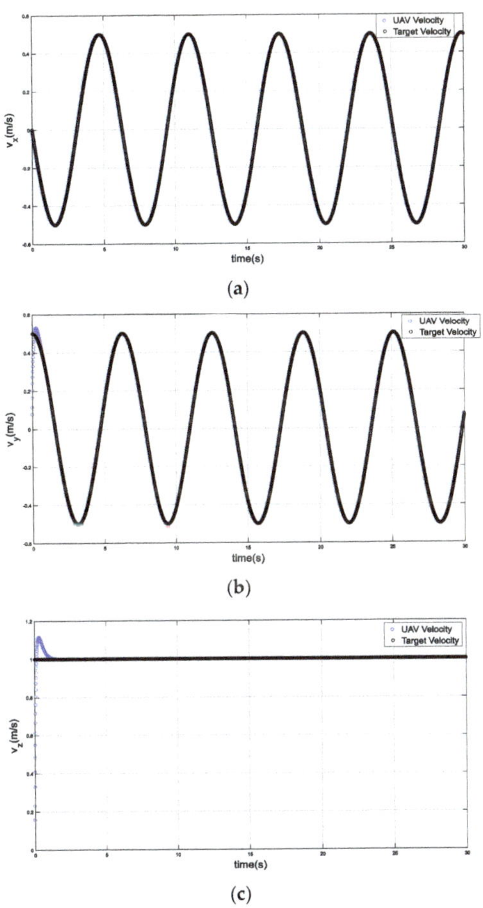

Figure 14. Velocities of the drone and target on a helical path; (**a**) x-axis, (**b**) y-axis, (**c**) z-axis.

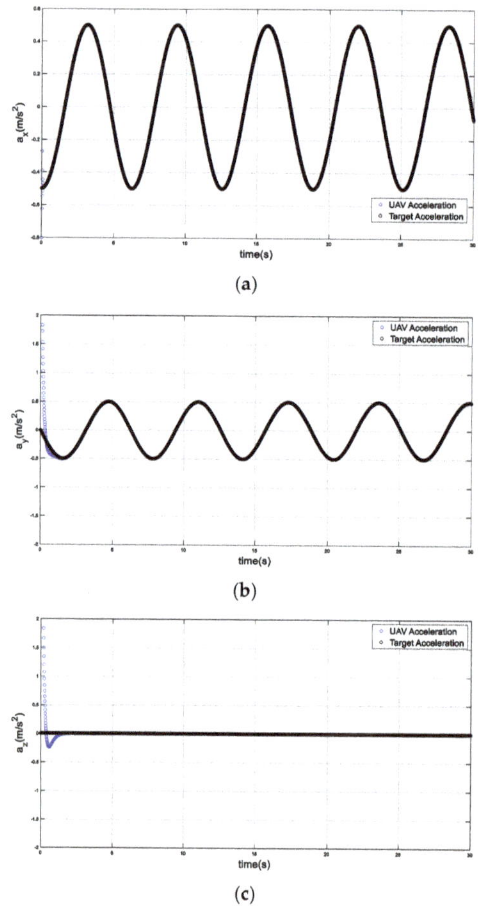

Figure 15. Accelerations of the drone and target on a helical path; (**a**) x-axis, (**b**) y-axis, (**c**) z-axis.

4.3. Performance Study on Edge Cases

More simulation studies are carried out to test the proposed technique in edge circumstances such as sudden stops or abrupt changes in the velocity and acceleration of the target, and disturbances on the UAV while in flight. Figure 16 illustrates a UAV tracking a target on a circular trajectory until it sharply changes direction after completing the circle. Figures 17 and 18 demonstrate a quick shift in velocity and acceleration. The attractive force adapted quickly to this change, providing a faster route to the UAV. The UAV could track the target's new velocity and acceleration in less than two seconds. Moreover, the UAV successfully and quickly responded to this steering, maintaining a straight route towards the target.

Another simulation was run, whereby the UAV goes in a circular path tracking a target, as shown in Figure 19. After completing a quarter circle, the target suddenly came to a complete stop. The UAV responded to the rapid change by decelerating dramatically, as shown in Figures 20 and 21. The UAV then approached the target at zero velocity and acceleration in 1.5 s.

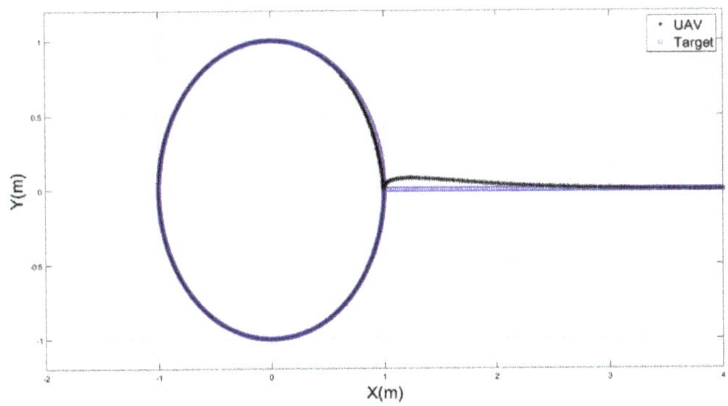

Figure 16. The performance of a UAV throughout sudden steering on the target path.

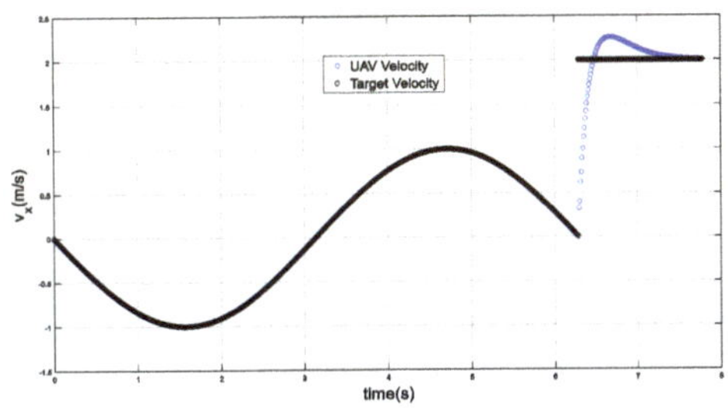

(a)

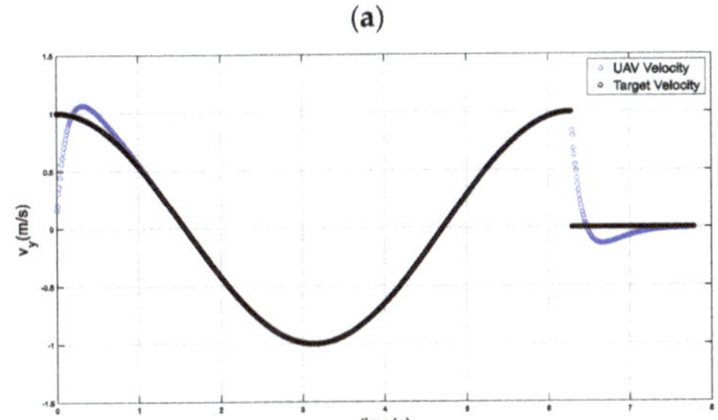

(b)

Figure 17. UAV and target velocities in a sudden direction change scenario; (a) x-axis, (b) y-axis.

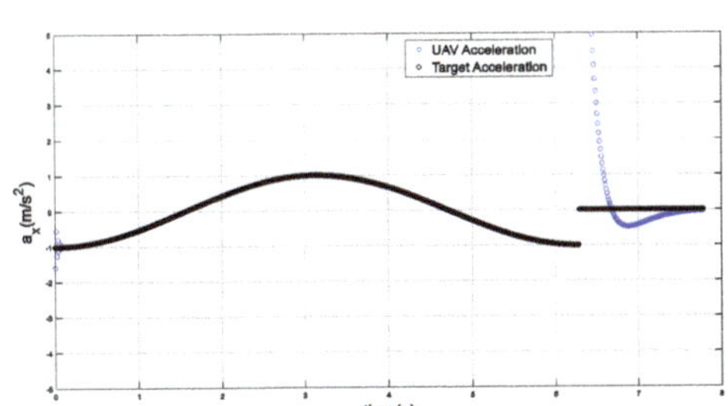

(a)

Figure 18. Cont.

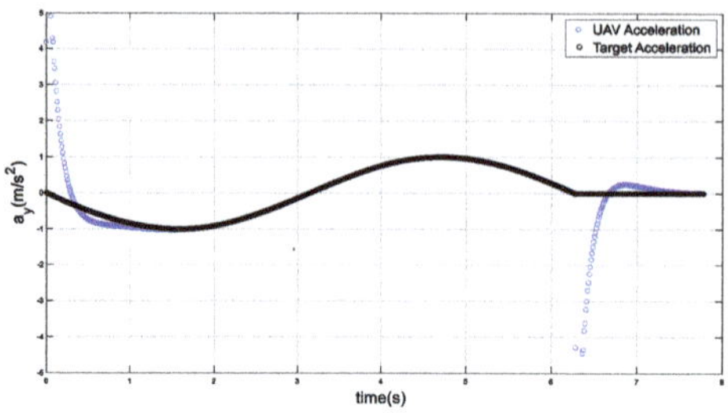

(**b**)

Figure 18. UAV and target accelerations in a sudden direction change scenario; (**a**) x-axis, (**b**) y-axis.

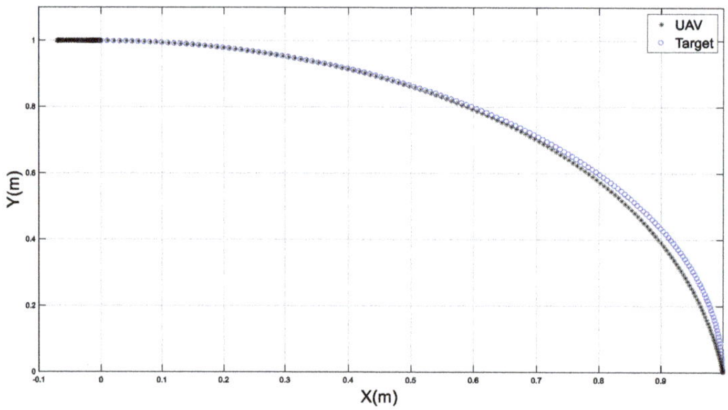

Figure 19. The performance of a UAV tracking a target on a circular path and then stopping.

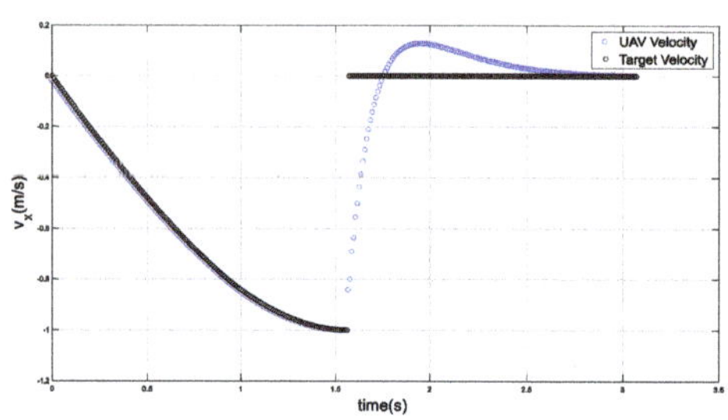

(**a**)

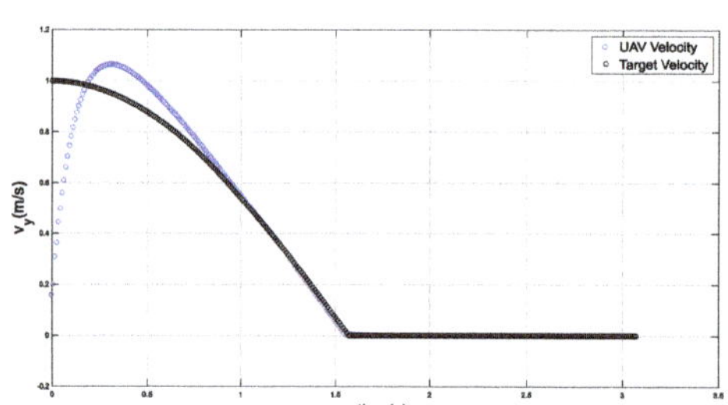

(**b**)

Figure 20. UAV and target velocities in a sudden stop scenario; (**a**) x-axis, (**b**) y-axis.

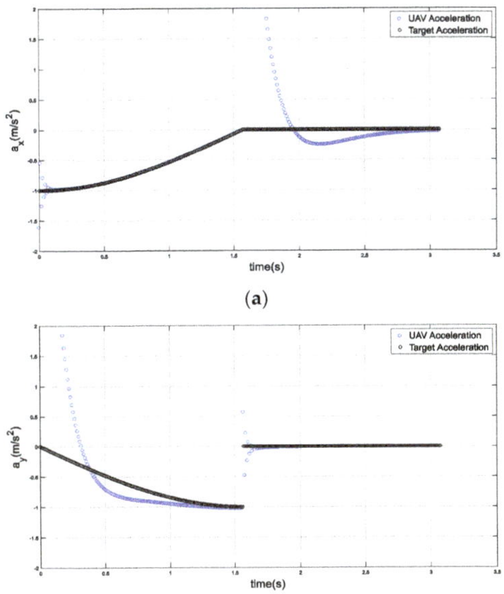

(**b**)

Figure 21. UAV and target accelerations in a sudden stop scenario; (**a**) x-axis, (**b**) y-axis.

The last simulation is carried out to examine the performance of the UAV when it is subjected to a disturbance of a stochastic force while it is following a target on a circular trajectory. Starting at position $x = 1$ and $y = 0$, the UAV tracked a target on a circular path with initial zero velocities and accelerations. After completing a quarter circle, a disturbance of a stochastic force of 120 N was applied for 0.3 s when the UAV was at $y = 1$ and $x = 0$, as shown in Figure 22. The UAV effectively adapted to this change and resumed its circular flight within one second. The UAV returned to accurately track the target's velocity and acceleration, as seen in Figures 23 and 24.

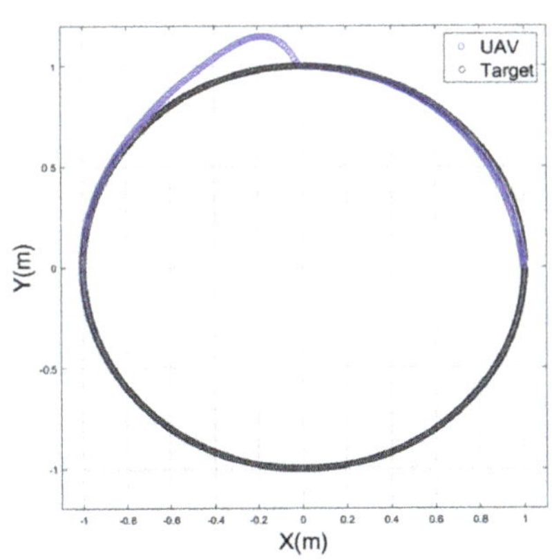

Figure 22. The response of a UAV to an external force while tracking a target on a circular path.

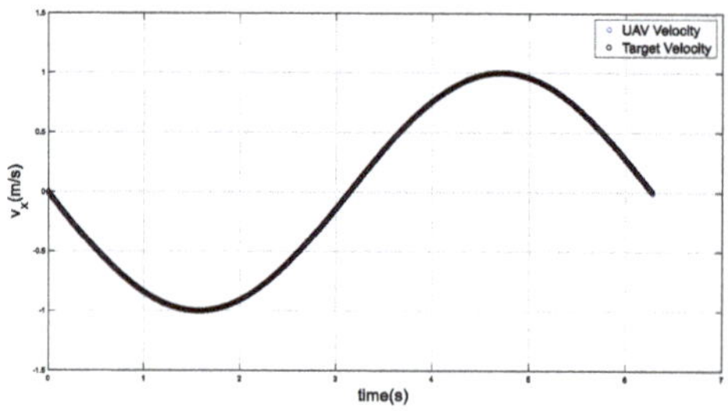

(**a**)

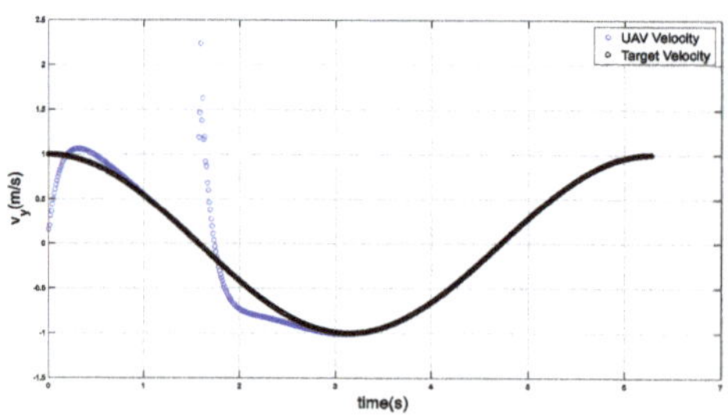

(**b**)

Figure 23. UAV and target velocities in an applied disturbance scenario; (**a**) x-axis, (**b**) y-axis.

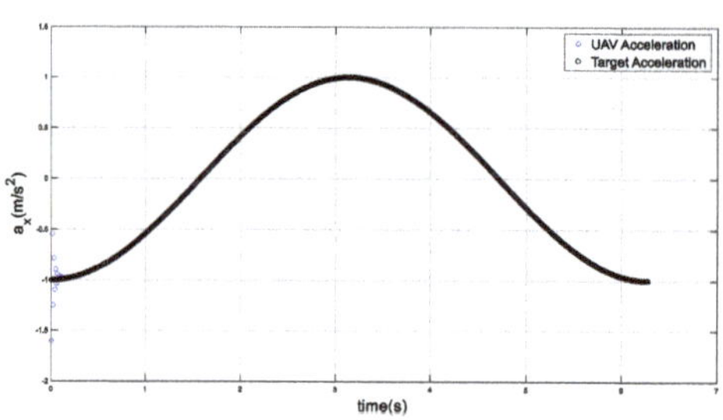

(**a**)

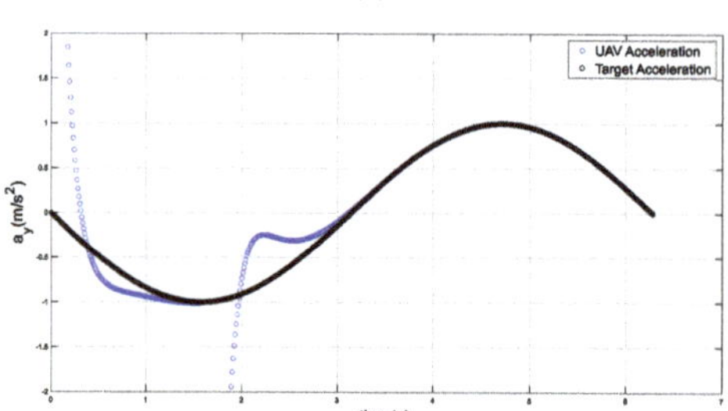

(**b**)

Figure 24. UAV and target accelerations in an applied disturbance scenario; (**a**) x-axis, (**b**) y-axis.

5. Experimental Setup and Results

The proposed potential field path planning method was evaluated using Qdrone from Quanser (Markham, ON, Canada), as well as an internal motion tracking system from Vicon (Oxford, UK), as shown in Figure 25. The system accurately positions a moving body, such as a drone, in 3D space. The cameras of the Vicon system are sensitive to all light in their spectrum, which might result in data noise. This would lead to inaccuracy in marker tracking, lowering the quality of motion capture data. However, the system has addressed these issues by incorporating proper noise filters. A computer was used as a ground control station (GCS) to perform the network and computing tasks. Simulink R2024 was used to implement the drone–computer communications, Vicon–computer communications, and control implementations, all using Quanser's Quarc toolbox.

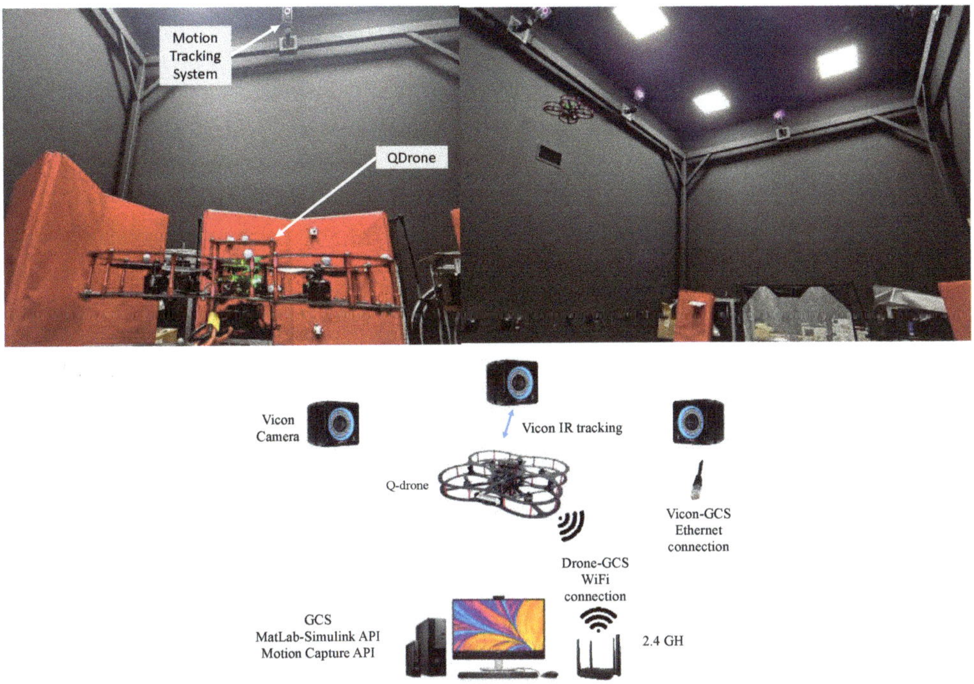

Figure 25. Experimental Setup of Qdrone and the Vicon motion tracking system.

The goal of the experiments is to assess the performance of the proposed path planning system, which was improved by the acceleration term, and to compare it to the performance of the conventional potential field method, which only proposes the position and velocity components. To ensure fair comparisons, each experiment began at the same time and location. The motion of the drone was tested to follow a virtual target along defined paths of positions, velocities, and accelerations. Various path scenarios (i.e., circular, infinite, and helical) have been proposed to examine the efficiency of drone motion. The suggested path planning approach is integrated as a high-level controller that arranges the UAV route. The adopted drone was tested using a robust low-level controller, as stated in [1]. This controller demonstrated robustness against several types of disturbances.

Accurate position, velocity, and acceleration measurements are required to properly implement both acceleration-improved and conventional potential field path-planning. Position measurements from the Vicon system were used directly because of their high accuracy, which is deemed to be 0.02 mm by the manufacturer. To obtain accurate velocity and acceleration estimates, the measurements from the motion tracking system and the drone's inertial measurement unit (IMU) were fused using a complementary filter as used in [1,33], as follows:

$$\begin{cases} \hat{a} = k_1(v - \hat{v}) + ge_3 + Qa \\ \dot{Q} = QS(\Omega - b) + k_v(v - \hat{v})a^T \\ \hat{v} = v + \frac{1}{2}\int (Qa + ge_3) + k_2(p - \hat{p}) \end{cases} \quad (20)$$

where $\hat{a}$ and $\hat{v}$ are the estimated accelerations and velocities, respectively. v and p are the velocity and position of the drone, respectively. The actual positions and velocities were determined using the indoor motion-tracking system. k_1, k_2, and k_v are positive gains of the filter. $Q \in \mathbb{R}^{3\times3}$ is a virtual rotation matrix and Ω is the angular speed measured by the gyroscope. The gyroscope measurements were corrected using gyro bias b. The local gravity vector in the inertial frame was given by $ge_3 = \begin{bmatrix} 0 & 0 & g \end{bmatrix}^T$.

For all the experimental scenarios that used the improved acceleration-based potential field, the optimized attractive force parameters were as follows:

$$\begin{cases} i = 2 \\ j = 2 \\ k = 2 \end{cases} \quad (21)$$

$$\begin{cases} \delta_a = 20 \\ \delta_b = 8 \\ \delta_c = 0.2 \end{cases} \quad (22)$$

These parameters were obtained in a manner similar to that of the simulation process, as discussed in Section 4.1. To make fair comparisons with the conventional potential field method, the optimized parameters were determined by [17], as follows:

$$\begin{cases} i = 2 \\ j = 2 \end{cases} \quad (23)$$

$$\begin{cases} \delta_a = 35 \\ \delta_b = 10 \end{cases} \quad (24)$$

In a circular path scenario, the target was moving in a 1.5 m circle at a height of 1 m. Furthermore, the target should move at velocities of $[-0.4, 0.4]$ m and an acceleration of $[-0.1, 0.1]$ $\mathrm{m/s^2}$. Figure 26a,b show how the drone tracked the target while accounting for and ignoring the acceleration term, respectively.

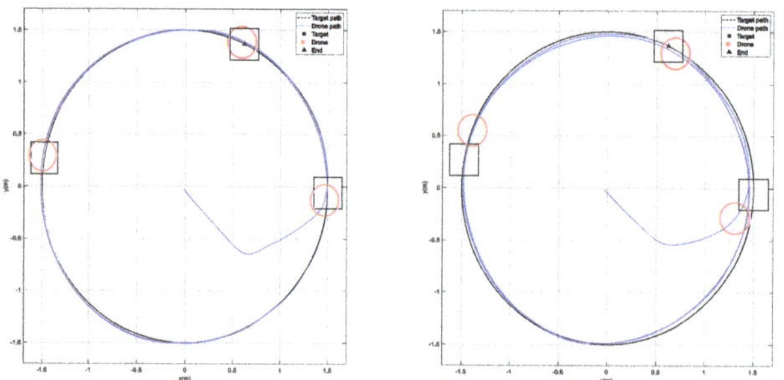

(a) (b)

Figure 26. Circular path tracking. (**a**) Improved potential field with acceleration. (**b**) Conventional potential field.

The drone was able to transition from the origin to the target more efficiently and quickly than the conventional method, as shown in Figures 27–29. The drone accurately tracked the target's position, speed, and acceleration, allowing for a more accurate landing. It is worth noting that the short-period spikes seen on some curves were due to Vicon drone miss coverage at certain points. Consequently, when the drone entered an area not covered by cameras, the Vicon system provided less accurate positioning, as shown in Figure 28b.

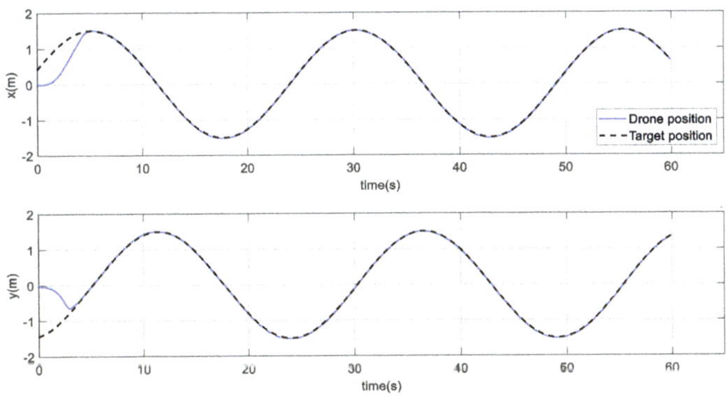

(**a**)

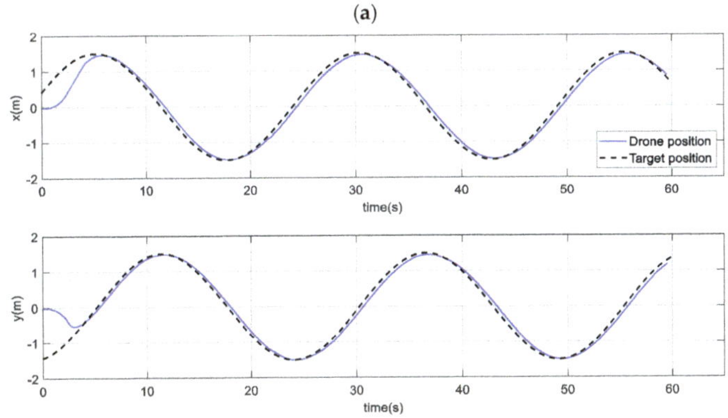

(**b**)

Figure 27. Drone and target positions on a circular path. (**a**) Improved method. (**b**) Conventional method.

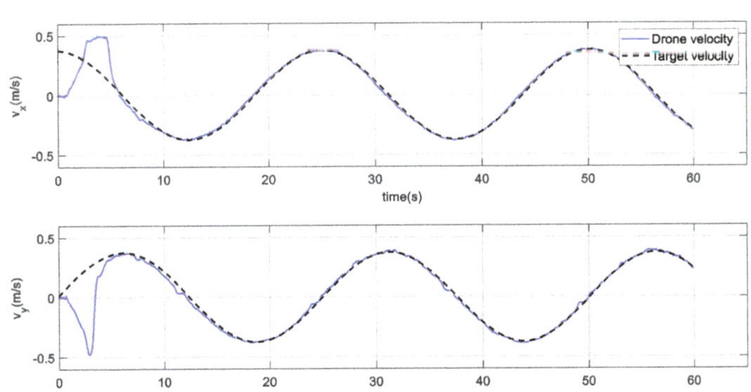

(**a**)

Figure 28. *Cont.*

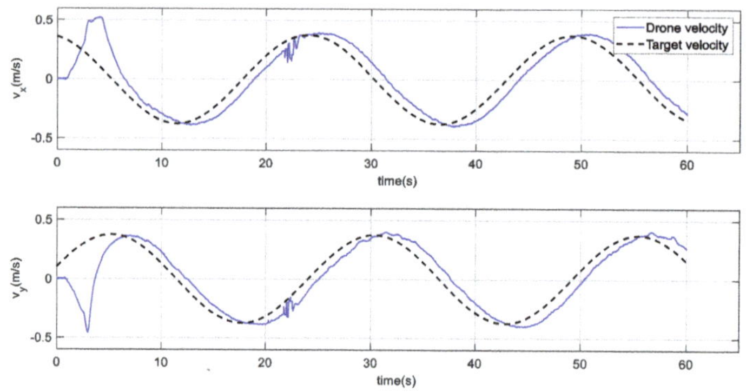

(**b**)

Figure 28. Drone and target velocities on a circular path. (**a**) Improved method. (**b**) Conventional method.

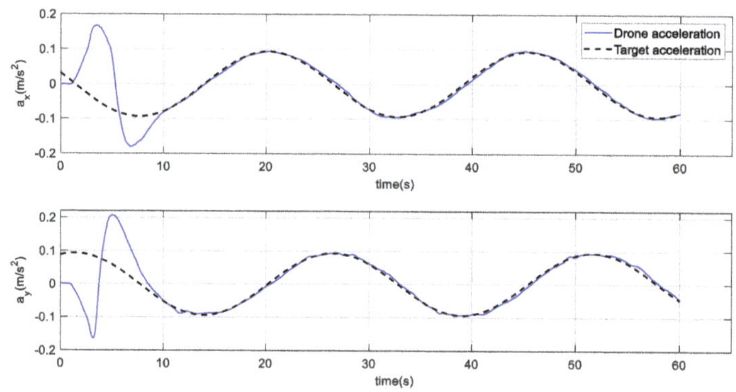

(**a**)

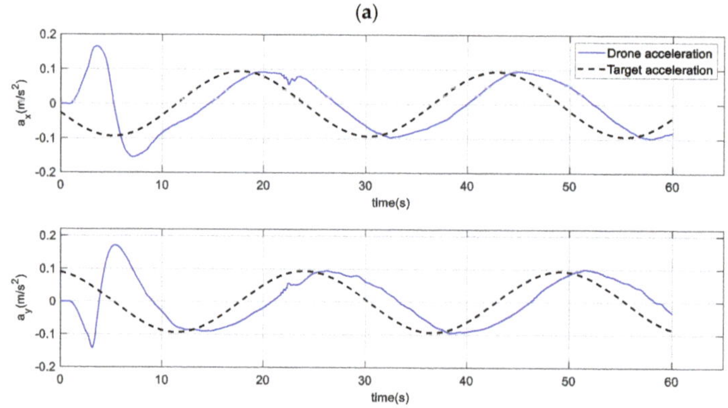

(**b**)

Figure 29. Drone and target accelerations on a circular path. (**a**) Improved method. (**b**) Conventional method.

Table 2 shows the mean square error (MSE) of positions, velocities, and accelerations for both approaches. The table clearly shows how the drone path was improved using the proposed method compared to the conventional potential field. The performance of the drone path with the conventional method lagged behind that of the improved approach in terms of position, velocity, and acceleration, with percentage differences of 54.45%, 48.73%, and 53.15%, respectively.

Table 2. MSE of position, velocity, and acceleration for the two methods on a circular path.

	x (m)	y (m)	v_x (m/s)	v_y (m/s)	a_x (m/s^2)	a_y (m/s^2)
Improved method	0.0320	0.0536	0.0064	0.0102	0.0020	0.0023
Conventional method	0.0881	0.1050	0.0146	0.0184	0.0047	0.0045
Difference % (between the two methods)	54.45		48.73		53.15	

In another scenario, the drone must follow the infinite path depicted in Figure 30. With similar gains, the Figure shows that the performance of the drone path using the proposed method was significantly better than that of the conventional method. Figures 31–33 demonstrate how the drone maintained accurate tracking of the position, velocity, and acceleration along the infinite path. The acceleration term in the potential field attractive force enables the drone to quickly compensate for the shortage of position and velocity terms. Again, due to the limited space size, one or two Vicon cameras missed the drone coverage. As a result, the drone oscillated for a relatively very short period, as shown in certain figures.

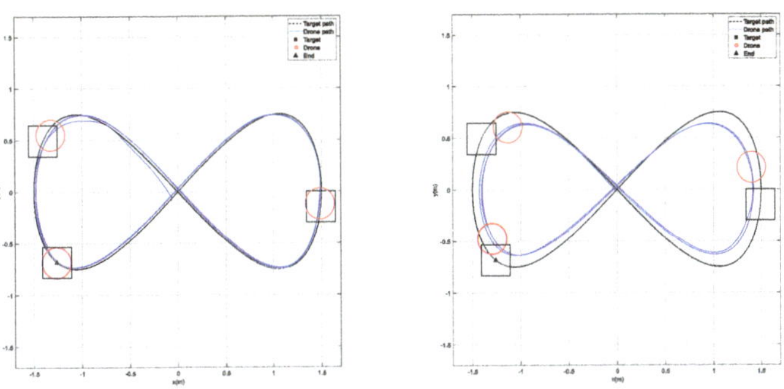

(a) (b)

Figure 30. Infinite path tracking. (**a**) Improved potential field with acceleration. (**b**) Conventional potential field.

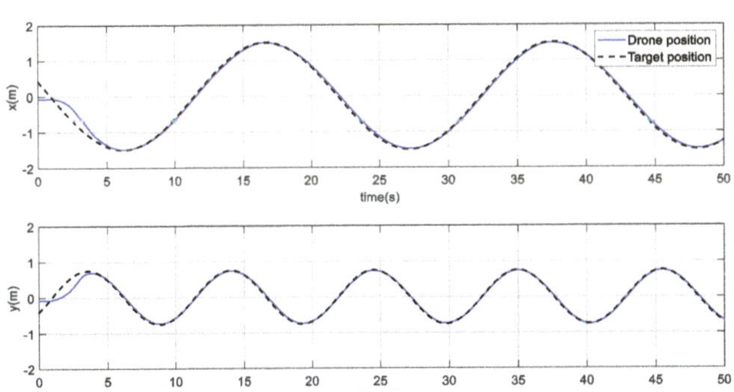

(a)

Figure 31. *Cont.*

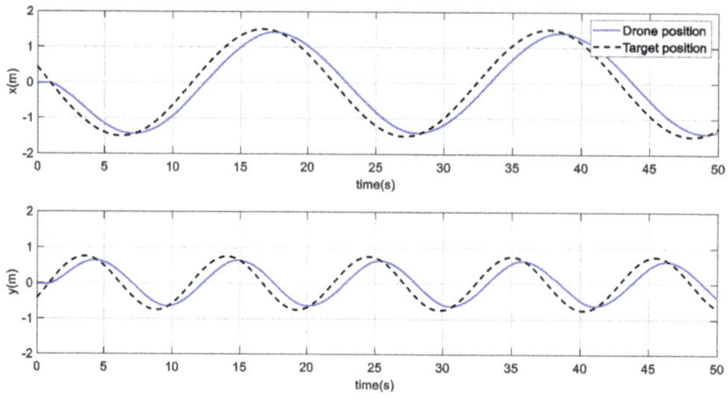

(**b**)

Figure 31. Drone and target positions on an infinite path. (**a**) Improved method. (**b**) Conventional method.

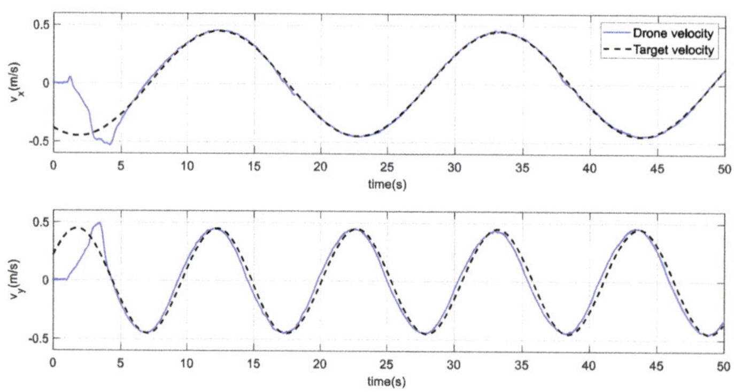

(**a**)

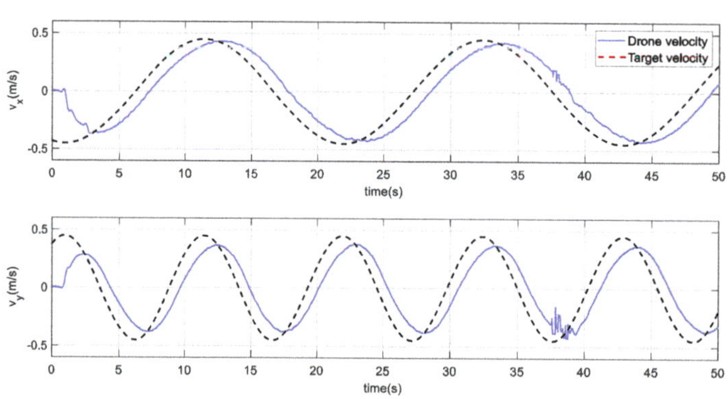

(**b**)

Figure 32. Drone and target velocities on an infinite path. (**a**) Improved method. (**b**) Conventional method.

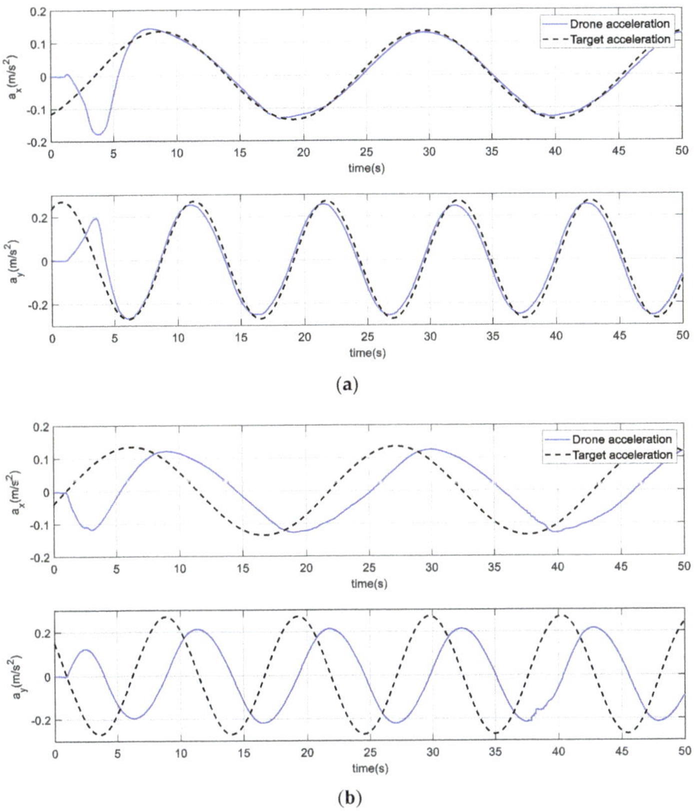

Figure 33. Drone and target accelerations on an infinite path. (**a**) Improved method. (**b**) Conventional method.

The proposed method performed better for drone positioning on an infinite path. Table 3 shows that the improved method has a significantly lower MSE for position, velocity, and acceleration than the conventional method. The table also shows the significant differences between the two methods.

Table 3. MSE of position, velocity, and acceleration for the two methods on an infinite path.

	x (m)	y (m)	v_x (m/s)	v_y (m/s)	a_x (m/s^2)	a_y (m/s^2)
Improved method	0.0066	0.0041	0.0088	0.0086	0.0018	0.0052
Conventional method	0.0952	0.0745	0.0209	0.0324	0.0082	0.0539
Difference % (between the two methods)	93.57		68.09		89.9	

To expand the evaluation of performance in 3D space, the virtual target was moving along a helical path. As shown in Figure 34a, the drone was accurately positioned over the target in three directions and performed better than the conventional method, owing to the improved potential field attractive force. Over a helical path of a 1.5 m radius, the drone tracked the target position more accurately, as shown in Figure 35a. Furthermore, the drone reached the target's velocity and acceleration with very small differences, as shown in Figures 36a and 37a, respectively.

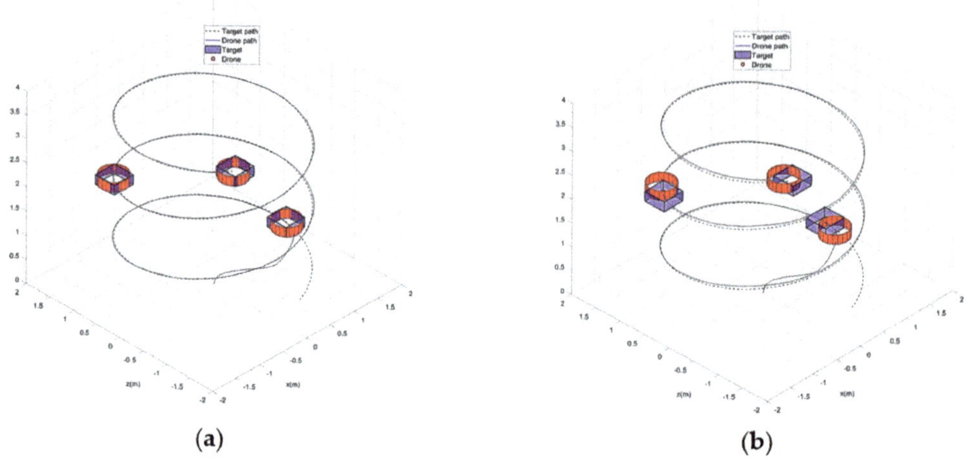

Figure 34. Helical path tracking. (**a**) Improved potential field with acceleration. (**b**) Conventional potential field.

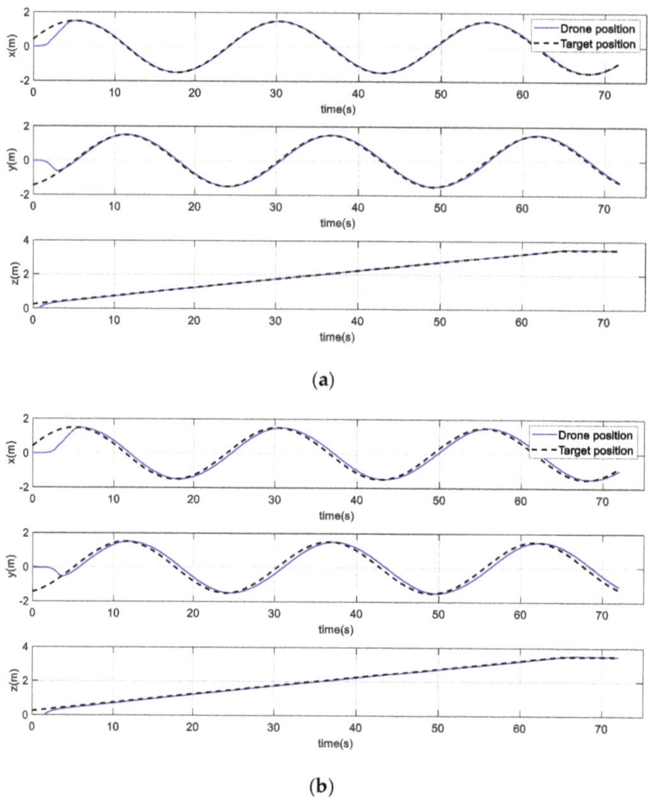

Figure 35. Drone and target positions on a helical path. (**a**) Improved method. (**b**) Conventional method.

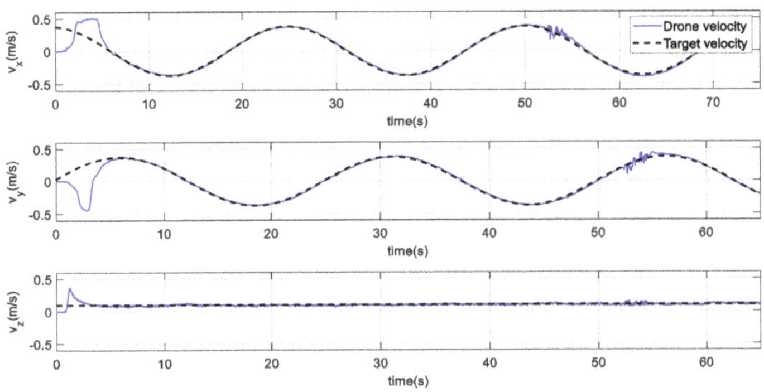

(a)

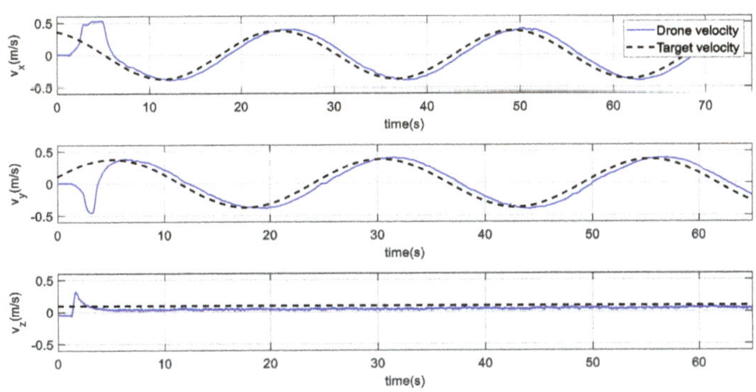

(b)

Figure 36. Drone and target velocities on a helical path. (**a**) Improved method. (**b**) Conventional method.

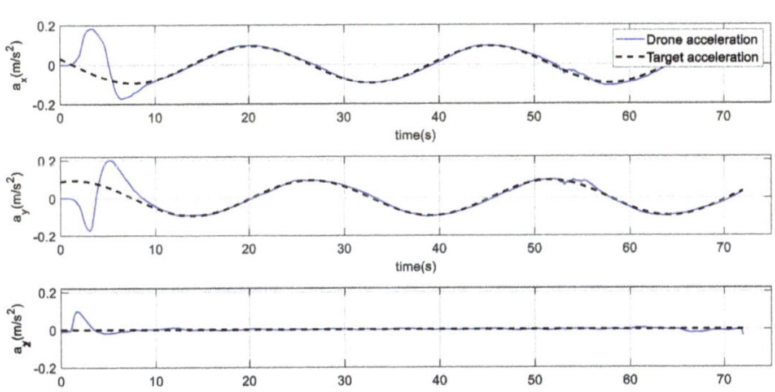

(a)

Figure 37. *Cont.*

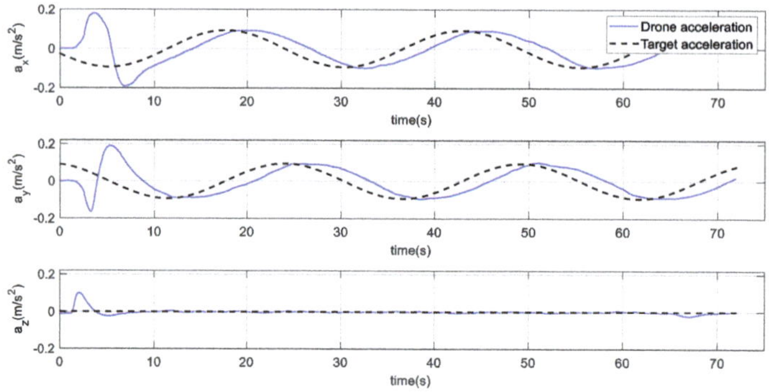

(b)

Figure 37. Drone and target accelerations on a helical path. (**a**) Improved method. (**b**) Conventional method.

Table 4 shows the MSE in the positions, velocities, and accelerations for the drone on a helical path using the two methods. The improved potential field method outperformed the conventional potential field. The table also shows how the drone path is improved by approximately 200% over the conventional method along all three axes.

Table 4. MSE of position, velocity, and acceleration for the two methods on a helical path.

	x (m)	y (m)	z (m)	v_x (m/s)	v_y (m/s)	v_z (m/s)	a_x (m/s^2)	a_y (m/s^2)	a_z (m/s^2)
Improved PF	0.0236	0.0478	0.0017	0.0057	0.0091	0.0011	0.0017	0.0020	0.0002
Conventional method	0.0636	0.0830	0.0034	0.0127	0.0157	0.0042	0.0044	0.0041	0.0004
Difference % (between the two methods)		49.02			47.67			56.32	

Table 5 shows the rising times for each path using both approaches. The data clearly illustrate that the proposed ABPF method achieved a faster response of UAV than the conventional PF. As a result, the UAV could merge with the target path 1.5 s faster for the circular path, 1.6 s for the infinite paths, and 1.3 s for the helical path. The experiments for each scenario utilizing the suggested ABPF approach are also demonstrated in videos that can be found in the Supplementary Materials.

Table 5. Rising time for both methods in different paths.

	Axis	Circular Path (s)	Infinite Path (s)	Helical Path (s)
	X	5.18	6.28	4.89
Conventional PF	Y	3.41	4.08	3.32
	Z	-	-	3.31
	X	3.79	4.71	4.26
Improved PF	Y	3.00	3.77	3.16
	Z	-	-	2.05

6. Conclusions

This paper proposes a novel method for an attractive potential field model that considers the relative acceleration, velocity, and position between a UAV and a target in a highly dynamic path. The new model was developed and deployed in several accelerated path scenarios for soft UAV landings. The generated path of the UAV using the proposed method was compared with that generated by the classic PF method under comparable conditions. The UAV's performance was evaluated in simulated and experimental scenarios, including complex trajectories such as circular, infinite, and helical trajectories. In terms of the accuracy of the average position, velocity, and acceleration, the proposed PF approach outperformed the classical approach by approximately 50% on the circular and helical paths. Furthermore, the performance of the UAV utilizing the developed method surpassed 67% in the infinite path under similar conditions. The proposed ABPF approach provides a more responsive motion to integrate with the target path than the classic PF. Furthermore, the attractive force was adapted effectively in edge circumstances, such as unexpected pauses or sudden direction changes of the target, as well as to disturbances. The proposed technique only looked at the attractive force of the potential field for an accelerating target. Therefore, the repulsive force for accelerated obstacles could be derived in future works for the free-collision path of the UAV. Furthermore, future directions could include discussing the applicability of the ABPF method in real-world outdoor conditions or assessing its effectiveness on various UAV platforms.

Supplementary Materials: The following supporting information can be downloaded at: https://www.mdpi.com/article/10.3390/electronics14010176/s1. Videos S1–S3: Videos of experiments.

Author Contributions: Conceptualization: M.R.H. and M.H.G.; methodology: M.R.H. and M.H.G.; software: M.R.H.; validation: M.R.H. and M.H.G.; resources: A.B.Y.; data curation: M.R.H. and M.H.G.; writing—original draft preparation: M.R.H., M.H.G., A.B.Y. and M.A.G.; writing—review and editing: M.R.H., M.H.G., A.B.Y. and M.A.G.; visualization: M.R.H.; supervision: A.B.Y. and M.A.G. All authors have read and agreed to the published version of the manuscript.

Funding: This research received no external funding.

Data Availability Statement: All test cases are described in detail in this paper. The data will be made available upon reasonable request from the corresponding author.

Acknowledgments: The authors thank the people in the Department of Aerospace Engineering at San Diego State University for facilitating the experiments in the SPACE Lab. The corresponding author received a 9-month Fulbright research Award from the Binational Fulbright Commission in Jordan to pursue this research at San Diego State University.

Conflicts of Interest: The authors declare no conflicts of interest.

References

1. Hayajneh, M.; Al Mahasneh, A. Guidance, Navigation and Control System for Multi-Robot Network in Monitoring and Inspection Operations. *Drones* **2022**, *6*, 332. [CrossRef]
2. Yang, Y.; Xiong, X.; Yan, Y. UAV Formation Trajectory Planning Algorithms: A Review. *Drones* **2023**, *7*, 62. [CrossRef]
3. Liu, L.; Yao, J.; He, D.; Chen, J.; Huang, J.; Xu, H.; Wang, B.; Guo, J. Global dynamic path planning fusion algorithm combining jump-A* algorithm and dynamic window approach. *IEEE Access* **2021**, *9*, 19632–19638. [CrossRef]
4. Dobrevski, M.; Skočaj, D. Dynamic Adaptive Dynamic Window Approach. *IEEE Trans. Robot.* **2024**, *40*, 3068–3081. [CrossRef]
5. Kobayashi, M.; Motoi, N. Local path planning: Dynamic window approach with virtual manipulators considering dynamic obstacles. *IEEE Access* **2022**, *10*, 17018–17029. [CrossRef]
6. Pengfei, J.; Yu, C.; Aihua, W.; Zhenqian, H.; Yichong, W. Optimal Path Planning for Multi-UAV Based on Pseudo-spectral Method. In Proceedings of the 2020 International Conference on Big Data, Artificial Intelligence and Internet of Things Engineering (ICBAIE), Fuzhou, China, 12–14 June 2020; pp. 417–422.

7. Li, J.; Xiong, Y.; She, J.; Wu, M. A path planning method for sweep coverage with multiple UAVs. *IEEE Internet Things J.* **2020**, *7*, 8967–8978. [CrossRef]
8. Xia, Q.A.L.S.; Guo, M.; Wang, H.; Zhou, Q.; Zhang, X. Multi-UAV trajectory planning using gradient-based sequence minimal optimization. *Robot. Auton. Syst.* **2021**, *137*, 103728. [CrossRef]
9. Li, S.; Chen, Y.; Yang, Y. Multi-rotor UAV path planning based on Model Predictive Control and Control Barrier Function. In Proceedings of the 36th Chinese Control and Decision Conference (CCDC), Xi'an, China, 25–27 May 2024; pp. 1141–1146.
10. Wu, W.; Li, J.; Wu, Y.; Ren, X.; Tang, Y. Multi-UAV Adaptive Path Planning in Complex Environment Based on Behavior Tree. In Proceedings of the International Conference on Collaborative Computing: Networking, Applications and Worksharing, Shanghai, China, 16–18 October 2020; pp. 494–505.
11. Tran, N.Q.H.; Prodan, I.; Grøtli, E.I.; Lefèvre, L. Potential-field constructions in an MPC framework: Application for safe navigation in a variable coastal environment. *IFAC-Pap.* **2018**, *51*, 307–312. [CrossRef]
12. Li, J.; Sun, J.; Liu, L.; Xu, J. Model predictive control for the tracking of autonomous mobile robot combined with a local path planning. *Meas. Control.* **2021**, *54*, 1319–1325. [CrossRef]
13. Chen, X.; Zhang, J. The three-dimension path planning of UAV based on improved artificial potential field in dynamic environment. In Proceedings of the 5th International Conference on Intelligent Human-Machine Systems and Cybernetics, Hangzhou, China, 26–27 August 2013; Volume 2, pp. 144–147.
14. Chengqing, L.; Ang, M.H.; Krishnan, H.; Yong, L.S. Virtual obstacle concept for local-minimum-recovery in potential-field based navigation. In Proceedings of the IEEE International Conference on Robotics and Automation. Symposia Proceedings, Paris, France, 31 May–31 August 2020; Volume 2, pp. 983–988.
15. Zou, X.-Y.; Zhu, J. Virtual local target method for avoiding local minimum in potential field based robot navigation. *J. Zhejiang Univ. Sci. A* **2003**, *4*, 264–269. [CrossRef]
16. Garibeh, M.H.; Jaradat, M.A.; Alshorman, A.M.; Hayajneh, M.; Younes, A.B. A real-time fuzzy motion planning system for unmanned aerial vehicles in dynamic 3D environments. *Appl. Soft Comput.* **2024**, *150*, 110995. [CrossRef]
17. Garibeh, M.H.; Alshorman, A.M.; Jaradat, M.A.; Ahmad, B.Y.; Khaleel, M. Motion planning of unmanned aerial vehicles in dynamic 3D space: A potential force approach. *Robotica* **2022**, *40*, 3604–3630. [CrossRef]
18. Yao, P.; Wang, H.; Su, Z. Real-time path planning of unmanned aerial vehicle for target tracking and obstacle avoidance in complex dynamic environment. *Aerosp. Sci. Technol.* **2015**, *47*, 269–279. [CrossRef]
19. Khatib, O. Real-time obstacle avoidance for manipulators and mobile robots. *Int. J. Robot. Res.* **1986**, *5*, 90–98. [CrossRef]
20. Ge, S.S.; Cui, Y.J. Dynamic motion planning for mobile robots using potential field method. *Auton. Robot.* **2002**, *13*, 207–222. [CrossRef]
21. Garibeh, M.H.; Jaradat, M.A.K.; Rawashdeh, N.A. A potential field simulation study for mobile robot path planning in dynamic environments. In Proceedings of the 20th International Conference on Research and Education in Mechatronics (REM), Wels, Austria, 23–24 May 2019; pp. 1–8.
22. Jayaweera, H.M.; Hanoun, S. A dynamic artificial potential field (D-APF) UAV path planning technique for following ground moving targets. *IEEE Access* **2020**, *8*, 192760–192776. [CrossRef]
23. Hayajneh, M.R.; Badawi, A.R.E. Automatic UAV wireless charging over solar vehicle to enable frequent flight missions. In Proceedings of the 3rd International Conference on Automation, Control and Robots, Prague, Czech Republic, 11–13 October 2019; pp. 44–49.
24. Yu, W.; Lu, Y. UAV 3D environment obstacle avoidance trajectory planning based on improved artificial potential field method. *J. Phys. Conf. Ser.* **2021**, *1885*, 022020. [CrossRef]
25. Keyu, L.; Yonggen, L.; Yanchi, Z. Dynamic obstacle avoidance path planning of UAV Based on improved APF. In Proceedings of the 5th International Conference on Communication, Image and Signal Processing (CCISP), Chengdu, China, 13–15 November 2020; pp. 159–163.
26. Jayaweera, H.M.; Hanoun, S. Path planning of unmanned aerial vehicles (UAVs) in windy environments. *Drones* **2022**, *6*, 101. [CrossRef]
27. Thangaraj, M.; Sangam, R.S. Intelligent UAV path planning framework using artificial neural network and artificial potential field. *Indones. J. Electr. Eng. Comput. Sci.* **2023**, *29*, 1192. [CrossRef]
28. Feng, J.; Zhang, J.; Zhang, G.; Xie, S.; Ding, Y.; Liu, Z. UAV dynamic path planning based on obstacle position prediction in an unknown environment. *IEEE Access* **2021**, *9*, 154679–154691. [CrossRef]
29. Du, Y.; Zhang, X.; Nie, Z. A real-time collision avoidance strategy in dynamic airspace based on dynamic artificial potential field algorithm. *IEEE Access* **2019**, *7*, 169469–169479. [CrossRef]
30. BinKai, Q.; Mingqiu, L.; Yang, Y.; XiYang, W. Research on UAV path planning obstacle avoidance algorithm based on improved artificial potential field method. *J. Phys. Conf. Ser.* **2021**, *1948*, 012060. [CrossRef]
31. Ortner, R.; Kurmi, I.; Bimber, O. Acceleration-aware path planning with waypoints. *Drones* **2021**, *5*, 143. [CrossRef]

32. Yin, L.; Yin, Y.; Lin, C.-J. A new potential field method for mobile robot path planning in the dynamic environments. *Asian J. Control* **2009**, *11*, 214–225. [CrossRef]
33. Hayajneh, M.; Melega, M.; Marconi, L. Design of autonomous smartphone based quadrotor and implementation of navigation and guidance systems. *Mechatronics* **2018**, *49*, 119–133. [CrossRef]

electronics

MDPI

Article

GLBWOA: A Global–Local Balanced Whale Optimization Algorithm for UAV Path Planning

Qiwu Wu [1,†], Weicong Tan [2,*,†], Renjun Zhan [1], Lingzhi Jiang [2], Li Zhu [1,3] and Husheng Wu [1]

1. School of Equipment Management and Support, Engineering University of PAP, Xi'an 710086, China; cli@hunnu.edu.cn (Q.W.); zhanrenjun@aliyun.com (R.Z.); zhuli_cnrs@foxmail.com (L.Z.); wuhusheng0421@163.com (H.W.)
2. School of Information Engineering, Engineering University of PAP, Xi'an 710086, China; jianglingzhi1123@ustb.edu.cn
3. Key Laboratory of Counter-Terrorism Command & Information Engineering (Engineering University of PAP), Ministry of Education, Xi'an 710086, China

* Correspondence: tanweicong_pap@163.com

† These authors contributed equally to this work.

Abstract: To tackle the challenges of path planning for unmanned aerial vehicle (UAV) in complex environments, a global–local balanced whale optimization algorithm (GLBWOA) has been developed. Initially, to prevent the population from prematurely converging, a bubble net attack enhancement strategy is incorporated, and mutation operations are introduced at different stages of the algorithm to mitigate early convergence. Additionally, a failure parameter test mutation mechanism is integrated, along with a predefined termination rule to avoid excessive computation. The algorithm's convergence is accelerated through mutation operations, further optimizing performance. Moreover, a random gradient-assisted optimization approach is applied, where the negative gradient direction is identified during each iteration, and an appropriate step size is selected to enhance the algorithm's exploration capability toward finding the optimal solution. The performance of GLBWOA is benchmarked against several other algorithms, including SCA, BWO, BOA, and WOA, using the IEEE CEC2017 test functions. The results indicate that the GLBWOA outperforms other algorithms. Path-planning simulations are also conducted across four benchmark scenarios of varying complexity, revealing that the proposed algorithm achieves the lowest average total cost for flight path planning and exhibits high convergence accuracy, thus validating its reliability and superiority.

Keywords: whale optimization algorithms; complex environment; path planning; multiple strategies; digital elevation model

1. Introduction

Unmanned aerial vehicles and other intelligent agents have become the focal point of research in recent years, with their applications expanding across various domains, including military operations [1], agriculture [2], environmental monitoring [3], and particularly in emergency rescue [4] and logistics distribution [5]. The establishment of a safe flight path is crucial for the successful execution of missions. However, the task of planning a safe flight path for UAVs within complex environments presents considerable challenges. Such environments may encompass rugged mountainous terrain, urban structures, and geographical obstacles such as waterfalls, in addition to being influenced by dynamic factors like weather fluctuations and traffic conditions. Consequently, the development of efficient, safe, and feasible flight paths for UAVs has emerged as a pressing issue that necessitates urgent attention under these intricate conditions.

Currently, the predominant approach to unmanned aerial vehicle (UAV) path planning involves transforming the environmental model [6] into a mathematical framework. This allows for the development of a safe, feasible, and stable flight path from the initial point to the destination, utilizing algorithms within specified constraints [7,8].

Intelligent algorithms utilized for autonomous UAV path planning can be categorized into three primary groups: traditional optimization algorithms, intelligent optimization algorithms, and machine learning algorithms. Traditional optimization algorithms have been extensively employed in various path-planning applications. Among these, the A* algorithm [9,10], recognized as a classical heuristic search algorithm, is particularly favored due to its straightforward implementation. However, its efficacy diminishes significantly when applied to large-scale and high-dimensional spaces, thereby constraining its capacity to address trajectory planning challenges that involve multiple constraints. The rapidly exploring random tree (RRT) algorithm [11,12] represents a notable path-planning technique based on spatial sampling, which does not necessitate the discretization of the flight environment, resulting in a more rapid search process. Nonetheless, this method often struggles to yield optimal trajectories. The artificial potential field method [13,14] is appreciated for its rapid computational speed and effective real-time performance in path planning; however, in expansive and high-dimensional spatial environments, it may encounter issues such as local oscillations and local minima, which can render the generated paths impractical. Collectively, these observations underscore the limitations of traditional optimization algorithms in effectively addressing multi-constraint path-planning problems, as they often fail to achieve a satisfactory balance between accuracy and time efficiency.

In recent years, numerous scholars have investigated and developed intelligent optimization algorithms inspired by biological behaviors observed in nature, as well as principles derived from mathematical functions, to address UAV path-planning challenges. Notable algorithms in this domain include the social spider algorithm (SSA) [15], grey wolf optimization (GWO) [16], beluga whale optimization (BWO) algorithm [17,18], sine cosine algorithm (SCA) [19], and butterfly optimization algorithm (BOA) [20–22], among others. These algorithms are capable of rapidly identifying optimal paths by employing a variety of search strategies and executing multiple iterations. However, it is important to note that many intelligent optimization algorithms are probabilistic stochastic search methods characterized by a significant degree of randomness when applied to specific engineering problems. Consequently, the interplay between global optimization and local optimization tends to be weak. Therefore, a primary challenge faced by many intelligent algorithms is to prevent convergence to local optima and to enhance the global convergence rate as much as possible.

Introduced by Mirjalili S et al. in 2016, the whale optimization algorithm [23] is a metaheuristic method that emulates the feeding behaviors of humpback whales. By emulating three predation tactics of humpback whales—encircling prey, bubble net feeding, and searching for food—the algorithm seeks the optimal solution. These strategies are characterized by robust search capabilities and computational stability. Jiang R [24] et al. proposed the whale army optimization algorithm, which introduces the armed forces procedure and adjusts the establishment of key parameters and foundation principles of the original whale algorithm, which is comparable to the traditional whale optimization algorithm as well as other high-performance group intelligent algorithms. The algorithm has faster convergence speed under lower computational complexity. Huang Y [25] et al. introduced a whale optimization algorithm designed for the path-planning challenges of autonomous underwater vehicles. This approach integrates segmented learning with an adaptive operator selection strategy, employing a dynamic partitioning method and a weighted mean scheme to create virtual individuals. These virtual entities are then incorporated into the whale optimization framework to form an evolutionary pool. As a result, the algorithm's optimization performance is enhanced. Simulation results demonstrate that the proposed method exhibits greater robustness and search capability compared to other comparative algorithms. Guo W [26] et al. proposed an improved whale optimization algorithm based on wavelet mutation strategy and social learning, designed a new linear incremental probability to improve the global exploitation ability, introduced an adaptive neighborhood learning strategy to promote the exchange of information between individuals, and integrated the Morlet wavelet mutation mechanism to avoid the algorithm falling into local optimality. Wang C [27] and colleagues introduced an adaptive adjustment mechanism based on the whale optimization algorithm. This mechanism dynamically modifies the search process during iterations by incorporating controllable variables and utilizing a differential mutation evolutionary strategy. These enhancements effectively balance the algorithm's global and local optimality. Ultimately, the algorithm was applied to the path-planning problem, demonstrating superior performance compared to the original whale algorithm and six other advanced intelligent optimization methods. The proposed algorithm, along with the six high-performance optimization techniques, exhibited improved convergence speed, greater accuracy, and enhanced stability. The study presented in [28] introduced a novel whale optimization algorithm (NWOA) aimed at addressing the robot path-planning challenge within highly complex dynamic environments. This approach employs an adaptive strategy to hasten the algorithm's convergence. Additionally, it incorporates virtual obstacles to improve the algorithm's capacity to evade local optima and introduces a potential field factor to boost the robot's performance in obstacle avoidance. Simulation comparisons demonstrate the advantages of the proposed algorithm. The authors of [29] proposed an enhanced whale optimization algorithm to realize the path planning of UAV weather detection missions in complex environments and introduced real-time boundary processing, quasi-opposite-based learning, and an enhanced search mechanism into the standard whale optimization algorithm, which improves the convergence speed of the algorithm and the ability of global optimization, and the simulations show that the algorithm gives a higher-quality path plan than the other improved algorithms.

Furthermore, with the rapid advancements in key machine learning techniques, an increasing number of researchers have begun exploring their application to path-planning challenges [30–32]. As a result, the quest for more efficient and robust path-planning algorithms has become a critical area of research that warrants comprehensive investigation.

The aforementioned paper proposes various enhancement strategies for the whale optimization algorithm, resulting in varying degrees of improved optimization performance. However, it continues to encounter challenges pertaining to the accuracy of optimal value searches and the balance between global and local exploration capabilities. To address these issues, we introduce a global–local balanced whale optimization algorithm (GLBWOA) that incorporates three principal enhancement strategies:

- We propose an enhancement strategy for the bubble net attack, enabling individuals to possess the requisite capability to escape their current position at various stages. This approach aims to increase the algorithm's likelihood of transcending local optima.
- We present the failure parameter test mutation mechanism, which involves predefined trigger conditions. When the algorithm encounters a local optimum or exhibits slow progress, the mutation operation is activated to enhance its global search capability and its ability to escape from local optima.
- Inspired by the directional variations of the gradient vector, we propose a stochastic gradient-assisted optimization method that integrates the gradient into the conventional whale optimization algorithm to enhance its optimization performance. Furthermore, an energy reduction scheme is introduced to improve the algorithm's local exploration capabilities.

Ultimately, the algorithm introduced in this study is utilized for path planning in UAVs across various complex environments, demonstrating its effectiveness.

The remainder of this paper is organized as follows: Section 2 outlines the steps involved in formulating the objective function; Section 3 details the design of the improved algorithm; and Section 4 presents the simulation of the algorithms using the test function, along with the implementation of path-planning problems and their comparative results. Finally, we conclude the paper with a summary of our findings.

2. Problem Description

This research investigates the challenge of path planning for unmanned aerial vehicles through the formulation of a comprehensive cost function that assigns specific weights to different constraints. This methodology considers a wide array of constraints and seeks to determine the optimal trajectory by minimizing the associated cost function [33]. The constraints considered are more comprehensive than the cost function designed in the literature [34], and the comprehensive cost function in this paper can be flexible by adding constraints and adjusting weights at any time according to the different task requirements.

2.1. Restrictive Condition

UAVs prioritize range length when performing missions, and shorter ranges can greatly reduce fuel consumption to improve endurance. A UAV is usually controlled by a ground control station to fly sequentially along waypoints planned in a search map to form a flight path X_i. Each waypoint is a node of the path searched on a known map, with coordinates set to $M_{ij} = (x_{ij}, y_{ij}, z_{ij})$. The range length cost function F_1 can be obtained by accumulating the Euclidean distance between every two nodes:

$$F_1(Path_i) = \sum_{j=1}^{n-1} \left\| M_{ij}\vec{M}_{i,j+1} \right\|, \tag{1}$$

In addition to the duration of the flight, it is imperative to account for potential threats posed by obstacles encountered during the flight. The designated flight path must be designed to enable the UAV to navigate around these obstacles, thereby ensuring safe operational conditions throughout the flight. Let α represent the set of all potential threats, with the threat posed by obstacles being modeled as a cylinder characterized by a projection center coordinate O_α and a radius R_α. The UAV has a diameter denoted as D, while the length of the safety buffer is represented by S. Furthermore, the distance between the path, denoted as $\left\| M_{ij}\vec{M}_{i,j+1} \right\|$, is directly established by any two flight points of the UAV. The distance between the path and the center coordinate is d_α, as shown in Figure 1. Considering the above conditions, the threat cost function F_2 constitutes:

$$\begin{cases} F_2(Path_i) = \sum\limits_{j=1}^{n-1} \sum\limits_{\alpha=1}^{\alpha} K_\alpha(M_{ij}\vec{M}_{i,j+1}), \\ K_\alpha(M_{ij}\vec{M}_{i,j+1}) = \begin{cases} 0, & \text{if } d_\alpha > S + D + R_\alpha \\ (S + D + R_\alpha) - d_\alpha, & \text{if } D + R_\alpha < d_\alpha \leq S + D + R_\alpha \\ \infty, & \text{if } d_\alpha \leq D + R_\alpha. \end{cases} \end{cases} \tag{2}$$

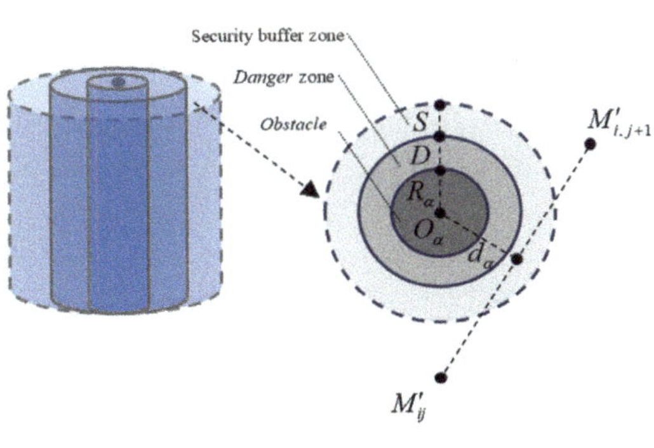

Figure 1. Cylindrical obstacle threat.

In certain scenarios, such as aerial photography and experimental missions, an unmanned aerial vehicle (UAV) is required to operate within designated airspace. Flying at excessive altitudes can compromise the resolution of aerial imagery, while insufficient altitudes pose unnecessary risks to ground personnel, flora, and fauna and may obstruct the field of view during filming. Therefore, the operational flight altitude is typically constrained within two defined limits, as illustrated in Figure 2. This approach enables the efficient allocation and utilization of airspace resources, reducing potential conflicts and interference. During flight operations, the actual altitude is determined by both the terrain elevation and the prescribed altitude limits. The following guidelines outline how to calculate the altitude cost at a given point within the specified range:

$$H_{ij} = \begin{cases} \left| h_{ij} - \frac{(h_{\max}+h_{\min})}{2} \right|, & \text{if } h_{\min} \le h_{ij} \le h_{\max} \\ \infty, & \text{otherwise,} \end{cases} \tag{3}$$

where the rule restricts the UAV to flying at the average of the two extremes and specifies that the cost of flying increases accordingly as the distance traveled away from the average altitude is increased, thus constituting the altitude cost function F_3:

$$F_3(Path_i) = \sum_{j=1}^{n} H_{ij}. \tag{4}$$

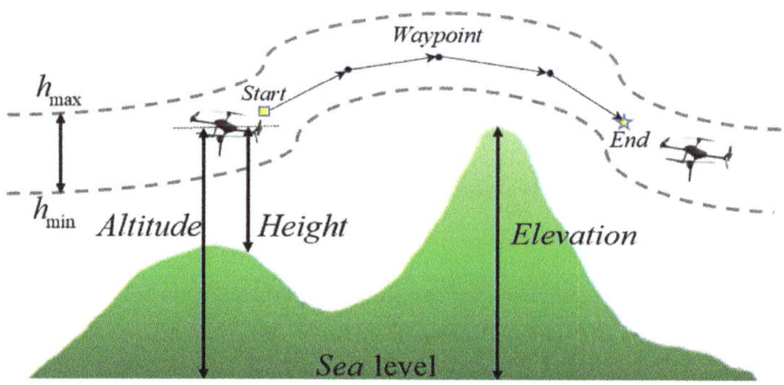

Figure 2. Altitude cost explanation.

Smoothing cost is an important consideration in UAV path planning and is a cost introduced to ensure that the flight path of the UAV is as smooth as possible to avoid sharp steering or altitude changes that lead to increased difficulty in controlling the airframe and accelerated fuel consumption. As shown in Figure 3, the smoothing cost includes the fuselage steering cost and the climb cost, where ψ_{ij} stands for the steering angle and $\theta_{i,j+1}$ stands for the climb angle. According to the UAV performance constraints, the maximum steering angle and maximum climb angle cannot exceed $\psi_{\max}$ and $\theta_{\max}$. Taking z as a unit vector in the direction of the z coordinate axis, the climb angle θ_{ij} can be expressed as:

$$\theta_{ij} = \arctan\left(\frac{z_{i,j+1} - z_{ij}}{\left\| \overrightarrow{M'_{ij}M'_{i,j+1}} \right\|} \right), \tag{5}$$

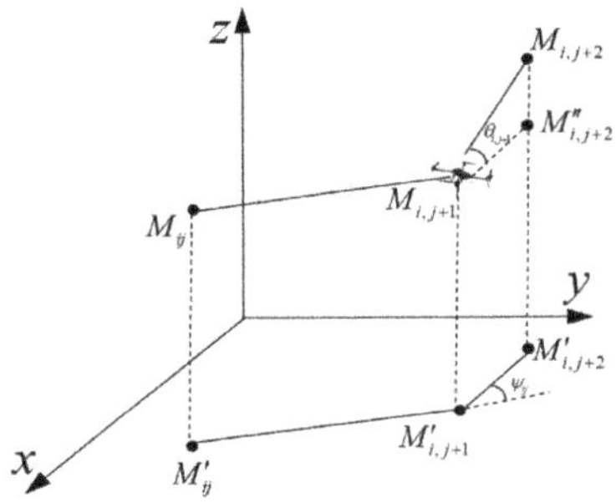

Figure 3. Calculation of turning and climbing angles.

The steering angle ψ_{ij} is expressed as

$$\psi_{ij} = \arctan\left(\frac{\left\| \overrightarrow{M'_{ij}M'_{i,j+1}} \times \overrightarrow{M'_{i,j+1}M'_{i,j+2}} \right\|}{\overrightarrow{M'_{ij}M'_{i,j+1}} \cdot \overrightarrow{M'_{i,j+1}M'_{i,j+2}}}\right), \tag{6}$$

The smoothing cost can be expressed as

$$F_4(Path_i) = \sigma_1 \sum_{j=1}^{n-2} \psi_{ij} + \sigma_2 \sum_{j=1}^{n-1} \left|\theta_{ij} - \theta_{i,j-1}\right|, \tag{7}$$

where σ_1 and σ_2 denote the cost coefficients for the steering angle and climb angle, respectively.

2.2. Integrated Cost Function

To ensure the UAV reaches its target safely and efficiently, the planned path must guide the UAV through collision-free flight, taking into account factors such as total path length cost, threat cost, altitude cost, and smoothing cost. The total cost function is formulated as follows:

$$F_{\cos t}(Path_i) = \sum_{\alpha=1}^{4} w_\alpha F_\alpha(Path_i), \tag{8}$$

where F_1 to F_4 denote the costs of trajectory length, obstacle threat, navigational altitude, and path smoothing, respectively, and w_α is a weighting factor corresponding to the different costs.

2.3. Environmental Model

The path planning scenarios are derived from two distinct terrains located on Christmas Island, Australia [35], as depicted in Figure 4a,b. These scenarios employ authentic digital elevation model (DEM) maps obtained from LiDAR sensors. Each scenario is classified into simple and complex categories based on the number of obstacles present. The simple scenario is characterized by the presence of three cylindrical obstacles, whereas the complex scenario is designed to incorporate at least twice the number of structural obstacles found in the simple scenario. This differentiation aims to assess the performance of the path-planning algorithm under varying environmental conditions, leading to the establishment of four benchmark scenarios.

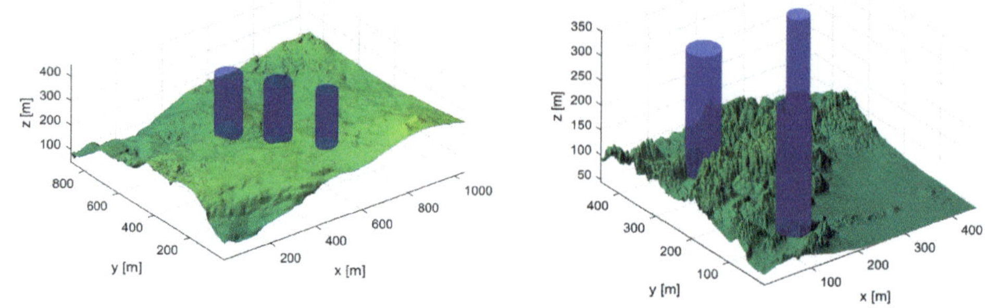

(**a**) Terrain model 1 (**b**) Terrain model 2

Figure 4. Terrain environment model for UAV path planning. (Blue cylinders are artificially added obstacles).

3. Algorithm Design

Among various swarm intelligence algorithms, the whale optimization algorithm (WOA) is known for its simplicity and minimal parameter requirements. However, it exhibits certain limitations when addressing the complex optimization challenges of UAV path planning. Therefore, this paper focuses on the analysis and enhancement of the WOA. In this subsection, after reviewing the standard WOA, we propose an improved global–local equilibrium whale optimization algorithm by integrating multiple strategies. These enhancements enable the algorithm to more efficiently identify optimal paths in UAV path-planning tasks, particularly in complex terrain environments.

3.1. Standard Whale Optimization Algorithm

The whale optimization algorithm mimics the unique hunting behavior of humpback whales. According to the feeding characteristics of whales, the whale's feeding behavior is divided into three phases: constricted encircling feeding, bubble net attack, and stochastic search, and the specific analyses are described as follows:

3.1.1. Constriction-Enclosed Predation Phase

In nature, whales can find the location of prey and encircle them for predation, and the algorithm assumes that the optimal individual of the current population is the prey, and all other whales in the population encircle the location of the optimal whale to update their position, which is updated by Equations (9) and (10):

$$D = |C \cdot X^*(t) - X(t)|, \tag{9}$$

$$X(t+1) = X^*(t) - A \cdot D, \tag{10}$$

where t is the number of iterations; D denotes the bracketing step; A and C represent the coefficient vectors; $X^*(t)$ is the optimal position vector of the population; $X(t)$ is the position vector of the current population; A and C are updated by Equations (11) and (12):

$$A = 2a \cdot r_1 - a, \tag{11}$$

$$C = 2 \cdot r_2, \tag{12}$$

r_1 and r_2 are random numbers in the range [0,1]; the value of a decreases linearly from 2 to 0, denoted by:

$$a = 2 - 2 \cdot \frac{t}{T_{Max}}, \tag{13}$$

T_{Max} is the maximum number of iterations.

3.1.2. Bubble Network Attack Phase

Humpback whales swim towards their prey in a spiral trajectory when hunting, and in the whale optimization algorithm, individual whales update their position by using Equations (14) and (15):

$$D' = |X^*(t) - X(t)|, \tag{14}$$

$$X(t+1) = D' \cdot e^{bl} \cos(2\pi l) + X^*(t), \tag{15}$$

where b is a constant to change the shape of the spiral, usually set to l; l is a random number in between $[-1, 1]$.

The development phase of the whale optimization algorithm consists of two phases: shrinking encirclement and bubble net attack. When $|A| < 1$, as the whale swims along the spiral trajectory around the prey in the shrinking encirclement, the whale has a 50% possibility of choosing to encircle the prey and a 50% possibility of choosing the bubble net attack, which is obtained by Equation (16):

$$X(t+1) = \begin{cases} X^*(t) - A \cdot D, & p < 0.5 \\ D' \cdot e^{bl} \cos(2\pi l) + X^*(t), & p \geq 0.5 \end{cases} \tag{16}$$

where p is a random number between [0,1].

3.1.3. Random Search Phase

Whales randomly search and feed based on their position when $|A| \geq 1$. In the WOA, whales update their position by Equations (17) and (18):

$$D = \left| C \cdot X^{\text{rand}}(t) - X(t) \right|, \tag{17}$$

$$X(t+1) = X^{\text{rand}}(t) - A \cdot D, \tag{18}$$

where $X^{rand}(t)$ is a randomly selected whale position vector.

3.2. Global–Local Balanced Whale Optimization Algorithm

WOA conducts global exploration through a stochastic search strategy after initializing the population. However, this approach may result in insufficient global search capability. As the algorithm progresses, local search is performed during the encircling predation and spiral updating phases, but the linearly decreasing convergence factor can cause an imbalance between global and local search. Consequently, the algorithm tends to fall into local optima in its later stages. To overcome these shortcomings, this subsection introduces a global–local equalization whale optimization algorithm. A bubble net attack enhancement strategy is implemented to prevent the algorithm from getting trapped in local optima, and a failure parameter test variation mechanism is incorporated to strengthen its global search capability. In the algorithm's later stages, a stochastic gradient-assisted optimization strategy is employed to further enhance its search performance. The three proposed improvement strategies are elaborated on in the following sections.

3.2.1. Bubble Net Attack Enhancement Strategy

In the standard whale optimization algorithm, the same spiral attack and contraction encircling strategy is used for all individuals during the exploitation phase to update positions. However, this approach does not account for the fact that the ability of an individual to escape its current position varies at different stages of the optimization process. Relying solely on these two modes of position updating can hinder the algorithm's ability to escape local optima, particularly when it begins to converge prematurely. To prevent the population from entering an aggregation state, which can cause WOA to become trapped in a local optimum, a variation method is introduced to enhance the bubble net attack. A new variation operation is applied to update the position of the optimal whale individual when the random number is less than or equal to 0.6, while the original position update method remains unchanged. The variation formula is presented in Equation (19).

$$X_{i,j}(t+1) = X_{i,j}(t) + r_5 \times (X_{be,j}(t) - X_{i,j}(t)), \tag{19}$$

where $X_{be,j}(t)$ is the optimal solution of the jth dimension of the current iteration, r_5 is a random number.

3.2.2. Failed Parameter Test Variation Mechanism

In optimization algorithms, termination criteria dictate when to stop the iterative process. Selecting appropriate termination criteria helps prevent over-computation while ensuring that the algorithm finds a satisfactory solution within a reasonable time frame. Based on the analysis above, to enhance the algorithm's performance, a failure parameter test variation mechanism is proposed. This mechanism triggers mutation operations by setting the following two termination conditions for the algorithm's execution:

1. A better value is not found for several consecutive iterations. For example, when the algorithm runs for 5 consecutive iterations without finding a better value, the mutation operation is triggered.
2. The change in the objective function value is less than a preset threshold. For example, the preset threshold parameter is set to 10^{-6}, and when the difference between the objective function value of the current iteration and the objective function value of the previous iteration is less than 10^{-6}, the variation operation is triggered.

The specific formula for the mutation operation is as follows:

Calculate the mutation step based on the current number of iterations t and the maximum number of iterations T:

$$step_size = \left(\frac{ub - lb}{t/T}\right) \cdot randn(1, \dim), \tag{20}$$

Calculate the variation vector:

$$m = step_size \cdot ((rand(1, \dim)) \cdot 2 - 1) \cdot \left(\frac{1}{randn(1, \dim) \mid}\right)^{\beta}, \tag{21}$$

where $\beta = 1.5$.

Apply the variation vector to the current whale position and perform a boundary check:

$$X_{i,j}(t+1) = X_{i,j}(t) + m \tag{22}$$

By introducing the above mutation operations, the aim is to increase the population diversity and avoid falling into local optimal solutions, thus improving the algorithm's global search capability and convergence speed.

3.2.3. Stochastic Gradient-Assisted Optimization Method

The standard whale optimization algorithm runs with incomplete local exploration. The fusion of gradient into a swarm intelligence algorithm to form a hybrid algorithm aims at combining the advantages of the two to improve the algorithm's performance in optimization. The change in the independent variable along the direction of the gradient vector can maximize the change in the function value. In the algorithm, the objective function is the optimization goal. Given the above analysis, a stochastic gradient-assisted optimization [36] method is proposed, in which after determining the negative gradient direction in each iteration, a suitable step size $step^{t+1}$ is chosen so that the objective function value can be reduced to the maximum extent to enhance the exploration ability of the algorithm for the optimal solution. The specific operation is as follows:

$$X_i^{t+1} = X_i^t - step^{t+1} \cdot \nabla f(X_i^t), \tag{23}$$

where $-\nabla f(x_i^t)$ denotes the negative gradient direction, and $step$ denotes the optimal step size along that direction. X_i^{t+1} is the i individual in the $t+1$ iteration. The gradient direction is defined as shown in Equation (24):

$$\nabla f = \frac{\partial f}{\partial X_1^t}\vec{e_1} + \frac{\partial f}{\partial X_2^t}\vec{e_2} + \cdots + \frac{\partial f}{\partial X_{Dim}^t}\vec{e}_{Dim}, \tag{24}$$

where Dim denotes the dimension of the optimization problem to be solved. $\vec{e_l}(i = 1, 2, \cdots Dim)$ is a set of unit orthogonal vectors. In order to enhance the ability of the swarm intelligence algorithm to solve the optimization problem, so that the hybrid algorithm is still able to solve the problem independently of the mathematical properties of the problem, the gradient is approximated using the forward difference formulae viewed as a definitional derivation. The formula is shown in Equation (25).

$$\frac{\partial f}{\partial X_i^t} \approx \frac{f(X_i^t + \varepsilon) - f(X_i^t)}{\varepsilon}, \tag{25}$$

where ε is a small positive number set to 10^{-6}.

The step size along the negative gradient direction is obtained by the line search method, as shown in Equation (26).

$$step^{t+1} = \begin{cases} step^t\varsigma, & \text{if } f(X_i^t - step^t\varsigma\nabla f(X_i^t)) \le f\left(X_i^t - \frac{step^t}{\varsigma} \cdot \nabla f(X_i^t)\right) \\ \frac{step^t}{\varsigma}, & \text{else} \end{cases} \tag{26}$$

where ς is a scale factor and ς is set to 1.8.

3.3. Algorithmic Process

In this paper, a global local balanced whale optimization algorithm is proposed. Firstly, the original population initialization as well as the random search strategy are used, followed by a bubble attack enhancement strategy designed to improve the ability to jump out of the local optimum by introducing a mutation method while the original helix updating method remains unchanged in the bubble net predation phase. After that, a failure parameter test mutation mechanism is introduced, conditions are set to trigger the termination of the algorithm to avoid over-computation, and the global search ability is improved and the algorithm convergence speed is accelerated by increasing the mutation operation. Finally, the stochastic gradient is used to assist in the optimization search, so that the algorithm searches the global optimal value as much as possible, and balances the global and local exploration ability of the algorithm. The pseudo-code of the algorithm is shown in Algorithm 1. The specific flow of the algorithm is shown in Figure 5.

3.4. Computational Complexity

Computational complexity encompasses both time complexity and space complexity. Time complexity constitutes a fundamental component of algorithm analysis, serving as a metric for both the performance and computational efficiency of algorithms. In this context, let N represent the population size, n denote the dimension of the search space, and Max_iter signify the maximum number of iterations. The time complexity of the conventional whale optimization algorithm can be articulated as $T_{woa} = O(N \times n \times Max\_iter) = O(n)$. The generalized bubble whale optimization algorithm (GLBWOA) enhances the standard WOA by integrating three distinct strategies, one of which is the bubble net attack enhancement strategy that does not introduce additional nested loops. As a result, the time complexity for this strategy remains $T_1 = O(N \times n \times Max\_iter) = O(n)$. Let t_1 denote the cycle running time for formulas (20), (21), and (22), while t_2 represents the time required for fitness evaluations. Consequently, the time complexity associated with the failure parameter test mutation mechanism can be expressed as $T_2 = O(N \times n \times (t_1 + t_2)) = O(n)$. Furthermore, let t_3 indicate the time required for executing boundary constraint operations within the stochastic gradient-assisted optimization method. Thus, the time complexity for this method is $T_3 = O(N \times n \times t3) = O(n)$. In conclusion, the overall time complexity of GLBWOA can be formulated as $T_{GLBWOA} = T_1 + Max\_iter(T_2 + T_3) = O(n)$. When juxtaposed with the standard WOA, it is apparent that the time complexity remains invariant, thereby preserving the execution efficiency of the algorithm. The subsequent section will assess the performance of GLBWOA through a series of function set tests and path-planning simulations and further analyze the optimization efficiency of the algorithm by documenting its actual running time in path-planning simulations.

Algorithm 1: GLBWOA

Set parameters, population size, number of iterations, etc.
Initialize the population.
Calculate the fitness value of the initial population.
Find the current optimal individual and the optimal value.
Main loop
For 1:N
    Use Equations (11)–(13) to update the whale algorithm parameters
  If $p < 0.5$
      If $|A| \geq 1$
        Equation (18) is used to update the random search phase stage.
      else
        Equation (10) is used to update the closed predator stage.
      end
    else
      If $rand > 0.6$
        Equation (15) is used to update the bubble net attack.
      else
        Equation (19) update enhanced bubble network attack strategy.
    end
Calculate the fitness value of each individual, and select the optimal individual and the optimal value at this time.
Record the number of optimal value update failures and calculate the difference between the current best fitness and the global best fitness.
    If Value of difference > 10^{-6} or the number of optimal value update failures > 5
      Using the Formula (20)–(21) to update the mutation parameters.
      Equation (22) is used to update the failed mutation formula.
    end
    Set the gradient step factor.
    Using Equation (24) to update the negative gradient direction
    Equation (26) is used to update the gradient step size.
    Equation (23), update the gradient-assisted optimization formula.
Using the greedy algorithm, the optimal individual is compared. If the fitness value of the optimal individual after auxiliary optimization is better, the individual is replaced by the original individual.
end
Output the optimal solution, the optimal value.

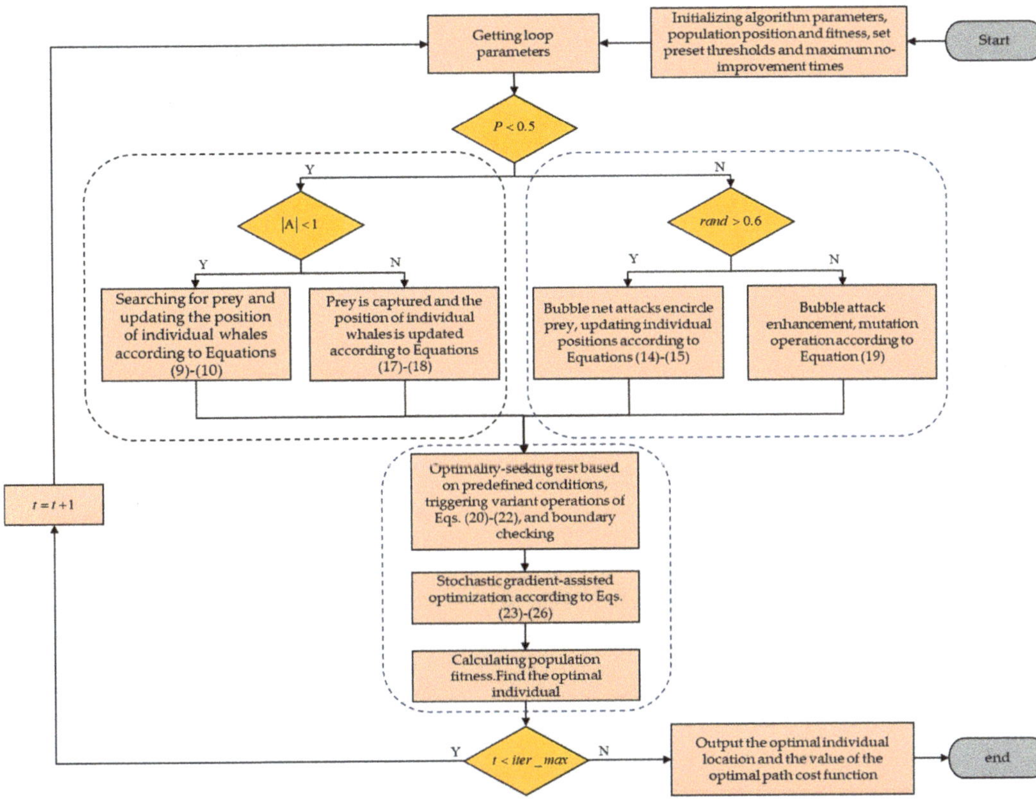

Figure 5. Global–local balanced whale optimization algorithm process.

Space complexity is a measure of the amount of storage space temporarily occupied by an algorithm during operation and is an important indicator of an algorithm's merit. The space complexity of standard WOA is $S_{WOA} = O(N \times n) + O(Max\_iter) = O(n)$. In GLBWOA, the space complexity of the position matrix is $S_1 = O(N \times n)$, the space complexity of the fitness storage is $S_2 = O(N)$, the space complexity of the leader information is $S_3 = O(n) + O(1)$, the space complexity of the convergence curve storage is $S_4 = O(Max\_iter)$, and the space complexity of the other temporary variables is $S_5 = O(1)$, so the overall space complexity of GLBWOA is $S_{GLBWOA} = O(N \times n) + O(N) + O(Max\_iter) = O(n)$, which shows that the space complexity of GLBWOA is consistent with that of the WOA in the large-scale problems. Space complexity is the same.

4. Simulation and Discussion

In this subsection, the test function is used to assess the optimization capabilities of the proposed algorithm, and the optimal path is identified within the actual elevation map. The superiority of the GLBWOA is demonstrated through a comparative analysis with other leading high-performance metaheuristic algorithms via numerical simulations. All simulations conducted in this study were performed on a Windows 11 platform equipped with a 13th Generation Intel Core™ i9-13900HX processor operating at 2.20 GHz. Additionally, MATLAB 2024a software was employed for the simulations.

4.1. Optimization Performance Test

The IEEE CEC2017 function is utilized to evaluate the optimization performance of the GLBWOA. In addition to comparing it with the basic WOA, three advanced intelligent optimization algorithms—BWO, SCA, and BOA—are also employed for comparative analysis. To ensure a fair evaluation, all algorithms are configured to operate in dimensions of 30, 50, and 100. Simulations are conducted across these varying dimensions, with a maximum evaluation time set to 10,000 times the dimensionality. The population size is fixed at 30, and the maximum number of iterations is limited to 500. In this study, each algorithm is executed independently for 30 trials, and metrics such as the optimal value, mean, and standard deviation are recorded to assess the optimization performance of the algorithms.

The CEC2017 function test set contains four types of functions, where F1 to F3 are single-peak functions, F4 to F10 are basic multi-peak functions, F11 to F20 are hybrid functions, and F21 to F30 are composite functions. The performance of the algorithms tested on the different function types will be analyzed in turn below.

From the data presented in Table 1, it is evident that, for the single-peak function, the GLBWOA can reach the theoretical optimum more efficiently than the other algorithms within a limited number of iterations. This suggests that GLBWOA possesses a stronger convergence capability. However, it is also observed that the stability of the optimization search conducted by GLBWOA slightly diminishes under high-dimensional conditions.

Table 1. Algorithm test results. Significant values are in bold.

Func	Alg	d = 30			d = 50			d = 100		
		Best	Ave	Std	Best	Ave	Std	Best	Ave	Std
F1	Ours	**4.9E + 04**	**1.4E + 05**	**6.6E + 04**	**1.0E + 03**	**9.3E + 03**	**8.1E + 03**	**5.7E + 03**	**2.7E + 04**	**2.2E + 04**
	WOA	2.1E + 09	5.3E + 09	2.1E + 09	1.3E + 10	2.0E + 10	4.6E + 09	9.0E + 10	1.1E + 11	1.0E + 10
	BWO	4.0E + 10	5.3E + 10	5.8E + 09	9.4E + 10	1.1E + 11	4.7E + 09	2.5E + 11	2.6E + 11	6.9E + 09
	SCA	1.2E + 10	2.0E + 10	5.1E + 09	5.0E + 10	6.6E + 10	7.9E + 09	1.8E + 11	2.1E + 11	1.5E + 10
	BOA	3.7E + 10	5.3E + 10	6.7E + 09	8.6E + 10	1.1E + 11	9.6E + 09	2.3E + 11	2.6E + 11	1.2E + 10
F2	Ours	**2.0E + 02**	**5.2E + 03**	**2.3E + 04**	**4.2E + 02**	**1.3E + 11**	**7.2E + 11**	**7.2E + 32**	**6.8E + 47**	3.7E + 48
	WOA	2.2E + 26	5.7E + 34	1.4E + 35	7.0E + 62	4.8E + 76	2.0E + 77	9.4E + 146	1.9E + 175	**6.6E + 04**
	BWO	2.0E + 41	4.8E + 46	1.9E + 47	6.1E + 69	1.2E + 80	4.6E + 80	3.2E + 162	5.2E + 172	**6.6E + 04**
	SCA	1.3E + 33	2.6E + 38	8.6E + 38	1.9E + 64	8.5E + 70	2.8E + 71	1.7E + 150	5.8E + 167	**6.6E + 04**
	BOA	3.0E + 41	1.6E + 53	3.5E + 53	3.4E + 80	3.2E + 93	9.9E + 93	7.5E + 185	1.7E + 197	**6.6E + 04**
F3	Ours	**5.8E + 03**	**3.4E + 04**	2.3E + 04	**5.4E + 04**	**1.1E + 05**	**3.1E + 04**	**2.5E + 05**	4.3E + 05	1.0E + 05
	WOA	1.4E + 05	2.7E + 05	7.8E + 04	1.8E + 05	3.1E + 05	1.2E + 05	7.6E + 05	9.2E + 05	1.1E + 05
	BWO	7.0E + 04	8.2E + 04	**4.6E + 03**	1.6E + 05	2.4E + 05	3.5E + 04	3.4E + 05	**3.8E + 05**	**4.0E + 04**
	SCA	6.5E + 04	8.9E + 04	1.7E + 04	1.5E + 05	2.2E + 05	3.2E + 04	4.0E + 05	6.1E + 05	9.5E + 04
	BOA	6.6E + 04	8.0E + 04	6.2E + 03	1.7E + 05	3.7E + 05	1.6E + 05	3.2E + 05	5.7E + 05	3.5E + 05

Table 2 presents the test data for the algorithms applied to the multi-peak function with local extreme points. The optimal and average values achieved through GLBWOA optimization are superior across different dimensions, demonstrating the algorithm's robust capability to escape local optima. Notably, in function F4, GLBWOA significantly outperforms other algorithms across various performance indicators, underscoring its excellent stability.

Table 2. Algorithm test results. Significant values are in bold.

Func	Alg	d = 30			d = 50			d = 100		
		Best	Ave	Std	Best	Ave	Std	Best	Ave	Std
F4	Ours	**4.9E + 02**	**5.2E + 02**	**2.0E + 01**	**5.0E + 02**	**6.7E + 02**	**6.7E + 01**	**9.7E + 02**	**1.1E + 03**	**8.9E + 01**
	WOA	8.2E + 02	1.3E + 03	4.0E + 02	2.6E + 03	4.5E + 03	1.2E + 03	1.4E + 04	2.1E + 04	3.6E + 03
	BWO	9.4E + 03	1.3E + 04	1.3E + 03	2.7E + 04	3.4E + 04	2.9E + 03	6.7E + 04	9.8E + 04	8.6E + 03
	SCA	1.8E + 03	3.3E + 03	1.2E + 03	9.1E + 03	1.3E + 04	2.4E + 03	3.9E + 04	5.3E + 04	8.4E + 03
	BOA	1.5E + 04	2.1E + 04	3.9E + 03	3.1E + 04	4.0E + 04	4.0E + 03	9.1E + 04	1.1E + 05	1.0E + 04

Table 2. *Cont.*

Func	Alg	d = 30			d = 50			d = 100		
		Best	Ave	Std	Best	Ave	Std	Best	Ave	Std
F5	Ours	**6.4E + 02**	**7.0E + 02**	3.7E + 01	**8.0E + 02**	**8.6E + 02**	4.0E + 01	**1.2E + 03**	**1.3E + 03**	6.8E + 01
	WOA	7.8E + 02	8.7E + 02	4.9E + 01	1.0E + 03	1.1E + 03	9.0E + 01	1.8E + 03	1.9E + 03	1.5E + 02
	BWO	9.0E + 02	9.3E + 02	**1.7E + 01**	1.2E + 03	1.2E + 03	**1.6E + 01**	2.0E + 03	2.1E + 03	**2.3E + 01**
	SCA	7.8E + 02	8.2E + 02	2.1E + 01	1.1E + 03	1.1E + 03	3.9E + 01	1.9E + 03	2.1E + 03	1.1E + 02
	BOA	8.9E + 02	9.3E + 02	1.9E + 01	1.2E + 03	1.2E + 03	2.3E + 01	2.0E + 03	2.1E + 03	3.7E + 01
F6	Ours	**6.3E + 02**	**6.4E + 02**	6.4E + 00	**6.4E + 02**	**6.5E + 02**	5.4E + 00	**6.5E + 02**	**6.6E + 02**	3.7E + 00
	WOA	6.6E + 02	6.8E + 02	1.3E + 01	6.9E + 02	7.0E + 02	7.9E + 00	6.9E + 02	7.1E + 02	1.2E + 01
	BWO	6.8E + 02	6.9E + 02	5.6E + 00	6.9E + 02	7.0E + 02	**3.8E + 00**	7.1E + 02	7.1E + 02	**2.2E + 00**
	SCA	6.5E + 02	6.7E + 02	1.0E + 01	6.7E + 02	6.9E + 02	6.9E + 00	7.0E + 02	7.1E + 02	4.8E + 00
	BOA	6.8E + 02	6.9E + 02	**5.2E + 00**	6.9E + 02	7.0E + 02	5.7E + 00	7.1E + 02	7.1E + 02	2.7E + 00
F7	Ours	**9.8E + 02**	**1.2E + 03**	8.2E + 01	**1.4E + 03**	**1.6E + 03**	8.4E + 01	**2.9E + 03**	**3.2E + 03**	2.6E + 02
	WOA	1.1E + 03	1.3E + 03	7.6E + 01	1.7E + 03	1.9E + 03	8.3E + 01	3.5E + 03	3.8E + 03	1.5E + 02
	BWO	1.3E + 03	1.4E + 03	**2.9E + 01**	1.8E + 03	2.0E + 03	5.7E + 01	3.8E + 03	3.9E + 03	6.3E + 01
	SCA	1.1E + 03	1.3E + 03	6.0E + 01	1.7E + 03	1.9E + 03	9.6E + 01	3.8E + 03	4.2E + 03	2.5E + 02
	BOA	1.3E + 03	1.4E + 03	3.0E + 01	1.9E + 03	2.0E + 03	**5.4E + 01**	3.8E + 03	4.0E + 03	**6.3E + 01**
F8	Ours	**9.0E + 02**	**9.5E + 02**	2.9E + 01	**1.1E + 03**	**1.2E + 03**	4.5E + 01	**1.6E + 03**	**1.7E + 03**	7.9E + 01
	WOA	9.9E + 02	1.1E + 03	5.0E + 01	1.3E + 03	1.4E + 03	8.6E + 01	2.3E + 03	2.4E + 03	8.9E + 01
	BWO	1.1E + 03	1.1E + 03	**1.9E + 01**	1.5E + 03	1.5E + 03	**2.1E + 01**	2.5E + 03	2.6E + 03	**3.1E + 01**
	SCA	1.1E + 03	1.1E + 03	2.2E + 01	1.4E + 03	1.5E + 03	3.8E + 01	2.2E + 03	2.4E + 03	7.6E + 01
	BOA	1.1E + 03	1.1E + 03	2.1E + 01	1.4E + 03	1.5E + 03	3.3E + 01	2.5E + 03	2.6E + 03	4.0E + 01
F9	Ours	**3.4E + 03**	**5.5E + 03**	1.2E + 03	**1.1E + 04**	**1.4E + 04**	**1.6E + 03**	**2.1E + 04**	**2.5E + 04**	**2.0E + 03**
	WOA	5.5E + 03	1.2E + 04	4.5E + 03	2.4E + 04	4.2E + 04	1.2E + 04	5.8E + 04	7.8E + 04	1.7E + 04
	BWO	8.1E + 03	1.1E + 04	**1.1E + 03**	3.3E + 04	3.9E + 04	2.3E + 03	7.5E + 04	8.1E + 04	3.4E + 03
	SCA	6.3E + 03	8.7E + 03	1.7E + 03	2.4E + 04	3.3E + 04	5.5E + 03	7.7E + 04	9.5E + 04	1.1E + 04
	BOA	8.9E + 03	1.1E + 04	1.3E + 03	3.5E + 04	4.0E + 04	2.7E + 03	7.6E + 04	8.4E + 04	4.4E + 03
F10	Ours	**3.7E + 03**	**5.4E + 03**	7.9E + 02	**5.8E + 03**	**8.2E + 03**	9.0E + 02	**1.4E + 04**	**1.7E + 04**	1.5E + 03
	WOA	6.6E + 03	7.6E + 03	5.1E + 02	1.1E + 04	1.3E + 04	1.1E + 03	2.6E + 04	3.0E + 04	1.5E + 03
	BWO	8.6E + 03	8.9E + 03	**2.3E + 02**	1.4E + 04	1.5E + 04	**4.8E + 02**	3.1E + 04	3.2E + 04	5.4E + 02
	SCA	7.3E + 03	8.9E + 03	4.4E + 02	1.4E + 04	1.5E + 04	5.3E + 02	3.2E + 04	3.3E + 04	**4.4E + 02**
	BOA	8.7E + 03	9.3E + 03	2.9E + 02	1.5E + 04	1.6E + 04	4.4E + 02	3.1E + 04	3.3E + 04	7.4E + 02

Table 3 presents the test data for the algorithm applied to hybrid functions. Each function is either rotated or shifted and comprises three or more CEC2017 benchmark functions, with each subfunction assigned a specific weight. The difficulty of solving these functions has significantly increased compared to the previous ones. For the GLBWOA, its optimization accuracy remains unaffected by rotation or displacement. However, the individual indices for F20 are slightly lower than those of the other algorithms. In contrast, the optimal and average values for the other nine functions are considerably higher than those of the comparison algorithms. This demonstrates GLBWOA's strong global exploration capability and its superior ability to identify optimal solutions.

Table 3. Algorithm test results. Significant values are in bold.

Func	Alg	d = 30			d = 50			d = 100		
		Best	Ave	Std	Best	Ave	Std	Best	Ave	Std
F11	Ours	**1.1E + 03**	**1.2E + 03**	**5.0E + 01**	**1.3E + 03**	**1.4E + 03**	**8.1E + 01**	**9.0E + 03**	**1.9E + 04**	**1.3E + 04**
	WOA	3.7E + 03	1.0E + 04	4.3E + 03	4.1E + 03	8.5E + 03	2.2E + 03	1.5E + 05	2.8E + 05	1.2E + 05
	BWO	5.3E + 03	8.0E + 03	1.4E + 03	2.0E + 04	2.3E + 04	1.4E + 03	2.3E + 05	3.6E + 05	8.3E + 04
	SCA	2.4E + 03	4.0E + 03	1.0E + 03	7.0E + 03	1.2E + 04	2.5E + 03	1.1E + 05	1.8E + 05	3.7E + 04
	BOA	3.5E + 03	8.3E + 03	2.6E + 03	1.8E + 04	2.4E + 04	2.8E + 03	1.7E + 05	4.1E + 05	2.4E + 05

Table 3. *Cont.*

Func	Alg	d = 30			d = 50			d = 100		
		Best	Ave	Std	Best	Ave	Std	Best	Ave	Std
F12	Ours	**1.6E + 06**	**5.1E + 06**	**2.6E + 06**	**2.9E + 06**	**1.1E + 07**	**6.8E + 06**	**7.5E + 06**	**3.4E + 07**	**1.6E + 07**
	WOA	1.6E + 08	4.7E + 08	2.3E + 08	2.1E + 09	4.7E + 09	1.9E + 09	1.7E + 10	2.8E + 10	5.8E + 09
	BWO	8.4E + 09	1.2E + 10	1.5E + 09	4.4E + 10	6.5E + 10	8.9E + 09	1.5E + 11	1.9E + 11	1.2E + 10
	SCA	1.5E + 09	2.9E + 09	9.3E + 08	1.3E + 10	2.2E + 10	4.7E + 09	8.0E + 10	1.0E + 11	1.2E + 10
	BOA	4.8E + 09	1.4E + 10	4.2E + 09	5.0E + 10	8.3E + 10	1.7E + 10	1.4E + 11	2.0E + 11	2.3E + 10
F13	Ours	**1.8E + 04**	**6.2E + 04**	**5.0E + 04**	**1.3E + 04**	**4.3E + 04**	**3.3E + 04**	**1.1E + 04**	**2.5E + 04**	**8.1E + 03**
	WOA	1.6E + 06	1.9E + 07	4.5E + 07	1.2E + 08	6.0E + 08	3.7E + 08	1.2E + 09	2.7E + 09	1.1E + 09
	BWO	9.7E + 08	6.4E + 09	2.4E + 09	1.1E + 10	3.8E + 10	9.6E + 09	2.9E + 10	4.3E + 10	4.7E + 09
	SCA	1.7E + 08	1.1E + 09	5.9E + 08	3.4E + 09	6.4E + 09	1.7E + 09	1.3E + 10	1.8E + 10	3.6E + 09
	BOA	3.2E + 09	1.4E + 10	6.6E + 09	3.0E + 10	4.8E + 10	1.2E + 10	3.6E + 10	4.8E + 10	5.4E + 09
F14	Ours	**2.1E + 04**	**3.4E + 05**	**2.9E + 05**	**1.1E + 05**	**5.5E + 05**	**2.3E + 05**	**7.0E + 05**	**2.0E + 06**	**8.3E + 05**
	WOA	5.0E + 04	1.9E + 06	2.0E + 06	8.2E + 05	6.0E + 06	3.9E + 06	8.0E + 06	1.9E + 07	7.7E + 06
	BWO	1.2E + 06	3.9E + 06	2.1E + 06	8.6E + 06	5.6E + 07	2.5E + 07	4.6E + 07	7.7E + 07	1.9E + 07
	SCA	1.3E + 05	1.1E + 06	9.8E + 05	2.1E + 06	8.2E + 06	4.3E + 06	2.0E + 07	6.2E + 07	3.1E + 07
	BOA	8.3E + 04	3.6E + 06	3.3E + 06	2.1E + 07	1.3E + 08	9.6E + 07	4.2E + 07	1.4E + 08	7.0E + 07
F15	Ours	**3.8E + 03**	**1.6E + 04**	**1.0E + 04**	**7.9E + 03**	**2.2E + 04**	**9.5E + 03**	**8.7E + 03**	**1.9E + 04**	**6.2E + 03**
	WOA	9.7E + 04	1.4E + 07	3.6E + 07	1.9E + 06	5.2E + 07	4.9E + 07	1.1E + 08	4.7E + 08	3.0E + 08
	BWO	6.4E + 07	3.5E + 08	2.4E + 08	3.0E + 09	6.0E + 09	1.4E + 09	1.9E + 10	2.4E + 10	2.3E + 09
	SCA	5.0E + 06	5.3E + 07	5.4E + 07	2.8E + 08	1.1E + 09	4.5E + 08	2.9E + 09	6.6E + 09	1.6E + 09
	BOA	4.0E + 07	7.1E + 08	6.9E + 08	2.8E + 09	7.9E + 09	3.2E + 09	1.5E + 10	2.4E + 10	4.8E + 09
F16	Ours	**2.6E + 03**	**3.1E + 03**	3.9E + 02	**2.9E + 03**	**4.1E + 03**	5.2E + 02	**5.4E + 03**	**7.0E + 03**	**8.3E + 02**
	WOA	2.9E + 03	4.3E + 03	4.9E + 02	4.8E + 03	6.6E + 03	1.0E + 03	1.2E + 04	1.7E + 04	3.2E + 03
	BWO	4.4E + 03	5.6E + 03	**3.2E + 02**	7.1E + 03	8.8E + 03	8.6E + 02	2.0E + 04	2.3E + 04	1.1E + 03
	SCA	3.3E + 03	4.2E + 03	1.8E + 03	5.6E + 03	6.3E + 03	**3.6E + 02**	1.3E + 04	1.5E + 04	1.1E + 03
	BOA	4.7E + 03	7.8E + 03	9.3E + 02	8.0E + 03	1.1E + 04	1.6E + 03	2.3E + 04	2.6E + 04	1.9E + 03
F17	Ours	**2.0E + 03**	**2.4E + 03**	2.3E + 02	**2.8E + 03**	**3.7E + 03**	**3.6E + 02**	**4.9E + 03**	**5.9E + 03**	**7.3E + 02**
	WOA	2.1E + 03	2.8E + 03	3.5E + 02	3.9E + 03	4.9E + 03	7.9E + 02	9.6E + 03	3.7E + 04	2.9E + 04
	BWO	3.6E + 03	4.3E + 03	4.7E + 02	5.0E + 03	7.6E + 03	1.6E + 03	3.9E + 05	5.6E + 06	3.4E + 06
	SCA	2.4E + 03	2.8E + 03	**1.9E + 02**	4.1E + 03	5.1E + 03	4.8E + 02	1.5E + 04	6.5E + 04	5.4E + 04
	BOA	3.8E + 03	1.1E + 04	9.8E + 03	5.3E + 03	1.7E + 04	1.3E + 04	1.2E + 06	1.8E + 07	1.7E + 07
F18	Ours	**1.3E + 05**	**1.2E + 06**	**1.3E + 06**	**2.0E + 05**	**3.5E + 06**	**2.4E + 06**	**1.8E + 06**	**3.1E + 06**	**1.0E + 06**
	WOA	1.2E + 06	1.1E + 07	8.1E + 06	2.6E + 06	5.0E + 07	4.3E + 07	8.9E + 06	2.1E + 07	1.0E + 07
	BWO	5.0E + 06	3.6E + 07	1.6E + 07	6.5E + 07	1.5E + 08	3.9E + 07	7.6E + 07	2.1E + 08	6.2E + 07
	SCA	1.7E + 06	1.9E + 07	1.4E + 07	2.5E + 07	7.3E + 07	3.8E + 07	3.5E + 07	1.2E + 08	5.5E + 07
	BOA	4.9E + 06	9.4E + 07	1.1E + 08	3.8E + 07	2.1E + 08	1.2E + 08	7.3E + 07	2.5E + 08	1.2E + 08
F19	Ours	**2.8E + 03**	**1.6E + 04**	**1.8E + 04**	**7.5E + 03**	**6.1E + 04**	**5.7E + 04**	**1.6E + 04**	**2.5E + 05**	**2.2E + 05**
	WOA	1.2E + 06	2.0E + 07	1.6E + 07	3.0E + 06	2.2E + 07	2.2E + 07	2.6E + 08	5.3E + 08	2.5E + 08
	BWO	1.4E + 08	5.2E + 08	2.4E + 08	1.2E + 09	3.3E + 09	9.4E + 08	1.2E + 10	2.3E + 10	2.7E + 09
	SCA	2.9E + 07	1.2E + 08	7.5E + 07	2.2E + 08	7.3E + 08	3.2E + 08	2.4E + 09	5.4E + 09	1.4E + 09
	BOA	8.8E + 07	8.9E + 08	6.8E + 08	5.8E + 08	4.2E + 09	1.8E + 09	1.6E + 10	2.5E + 10	4.1E + 09
F20	Ours	**2.4E + 03**	**2.8E + 03**	2.1E + 02	3.1E + 03	**3.6E + 03**	2.7E + 02	**4.7E + 03**	**5.8E + 03**	5.6E + 02
	WOA	2.5E + 03	3.0E + 03	2.3E + 02	**2.9E + 03**	4.0E + 03	4.3E + 02	5.7E + 03	7.2E + 03	6.4E + 02
	BWO	2.8E + 03	3.1E + 03	**1.2E + 02**	3.5E + 03	4.1E + 03	**1.8E + 02**	7.3E + 03	7.8E + 03	**2.3E + 02**
	SCA	2.6E + 03	3.0E + 03	1.7E + 02	3.9E + 03	4.3E + 03	2.3E + 02	7.1E + 03	8.0E + 03	3.4E + 02
	BOA	2.8E + 03	3.1E + 03	1.3E + 02	3.6E + 03	4.3E + 03	2.4E + 02	7.5E + 03	8.1E + 03	2.8E + 02

F21–F30 are composite functions that consist of at least three hybrid functions or CEC2017 benchmark functions that have been rotated and shifted. Each subfunction includes additional bias values and a weight, which further complicates the optimization challenges faced by the algorithms. Table 4 presents the test data for each algorithm within the composite function. The simulation results indicate that, across various dimensions, the GLBWOA demonstrates superior performance in identifying optimal solutions. It excels in both optimal value and average value metrics, particularly in functions F25, F28, and F30, where GLBWOA's performance indices significantly surpass those of other algorithms. This suggests that GLBWOA enhances local search capabilities compared to the WOA, leading to improved solution accuracy and a robust ability to avoid local optima, thereby facilitating the discovery of optimal solutions. Even when other algorithms exhibit low search accuracy or fail to converge, GLBWOA consistently maintains high solution accuracy.

To verify whether there is a significant difference between GLBWOA and the other algorithms, the experimental data were statistically analyzed using the Wilcoxon rank sum test [37]. For each test function, the Wilcoxon rank sum test was performed by combining the results of 30 independent optimization searches for GLBWOA with the results of 30 independent optimization searches for WOA, BWO, SCA, and BOA, respectively, at a significance level of 5%, with all algorithmic dimensions set to 30, 50, and 100 cases simultaneously, the population size set to 30, and the number of iterations set to 500 generations. The p-value of the test result is less than 0.05, indicating that there is a significant difference between the compared algorithms, and vice versa there is no significant difference. The symbols '<' '>', and '=' indicate that the performance of GLBWOA is better, worse, and equivalent to the comparison algorithms, respectively. The results in Table 5 show that almost all p-values are less than 5%, indicating that GLBWOA's ability to find the best is better than the remaining four comparison algorithms.

Table 4. Algorithm test results. Significant values are in bold.

Func	Alg	d = 30			d = 50			d = 100		
		Best	Ave	Std	Best	Ave	Std	Best	Ave	Std
F21	Ours	**2.4E + 03**	**2.5E + 03**	4.8E + 01	**2.6E + 03**	**2.7E + 03**	6.7E + 01	**3.2E + 03**	**3.5E + 03**	1.8E + 02
	WOA	2.5E + 03	2.6E + 03	6.5E + 01	2.8E + 03	3.1E + 03	1.1E + 02	4.1E + 03	4.4E + 03	2.0E + 02
	BWO	2.6E + 03	2.7E + 03	3.5E + 01	3.1E + 03	3.2E + 03	5.8E + 01	4.5E + 03	4.8E + 03	9.3E + 01
	SCA	2.6E + 03	2.6E + 03	**2.5E + 01**	2.9E + 03	3.0E + 03	**5.0E + 01**	4.1E + 03	4.2E + 03	**8.8E + 01**
	BOA	2.5E + 03	2.7E + 03	5.9E + 01	3.1E + 03	3.3E + 03	8.4E + 01	4.5E + 03	4.9E + 03	1.7E + 02
F22	Ours	**2.3E + 03**	**4.4E + 03**	2.5E + 03	**8.5E + 03**	**1.0E + 04**	9.5E + 02	**1.8E + 04**	**2.0E + 04**	1.3E + 03
	WOA	3.1E + 03	8.1E + 03	1.8E + 03	1.3E + 04	1.5E + 04	1.1E + 03	2.9E + 04	3.2E + 04	1.5E + 03
	BWO	7.4E + 03	8.7E + 03	**6.5E + 02**	1.5E + 04	1.7E + 04	6.9E + 02	3.4E + 04	3.5E + 04	**5.0E + 02**
	SCA	4.2E + 03	9.7E + 03	1.9E + 03	1.6E + 04	1.7E + 04	**4.5E + 02**	3.4E + 04	3.5E + 04	6.9E + 02
	BOA	5.0E + 03	7.2E + 03	1.5E + 03	1.3E + 04	1.7E + 04	9.0E + 02	3.4E + 04	3.6E + 04	5.9E + 02
F23	Ours	**2.8E + 03**	**2.9E + 03**	6.8E + 01	**3.1E + 03**	**3.3E + 03**	1.4E + 02	**3.8E + 03**	**4.1E + 03**	1.7E + 02
	WOA	2.9E + 03	3.2E + 03	1.2E + 02	3.4E + 03	3.8E + 03	1.9E + 02	4.9E + 03	5.3E + 03	2.6E + 02
	BWO	3.2E + 03	3.3E + 03	5.8E + 01	4.0E + 03	4.1E + 03	9.4E + 01	5.9E + 03	6.1E + 03	1.3E + 02
	SCA	3.0E + 03	3.1E + 03	**3.9E + 01**	3.5E + 03	3.7E + 03	**8.1E + 01**	5.1E + 03	5.3E + 03	**1.2E + 02**
	BOA	3.2E + 03	3.6E + 03	1.7E + 02	4.1E + 03	4.7E + 03	2.8E + 02	6.2E + 03	6.7E + 03	3.2E + 02
F24	Ours	**3.0E + 03**	**3.1E + 03**	8.3E + 01	**3.3E + 03**	**3.5E + 03**	1.4E + 02	**4.5E + 03**	**5.1E + 03**	**2.5E + 02**
	WOA	3.1E + 03	3.3E + 03	8.8E + 01	3.6E + 03	3.9E + 03	1.5E + 02	6.1E + 03	6.8E + 03	4.7E + 02
	BWO	3.4E + 03	3.6E + 03	1.0E + 02	4.1E + 03	4.5E + 03	1.5E + 02	8.7E + 03	9.3E + 03	4.3E + 02
	SCA	3.2E + 03	3.3E + 03	**3.7E + 01**	3.7E + 03	3.9E + 03	**7.1E + 01**	6.8E + 03	7.3E + 03	2.9E + 02
	BOA	3.5E + 03	4.1E + 03	2.9E + 02	4.9E + 03	5.5E + 03	3.3E + 02	9.7E + 03	1.3E + 04	1.3E + 03
F25	Ours	**2.9E + 03**	**2.9E + 03**	**2.1E + 01**	**3.1E + 03**	**3.2E + 03**	**3.1E + 01**	**3.6E + 03**	**3.8E + 03**	**8.7E + 01**
	WOA	3.1E + 03	3.2E + 03	7.7E + 01	4.3E + 03	5.4E + 03	6.9E + 02	9.5E + 03	1.1E + 04	1.0E + 03
	BWO	4.0E + 03	4.5E + 03	2.0E + 02	1.2E + 04	1.4E + 04	9.2E + 02	2.6E + 04	2.8E + 04	1.0E + 03
	SCA	3.3E + 03	3.6E + 03	2.2E + 02	6.7E + 03	9.0E + 03	1.3E + 03	1.8E + 04	2.2E + 04	2.0E + 03
	BOA	4.8E + 03	5.8E + 03	5.3E + 02	1.4E + 04	1.6E + 04	8.6E + 02	2.8E + 04	3.0E + 04	1.6E + 03
F26	Ours	**2.8E + 03**	**5.6E + 03**	1.8E + 03	**4.0E + 03**	**1.0E + 04**	2.2E + 03	**2.1E + 04**	**2.5E + 04**	2.1E + 03
	WOA	6.8E + 03	8.6E + 03	1.0E + 03	1.2E + 04	1.5E + 04	1.8E + 03	2.9E + 04	3.8E + 04	3.7E + 03
	BWO	9.2E + 03	1.1E + 04	**5.0E + 02**	1.6E + 04	1.7E + 04	**4.3E + 02**	4.8E + 04	5.1E + 04	**1.3E + 03**
	SCA	6.8E + 03	7.9E + 03	5.4E + 02	1.2E + 04	1.4E + 04	8.1E + 02	3.6E + 04	4.2E + 04	3.0E + 03
	BOA	1.0E + 04	1.2E + 04	8.3E + 02	1.7E + 04	1.8E + 04	7.0E + 02	5.3E + 04	5.8E + 04	2.2E + 03

Table 4. *Cont.*

Func	Alg	d = 30			d = 50			d = 100		
		Best	Ave	Std	Best	Ave	Std	Best	Ave	Std
F27	Ours	**3.2E + 03**	**3.3E + 03**	**2.9E + 01**	**3.6E + 03**	**3.9E + 03**	2.6E + 02	**3.8E + 03**	**4.3E + 03**	**3.2E + 02**
	WOA	3.3E + 03	3.5E + 03	1.4E + 02	4.0E + 03	4.9E + 03	6.6E + 02	5.0E + 03	6.5E + 03	1.0E + 03
	BWO	3.6E + 03	4.0E + 03	1.7E + 02	4.7E + 03	6.3E + 03	4.5E + 02	1.0E + 04	1.2E + 04	7.2E + 02
	SCA	3.4E + 03	3.6E + 03	6.9E + 01	4.6E + 03	5.0E + 03	**2.4E + 02**	7.6E + 03	8.7E + 03	6.7E + 02
	BOA	3.8E + 03	4.4E + 03	3.0E + 02	5.5E + 03	7.1E + 03	8.2E + 02	1.3E + 04	1.5E + 04	1.3E + 03
F28	Ours	**3.3E + 03**	**3.3E + 03**	**2.3E + 01**	**3.4E + 03**	**3.5E + 03**	**6.1E + 01**	**3.8E + 03**	**4.0E + 03**	**1.5E + 02**
	WOA	3.7E + 03	4.0E + 03	2.9E + 02	5.3E + 03	6.2E + 03	5.2E + 02	1.1E + 04	1.5E + 04	1.4E + 03
	BWO	5.7E + 03	6.5E + 03	3.8E + 02	1.2E + 04	1.2E + 04	4.9E + 02	2.6E + 04	2.8E + 04	8.4E + 02
	SCA	3.9E + 03	4.5E + 03	4.7E + 02	7.3E + 03	8.9E + 03	1.0E + 03	2.4E + 04	2.7E + 04	2.6E + 03
	BOA	6.9E + 03	8.1E + 03	5.1E + 02	1.3E + 04	1.5E + 04	8.1E + 02	3.4E + 04	3.7E + 04	1.8E + 03
F29	Ours	**3.6E + 03**	**4.2E + 03**	3.0E + 02	**4.4E + 03**	**5.2E + 03**	**5.2E + 03**	**7.3E + 03**	**8.9E + 03**	**7.5E + 02**
	WOA	4.3E + 03	5.4E + 03	5.8E + 02	7.2E + 03	9.4E + 03	9.4E + 03	1.4E + 04	2.0E + 04	2.7E + 03
	BWO	6.0E + 03	7.1E + 03	6.4E + 02	1.2E + 04	3.0E + 04	3.0E + 04	1.1E + 05	4.3E + 05	2.0E + 05
	SCA	4.6E + 03	5.2E + 03	**2.4E + 02**	6.6E + 03	9.2E + 03	9.2E + 03	1.9E + 04	3.2E + 04	8.0E + 03
	BOA	6.5E + 03	1.2E + 04	4.7E + 03	1.3E + 04	2.8E + 05	2.8E + 05	1.6E + 05	1.1E + 06	7.5E + 05
F30	Ours	**6.7E + 04**	**5.3E + 05**	**2.7E + 05**	**2.9E + 06**	**6.5E + 06**	**1.7E + 06**	**1.4E + 06**	**4.0E + 06**	**1.6E + 06**
	WOA	5.7E + 06	6.6E + 07	4.9E + 07	1.3E + 08	3.1E + 08	1.1E + 08	8.6E + 08	2.8E + 09	1.3E + 09
	BWO	2.8E + 08	1.1E + 09	4.7E + 08	3.4E + 09	5.2E + 09	9.0E + 08	3.2E + 10	4.1E + 10	2.8E + 09
	SCA	5.2E + 07	1.8E + 08	7.3E + 07	5.3E + 08	1.2E + 09	3.5E + 08	8.7E + 09	1.3E + 10	2.7E + 09
	BOA	2.9E + 08	1.4E + 09	1.1E + 09	2.2E + 09	7.8E + 09	2.9E + 09	2.5E + 10	4.0E + 10	6.5E + 09

The primary objective of the improved algorithm is to find the best solution as quickly as possible. As depicted in Figure 6, which showcases the average convergence curve derived from the function tests, the GLBWOA demonstrates superior global search capabilities relative to four other high-performance optimization algorithms. It exhibits an improved capacity to evade local optima and achieves swift convergence across all 30 optimization functions. These findings indicate that GLBWOA is not only proficient in rapidly identifying superior solutions but also excels in addressing complex, multi-constraint problems with increased efficiency.

Table 5. Results of the Wilcoxon rank sum test. Significant values are in bold.

Func	d = 30				d = 50				d = 100			
	BWO	SCA	BOA	WOA	BWO	SCA	COA	WOA	BWO	SCA	BOA	WOA
F1	3.0E − 11	3.0E − 11	3.0E − 11	3.0E − 11	3.0E − 11	3.0E − 11	3.0E − 11	3.0E − 11	3.0E − 11	3.0E − 11	3.0E − 11	3.0E − 11
F2	3.0E − 11	3.0E − 11	3.0E − 11	3.0E − 11	3.0E − 11	3.0E − 11	3.0E − 11	3.0E − 11	3.0E − 11	3.0E − 11	3.0E − 11	3.0E − 11
F3	8.5E − 09	2.7E − 09	9.3E − 09	3.0E − 11	4.5E − 11	8.2E − 11	9.9E − 11	4.1E − 11	3.9E − 02	7.7E − 08	2.3E − 01	3.0E − 11
F4	3.0E − 11	3.0E − 11	3.0E − 11	3.0E − 11	3.0E − 11	3.0E − 11	3.0E − 11	3.0E − 11	3.0E − 11	3.0E − 11	3.0E − 11	3.0E − 11
F5	3.0E − 11	1.3E − 10	3.0E − 11	3.7E − 11	3.0E − 11	3.0E − 11	3.0E − 11	3.0E − 11	3.0E − 11	3.0E − 11	3.0E − 11	3.0E − 11
F6	3.0E − 11	1.2E − 10	3.0E − 11	3.0E − 11	3.0E − 11	3.0E − 11	3.0E − 11	3.0E − 11	3.0E − 11	3.0E − 11	3.0E − 11	3.0E − 11
F7	3.0E − 11	5.5E − 06	3.0E − 11	7.1E − 09	3.0E − 11	4.1E − 11	3.0E − 11	3.0E − 11	3.5E − 10	6.1E − 11	1.2E − 10	2.2E − 09
F8	3.0E − 11	3.0E − 11	3.0E − 11	6.7E − 11	3.0E − 11	3.0E − 11	3.0E − 11	3.0E − 11	3.0E − 11	3.0E − 11	3.0E − 11	3.0E − 11
F9	3.0E − 11	2.7E − 09	3.0E − 11	1.5E − 10	3.0E − 11	3.0E − 11	3.0E − 11	3.0E − 11	3.0E − 11	3.0E − 11	3.0E − 11	3.0E − 11
F10	3.0E − 11	3.0E − 11	3.0E − 11	8.2E − 11	3.0E − 11	3.0E − 11	3.0E − 11	3.0E − 11	3.0E − 11	3.0E − 11	3.0E − 11	3.0E − 11
F11	3.0E − 11	3.0E − 11	3.0E − 11	3.0E − 11	3.0E − 11	3.0E − 11	3.0E − 11	3.0E − 11	3.0E − 11	3.0E − 11	3.0E − 11	3.0E − 11
F12	3.0E − 11	3.0E − 11	3.0E − 11	3.0E − 11	3.0E − 11	3.0E − 11	3.0E − 11	3.0E − 11	3.0E − 11	3.0E − 11	3.0E − 11	3.0E − 11
F13	3.0E − 11	3.0E − 11	3.0E − 11	3.0E − 11	3.0E − 11	3.0E − 11	3.0E − 11	3.0E − 11	3.0E − 11	3.0E − 11	3.0E − 11	3.0E − 11
F14	3.0E − 11	3.4E − 05	1.1E − 08	3.6E − 05	3.0E − 11	3.0E − 11	3.0E − 11	4.5E − 11	3.0E − 11	3.0E − 11	3.0E − 11	3.0E − 11
F15	3.0E − 11	3.0E − 11	3.0E − 11	3.0E − 11	3.0E − 11	3.0E − 11	3.0E − 11	3.0E − 11	3.0E − 11	3.0E − 11	3.0E − 11	3.0E − 11
F16	3.0E − 11	1.3E − 10	3.0E − 11	1.4E − 07	3.0E − 11	3.0E − 11	3.0E − 11	5.0E − 11	3.0E − 11	3.0E − 11	3.0E − 11	3.0E − 11
F17	3.0E − 11	7.1E − 08	3.0E − 11	5.6E − 05	3.0E − 11	4.1E − 11	3.0E − 11	1.3E − 10	3.0E − 11	3.0E − 11	3.0E − 11	3.0E − 11
F18	3.3E − 11	6.7E − 11	3.3E − 11	9.3E − 09	3.0E − 11	3.0E − 11	3.0E − 11	2.9E − 10	3.0E − 11	3.0E − 11	3.0E − 11	3.0E − 11
F19	3.0E − 11	3.0E − 11	3.0E − 11	3.0E − 11	3.0E − 11	3.0E − 11	3.0E − 11	3.0E − 11	3.0E − 11	3.0E − 11	3.0E − 11	3.0E − 11
F20	3.5E − 07	3.6E − 04	3.8E − 07	9.0E − 04	1.4E − 09	8.2E − 11	2.0E − 10	6.4E − 05	3.0E − 11	3.0E − 11	3.0E − 11	3.2E − 09
F21	3.0E − 11	6.1E − 11	6.1E − 11	5.6E − 10	3.0E − 11	3.7E − 11	3.0E − 11	3.7E − 11	3.0E − 11	3.0E − 11	3.0E − 11	3.0E − 11
F22	6.7E − 10	3.5E − 09	5.9E − 04	8.5E − 09	3.0E − 11	3.0E − 11	3.0E − 11	3.0E − 11	3.0E − 11	3.0E − 11	3.0E − 11	3.0E − 11
F23	3.0E − 11	2.9E − 10	3.0E − 11	3.5E − 10	3.0E − 11	5.0E − 11	3.0E − 11	2.9E − 10	3.0E − 11	3.0E − 11	3.0E − 11	3.0E − 11
F24	3.0E − 11	2.8E − 08	3.0E − 11	5.1E − 08	3.0E − 11	1.1E − 10	3.0E − 11	2.6E − 10	3.0E − 11	3.0E − 11	3.0E − 11	3.0E − 11
F25	3.0E − 11	3.0E − 11	3.0E − 11	3.0E − 11	3.0E − 11	3.0E − 11	3.0E − 11	3.0E − 11	3.0E − 11	3.0E − 11	3.0E − 11	3.0E − 11
F26	3.0E − 11	1.6E − 08	3.0E − 11	1.4E − 09	3.0E − 11	2.9E − 10	3.0E − 11	1.5E − 10	3.0E − 11	3.0E − 11	3.0E − 11	4.1E − 11
F27	3.0E − 11	3.0E − 11	3.0E − 11	6.7E − 11	3.0E − 11	3.3E − 11	3.0E − 11	1.4E − 09	3.0E − 11	3.0E − 11	3.0E − 11	3.7E − 11
F28	3.0E − 11	3.0E − 11	3.0E − 11	3.0E − 11	3.0E − 11	3.0E − 11	3.0E − 11	3.0E − 11	3.0E − 11	3.0E − 11	3.0E − 11	3.0E − 11
F29	3.0E − 11	4.1E − 11	3.0E − 11	2.9E − 10	3.0E − 11	3.0E − 11	3.0E − 11	3.0E − 11	3.0E − 11	3.0E − 11	3.0E − 11	3.0E − 11
F30	3.0E − 11	3.0E − 11	3.0E − 11	3.0E − 11	3.0E − 11	3.0E − 11	3.0E − 11	3.0E − 11	3.0E − 11	3.0E − 11	3.0E − 11	3.0E − 11
</=/>	**30/0/0**	**30/0/0**	**30/0/0**	**30/0/0**	**30/0/0**	**30/0/0**	**30/0/0**	**30/0/0**	**30/0/0**	**30/0/0**	**29/0/1**	**30/0/0**

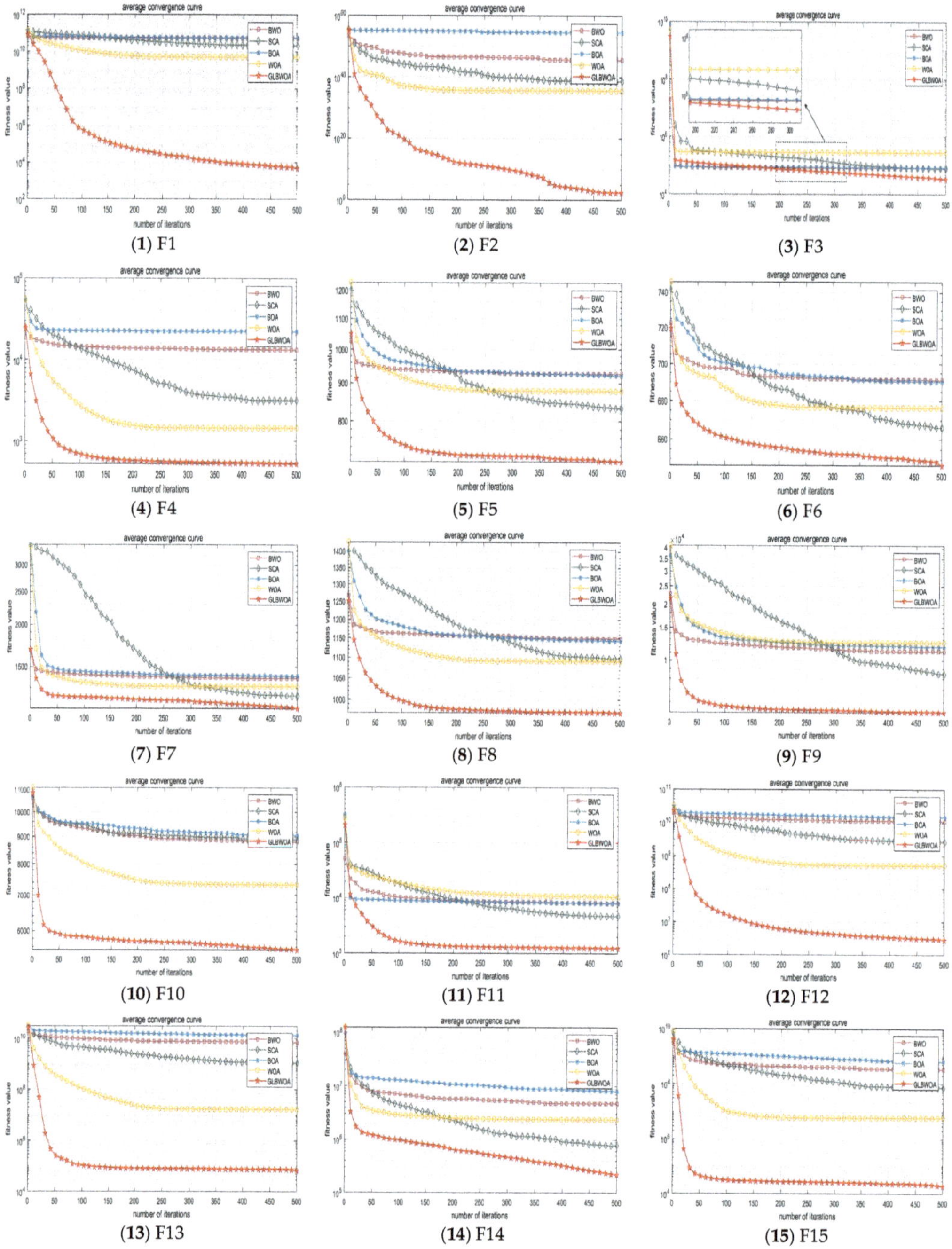

(1) F1 **(2)** F2 **(3)** F3
(4) F4 **(5)** F5 **(6)** F6
(7) F7 **(8)** F8 **(9)** F9
(10) F10 **(11)** F11 **(12)** F12
(13) F13 **(14)** F14 **(15)** F15

Figure 6. *Cont.*

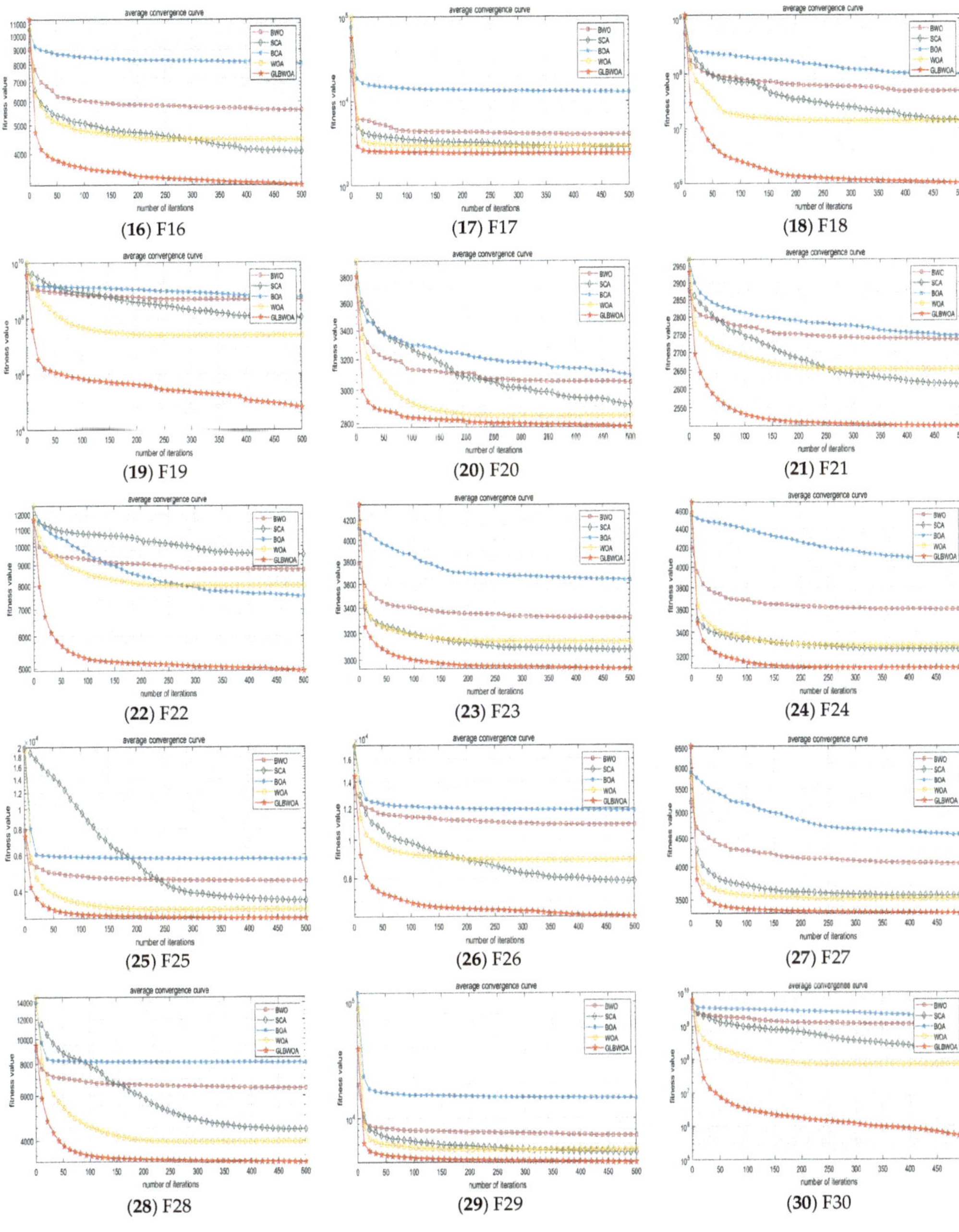

Figure 6. Average convergence curves of the algorithms.

In the analysis of convergence curves for thirty functions, the global best water wave optimization algorithm demonstrates superior convergence accuracy, particularly in the context of multi-modal functions. Specifically, in the case of function 3, while the initial fitness of GLBWOA is marginally higher than that of competing algorithms, it is observed that, as the number of iterations increases, the other four algorithms tend to converge prematurely, resulting in entrapment within local optima. In contrast, GLBWOA maintains its capacity for continuous exploration of optimal solutions, thereby achieving enhanced optimization outcomes in the later stages of iteration, attributable to its distinct optimization strategies.

The findings indicate that the GLBWOA demonstrates significant efficiency in identifying optimal solutions across both low- and high-dimensional spaces. In comparison to other high-performance algorithms, GLBWOA exhibits superior capabilities in escaping local optima and possesses enhanced local search abilities.

4.2. Path-Planning Simulation

The simulations were conducted in two environments with different terrain structures on Christmas Island, Australia, where Map 1 has an extent of 1045 × 879 × Z m and Map 2 has an extent of 450 × 450 × Z m. The scenarios were classified as simple and complex according to the number and position of threatening cylinders, while the waypoints are selected as $n = 10$. To make a fair comparison, all the algorithmic parameters were unified, the population size is set to 30, and the maximum number of iterations is set to 200. Due to the stochastic nature of the metaheuristic algorithms, each algorithm is repeated independently 30 times to better illustrate the performance of the algorithms and ensure the reliability of the results, the total cost $F_{cost}(Path_i)$ is used as the main performance index of path planning, and according to the realistic flight requirements, the weighting coefficients of each cost function are set to $w_1 = 10$, $w_2 = 100$, $w_3 = 10$, $w_4 = 50$. The constraint parameters of the simulations are shown in Table 6.

Table 6. Constraint parameter setting.

Parameter	Numerical Value
UAV size D/m	10
Dangerous distance S/m	$2 \times D$
Maximum height h_{max}/m	200
Minimum height h_{min}/m	100
Maximum steering angle $\psi_{max}/(^\circ)$	45
Maximum angle of climb $\theta_{max}/(^\circ)$	45

The obstacle parameters for scenario 1 are shown in Table 7. Assuming that the starting point of the path is (200, 100, 150) and the end point is set to (800, 800, 150), the optimal path between the two points is planned. As shown in Figure 7, the best effect of path planning in scenario 1 is demonstrated. From the top view in Figure 7a and the side view in Figure 7b, it can be seen that all the algorithms can generate feasible paths that satisfy the requirements of five constraints, namely, path length, obstacle threat, height limitation, climb angle, and steering angle, and in order to observe the paths avoiding obstacles in a more intuitive manner, we chose to hide the terrain structure for observation. As shown in Figure 7c, it can be seen that the generated path can effectively avoid collision, and the path is smoother, in line with the real flight needs.

Table 7. Scenario 1 Parameter Setting.

Number	Location Coordinates /m	Threat Radius R/m
1	(400, 500, 200)	50
2	(600, 200, 200)	40
3	(500, 350, 200)	50

According to the distribution of terrain peaks, terrain 1 complex environment obstacles are set as in Table 8, with the same start and end points as above. Figure 8 shows the path-planning effect in the complex scene of terrain 1 and, with the increase in obstacles, the complexity of path solving rises, and the difficulty of algorithms to solve the optimal path increases. It can be seen that all the algorithms generate paths that can guide the UAV to fly safely without collision, but different algorithms generate paths with large differences, among which BWO generates paths with more sharp turns, and the difficulty of actual flight is higher. BOA has the highest average total cost of planning and does not find the optimal path while, in comparison, the paths generated by SCA, WOA, and GLBWOA are more suitable for the actual flight of UAV, and GLBWOA has the fastest convergence speed among the three. The optimal path can be found in about 10 generations of iterations, and the average total cost is the lowest as in the case of WOA, reflecting the superiority of the algorithms proposed in this paper.

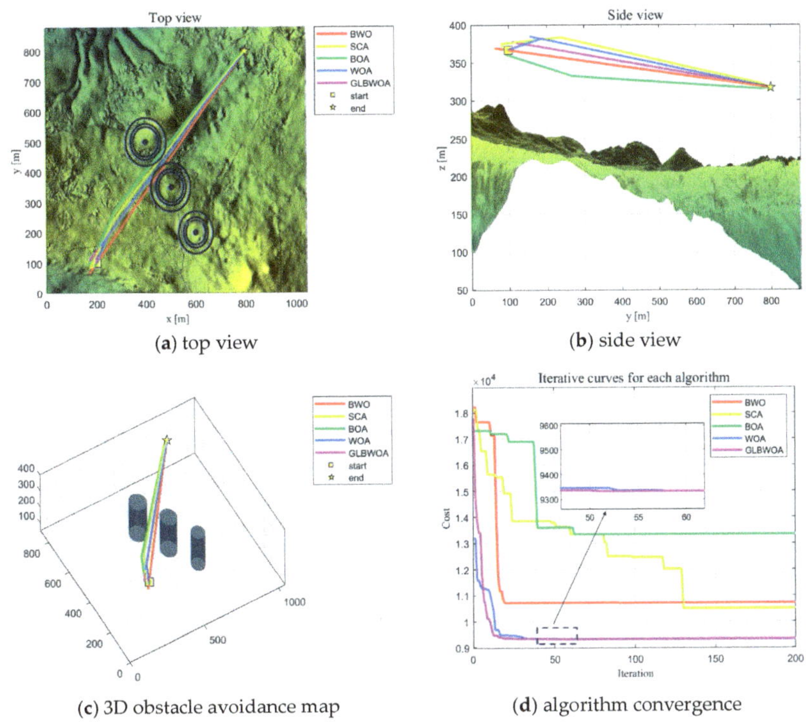

(**a**) top view (**b**) side view

(**c**) 3D obstacle avoidance map (**d**) algorithm convergence

Figure 7. Path Planning in Scenario 1 (n = 10).

Table 8. Scenario 2 Parameter Setting.

Number	Location Coordinates /m	Threat Radius R/m
1	(400, 600, 200)	50
2	(300, 350, 100)	40
3	(500, 430, 150)	35
4	(200, 180, 200)	40
5	(200, 550, 200)	40
6	(650, 750, 150)	50
7	(820, 400, 175)	30
8	(730, 560, 200)	50
9	(450, 210, 200)	30

The path-planning simulation is continued under terrain 2 to further test the ability of the algorithm proposed in this paper to plan paths, where the path starting point is set to (10, 10, 200) and the end point is set to (400, 400, 150). The simple scenario obstacles are set as in Table 9, and the solved paths are shown in Figure 9, and it can be observed in Figure 9a,b that the paths generated by the GLBWOA are smoother in terms of path changes and without abrupt changes, which is better than the remaining four algorithms.

From Figure 9c, it can be seen that BOA and BWO fall into the local optimum at the early stage of the algorithm, which ultimately leads to premature convergence and planning paths with higher total cost, while GLBWOA has better optimality searching performance by quickly escaping after falling into the local extremes and continuously searching for the globally optimal paths on an ongoing basis. From Figure 9d, it is evident that the algorithm introduced in this study can swiftly escape local optima encountered during the initial stages. In contrast, other algorithms tend to remain trapped in local optima for extended durations throughout their iterations. This suggests that incorporating the bubble network attack enhancement strategy significantly improves the ability to escape local optima. A closer examination of the average convergence curve during the early iterations of the GLBWOA reveals that the algorithm activates the variance mechanism shortly after becoming stuck in a local optimum, enabling it to quickly identify the global optimum. This indicates that implementing the failure parameter testing mechanism markedly enhances the algorithm's global search capabilities.

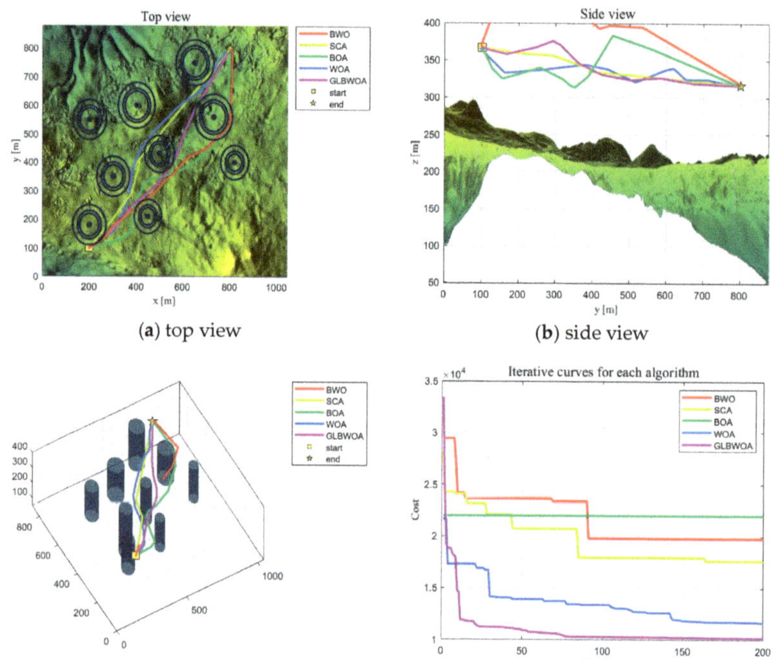

(**a**) top view (**b**) side view

(**c**) 3D obstacle avoidance map (**d**) algorithm convergence

Figure 8. Path Planning in Scenario 2 (n = 10).

Table 9. Scenario 3 Parameter Setting.

Number	Location Coordinates /*m*	Threat Radius *R*/*m*
1	(100, 300, 100)	30
2	(300, 300, 100)	20
3	(100, 50, 100)	30

In the terrain 2 complex obstacle scenario to solve the safe flight path, the start and end points are the same as above, the obstacle parameters are set as in Table 10, and the results are shown in Figure 10, which shows that the related algorithms all give their respective path-planning results and the planned paths avoid the peaks and threat sources in the environment. It can be observed that although the scheme given by GLBWOA sacrifices the path length cost to plan the paths, the planned paths effectively reduce the altitude changes and steering adjustments during the flight of the UAV and at the same time effectively avoid the obstacles, thus reducing the total cost, and the total cost is the lowest amongst the five algorithms. From Figure 10d, it can be seen that the BWO and WOA gradually begin to converge after around 30 generations of iterations, but GLBWOA is still searching for the globally optimal path, demonstrating that the algorithms have strong local exploration ability and global exploration performance, indicating that the introduction of the gradient kinetic energy strategy in the algorithms can escape from the local minima. The design of the update method effectively prevents the algorithm from missing the globally optimal solution.

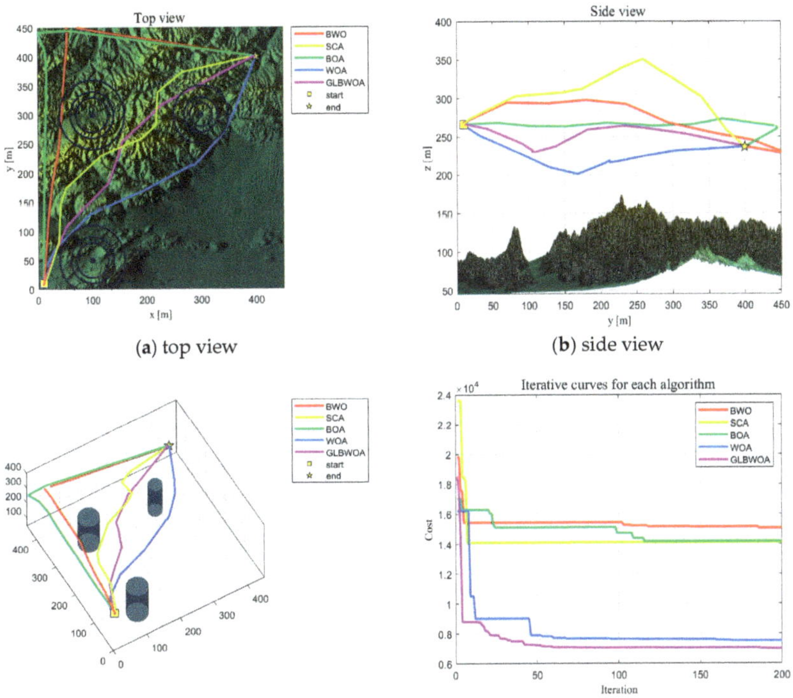

(**a**) top view (**b**) side view

(**c**) 3D obstacle avoidance map (**d**) algorithm convergence

Figure 9. Path Planning in Scenario 3 (n = 10).

Table 10. Scenario 4 Parameter Setting.

Number	Location Coordinates /*m*	Threat Radius *R*/*m*
1	(300, 300, 100)	30
2	(200, 100, 100)	20
3	(100, 200, 100)	30
4	(300, 100, 100)	20
5	(200, 50, 100)	20
6	(150, 350, 100)	30

The flight data for path planning for the four benchmark scenarios are presented in Table 11. GLBWOA, along with the other algorithms, successfully generated collision-free UAV flight paths, and GLBWOA excelled in the optimal flight cost and average flight cost metrics. The only exception is in the terrain 1 simple obstacle scenario, where the total flight cost of GLBWOA is the same as the standard WOA. However, in the other three benchmark scenarios, the total flight cost of GLBWOA is reduced by 19%, 10.6%, and 24.9%, respectively, compared to the standard WOA. In addition, the improvements in convergence speed, accuracy, and stability highlight the effectiveness of the proposed enhancement strategy. Meanwhile, Table 11 shows the average running time of each algorithm to determine the optimal path in 30 independent runs. It is clear that the GLBWOA has a slightly longer running time compared to the other algorithms but it is within an acceptable range. Although the extension of time is still within acceptable limits, it poses a limitation in application settings where the optimal path solution is required to be found in the shortest possible time. Therefore, our future research efforts will aim to reduce the running time of the algorithm while maintaining its performance level.

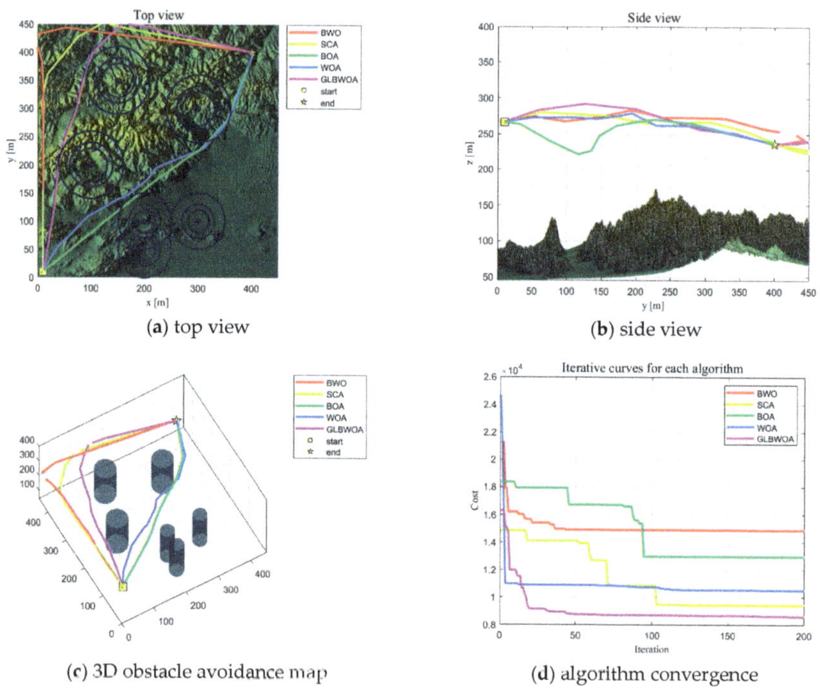

Figure 10. Path Planning in Scenario 4 (n = 10).

Table 11. Results of path-planning simulations. Significant values are in bold.

Alg	Scenario 1			Scenario 2			Scenario 3			Scenario 4		
	Best	Mean	Ave-Time	Best	Mean	Ave-Time	Best	Mean	Ave-Time	Best	Mean	Ave-Time
Ours	**9330.37**	**9350.6**	0.6597 s	**10,185.1**	**11,381.5**	1.3252 s	**6989.56**	**7211.2**	0.8263 s	**8637.54**	**8900.2**	1.3124 s
WOA	**9330.37**	9354.8	0.3390 s	12,644.5	12,774.6	**0.7153 s**	7817.26	8102.6	0.3634 s	11,514.3	11,902.6	**0.4532 s**
SCA	10,508.4	10,646.3	**0.3217 s**	17,588.3	18,363.2	0.7194 s	14,100.4	14,908.3	**0.3544 s**	9463.38	9779.6	0.5226 s
BWO	10,708.4	11,206.2	0.3696 s	19,799.7	19,828.3	0.7852 s	15,042.2	15,900.1	0.4290 s	14,921.2	15,112.3	0.6468 s
BOA	13,350.7	13,820.5	0.6195 s	21,975.4	22,131.8	1.1082 s	14,170.8	15,192.4	0.7109 s	12,984.4	13,155.7	0.8866 s

5. Conclusions

This study introduces a novel global–local balanced whale optimization algorithm designed to address the path-planning challenges faced by unmanned aerial vehicles in complex environments. A three-dimensional spatial model is constructed using digital elevation models, and a total cost function is formulated by integrating mission requirements with relevant constraints. To enhance the traditional whale optimization algorithm, a bubble net attack enhancement scheme is proposed to improve the algorithm's ability to escape local optima. This enhancement is achieved through a mutation operation governed by predefined conditions, recognizing that an individual's capacity to overcome its current position varies at different stages of the optimization process. Additionally, a failure parameter testing mutation mechanism is incorporated to accelerate the algorithm's convergence rate. In the later phases of optimization, a stochastic gradient-assisted search strategy is employed to reinforce the algorithm's global search capabilities. The optimization performance of GLBWOA is evaluated using the CEC2017 function test set, where it demonstrates superior performance compared to four other high-performance algorithms across all metrics, indicating that the proposed strategies effectively balance the global and local search capabilities of the algorithm. In four benchmark scenarios, GLBWOA consistently achieves a lower average total flight cost and exhibits more accurate and faster convergence under identical algorithmic parameters. Future research will further assess the algorithm's performance by considering the impact of dynamic obstacles, weather variations, and other complex conditions on the UAV path-planning problem. Additionally, efforts will be made to implement the algorithm in real UAVs to conduct path planning in real-world environments, thereby validating its practical effectiveness.

Author Contributions: Conceptualization, Q.W. and W.T.; methodology, Q.W. and W.T.; software, W.T.; validation, Q.W. and W.T.; formal analysis, W.T.; investigation, W.T.; resources, L.Z.; data curation, H.W.; writing—original draft preparation, W.T.; writing—review and editing, Q.W. and W.T.; visualization, W.T.; supervision, W.T.; project administration, L.J.; funding acquisition, Q.W. and R.Z. All authors have read and agreed to the published version of the manuscript.

Funding: This research was funded by the National Defense Science and Technology Innovation project, grant number ZZKY20223103; the Basic Frontier Innovation Project at the Engineering University of PAP, grant number WJY202429; the Basic Frontier Innovation Project at the Engineering University of PAP, grant number WJY202408; Key project of National Social Science Foundation, grant number 2023-SKJJ-A-116.

Data Availability Statement: The original contributions presented in the study are included in the article, further inquiries can be directed to the corresponding author.

Conflicts of Interest: The authors declare no conflicts of interest.

References

1. Elmeseiry, N.; Alshaer, N.; Ismail, T. A detailed survey and future directions of unmanned aerial vehicles (uavs) with potential applications. *Aerospace* **2021**, *8*, 363. [CrossRef]
2. Tsouros, D.C.; Bibi, S.; Sarigiannidis, P.G. A review on UAV-based applications for precision agriculture. *Information* **2019**, *10*, 349. [CrossRef]
3. Asadzadeh, S.; de Oliveira, W.J.; de Souza Filho, C.R. UAV-based remote sensing for the petroleum industry and environmental monitoring: State-of-the-art and perspectives. *J. Pet. Sci. Eng.* **2022**, *208*, 109633. [CrossRef]
4. Tang, P.; Li, J.; Sun, H. A Review of Electric UAV Visual Detection and Navigation Technologies for Emergency Rescue Missions. *Sustainability* **2024**, *16*, 2105. [CrossRef]
5. Du, P.; He, X.; Cao, H.; Garg, S.; Kaddoum, G.; Hassan, M.M. AI-based energy-efficient path planning of multiple logistics UAVs in intelligent transportation systems. *Comput. Commun.* **2023**, *207*, 46–55. [CrossRef]
6. Aggarwal, S.; Kumar, N. Path planning techniques for unmanned aerial vehicles: A review, solutions, and challenges. *Comput. Commun.* **2020**, *149*, 270–299. [CrossRef]
7. Zhao, Y.; Zheng, Z.; Liu, Y. Survey on computational-intelligence-based UAV path planning. *Knowl.-Based Syst.* **2018**, *158*, 54–64. [CrossRef]
8. Tisdale, J.; Kim, Z.; Hedrick, J.K. Autonomous UAV path planning and estimation. *IEEE Robot. Autom. Mag.* **2009**, *16*, 35–42. [CrossRef]
9. Zhang, Z.; Jiang, J.; Wu, J.; Zhu, X. Efficient and optimal penetration path planning for stealth unmanned aerial vehicle using minimal radar cross-section tactics and modified A-Star algorithm. *ISA Trans.* **2023**, *134*, 42–57. [CrossRef]
10. Zhen, R.; Gu, Q.; Shi, Z.; Suo, Y. An improved A-star ship path-planning algorithm considering current, water depth, and traffic separation rules. *J. Mar. Sci. Eng.* **2023**, *11*, 1439. [CrossRef]
11. Hao, K.; Yang, Y.; Li, Z.; Liu, Y.; Zhao, X. CERRT: A Mobile Robot Path Planning Algorithm Based on RRT in Complex Environments. *Appl. Sci.* **2023**, *13*, 9666. [CrossRef]
12. Xin, P.; Wang, X.; Liu, X.; Wang, Y.; Zhai, Z.; Ma, X. Improved bidirectional RRT* algorithm for robot path planning. *Sensors* **2023**, *23*, 1041. [CrossRef] [PubMed]
13. Zhao, W.; Li, L.; Wang, Y.; Zhan, H.; Fu, Y.; Song, Y. Research on A Global Path-Planning Algorithm for Unmanned Arial Vehicle Swarm in Three-Dimensional Space Based on Theta*–Artificial Potential Field Method. *Drones* **2024**, *8*, 125. [CrossRef]

14. Chen, Y.-B.; Luo, G.-C.; Mei, Y.-S.; Yu, J.-Q.; Su, X.-l. UAV path planning using artificial potential field method updated by optimal control theory. *Int. J. Syst. Sci.* **2016**, *47*, 1407–1420. [CrossRef]
15. Xue, J.; Shen, B. A novel swarm intelligence optimization approach: Sparrow search algorithm. *Syst. Sci. Control. Eng.* **2020**, *8*, 22–34. [CrossRef]
16. Yu, X.; Jiang, N.; Wang, X.; Li, M. A hybrid algorithm based on grey wolf optimizer and differential evolution for UAV path planning. *Expert Syst. Appl.* **2023**, *215*, 119327. [CrossRef]
17. Zhong, C.; Li, G.; Meng, Z. Beluga whale optimization: A novel nature-inspired metaheuristic algorithm. *Knowl.-Based Syst.* **2022**, *251*, 109215. [CrossRef]
18. Houssein, E.H.; Sayed, A. Dynamic candidate solution boosted beluga whale optimization algorithm for biomedical classification. *Mathematics* **2023**, *11*, 707. [CrossRef]
19. Mirjalili, S. SCA: A sine cosine algorithm for solving optimization problems. *Knowl.-Based Syst.* **2016**, *96*, 120–133. [CrossRef]
20. Arora, S.; Singh, S. Butterfly optimization algorithm: A novel approach for global optimization. *Soft Comput.* **2019**, *23*, 715–734. [CrossRef]
21. Arora, S.; Singh, S. An improved butterfly optimization algorithm with chaos. *J. Intell. Fuzzy Syst.* **2017**, *32*, 1079–1088. [CrossRef]
22. Mortazavi, A.; Moloodpoor, M. Enhanced butterfly optimization algorithm with a new fuzzy regulator strategy and virtual butterfly concept. *Knowl.-Based Syst.* **2021**, *228*, 107291. [CrossRef]
23. Mirjalili, S.; Lewis, A. The whale optimization algorithm. *Adv. Eng. Softw.* **2016**, *95*, 51–67. [CrossRef]
24. Jiang, R.; Yang, M.; Wang, S.; Chao, T. An improved whale optimization algorithm with armed force program and strategic adjustment. *Appl. Math. Model.* **2020**, *81*, 603–623. [CrossRef]
25. Huang, Y.; Li, Y.; Zhang, Z.; Sun, Q. A novel path planning approach for AUV based on improved whale optimization algorithm using segment learning and adaptive operator selection. *Ocean. Eng.* **2023**, *280*, 114591. [CrossRef]
26. Guo, W.; Liu, T.; Dai, F.; Xu, P. An improved whale optimization algorithm for forecasting water resources demand. *Appl. Soft Comput.* **2020**, *86*, 105925. [CrossRef]
27. Wang, C.-H.; Chen, S.; Zhao, Q.; Suo, Y. An efficient end-to-end obstacle avoidance path planning algorithm for intelligent vehicles based on improved whale optimization algorithm. *Mathematics* **2023**, *11*, 1800. [CrossRef]
28. Dai, Y.; Yu, J.; Zhang, C.; Zhan, B.; Zheng, X. A novel whale optimization algorithm of path planning strategy for mobile robots. *Appl. Intell.* **2023**, *53*, 10843–10857. [CrossRef]
29. Yin, S.; Yang, J.; Ma, L.; Fu, M.; Xu, K. An enhanced whale algorithm for three-dimensional path planning for meteorological detection of the unmanned aerial vehicle in complex environments. *IEEE Access* **2024**, *12*, 60039–60057. [CrossRef]
30. He, L.; Aouf, N.; Song, B. Explainable Deep Reinforcement Learning for UAV autonomous path planning. *Aerosp. Sci. Technol.* **2021**, *118*, 107052. [CrossRef]
31. de Castro, G.G.; Pinto, M.F.; Biundini, I.Z.; Melo, A.G.; Marcato, A.L.; Haddad, D.B. Dynamic path planning based on neural networks for aerial inspection. *J. Control. Autom. Electr. Syst.* **2023**, *34*, 85–105. [CrossRef]
32. Cui, Z.; Wang, Y. UAV path planning based on multi-layer reinforcement learning technique. *IEEE Access* **2021**, *9*, 59486–59497. [CrossRef]
33. Phung, M.D.; Ha, Q.P. Safety-enhanced UAV path planning with spherical vector-based particle swarm optimization. *Appl. Soft Comput.* **2021**, *107*, 107376. [CrossRef]
34. Liu, S.; Jin, Z.; Lin, H.; Lu, H. An improve crested porcupine algorithm for UAV delivery path planning in challenging environments. *Sci. Rep.* **2024**, *14*, 20445. [CrossRef] [PubMed]
35. Hou, J.; Van Dijk, A.I.; Renzullo, L.J. Merging Landsat and airborne LiDAR observations for continuous monitoring of floodplain water extent, depth and volume. *J. Hydrol.* **2022**, *609*, 127684. [CrossRef]
36. Cao, R.; Si, L.; Li, X.; Guang, Y.; Wang, C.; Tian, Y.; Pei, X.; Zhang, X. A conjugate gradient-assisted multi-objective evolutionary algorithm for fluence map optimization in radiotherapy treatment. *Complex Intell. Syst.* **2022**, *8*, 4051–4077. [CrossRef]
37. He, Y.; Wang, M. An improved chaos sparrow search algorithm for UAV path planning. *Sci. Rep.* **2024**, *14*, 366. [CrossRef]

electronics

MDPI

Article

Air Traffic Flow Prediction in Aviation Networks Using a Multi-Dimensional Spatiotemporal Framework

Cong Wu [1,2], Hui Ding [2], Zhongwang Fu [1] and Ning Sun [1,*]

1 Engineering Research Center of Wideband Wireless Communication Technology, Ministry of Education, Nanjing University of Posts and Telecommunications, Nanjing 210023, China; wucong@njupt.edu.cn (C.W.); b20010729@njupt.edu.cn (Z.F.)
2 State Key Laboratory of Air Traffic Management System, Nanjing 210014, China; dinghui@cetc.com.cn
* Correspondence: sunning@njupt.edu.cn

Abstract: A novel, multi-dimensional, spatiotemporal prediction framework is proposed to enhance air traffic flow prediction in increasingly complex aviation networks. This framework incorporates graph convolutional networks (GCNs) with multi-dimensional Long Short-Term Memory (LSTM) networks and multi-scale, temporal convolution, employing an attention mechanism to effectively capture spatiotemporal dependencies. By addressing irregular topologies and dynamic temporal trends, the framework models local air traffic patterns with improved accuracy. The experimental results demonstrate significant predictive accuracy improvements over traditional methods, particularly in accounting for the complex nature of air traffic flows. The model's scalability and adaptability extend its application to various aviation networks, encompassing all airspace units within three local networks, rather than focusing solely on airport traffic. These findings contribute to the development of more intelligent, accurate, and adaptive air traffic management systems, ultimately enhancing both operational efficiency and safety.

Keywords: air traffic flow prediction; spatiotemporal correlations; graph representation learning

1. Introduction

Air Traffic Flow Management (ATFM) is a crucial component for ensuring the efficient and safe operation of the global aviation system [1]. With the rapid expansion in air travel demand, the volume of flights continues to rise, leading to increased congestion in airspace, particularly around busy airports and along heavily trafficked routes [2]. The primary aim of ATFM is to optimize the allocation of airspace and airport resources to ensure that flights operate safely and efficiently, while minimizing delays and improving punctuality. Effective traffic flow management not only enhances the operational efficiency of the aviation network but also reduces airlines' operational costs and boosts passengers' satisfaction.

The operation of air traffic is dependent on the coordinated integration of routes, airspace, and traffic flow [3]. Routes are predefined paths that aircraft follow within the airspace, akin to highways in ground transportation, guiding them from departure to destination via specific waypoints. These routes create a structured network within the airspace, ensuring aircraft adhere to designated paths and avoid conflicts. The planning and adjustment of these routes are influenced by airspace capacity and the volume of air traffic. Airspace refers to the three-dimensional region in which aircraft operate, providing the spatial framework for routes. It is segmented and managed by national or regional aviation authorities, typically based on geographic location, altitude, and usage (e.g., commercial or military operations). Authorities adjust or restrict routes as necessary to ensure safe and efficient flight operations, preventing collisions and other safety incidents. Traffic flow pertains to the number of aircraft within a specific airspace or route section over a given time period [4]. The volume of traffic significantly impacts airspace congestion and management complexity. High traffic volumes lead to congestion, resulting in delays and an increased risk of mid-air conflicts. ATFM's central task is to optimize the traffic flow within the airspace by adjusting flight speeds and rescheduling departure and arrival times to ensure safe and efficient journeys.

Accurate traffic flow prediction is essential for effective ATFM, particularly as aviation networks become increasingly complex. By predicting air traffic volumes within specific airspaces, air traffic controllers can proactively identify potential congestion areas and develop strategies for optimizing routes and dynamically allocating resources to handle peak traffic periods and unexpected events. Improved prediction enhances air traffic control systems' intelligence, aiding route planning, airspace capacity distribution, and dynamic adjustments, thereby reducing delays, improving on-time performance, and enhancing economic returns and passenger satisfaction for airlines.

Artificial Intelligence (AI) is playing a key role in advancing air traffic flow prediction, addressing the increasing complexity of air traffic patterns and irregular airspace structures. AI enables aviation networks to manage the spatial and temporal dependencies of air traffic flow more effectively, allowing for more accurate and adaptive predictions. Traditional methods often struggle to capture the complex patterns of traffic in large, interconnected networks, but AI-based approaches can learn from vast data sources and adapt to dynamic conditions, offering intelligent traffic management solutions.

Recent research has explored novel methods and models to enhance air traffic flow prediction accuracy and efficiency. While traditional physical models [5,6] and shallow machine learning techniques such as Support Vector Regression (SVR) [7], neural networks (NN) [8–10], clustering algorithms [11], and boosting methods [12] have shown success in predicting traffic at individual airports or specific waypoints [13], these approaches often struggle to capture the complex spatiotemporal correlations associated with traffic fluctuations across broader aviation networks.

Central to AI's application in this field is the integration of advanced machine learning (ML) and deep learning (DL) techniques. In recent years, temporal dependencies have been modeled using Long Short-Term Memory (LSTM) networks, a class of recurrent neural networks (RNNs) designed to learn from and predict time series data. Studies have applied LSTM networks [14,15], RNNs [16], and causal graphs [17] to capture temporal dependencies in airspace traffic variations. However, predicting air traffic flow remains challenging due to periodic trends (e.g., normal versus peak flight periods, weekdays versus weekends) and random events. These models, while powerful, often face difficulties in managing multi-scale, temporal correlations within the same time series, limiting their ability to provide accurate predictions across varying temporal patterns.

To capture spatial correlations more effectively, some studies have proposed using gridded map methods to encode local air traffic flow conditions into novel two-dimensional [18] or three-dimensional [19] data representations. While this approach theoretically offers richer spatial information, the imposition of fixed-size, regular grid structures onto airspace can conflict with the operational logic of air traffic controllers [20], potentially increasing their workload and failing to reflect the irregularity of airspace structures.

Graph convolutional networks (GCNs) and related models have shown promise in modeling and analyzing traffic changes across the irregular topologies of multiple airspaces. Initial efforts [21,22] have employed GCN domain models to explore interactions between airspace nodes, revealing complex relationships. However, these studies have largely been limited to a small number of airspace nodes, making it challenging for the models to adaptively capture the complexities of non-Euclidean spatial structures in real-world aviation networks [23]. This limitation has hindered the broader application of these models in local aviation networks.

Despite the valuable insights provided by existing methodologies, there remains a need for advanced models that are capable of comprehensively addressing multi-scale, spatiotemporal correlations and irregular structures within the aviation network.

This study addresses existing gaps in air traffic flow prediction by proposing a novel, multi-dimensional, spatiotemporal prediction framework. The primary objectives are as follows:

1. To develop an integrated framework that combines GCNs with multi-dimensional, time-dependent modeling and multi-scale, temporal convolution, enhanced by an attention mechanism. This framework aims to capture complex spatiotemporal dependencies within air traffic networks, substantially improving predictive accuracy.
2. To incorporate advanced graph convolutional architectures that account for the irregular topologies that are characteristic of local aviation networks. This approach ensures accurate representation and the learning of the intricate spatial relationships among air traffic nodes.
3. To utilize the computational power of deep hybrid neural networks for modeling multi-scale, temporal dependencies, enabling the framework to predict air traffic flow with increased precision by capturing both specific periodic trends and short-term fluctuations.
4. To our knowledge, this is the first study to perform data collection and traffic flow prediction across all airspace units within three local aviation networks, rather than focusing solely on airport takeoff and landing traffic. This methodology is adaptable to other spatiotemporal data prediction tasks, such as weather prediction and pollution analysis.

By achieving these objectives, this study aims to enhance the accuracy, adaptability, and interpretability of air traffic flow predictions, thereby contributing to more optimized and intelligent air traffic management systems.

2. Materials and Methods

2.1. Multi-Dimensional, Spatiotemporal Prediction Framework

This paper proposes a multi-dimensional, spatiotemporal prediction framework that integrates spatial dependency modeling based on graph convolution, multi-dimensional time-dependent modeling, and multi-scale time domain convolution utilizing the attention mechanism, as demonstrated in Figure 1.

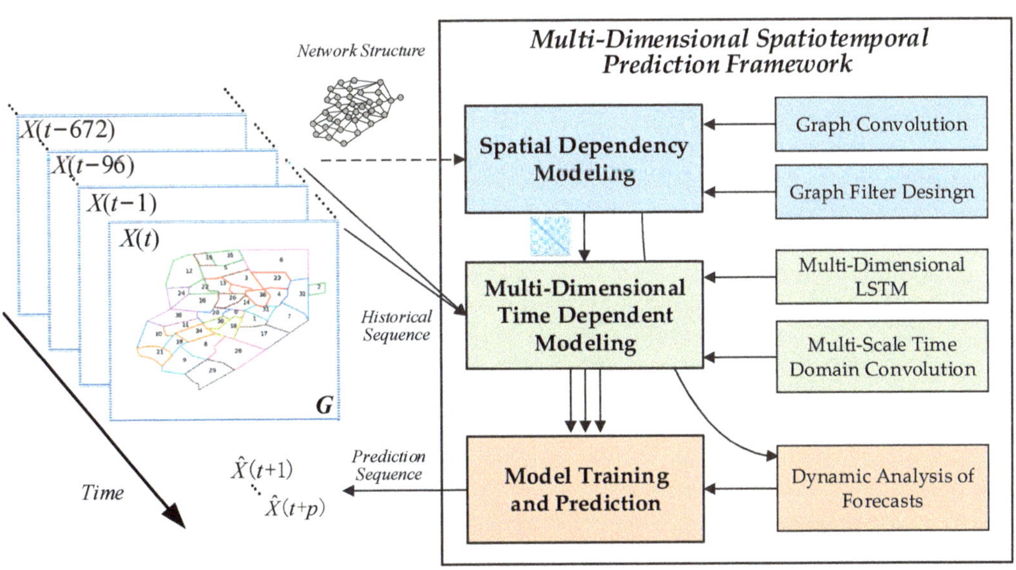

Figure 1. Architecture of multi-dimensional spatiotemporal prediction framework.

This technology aims to address the complex spatiotemporal correlations within air traffic flow networks. It incorporates airspace configuration and route coupling laws to extract the spatial characteristics inherent in the irregular topology observed in aviation networks. This is achieved through the construction of a graph convolutional network, facilitating a unified and structured characterization of local spatial relationships among nodes. In Figure 1, the number of each local aviation network node represents its ID.

To meet the practical requirements of intelligently predicting multi-dimensional, spatiotemporal states within aviation networks, this approach integrates the spatial and temporal dependencies of each node in the network dynamics. It extracts global components from real-time traffic flow data influenced by long-term spatial and temporal relationships while capturing local components that fluctuate with short-term specific events.

By leveraging the processing capabilities of graph convolutional networks and multi-dimensional recurrent neural networks, a deep hybrid neural network architecture is established. This network analyzes the multi-dimensional, spatiotemporal characteristics of air traffic flow from a hierarchical, multi-perspective standpoint. This enables the accurate prediction of future trends for each node within the aviation network and enhances the interpretability of the prediction methodology.

2.2. Spatial Dependency Modeling Based on Graph Convolution

This technique begins by constructing a topology graph G of the aviation network, based on the spatial structure of the aviation network and the coupling law of airway traffic flow. The vertices of the graph represent the airspace nodes, while the edges are used to describe the nearest neighbors and the distances between them. The relationship between the airspace nodes and the topology graph is represented by the normalized Laplace matrix L. This is defined in Equation (1), where D is the degree matrix of the graph G, and A is the adjacency matrix with the weighted adjacency matrix.

$$L = I_n - D^{-\frac{1}{2}} A D^{-\frac{1}{2}} \tag{1}$$

Given that the Laplace matrix L is a symmetric positive definite matrix, the eigenvalue decomposition yields $L = U\Lambda U^T$, where the matrix U is the matrix consisting of eigenvectors and the matrix Λ is the diagonal matrix consisting of eigenvalues. With reference to the Fourier transform of Euclidean space, the Fourier transform of the image is denoted as $\hat{x} = U^T x$, and the graph signal x is transformed into the corresponding spectral domain. In this domain, x represents the original feature of the entire graph composition. Consequently, the convolution of the graph signals x and y on the graph G is calculated as $*_G$, as shown in Equation (2).

$$x *_G y = U((UT\ x) \odot (UT\ y)) \tag{2}$$

The aforementioned calculations demonstrate that the current technique establishes graph features that describe local spatial relationships. From graph spectral theory, the convolution of the graph signal x (traffic flow data at a certain moment) is calculated on the graph G using the spectral filter g_θ, as shown in Equation (3).

$$g_\theta *_G x = g_\theta(L)x = g_\theta\left(U\Lambda U^T\right)x = U g_\theta(\Lambda) U^T x \tag{3}$$

To meet the requirements of the spatial relationship analysis, a graph convolution layer was proposed, based on the graph Fourier transform and the polynomial approximation. This extracts graph features embedded in the local spatial structure, as illustrated in Equation (4). In this equation, θ represents the polynomial coefficients, while K denotes the size of the local perceptual field of the graph filter. This field is defined as the set of nodes whose nearest neighbors are of an order less than K.

$$y = U\left(\sum_{k=0}^{K-1} \theta_k \Lambda^k\right) U^T x = \sum_{k=0}^{K-1} \theta_k L^k x \tag{4}$$

The objective of this technique is to characterize the spatial relationships of aviation networks through the application of a cluster analysis to the graphical features of local spatial relationships of aviation network nodes.

2.3. Multi-Dimensional, Time-Dependent Modeling

- Multi-Dimensional LSTM.

The state of aviation network traffic flow is influenced not only by recent specific events but also by strong, long-term cyclical patterns, such as daily and weekly cycles. This technique leverages the historical cyclical fluctuations in the aviation network state and the impact of random events by employing a temporal attention mechanism, as illustrated in Figure 2. The method combines the advantages of convolutional neural networks and recurrent neural networks in handling irregular spatiotemporal data to establish a dynamic spatiotemporal network based on deep hybrid neural networks. This network is designed to predict the operational state of each node in the aviation network under complex scenarios.

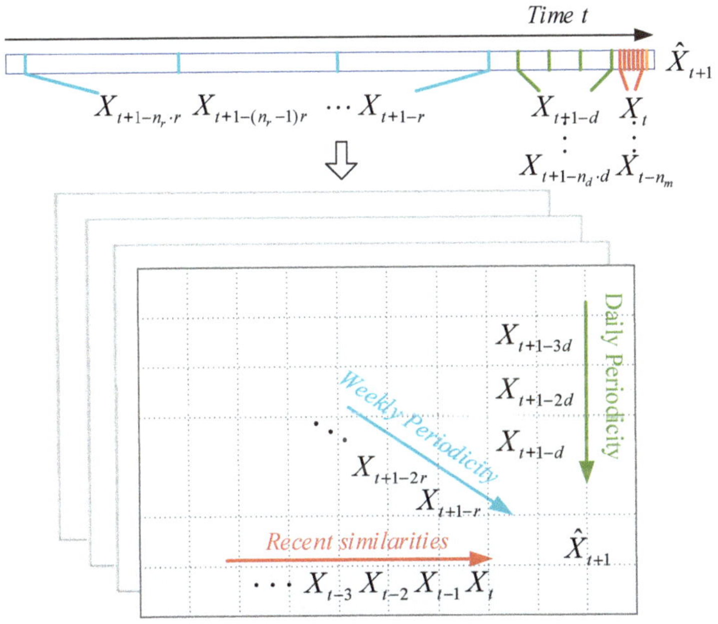

Figure 2. Schematic diagram of traffic flow timing concerns.

The implicit layer structure of the Long Short-Term Memory network unit is enhanced in order to construct the dynamic spatiotemporal network unit, as illustrated in Equation (5). This includes the input gate i, the forgetting gate f, the output gate o, and the memory unit c, which is used for storing and forgetting information. X represents the input data, $*_G$ represents the dynamic graph convolution operation, H represents the output of the unit, t represents the current moment, T represents the time interval, and j represents the time–attention selection parameter, which is used to select periods such as days, weeks, years, etc. W and b represent the corresponding control weights and deviations, while $\odot$ denotes the matrix dot product.

$$\begin{cases} i_t = \sigma\left(W_{xi} *_G X_t + W_{hi} \odot H_{t-1} + \sum_j W_{hi}^j \odot H_{t-jT} + b_i\right) \\ f_t = \sigma\left(W_{xf} *_G X_t + W_{hf} \odot H_{t-1} + \sum_j W_{hf}^j \odot H_{t-jT} + b_f\right) \\ c_t = f_t \odot c_{t-1} + i_t \odot tanh\left(W_{xc} *_G X_t + W_{hc} \odot H_{t-1} + \sum_j W_{hc}^j \odot H_{t-jT} + b_c\right) \\ o_t = \sigma\left(W_{xo} *_G X_t + W_{ho} \odot H_{t-1} + \sum_j W_{ho}^j \odot H_{t-jT} + b_o\right) \\ h_t = o_t \odot tanh(c_t) \end{cases} \tag{5}$$

This model proposes stacking multiple layers of dynamic spatiotemporal network units and utilizing the temporal attention mechanism to focus on historical cyclical information. This facilitates the automatic learning of the state fluctuation patterns of the aviation network and enables the accurate prediction of future trends. An objective function incorporating a regularization term was constructed to guide the training of the model.

- Multi-Scale Time Domain Convolution Based on the Attention Mechanism

The proposed technique converts the sequence of graphical features into one-dimensional lattice data that are formed by regular sampling on the time axis. This ensures that predictions made at previous moments do not leak future information, utilizing full convolution and causal convolution operations. The causal convolution of the filter f at moment t in the time series x is calculated as shown in Equation (6), where K is the filter size.

$$(f * x)(x_t) = \sum_{k=1}^{K} f(k) \cdot x_{t-K+k} \tag{6}$$

Causal convolution necessitates additional layers or larger filters to augment the receptive field, making it ineffective for processing extensive historical data. To address this limitation, the proposed approach employs dilation convolution to increase the receptive field of the convolution. For a one-dimensional input sequence, x, and a convolution kernel, $f : \{0, 1, \ldots, k-1\}$, the dilation convolution operation, F, is illustrated in Equation (7).

$$F(s) = (x *_d f)(s) = \sum_{i=0}^{k-1} f(i) \cdot x_{s-d \cdot i} \tag{7}$$

where d is the dilation factor, k is the convolution kernel size, and $s - d \cdot i$ denotes the position of adopting the previous layer of input data; the dilation factor controls the number of zeros to be inserted between each of the two inputs to achieve an increase in the length of the observed sequences, with essentially no change in the computational effort.

In traffic flow predicting, researchers have shown that traffic time series are influenced by key temporal characteristics in both recent and long-term historical data, such as daily cycles and weekdays versus weekends. However, canonical RNNs and existing models struggle with very long input sequences. For instance, peak hour traffic flows may be similar across consecutive weekdays, while weekday and holiday traffic patterns can differ significantly.

The value $Z^i(t)$ of the dilation causal convolution at the moment t of layer i is determined by the input value at the moment t of layer $i-1$ and the moments before that, as shown in Equation (8). Here, $Z(t)$ represents the time series data arranged in one dimension, and d, k, and f are the corresponding dilation rate, the size of the filter, and the parameters. In order to avoid information loss and information redundancy, the present technique sets $d_i = d_{i-1}k_{i-1}$ $(i > 1)$. According to the derivation, the receptive field (RF) of $Z^i(t)$ for the historical time series $Z(t)$ is calculated as shown in Equation (9).

$$Z^i(t) = \begin{cases} \sum_{j=0}^{k_{i-1}-1} f^{i-1}(j)\cdot Z^{i-1}(t - d_{i-1}\cdot j), & i > 1 \\ \sum_{j=0}^{k_0-1} f^0(j)\cdot Z(t-j), & i = 1 \end{cases} \tag{8}$$

$$RF(i) = d_{i-1}k_{i-1} = \prod_{j=0}^{i-1} k_j \tag{9}$$

2.4. *Dynamic Analysis of Prediction*

In the aforementioned process, the model learns static spatial dependencies. However, the occurrence of uncertainty events causes the spatial dependencies of the posture of some nodes in the aviation network to change over time. Consequently, the use of a fixed Laplace matrix is unable to capture such changes. In order to track the spatial dependencies of the nodes' posture changes under stochastic events, this technique introduces tensor decomposition into the deep learning framework. It was proposed that the global component $\mathcal{X}_Q$, which is determined by the structure of the whole network, and the local component $\mathcal{X}_S$, which is determined by a specific time period or event, should be extracted from the aviation network traffic data samples $\mathcal{X}$. This is shown in Equation (10), where $\mathcal{G}$ is the low-rank kernel tensor and $\times_i$ is denoted as the multiplication with each one-dimensional matrix U_i.

$$\mathcal{X} = \mathcal{G} \times_1 U_1 \times_2 U_2 \times \cdots \times_N U_N = \mathcal{X}_Q + \mathcal{X}_S \tag{10}$$

Combined with the event knowledge, this technique led us to propose a deep learning-based Laplace matrix estimator, which dynamically learns the Laplace matrix under the influence of a specific event based on the global and local components, i.e., the local Laplace matrix L_S. Through the above calculation, the spatiotemporal dependency of the aviation network under random events is represented by a new Laplace matrix, L, as shown in Equation (11), and the real-time estimated Laplace matrix is input to the graph convolution layer for feature extraction and prediction, where L_Q is the global Laplace matrix determined by the spatial structure of the aviation network, and F is the learned estimation function.

$$L = L_Q + L_S = L_Q + F(\mathcal{X}_Q, \mathcal{X}_S) \tag{11}$$

2.5. *Objective Function*

This technique employs a three-pronged approach to construct the objective function. Firstly, it incorporates regular terms to guide the model training. Secondly, it employs back propagation to guide the network parameter learning. Thirdly, it incorporates representation by minimizing the prediction error generated from the sample prediction results and the true values. Furthermore, it incorporates regular terms to constrain the model complexity and prevent the model from overfitting, as shown in Equation (12).

$$\min_{W,\Theta,\mathcal{F}} \sum_p \|X(t+p) - \hat{Z}(t+p)\|_2^2 + \alpha\|W\|_2^2 + \beta\|\Theta\|_2^2 + \gamma\|F\|_2^2 \tag{12}$$

where W, Θ, and F are network parameters, the latter three are L2 paradigm regularization terms, and α, β, and γ are the corresponding regularisation parameters used to balance the objectives of fitting the training and keeping the parameter values small.

3. Results

3.1. Datasets

- Spatial Structure of Three Local Aviation Networks

This study collected traffic flow data from three local aviation networks, referred to as Aviation Networks NS, NG, and NC, containing 36, 24, and 21 airspace units, respectively. The spatial relationships among the airspace units within these networks are depicted in Figures 3–5. Each polygon's center number corresponds to an airspace unit ID, with the horizontal and vertical axes representing latitude and longitude. As observed in Figures 3–5, the size of the airspace units is non-uniform, and their boundaries are irregular, significantly complicating spatial relationship modeling.

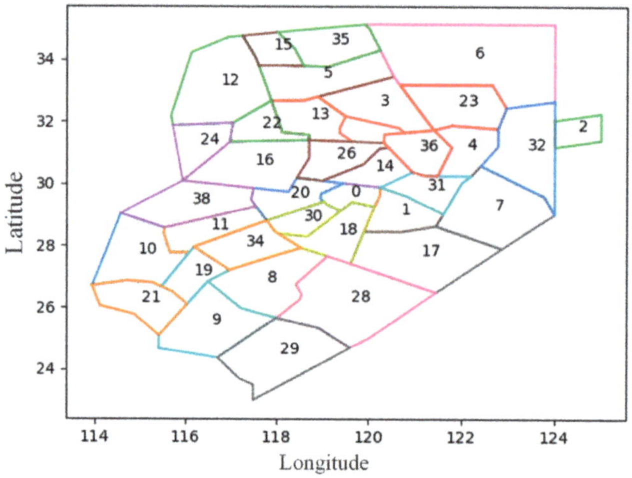

Figure 3. Spatial relationships between the airspace units of Aviation Network NS.

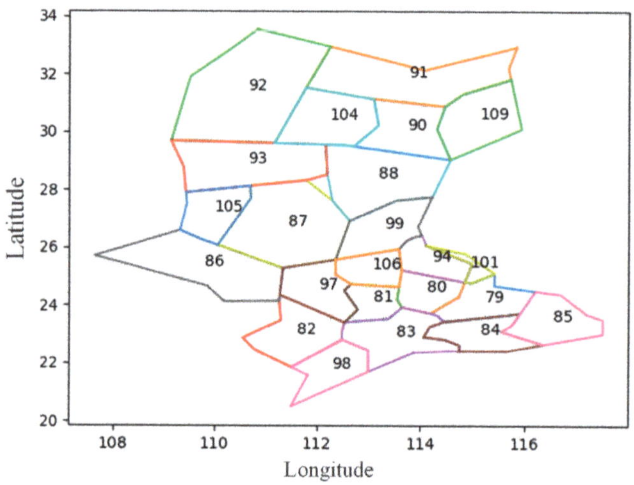

Figure 4. Spatial relationships between the airspace units of Aviation Network NG.

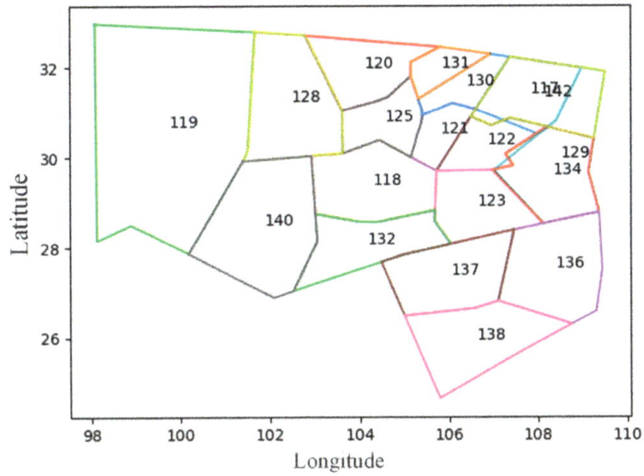

Figure 5. Spatial relationships between the airspace units of Aviation Network NC.

- Time Domain Characteristics of Traffic Flow in Each Airspace Unit

This study preprocesses ADS-B raw data for all aircraft within the aviation network, aggregating aircraft numbers within each airspace unit according to their real-time spatial location. Traffic data for each unit are aggregated every 15 min, spanning from 00:00 on 1 February 2021, to 19:00 on 18 May 2021, yielding 10,252 time intervals.

The daily traffic flow data (within 15 min) of typical airspace units of the three local aviation networks are presented in Figures 6–8. The traffic flow data for each airspace unit vary significantly, influenced not only by daily airspace traffic planning but also by other dynamic factors. Substantial differences are observed both between airspace units within the same aviation network and across different aviation networks.

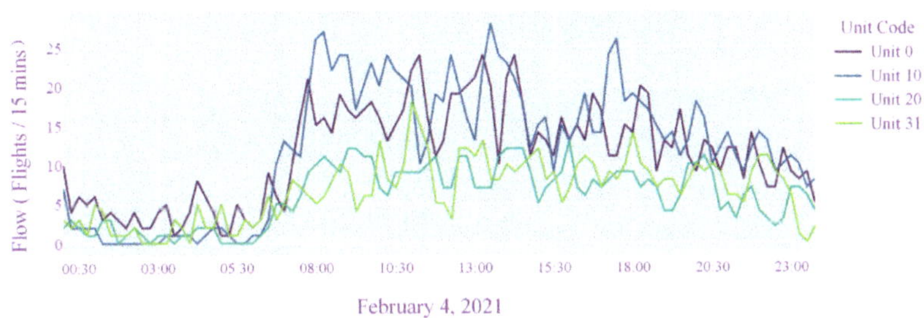

Figure 6. Daily traffic flow sequence of selected airspace units of Aviation Network NS.

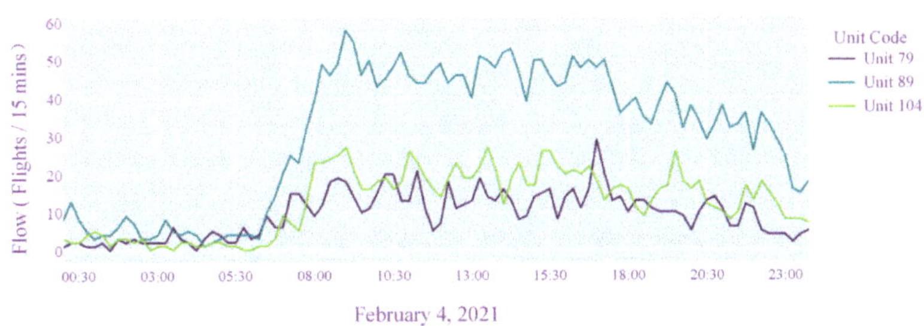

Figure 7. Daily traffic flow sequence of selected airspace units of Aviation Network NG.

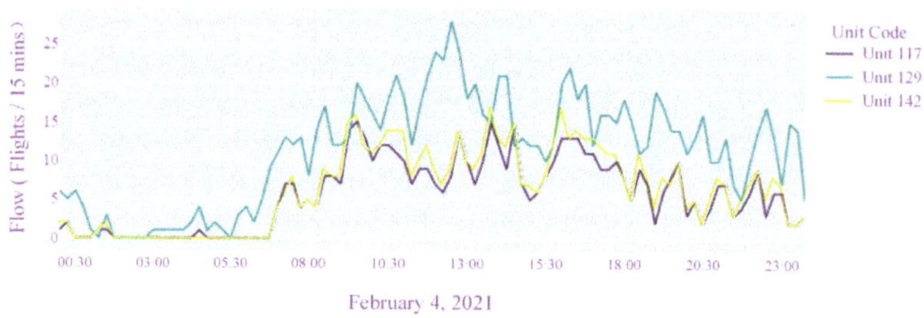

Figure 8. Daily traffic flow sequence of selected airspace units of Aviation Network NC.

Similarly, Figures 9–11 display the weekly traffic flow data (within 15 min) for typical airspace units. These figures highlight the presence of cyclical patterns in the weekly time series, albeit with a high degree of stochasticity.

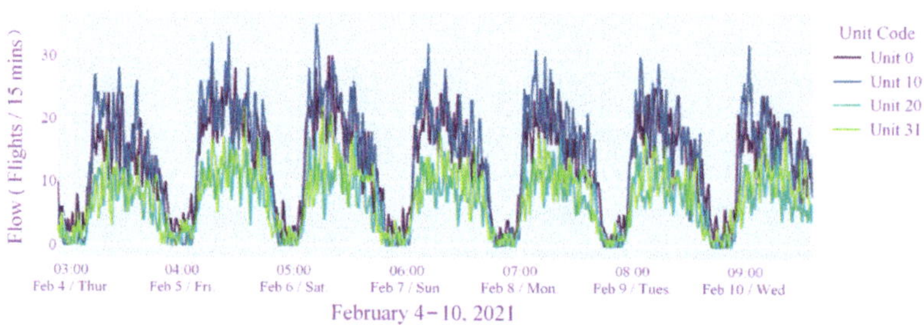

Figure 9. Weekly traffic flow sequence of selected airspace units of Aviation Network NS.

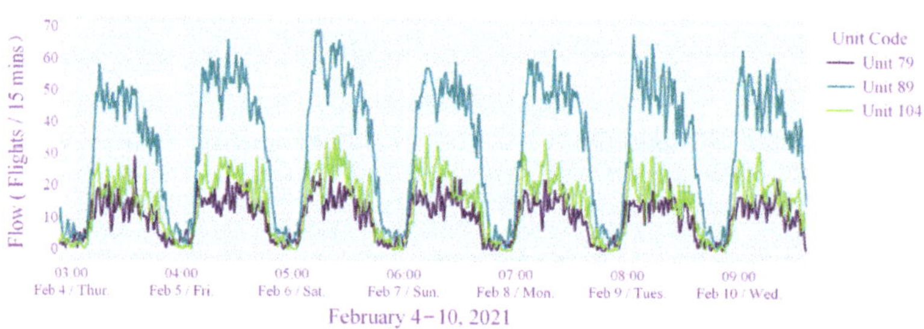

Figure 10. Weekly traffic flow sequence of selected airspace units of Aviation Network NG.

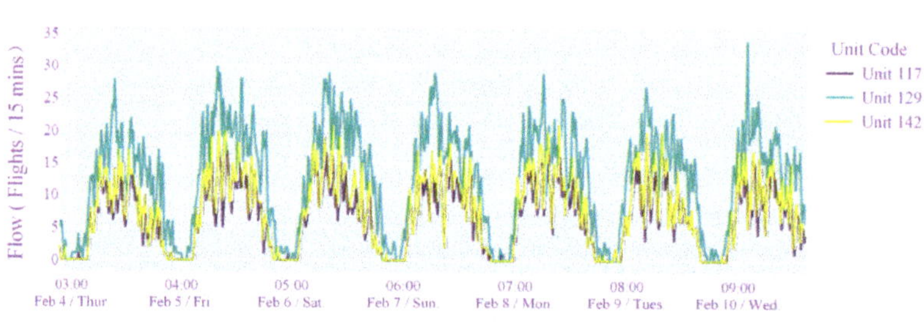

Figure 11. Weekly traffic flow sequence of selected airspace units of Aviation Network NC.

3.2. Evaluation Indicators

The following three metrics were employed in this paper to assess the predictive accuracy of the prediction model:

1. Root Mean Squared Error (*RMSE*).

$$RMSE = \sqrt{\frac{1}{MN}\sum_{j=1}^{M}\sum_{i=1}^{N}\left(y_i^j - \hat{y}_i^j\right)^2} \quad (13)$$

2. Mean Absolute Error (*MAE*).

$$MAE = \frac{1}{MN}\sum_{j=1}^{M}\sum_{i=1}^{N}\left|y_i^j - \hat{y}_i^j\right| \quad (14)$$

3. Weighted Mean Absolute Percentage Error (*WMAPE*).

$$WMAPE = \frac{\sum_{j=1}^{M}\sum_{i=1}^{N}\left|y_i^j - \hat{y}_i^j\right|}{\sum_{j=1}^{M}\sum_{i=1}^{N}\left|y_i^j\right|} \quad (15)$$

where y_i^j and $\hat{y}_i^j$ denote the real and predicted traffic flow information, respectively. M is the number of samples in the time series, and N is the number of airports. Three key indicators were used to evaluate prediction accuracy, with smaller values indicating higher accuracy.

To address instances where traffic flow data were minimal or zero, WMAPE was employed in place of the more commonly used Mean Absolute Percentage Error (MAPE) in these experimental evaluations. This choice is crucial for maintaining the accuracy and reliability of the performance metrics, particularly in datasets with significant variability in traffic volume, including periods of extremely low or zero traffic.

Although MAPE is widely utilized for error measurement, it has well-documented limitations when dealing with small denominators, often leading to inflated and misleading error values—particularly in scenarios with sparse traffic. This issue is of particular concern in air traffic flow prediction, where certain airspace units may experience low or zero traffic flow at specific times. Under such conditions, the standard MAPE can distort the overall error metrics, as it inadequately reflects the influence of these low traffic values.

In contrast, WMAPE offers a more stable and representative measure of prediction accuracy by adjusting for the relative magnitude of the data. By assigning weights to absolute errors based on the actual values of the data points, WMAPE mitigates the disproportionate influence of low or zero traffic values on the overall error calculation. Consequently, this approach provides a more balanced assessment of the model's performance across varying traffic conditions, from low-density traffic zones to high-volume airspace corridors.

3.3. Spatial Dependency Modeling

To model the spatial characteristics of the irregular topology in aviation networks, the spatial relationships between the airspace units of the three networks are represented using a graph structure as described in Section 2.2, shown in the left panels of Figures 12–14. Each node represents each airspace unit, and the line between two nodes represents whether there is a flight route connection. Each node's center number corresponds to an airspace unit ID. Importantly, spatial adjacency between airspace units does not necessarily imply a high correlation in traffic flow between them. For example, two adjacent airspaces may lack direct route connections.

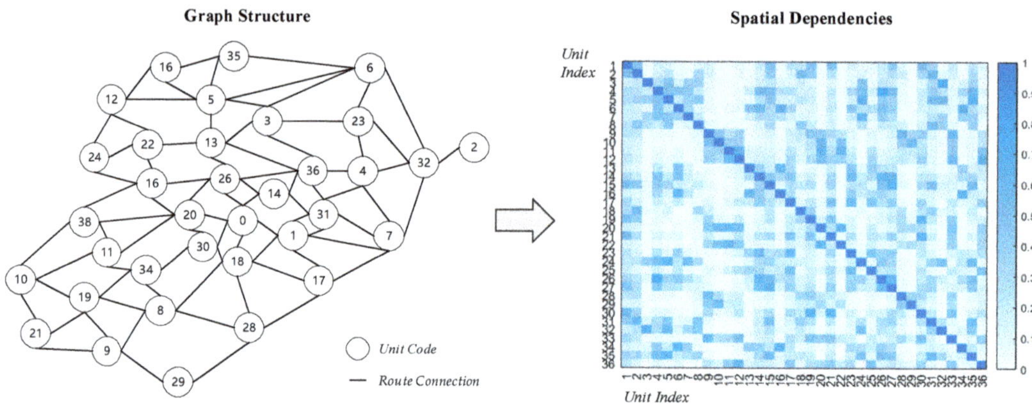

Figure 12. Airspace unit dependencies for Aviation Network NS.

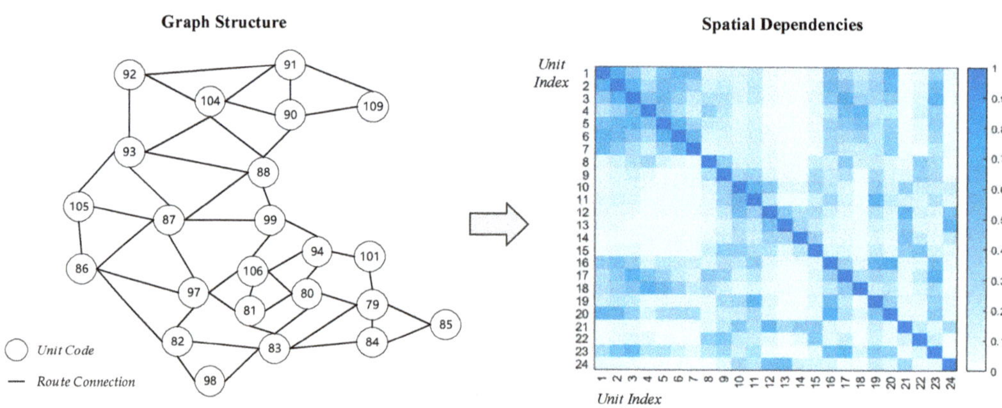

Figure 13. Airspace unit dependencies for Aviation Network NG.

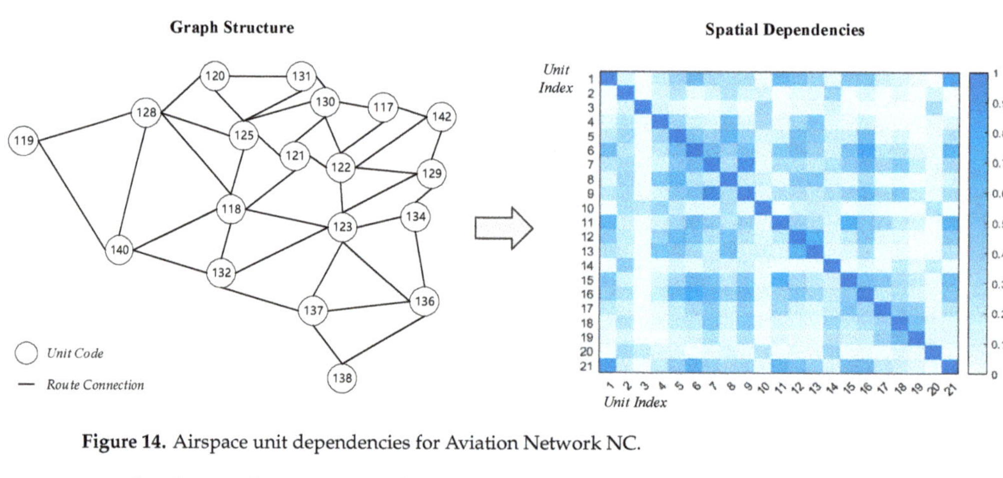

Figure 14. Airspace unit dependencies for Aviation Network NC.

Graph convolution was employed to model the spatial dependencies based on these topological relationships. The right panels of Figures 12–14 depict normalized spatial dependencies, where the axes represent airspace units, and each square indicates the dependency between two units. Darker colors represent stronger correlations.

3.4. Model Training

The dataset is divided into three sets, with a ratio of 7:1:2. The first 70% of the data serve as the training set, the middle 10% as the validation set, and the last 20% as the test set. The training processes for predicting the next 15 min, 1 h, and 3 h for Aviation Network NS are illustrated in Figures 15–17.

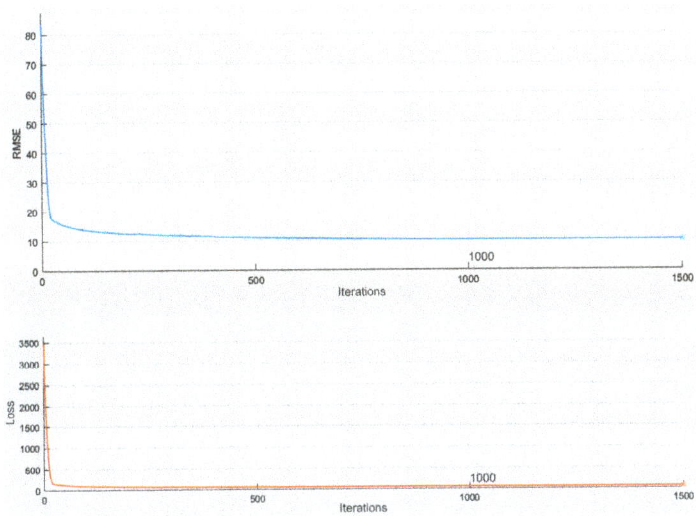

Figure 15. Aviation Network NS training process for predicting the next 15 min.

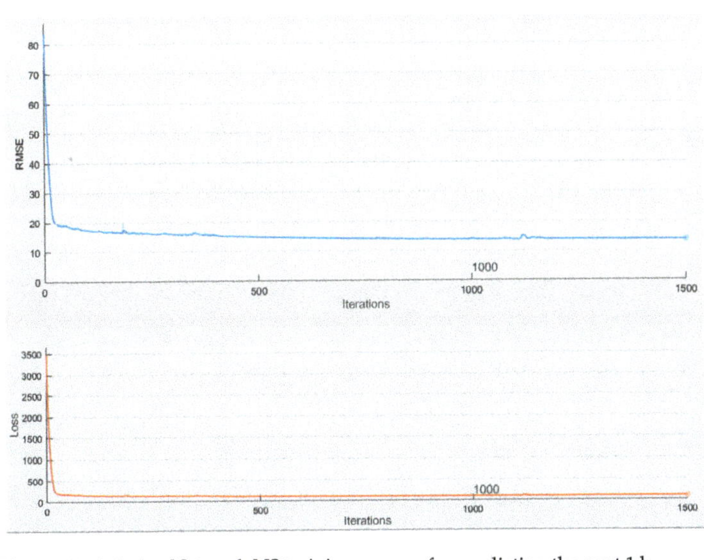

Figure 16. Aviation Network NS training process for predicting the next 1 h.

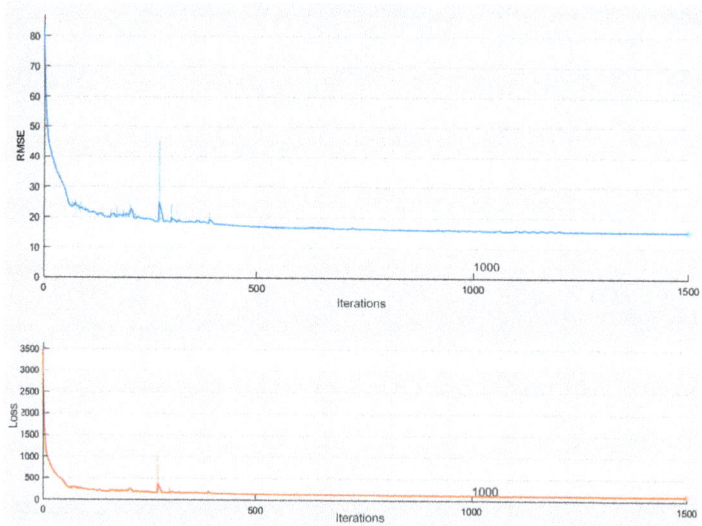

Figure 17. Aviation Network NS training process for predicting the next 3 h.

3.5. Comparative Analysis of Test Results

In this experiment, a multi-dimensional, spatiotemporal framework (MDSTF) model for network traffic prediction was constructed. Tables 1–3 present the results of predictions for the next 15 min, 1 h, and 3 h across the three aviation networks, comparing classical methods such as ARIMA, SVR, and BPNN. These methods are well-established and widely used across various domains due to their robustness and broad applicability, making them valuable benchmarks for this study. The results indicate that the proposed method demonstrates a significant advantage, especially in prediction accuracy, for the next 1 h (improved by approximately 1.6% to 4.9%) and for the next 3 h (improved by approximately 5.1% to 14.5%).

Table 1. Comparison of Aviation Network NS model prediction results.

Model	15 min			1 h			3 h		
	RMSE	MAE	WMAPE	RMSE	MAE	WMAPE	RMSE	MAE	WMAPE
ARIMA	2.92	3.87	19.66%	4.62	6.25	29.91%	7.19	9.85	43.13%
SVR	2.95	3.87	19.83%	4.53	6.13	29.86%	7.23	10.06	44.86%
BPNN	2.84	3.76	19.50%	4.14	5.58	27.65%	6.18	8.53	38.36%
MDSTF	**2.78**	**3.76**	**18.97%**	**3.87**	**5.35**	**25.92%**	**4.87**	**6.87**	**30.59%**

Table 2. Comparison of Aviation Network NG model prediction results.

Model	15 min			1 h			3 h		
	RMSE	MAE	WMAPE	RMSE	MAE	WMAPE	RMSE	MAE	WMAPE
ARIMA	3.34	4.49	18.99%	5.67	7.88	30.54%	9.14	13.07	45.74%
SVR	3.40	4.54	19.18%	5.54	7.67	30.15%	9.20	13.37	46.59%
BPNN	3.30	4.46	19.10%	4.99	6.95	27.77%	7.84	11.39	39.56%
MDSTF	**3.34**	**4.65**	**19.05%**	**4.88**	**6.80**	**26.15%**	**6.49**	**9.17**	**34.49%**

Table 3. Comparison of Aviation Network NC model prediction results.

Model	15 min			1 h			3 h		
	RMSE	MAE	WMAPE	RMSE	MAE	WMAPE	RMSE	MAE	WMAPE
ARIMA	2.90	3.94	20.26%	4.77	6.53	32.44%	7.14	9.93	44.48%
SVR	2.90	3.93	20.20%	4.65	6.42	32.46%	7.23	10.30	46.29%
BPNN	2.77	3.79	19.72%	4.13	5.81	29.45%	6.02	8.55	39.48%
MDSTF	**2.69**	**3.74**	**18.77%**	**3.85**	**5.43**	**27.55%**	**4.51**	**6.58**	**31.77%**

The analysis revealed that the traffic data values for numerous airspace units were insufficiently detailed, negatively impacting the prediction efficacy. This is demonstrated in Figures 18–20 and Table 4, which compare the relationship between the traffic flow of airspace units and the prediction accuracy. It was observed that when the average traffic flow of an airspace unit was greater than or equal to the median value of the corresponding aviation network, the prediction accuracy was relatively high. Specifically, for 15 min prediction, the accuracy exceeded the average by 2.2% to 3.1% and surpassed that of low-traffic prediction by 6.5% to 6.8%. For one-hour prediction, the accuracy was 1.9% to 3.2% higher than the average and 5.8% to 9.6% higher than that for low-flow airspace units.

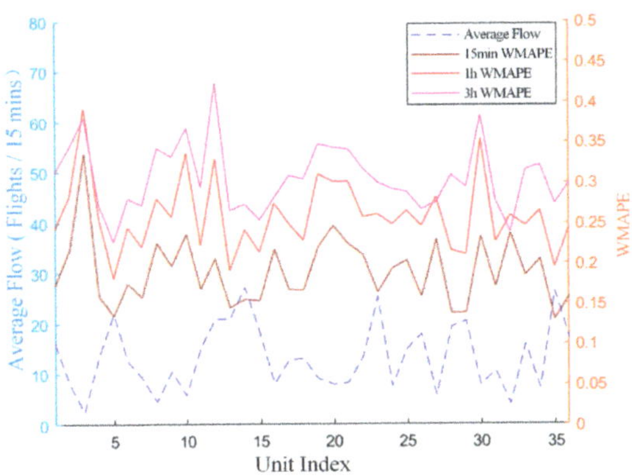

Figure 18. Comparison of average traffic and error in the airspace unit of the Aviation Network NS.

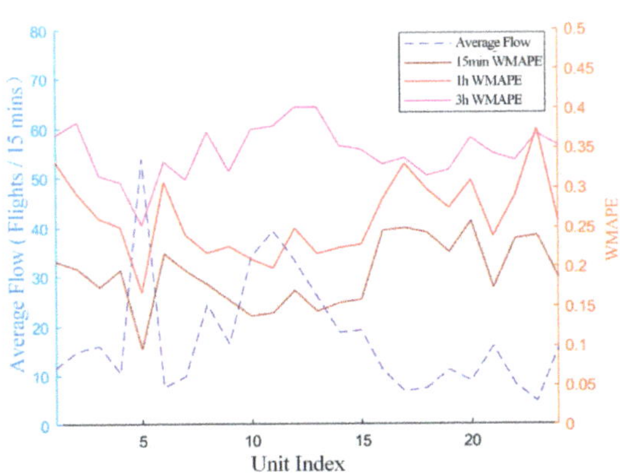

Figure 19. Comparison of average traffic and error in the airspace unit of the Aviation Network NG.

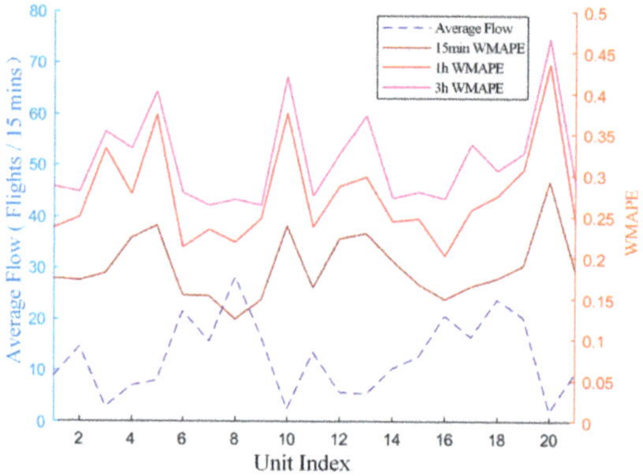

Figure 20. Comparison of average traffic and error in the airspace unit of the Aviation Network NC.

Table 4. Correlation analysis between airspace unit traffic flow and prediction error.

WMAPE (%)	15 min			1 h			3 h		
	$f \geq$ Median	$f <$ Median	Average	$f \geq$ Median	$f <$ Median	Average	$f \geq$ Median	$f <$ Median	Average
Network NS	16.79%	23.33%	18.97%	23.98%	29.80%	25.92%	29.60%	32.58%	30.59%
Network NG	15.91%	22.75%	19.05%	22.95%	29.93%	26.15%	35.33%	33.50%	34.49%
Network NC	16.53%	23.24%	18.77%	24.34%	33.98%	27.55%	28.56%	38.21%	31.77%

4. Discussion

The results of the proposed multi-dimensional, spatiotemporal prediction framework demonstrate substantial improvements over baseline models, highlighting the effectiveness of integrating GCNs, multi-dimensional LSTM networks, and attention mechanisms for air traffic flow prediction.

- Superior Predictive Performance.

The most notable outcome is the significant enhancement in prediction accuracy across all the evaluated metrics, particularly Mean Absolute Error (MAE), Root Mean Square Error (RMSE), and Weighted Mean Absolute Percentage Error (WMAPE). These improvements suggest that the proposed model is better equipped to capture the complexities of air traffic flow compared to traditional methods. Specifically, the incorporation of GCNs enables the model to capture the irregular, non-Euclidean spatial relationships between nodes in the aviation network—an area in which conventional Euclidean-based models often struggle.

Furthermore, the integration of multi-scale, temporal convolution enhances the model's capacity to capture temporal dependencies across varying scales, from short-term fluctuations to long-term trends. This is crucial for air traffic flow prediction, where interactions between different time scales (e.g., hourly, daily, weekly) can be highly complex.

- Scalability and Generalization.

The consistent performance of the proposed framework across diverse local aviation networks with varying characteristics highlights its scalability and generalization capabilities. Unlike models that require extensive design adjustments for specific datasets or environments, this framework demonstrates broad applicability across diverse network configurations, making it highly suitable for global air traffic management systems. Scalability is a critical feature, enabling deployment across a wide range of operational contexts, from smaller regional airspaces to large, complex international networks.

The robustness of the framework is further evidenced by its stable performance metrics across different network sizes and structures, indicating its ability to handle varying levels of complexity within aviation networks. This adaptability is a crucial advantage in real-world applications, where network structures can vary significantly across regions and countries.

5. Conclusions

In summary, the results of the proposed multi-dimensional, spatiotemporal prediction framework confirm its superiority over traditional models in predicting air traffic flow. By leveraging the strengths of GCNs, multi-dimensional LSTM networks, and attention mechanisms, the model is able to accurately capture the complex spatiotemporal dependencies that characterize air traffic networks.

5.1. Limitations

Despite the significant improvements achieved by the proposed multi-dimensional, spatiotemporal prediction framework, several limitations remain, highlighting potential areas for future research and enhancement.

- Handling Extreme Outlier Events.

While the model performs well across various scenarios, its ability to handle extreme outlier events, such as rare but impactful weather disruptions or large-scale airspace interference, is limited. These events often introduce abrupt, unpredictable changes in air traffic patterns that may not be fully captured by the current model's architecture. In particular, these outliers often lead to the formation of bottlenecks in the airspace, further complicating prediction efforts. The current model's ability to predict these bottlenecks, while functional, could be further improved to account for their often sporadic and complex nature.

- Computational Complexity.

The model's reliance on GCNs and LSTM networks introduces considerable computational demands, particularly in large-scale networks, which can hinder real-time applications. The high processing power and memory requirements pose challenges in environments where rapid inference is critical, such as in high-frequency air traffic control operations, where even minor delays in prediction could have operational consequences. This computational overhead also affects the model's ability to react quickly to emerging bottlenecks in the airspace.

- Data Availability and Quality.

The model's performance is highly dependent on the availability and quality of data. Inconsistent or sparse data across certain air traffic networks may result in reduced prediction accuracy. Furthermore, the model may struggle to generalize effectively in regions where historical data are either scarce or of low quality, due to missing records, sensor failures, or incomplete datasets. This limitation could restrict the model's applicability in less-developed regions with limited data infrastructures. Moreover, these data limitations make it challenging to accurately predict and address bottlenecks, particularly in regions with limited real-time monitoring capabilities.

5.2. Future Work

- Predicting Multiple Time Horizons.

Future research should explore the model's capacity for predicting air traffic flow over medium- and long-term horizons, contingent on the availability of such data. While some commercial companies offer these datasets, their high costs currently place them beyond the reach of this research. Medium-term predictions (weeks to months) and long-term predictions (months to years) are essential for strategic air traffic management, infrastructure planning, and policy development. Enhancing the model to incorporate broader seasonal trends, airport expansions, and shifting air traffic patterns will be key to developing more adaptive and future-oriented air traffic systems.

- Medium-Term Prediction: By incorporating techniques such as seasonal decomposition of time series (e.g., SARIMA models) alongside deep neural networks, the model can better capture medium-term periodicities in air traffic, such as fluctuations due to holidays, vacation seasons, or major events like the Olympics or trade conferences. Understanding these patterns can support more efficient scheduling, staffing, and resource allocation at airports.
- Long-Term Prediction: Long-term prediction can consider broader trends, such as global air travel demand shifts, fleet modernization, regulatory changes, and the rise of urban air mobility (e.g., drones or air taxis). Techniques such as multi-dimensional RNNs with extended time horizon capabilities, combined with macroeconomic and policy-based inputs, could be employed to predict long-term air traffic growth and flow changes, which are crucial for infrastructure investments and regulatory planning. This long-term prediction will also include an analysis of airspace bottlenecks caused by systemic issues such as increased air traffic demand and infrastructure constraints.
- Incorporating Anomaly Detection Mechanisms.

To address the limitations in handling extreme events, future work could integrate advanced anomaly detection algorithms into the prediction framework. These algorithms could identify and mitigate unusual events more effectively by flagging anomalous patterns before they propagate through the network. Unsupervised learning techniques, such as autoencoders or more sophisticated probabilistic models, could enhance the model's ability to detect and adjust for outlier events. Anomaly detection will also play a key role in the early identification of airspace bottlenecks, allowing for quicker interventions and more accurate traffic flow management.

- Model Optimization for Real-Time Applications.

Given the model's computational intensity, future research should focus on optimizing its architecture for faster inference times while maintaining accuracy. Techniques such as model pruning, which reduces the number of parameters, or knowledge distillation, which trains a smaller model to mimic the larger one, could make the framework more suitable for real-time air traffic management. These optimizations will improve the model's responsiveness, enabling it to predict and manage bottlenecks more effectively in real-time scenarios.

- Improved Data Fusion and Augmentation Techniques.

To overcome the limitations posed by inconsistent or sparse data, future work could focus on advanced data fusion and augmentation techniques. Incorporating external data sources such as weather prediction, satellite data, or even social media insights could provide additional context that improves the model's robustness. Synthetic data generation techniques, such as GANs (Generative Adversarial Networks), could also be employed to augment the training dataset in regions with limited historical data, thus enhancing the model's ability to generalize. These data enhancements will help refine bottleneck detection and prediction, particularly in regions with less-developed monitoring infrastructure.

Author Contributions: Methodology, C.W.; Formal analysis, Z.F.; Data curation, H.D.; Project administration, N.S. All authors have read and agreed to the published version of the manuscript.

Funding: This research was funded by the State Key Laboratory of Air Traffic Management System, China, grant number SKLATM202004.

Data Availability Statement: The original contributions presented in the study are included in the article, further inquiries can be directed to the corresponding author.

Conflicts of Interest: Author Hui Ding was employed by the State Key Laboratory of Air Traffic Management System, China. The remaining authors declare that the research was conducted in the absence of any commercial or financial relationships that could be construed as a potential conflict of interest.

References

1. Gui, G.; Zhou, Z.; Wang, J.; Liu, F.; Sun, J. Machine learning aided air traffic flow analysis based on aviation big data. *IEEE Trans. Veh. Technol.* **2020**, *69*, 4817–4826. [CrossRef]
2. Dalmau, R.; Genestier, B.; Anoraud, C.; Choroba, P.; Smith, D. A machine learning approach to predict the evolution of air traffic flow management delay. In Proceedings of the 14th USA/Europe Air Traffic Management Research and Development Seminar (ATM2021), New Orleans, LA, USA, 20–23 September 2021; Volume 8.
3. Ding, H.; Hu, M.; Xu, Q.; Tian, Y.; Yin, J. A Method to Optimize Routing Paths for City-Pair Airlines on Three-Layer Air Transport Networks. *Appl. Sci.* **2023**, *13*, 866. [CrossRef]
4. Isufaj, R.; Koca, T.; Piera, M.A. Spatiotemporal Graph Indicators for Air Traffic Complexity Analysis. *Aerospace* **2021**, *8*, 364. [CrossRef]
5. Chen, D.; Hu, M.; Ma, Y.; Yin, J. A network-based dynamic air traffic flow model for short-term en route traffic prediction. *J. Adv. Transp.* **2016**, *50*, 2174–2192. [CrossRef]
6. Chen, D.; Hu, M.; Zhang, H.; Yin, J.; Han, K. A network based dynamic air traffic flow model for en route airspace system traffic flow optimization. *Transp. Res. Part E Logist. Transp. Rev.* **2017**, *106*, 1–19. [CrossRef]
7. Yang, C.-H.; Lee, B.; Jou, P.-H.; Chung, Y.-F.; Lin, Y.-D. Analysis and Forecasting of International Airport Traffic Volume. *Mathematics* **2023**, *11*, 1483. [CrossRef]
8. Cheng, T.; Cui, D.; Cheng, P. Data mining for air traffic flow forecasting: A hybrid model of neural network and statistical analysis. In Proceedings of the 2003 IEEE International Conference on Intelligent Transportation Systems, Shanghai, China, 12–15 October 2003; IEEE: Piscataway, NJ, USA, 2003; Volume 1, pp. 211–215.
9. Qiu, F.; Li, Y. Air traffic flow of genetic algorithm to optimize wavelet neural network prediction. In Proceedings of the 2014 IEEE 5th International Conference on Software Engineering and Service Science, Beijing, China, 27–29 June 2014; IEEE: Piscataway, NJ, USA, 2014; pp. 1162–1165.
10. Zhang, Z.; Zhang, A.; Sun, C.; Xiang, S.; Guan, J.; Huang, X. Research on air traffic flow forecast based on ELM non-iterative algorithm. *Mob. Netw. Appl.* **2021**, *26*, 425–439. [CrossRef]
11. Murca, M.C.R.; Hansman, R.J. Identification, characterization, and prediction of traffic flow patterns in multi-airport systems. *IEEE Trans. Intell. Transp. Syst.* **2018**, *20*, 1683–1696. [CrossRef]
12. Hon, K. *Artificial Intelligence Prediction of Air Traffic Flow Rate at the Hong Kong International Airport*; IOP Conference Series: Earth and Environmental Science; IOP Publishing: Bristol, UK, 2021; Volume 865, p. 012051.
13. Tian, W.; Zhang, Y.; Zhang, Y.; Chen, H.; Liu, W. A Short-Term Traffic Flow Prediction Method for Airport Group Route Waypoints Based on the Spatiotemporal Features of Traffic Flow. *Aerospace* **2024**, *11*, 248. [CrossRef]
14. Zhou, R.; Qiu, S.; Li, M.; Meng, S.; Zhang, Q. Short-Term Air Traffic Flow Prediction Based on CEEMD-LSTM of Bayesian Optimization and Differential Processing. *Electronics* **2024**, *13*, 1896. [CrossRef]
15. Dursun, Ö.O. Air-traffic flow prediction with deep learning: A case study for Diyarbakır airport. *J. Aviat.* **2023**, *7*, 196–203. [CrossRef]
16. Yan, Z.; Yang, H.; Li, F.; Lin, Y. A Deep Learning Approach for Short-Term Airport Traffic Flow Prediction. *Aerospace* **2022**, *9*, 11. [CrossRef]
17. Du, W.; Chen, S.; Li, Z.; Cao, X.; Lv, Y. A spatial-temporal approach for multi-airport traffic flow prediction through causality graphs. In *IEEE Transactions on Intelligent Transportation Systems*; IEEE: Piscataway, NJ, USA, 2023.
18. Lin, Y.; Zhang, J.; Liu, H. Deep learning based short-term air traffic flow prediction considering temporal–spatial correlation. *Aerosp. Sci. Technol.* **2019**, *93*, 105113. [CrossRef]
19. Liu, H.; Lin, Y.; Chen, Z.; Guo, D.; Zhang, J.; Jing, H. Research on the air traffic flow prediction using a deep learning approach. *IEEE Access* **2019**, *7*, 148019–148030. [CrossRef]
20. Moreno, F.P.; Comendador, V.F.G.; Jurado, R.D.A.; Suárez, M.Z.; Janisch, D.; Valdés, R.M. Methodology of air traffic flow clustering and 3-D prediction of air traffic density in ATC sectors based on machine learning models. *Expert Syst. Appl.* **2023**, *223*, 119897. [CrossRef]
21. Zang, H.; Zhu, J.; Gao, Q. Deep learning architecture for flight flow spatiotemporal prediction in airport network. *Electronics* **2022**, *11*, 4058. [CrossRef]
22. Cai, K.; Shen, Z.; Luo, X.; Li, Y. Temporal attention aware dual-graph convolution network for air traffic flow prediction. *J. Air Transp. Manag.* **2023**, *106*, 102301. [CrossRef]
23. Shen, Z.; Cai, K.; Fang, Q.; Luo, X. Air Traffic Flow Prediction with Spatiotemporal Knowledge Distillation Network. *J. Adv. Transp.* **2024**, *2024*, 4349402. [CrossRef]

electronics

MDPI

Article

Full-Duplex Unmanned Aerial Vehicle Communications for Cellular Spectral Efficiency Enhancement Utilizing Device-to-Device Underlaying Structure

Yuetian Zhou [1,2] and Yang Li [2,*]

[1] Department of Mobile Communication and Terminal Technology, China Telecom Research Institute, Beijing 100033, China
[2] National Key Laboratory of Science and Technology on Communications, University of Electronic Science and Technology of China, Chengdu 611731, China
* Correspondence: ly1999@uestc.edu.cn

Abstract: Unmanned aerial vehicle (UAV) communications have gained recognition as a promising technology due to their unique characteristics of rapid deployment and flexible configuration. Meanwhile, device-to-device (D2D) and full-duplex (FD) technologies have emerged as promising methods for enhancing spectral efficiency and offloading traffic. One significant advantage of UAVs is their ability to partition suitable D2D pairs to increase cell capacity. In this paper, we present a novel network model in which UAVs are considered D2D pairs underlaying cellular networks, integrating FD into the communication links between UAVs to improve spectral efficiency. We then investigate a resource allocation problem for the proposed FD-UAV D2D underlaying structure model, with the objective of maximizing the system's sum rate. Specifically, the UAVs in our model operate in full-duplex mode as D2D users (DUs), allowing the reuse of both the uplink and downlink subcarrier resources of cellular users (CUs). This optimization challenge is formulated as a mixed-integer nonlinear programming problem, known for its NP-hard and intractable nature. To address this issue, we propose a heuristic algorithm (HA) that decomposes the problem into two steps: power allocation and user pairing. The optimal power allocation is solved as a nonlinear programming problem by searching among a finite set, while the user pairing problem is addressed using the Kuhn–Munkres algorithm. The numerical results indicate that our proposed FD-MaxSumCell-HA (full-duplex UAVs maximizing the cell sum rate with a heuristic algorithm) scheme for FD-UAV D2D underlaying models outperforms HD-UAV underlaying cellular networks, with improved access rates for UAVs in FD-MaxSumCell-HA compared to HD-UAV networks.

Keywords: UAV-aided networks; full duplex; D2D underlaying networks; Kuhn–Munkres algorithm; heuristic algorithm

1. Introduction

With the increase in mobile device usage and traffic, the spectrum has become increasingly limited. Given that device-to-device (D2D) communications can significantly enhance spectral efficiency by sharing spectrum resources with cellular users and effectively alleviate base station (BS) pressure through traffic offloading [1], it is considered a promising technique to address spectrum scarcity. Consequently, D2D communications in underlaying cellular networks have been widely investigated in recent years. Many important works have been focus on the resource allocation of D2D users (DUs) and cellular users (CUs) [2–8], which is mainly divided into three categories. The first category, like in Refs. [2–4], only allows DUs to reuse uplink subcarriers, which has a minimal affect on CUs. Ref. [3] considered a proportional fairness problem among users to guarantee the minimum individual user rate, and Ref. [4] aimed to improve energy efficiency while guaranteeing the required rate. The second category is downlink resource sharing for D2D [5,6].

In particular, Ref. [6] studied the balance of energy efficiency (EE) and spectral efficiency (SE) while DUs reuse the downlink subcarrier with CUs. The last category is joint uplink and downlink (JUAD) resource allocation [7,8]. Ref. [7] verified that the sum rate of JUAD is superior to that of the previous two, and Ref. [8] combined D2D communication with Non-Orthogonal Multiple Access technology to improve sum rate further. However, since D2D communication underlaying cellular networks needs to permit multiple DUs to share the same subcarrier with CUs, the mutual interference incurred by reusing the subcarrier will degrade the system capacity rather than improve it [9]. Thus, a more effective resource coordination scheme or other advanced technology needs to be developed to overcome this obstacle.

Unmanned aerial vehicle (UAV)-aided communications have been gaining more and more attention due to UAVs' unique characteristics, such as accessing LoS connections easily and flexible deployment. The increasingly sophisticated intelligent path planning [10] and resource management technologies [11] for UAVs make their deployment in actual networks feasible. Thus, it makes sense to integrate D2D technology into UAV-aided networks. D2D is expected to play an important role by leveraging UAVs' benefits [12–16], especially from the point of view of resource allocation, sum rate maximization, and coverage expansion. In Ref. [13], a UAV serves as a base station to maximize the sum rate for one device in D2D pairs, and a D2D link is used to extend coverage. Ref. [14] adds more constraints to maximize the sum rate, such as the power, altitude, location, and bandwidth of the UAV, but it only considers one D2D pair in which each device coexists in an underlaying manner. Refs. [14,15] focus on network energy harvesting aided by UAVs. Specifically, [15] considers a security system which aims to maximize secrecy energy efficiency, and ref. [14] tries to find an optimal transmit power vector which maximizes the sum rate of the system under minimum energy constraints. However, in the above maximization design, all communication links have unidirectional transmission, which may not meet the maximum capacity requirements of the 6G era of traffic explosion.

Due to the advances in self-interference (SI) cancellation techniques , full-duplex communications can be applied to cellular networks to potentially double the SE. The critical issue in full-duplex (FD) communications is their capability of canceling SI. In recent years, the SI cancellation techniques of analog, digital and antenna domains have been jointly applied to cancel SI by up to -125 dB [17–19], which makes FD a possible candidate 6G technology. Due to the same advantage as the two technologies above, combining D2D and FD is a effective way to further improve SE. Ref. [20] studied D2D underlaying cellular networks with FD BS to maximize the cell's rate; however, the system capacity gains were still significantly affected by strong residual SI (RSI). Certainly, in addition to the capability for self-interference cancellation, the level of RSI was affected by the transmit power of FD devices. In particular, lower transmit power results in decreased RSI. Since device-to-device (D2D) communication involves short-distance links and typically operates at low transmit power, integrating FD technology into D2D communications is a logical choice.

In the research domain of FD-D2D underlaying cellular networks, various scenarios have been explored. References [21,22] address a basic scenario involving a single FD-D2D pair and a single CU. Notably, ref. [21] presents a closed-form approximation for the sum rate. The research expands into multi-user scenarios in [23–25]. In [23], both perfect and statistical Channel State Information (CSI) estimations are analyzed, leading to the development of a heuristic algorithm that maximizes the sum rate for cellular uplink sharing. This algorithm employs 2D global searching and the Kuhn–Munkres algorithm. According to the numerical results in [24], FD-D2D underlay systems achieve significantly higher capacity gains than traditional half-duplex D2D (HD-D2D) systems, provided there is sufficient SI cancellation. Furthermore, ref. [25] presents centralized and distributed power control strategies aimed at maximizing the throughput of D2D links. Additional promising methods for integrating FD-D2D include FD-D2D underlaying cellular networks with base station MIMO antennas, as discussed in [26,27]. However, previous studies have primarily focused on uplink spectrum sharing, which can result in resource wastage in extreme scenarios.

Different from previous works, leveraging the technical characteristics of UAVs, D2D, and FD, we propose the FD-MaxSumCell-HA (full-duplex UAVs maximizing the cell sum rate with a heuristic algorithm) scheme for a novel model of FD-UAV-aided networks based on D2D underlaying networks to maximize the entire cell's sum rate, considering both uplink and downlink spectrum sharing. Specifically, the main contributions of this paper are summarized as follows:

1. We address the optimization problem of maximizing the sum rate within a novel system model where UAVs, considered as D2D pairs, operate in FD mode, enabling the joint reuse of both uplink and downlink subcarrier resources of CUs. To tackle this challenge, we propose a heuristic algorithm consisting of two key steps: optimal power allocation for each potential DU-CU pair and the development of a maximum weighted matching algorithm. In the power allocation step, we simplify computational complexity through one-dimensional searching, thereby mitigating the overall complexity of the proposed scheme.
2. We employ two metrics, specifically the sum rate of the cell and the access rate of D2D pairs, to evaluate the performance of the FD-MaxSumCell-HA scheme. Additionally, we introduce the FD-MaxSumCell-Rand (FD-D2D system maximizing the sum rate of the cell with random pairing) and HD-MaxSumCell-HA (HD-D2D system maximizing the sum rate of the cell with a heuristic algorithm) schemes as ideal benchmarks to evaluate the superiority of FD-MaxSumCell-HA.
3. This paper examines three scenarios in a parameter study for FD-MaxSumCell-HA: In the first scenario, only uplink users are present in the cell, utilizing uplink sharing. The second scenario involves exclusively downlink users in the cell, employing downlink sharing. In the third scenario, which closely resembles real mobile network conditions, both uplink and downlink users coexist in the cell, and JUAD sharing is implemented.

The rest of the paper is organized as follows. Section 2 will introduce the system model and formulate the optimization problem for FD-MaxSumCell-HA, and the heuristic algorithm of the proposed scheme is presented in Section 3. The parameter studies and numerical results are presented in Section 4. Finally, we will present our conclusions in Section 5.

2. System Model and Formulation

2.1. System Model

Figure 1 shows a cell of UAV-aided networks based on the structure of D2D underlaying networks. The UAVs are considered DUs, and the base station (BS) is positioned at the center of the cell, whereas the DUs and CUs are distributed randomly within the cell. There are three categories of resource allocation in Figure 1. The first is that the DU operates in FD mode and reuses the subcarrier with the CU like the DU1-CU5 pair and DU2-CU3 pair, where the DU1-CU5 pair reuses the uplink resource while the DU2-CU3 pair shares downlink. The second one is a traditional scenario where, like the DU3-CU4 pair, the DU reuses the resource with the CU in half-duplex (HD) mode. The last one is an unpaired CU, which uses resource alone like CU1 and CU2. Since FD-D2D can nearly the double spectral efficiency of the DU, in this paper, we consider a system that only includes FD-UAV and the CU, and assume that the CU operates in a traditional half-duplex FDD. It is worth mentioning that the UAV in this networks model is a mooring UAV, because the better load capacity of mooring UAVs enables them to load FD communication equipment, which is not achieved by non-mooring UAVs. In addition, mooring UAVs can provide wired backhaul to the local server, which is more suitable for the capacity of FD technology.

We use DUi and CUj to represent the UAV and CU distributed in the cell, respectively, and $i \in DU = \{1, 2, \ldots, Q\}$ and $j \in CU = \{1, 2, \ldots, P\}$. The two different UAVs in the D2D pair are noted as i_1 and i_2, respectively. Moreover, we assume that the entire carrier resource is occupied by CUs and pre-allocated equally among them. To avoid more sever interference and a complex coordinate scheme, we only consider a "one to one" scenario, where each subcarrier can be reused by only one DU, and each DU is limited to reusing a single subcarrier.

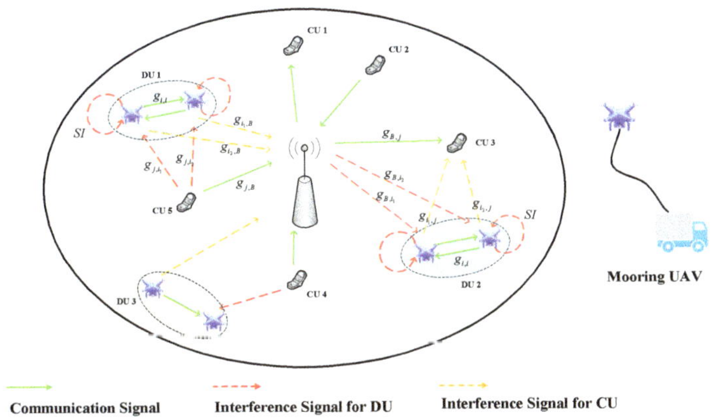

Figure 1. The cell model involves different kinds of user, such as an FD-D2D user, a traditional D2D user, and an unpaired CU.

The channels considered in this paper are those that experience path loss, slow shadowing, and fast fading. The channel gain between CUj and BS, denoted as $g_{j,B}$, for instance, is modeled as

$$g_{j,B} = G\beta_{j,B}\Gamma_{j,B}l_{j,B}^{-\alpha} \tag{1}$$

where $\beta_{j,B}$ represents the gain from fast fading, which follows an exponential distribution; $\Gamma j, B$ denotes the gain from slow fading, characterized by a log-normal distribution; G is the path loss constant; α is the path loss exponent; and lj, B is the distance between CUj and the BS. Similarly, the gains of the other channels shown in Figure 1 are denoted as $g_{B,j}$, $g_{i_1,B}$, $g_{i_2,B}$, g_{B,i_1}, g_{B,i_2}, g_{j,i_1}, g_{j,i_2}, $g_{i_1,j}$, $g_{i_2,j}$, and $g_{i,i}$. In particular, the reversible links between two devices in a D2D pair are transmitted at the same frequency and same time; thus, the gains of the two directions are all denoted as $g_{i,i}$. It is common knowledge that imperfect Channel State Information (CSI) can degrade system performance. However, as the imperfect CSI did not alter the performance order in the comparison of the proposed scheme, we assume, for convenience, that the BS possesses perfect CSI for all the involved links. The definitions of the channel-related parameters are summarized in Table 1. In practice, typical G2A channel models, including probabilistic LoS/NLoS models and 3GPP-suggested specifications, usually consider blockage distribution to determine LoS or NLoS conditions [10]. However, to quickly validate the network structure proposed in this paper, we made a trade-off between mathematical complexity and accuracy, so our adopted path loss model does not consider this aspect.

Table 1. Definitions of channel-related parameters.

Notation	Definition
$g_{B,j}$, $g_{i_1,B}$, $g_{i_2,B}$, g_{B,i_1}, g_{B,i_2}, g_{j,i_1}, g_{j,i_2}, $g_{i_1,j}$, $g_{i_2,j}$	The channel gain between the base station, CU, and DU. The subscript B represents the base station, j represents the CU, and i_1 and i_2 represent the DU.
β	The exponential distribution coefficient of fast fading.
Γ	The log-normal distribution coefficient of slow fading.
G	The constant coefficient of path loss.
α	The exponent coefficient of path loss.
l	The distance between the CU, DU, and BS.

To pair DUi and CUj, the binary variable $\rho_{i,j}$ is defined as a paired factor. If DUi reuses the same subcarrier (whether using the uplink or downlink) with CUj, then $\rho_{i,j} = 1$; otherwise, $\rho_{i,j} = 0$, $\rho^u_{i,j}$ is for uplink, while $\rho^d_{i,j}$ is for downlink. As shown in Figure 1, the interference scenario in FD-D2D systems is more complex than in traditional systems because of the residual SI of FD. We categorize the problem into two distinct cases: reusing the uplink and downlink of the CU. In the case of reusing the uplink, the SINR of CUj and the SINR of DUi can be expressed as

$$\gamma^u_j = \frac{p_j g_{j,B}}{\sum\limits_{i=1}^{Q} \rho^u_{i,j} p_i (g_{i_1,B} + g_{i_2,B}) + N_0} \tag{2}$$

$$\gamma^u_{i_1} = \frac{p_i g_{i,i}}{\sum\limits_{j=1}^{P} \rho^u_{i,j} (p_j g_{j,i_1} + p_i \cdot \eta) + N_0} \tag{3}$$

$$\gamma^u_{i_2} = \frac{p_i g_{i,i}}{\sum\limits_{j=1}^{P} \rho^u_{i,j} (p_j g_{j,i_2} + p_i \cdot \eta) + N_0} \tag{4}$$

where p_j and p_i denote the transmit power of CUj and DUi, respectively; η denotes the capability of self-interference suppression (SIS); and N_0 is the variance of zero mean Additive White Gaussian Noise. As for the case of reusing the downlink, the SINR of CUj and DUi can be, respectively, given by

$$\gamma^d_j = \frac{p_{B,j} g_{B,j}}{\sum\limits_{i=1}^{Q} \rho^d_{i,j} p_i (g_{i_1,j} + g_{i_2,j}) + N_0} \tag{5}$$

$$\gamma^d_{i_1} = \frac{p_i g_{i,i}}{\sum\limits_{j=1}^{P} \rho^d_{i,j} (p_{B,j} g_{B,i_1} + p_i \cdot \eta) + N_0} \tag{6}$$

$$\gamma^d_{i_2} = \frac{p_i g_{i,i}}{\sum\limits_{j=1}^{P} \rho^d_{i,j} (p_{B,j} g_{B,i_2} + p_i \cdot \eta) + N_0} \tag{7}$$

where $P_{B,j}$ stands for the power transmitted from the base station to CUj.

Hence, we can express the achievable rates for the uplink and downlink of CUj and its corresponding DUi as follows:

$$R^u_j = \log_2(1 + \gamma^u_j) \tag{8}$$

$$R^d_j = \log_2(1 + \gamma^d_j) \tag{9}$$

$$R^u_{i_1} = \log_2(1 + \gamma^u_{i_1}), \quad R^u_{i_2} = \log_2(1 + \gamma^u_{i_2}) \tag{10}$$

$$R^d_{i_1} = \log_2(1 + \gamma^d_{i_1}), \quad R^d_{i_2} = \log_2(1 + \gamma^d_{i_2}) \tag{11}$$

And the sum rate of the overall cell is

$$R_{\text{sum}} = \sum_{j=1}^{P} R^u_j + \sum_{j=1}^{P} R^d_j + \sum_{i=1}^{Q} R^u_i + \sum_{i=1}^{Q} R^d_i \tag{12}$$

where R^u_i is the sum of $R^u_{i_1}$ and $R^u_{i_2}$, and R^d_i is the sum of $R^d_{i_1}$ and $R^d_{i_2}$.

2.2. Problem Formulation

We investigate a resource allocation problem to maximize the sum rate of the overall system includes FD-D2D only while guaranteeing the quality of service (QoS) of both CUs and DUs. Thus, the optimization problem is presented as follows:

$$\mathcal{P}1: \max_{\rho_{i,j},\, p} R_{\text{sum}} \tag{13}$$

$$\text{s.t.} \quad \gamma_j^u \geq \gamma_j^{u,\text{req}},\ \gamma_j^d \geq \gamma_j^{d,\text{req}},\ \forall j \in \mathcal{C} \tag{13a}$$

$$\gamma_{i_1}^u \geq \gamma_i^{\text{req}},\ \gamma_{i_2}^u \geq \gamma_i^{\text{req}}\ \forall i \in \mathcal{D} \tag{13b}$$

$$\gamma_{i_1}^d \geq \gamma_i^{\text{req}},\ \gamma_{i_2}^d \geq \gamma_i^{\text{req}}\ \forall i \in \mathcal{D} \tag{13c}$$

$$0 \leq p_i \leq p_i^{\max},\ \forall i \in \mathcal{D} \tag{13d}$$

$$0 \leq p_j \leq p_j^{\max},\ \forall j \in \mathcal{C} \tag{13e}$$

$$0 \leq p_{B,j} \leq p_{B,j}^{\max},\ \forall j \in \mathcal{C} \tag{13f}$$

$$\sum_{i=1}^{Q} \rho_{i,j}^d + \rho_{i,j}^u \leq 1,\ \forall j \in \mathcal{C} \tag{13g}$$

$$\sum_{j=1}^{P} \rho_{i,j}^d + \rho_{i,j}^u \leq 1,\ \forall i \in \mathcal{D} \tag{13h}$$

$$\rho_{i,j}^d, \rho_{i,j}^u \in \{0,1\},\ \forall i \in \mathcal{D},\ \forall j \in \mathcal{C} \tag{13i}$$

where p is the transmit power set including p_i, p_j, and $p_{B,j}$. In $\mathcal{P}1$, constraints (13a–c) guarantee that the data rate of CUs and DUs is above the requirements, which satisfies the QoS. $\gamma_j^{u,\text{req}}$, $\gamma_j^{d,\text{req}}$, and γ_i^{req} denote the minimum SINR requirement of the uplink and downlink for CUs and DUs, respectively. (13d–f) are the power constraints, where $p_i^{\max}$, $p_j^{\max}$, and $p_{B,j}^{\max}$ are the maximum transmit power of DUi, CUj, and BS, respectively. The "one to one" reusing scenario is ensured by (13g,h), of which (13g) ensures that each subcarrier of CUj can be reused by only one DU, and Equation (13h) guarantees that any DUj can reuse at most one subcarrier of CUs.

As the network structure we proposed is a distributed system, it is assumed that the base station knows all the channel information for the calculations. The base station solves the optimization problem we modeled by using the algorithm we designed to perform power control and resource allocation for all DUs and CUs.

In practice, in actual network deployment, besides the data channels described in Figure 1, there are also control channels. DUs and CUs periodically upload CSI to the central base station via these control channels. Additionally, CUs can also transmit CSI to the base station through the data channel while performing the uplink service. It is worth mentioning that the denser the control channel's period, the more accurate the CSI the base station possesses. However, this also increases the system overhead and signaling interference. Conversely, the sparser the control channel's period, the lower the system overhead and signaling interference, but the CSI might not be updated promptly. If the CSI reporting period is too long, it can lead to inaccurate calculations by the base station, as the channel gain may have undergone random changes. Fortunately, due to the short-range communication characteristic of D2D, the CSI between two DUs in D2D pairs changes relatively slowly, allowing the control channel to be set with a larger period.

3. The Proposed Heuristic Algorithm

The problem $\mathcal{P}1$ is an MINLP, which is NP-hard and mathematically intractable. Therefore, we proposed a heuristic algorithm to decompose the $\mathcal{P}1$ into two subproblems to make the MINLP tractable, i.e., the power allocation and user pairing. First, the optimal power solution for each DUi matching each CUi is given by formulating the power allocation problem as nonlinear programming and searching for the optimal solution among a finite set. If the power solution can not only make the rate of DUi and CUj satisfy the QoS, but also improve the sum rate of the DUi-CUj pair compared with CUj, the reusing pair, DUi-CUj, will be regarded as a candidate option for the user pairing subproblem. Otherwise, it will be removed from the feasible option list. Then, we need to chose the most appropriate DU-CU pairs among the feasible candidates through maximum weight bipartite matching so that the sum rate of overall system can be maximized.

3.1. Power Allocation

To search for the optimal transmit power solution of each DU-CU pair, we simplify the problem $\mathcal{P}1$ to formulate an optimized problem $\mathcal{P}2$ which considers only one DU and one CU. The optimal objective is to maximize the rate of one DU-CU pair. For instance, when DUi reuses the uplink subcarrier of CUj, $\mathcal{P}2$ is given as

$$\mathcal{P}2: \max_{p_i, p_j} R^u_{i,j} \tag{14}$$

$$s.t. \quad \gamma^u_j \geq \gamma^{u,\text{req}}_j \tag{14a}$$

$$\gamma^u_{i_1} \geq \gamma^{\text{req}}_i, \ \gamma^u_{i_2} \geq \gamma^{\text{req}}_i \tag{14b}$$

$$0 \leq p_i \leq p^{\max}_i \tag{14c}$$

$$0 \leq p_j \leq p^{\max}_j \tag{14d}$$

where $R^u_{i,j} = R^u_j + R^u_{i_1} + R^u_{i_2}$, which indicates the sum rate of the pair DUi-CUj. It is evident that $\mathcal{P}2$ is a nonlinear programming problem that can be solved using geometric programming techniques. Since D2D is a type of short-range communication, to reduce the computational complexity, we set $g_{j,i_1} = g_{j,i_2} = g_{j,i}$, where $g_{j,i}$ is defined as the channel gain from CUj to the middle of two devices in D2D. Thus, we can obtain $\gamma^u_{i_1} = \gamma^u_{i_2} = \gamma^u_i$ using (2)–(4), and $R^u_{i_1} = R^u_{i_2} = R^u_i$, where γ^u_i is regarded as the SINR of D2D when reusing the uplink subcarrier of CU. As can be seen in Figure 2, l_1 is $\gamma^u_j = \gamma^{u,\text{req}}_j$, l_2 is $\gamma^u_i = \gamma^{\text{req}}_i$, l_3 is $p_j = p^{\max}_j$, and l_4 is $p_i = p^{\max}_i$, the region $\mathcal{R}$ delineates the feasible power allocation space for CUj and DUi.

When searching for the optimal power solution (p_i, p_j), we introduce the following lemmas.

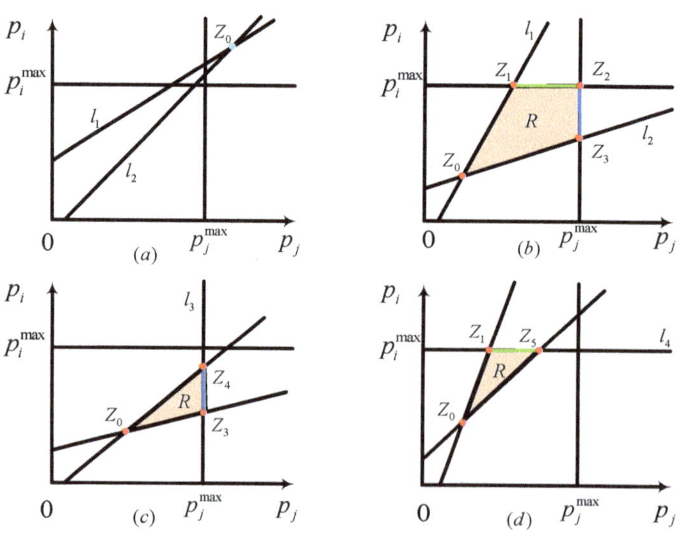

Figure 2. Feasible region for power allocation of each DU-CU pair in different situations.

Theorem 1. *In the optimal power solution, at least one component must be at its maximum value. Specifically, the optimal solution* (p_i^{op}, p_j^{op}) *will have either* $p_i^{op} = p_i^{\max}$ *or* $p_j^{op} = p_j^{\max}$.

Proof. Lemma 1 is proven by contradiction. $\mathcal{R}$ is a closed set like in Figure 2b–d or an empty set as in Figure 2a according to constraints in (14). For nonempty $\mathcal{R}$, the optimal power solution (p_i^{op}, p_j^{op}) obviously falls in $\mathcal{R}$, and it is assumed that p_i^{op} and p_j^{op} are below the maximum value. Then, if we substitute $(\alpha p_i^{op}, \alpha p_j^{op})$ for (p_i^{op}, p_j^{op}) in the objective function of $\mathcal{P}2$, in which $\forall \alpha > 1, \alpha \in R^+$, we can obtain

$$\begin{aligned} R_{i,j}^u(\alpha p_i^{op}, \alpha p_j^{op}) &= R_j^u(\alpha p_i^{op}, \alpha p_j^{op}) + 2 \cdot R_i^u(\alpha p_i^{op}, \alpha p_j^{op}) \\ &= log_2[(1 + \frac{p_j^{op} g_{j,B}}{p_i^{op}(g_{i_1,B} + g_{i_2,B}) + (N_0/\alpha)}) \times \\ &\quad (1 + \frac{p_i^{op} g_{i,i}}{p_j^{op} g_{j,i} + p_i^{op} \cdot \eta + (N_0/\alpha)})^2] \\ &> R_{i,j}^u(p_i^{op}, p_j^{op}). \end{aligned} \tag{15}$$

Using (15), we obtain $R_{i,j}^u(\alpha p_i^{op}, \alpha p_j^* op) > R_{i,j}^u(p_i^{op}, p_j^{op})$, while $\alpha > 1$. This obviously contradicts the assumption that (p_i^{op}, p_j^{op}) is the best possible solution. Thus, at least one component of the optimal solution (p_i^{op}, p_j^{op}) has to reach the maximum value $p_i^{\max}$ or $p_j^{\max}$. □

Lemma 1 illustrates that the optimal solution lies at the boundaries of the feasible region. As Figure 2 shows, there are four possible scenarios for the feasible region $\mathcal{R}$, which depend on different maximum transmit power levels, channel gains, and SINR requirements [2]. The most favorable solution exists at the line $\overline{Z_1Z_2}$, $\overline{Z_2Z_3}$, $\overline{Z_3Z_4}$ or the line $\overline{Z_1Z_5}$ in Figure 2. To further find the collection of potential optimal power solutions, we introduce Lemma 2 as follows.

Theorem 2. *If the feasible region* $\mathcal{R}$ *is limited, the most favorable solution* (p_i^{op}, p_j^{op}) *can only exist at the corners of* $\mathcal{R}$.

Proof. Let $\partial\mathcal{R}$ denote the boundary of $\mathcal{R}$. The region $\mathcal{R}$ is enclosed by four lines, which are l_1, l_2, l_3, and l_4. According to the conclusion of Lemma 1, we need to search for extreme points of objective function on $\partial\mathcal{R}$. Lemma 2 is demonstrated for the following cases:

(1) If the geometric programming situation is as in Figure 2c, $(p_i^{op}, p_j^{op}) \in \overline{Z_3Z_4}$. Since $R_{i,j}^u$ is a convex function [28], we have $\frac{\partial^2 R_{i,j}^u}{\partial {p_i}^2} \geq 0$; thus, the optimal solution can only exist at points Z_3 and Z_4.

(2) If the geometric programming situation is as in Figure 2d, $(p_i^{op}, p_j^{op}) \in \overline{Z_1Z_5}$. Since $R_{i,j}^u$ is a convex function, we have $\frac{\partial^2 R_{i,j}^u}{\partial {p_j}^2} \geq 0$; thus, the optimal solution can only exist at points Z_1 and Z_5.

(3) If the geometric programming situation is as in Figure 2b, $(p_i, p_j) \in \overline{Z_1Z_2}$ and $\overline{Z_2Z_3}$. Similar to (1) and (2), the optimal solution can only exist at points Z_1, Z_2, and Z_3.

Therefore, we conclude that the optimal solution (p_i^{op}, p_j^{op}) can only exist at the vertices of region $\mathcal{R}$. □

Based on the above lemmas, the possible objective points for the optimal power solution are indicated in Figure 2, which are Z_1 to Z_5. The coordinates of Z_0 and the slope of l_1 and l_2 determine whether there are solutions or not, which is illustrated in ref. [2]. We notate points $Z_0(p_j^{Z_0}, p_i^{Z_0})$, $Z_1(p_j^{Z_1}, p_i^{\max})$, $Z_2(p_j^{\max}, p_i^{\max})$, $Z_3(p_j^{\max}, p_i^{Z_3})$, $Z_4(p_j^{\max}, p_i^{Z_4})$, and $Z_5(p_j^{Z_5}, p_i^{\max})$. Since Z_1 to Z_5 are at the intersection of lines l_1, l_2, l_3, and l_4, we can obtain the values of $p_j^{Z_0}$, $p_i^{Z_0}$, $p_j^{Z_1}$, $p_i^{Z_3}$, $p_i^{Z_4}$, and $p_j^{Z_5}$ as follows:

$$p_j^{Z_0} = \frac{\gamma_j^{u,\text{req}} N_0 (g_{i,i} - \gamma_i^{\text{req}}\eta) + \gamma_j^{u,\text{req}}\gamma_i^{\text{req}} N_0 (g_{i_1,B} + g_{i_2,B})}{g_{j,B}(g_{i,i} - \gamma_i^{\text{req}}\eta) - \gamma_j^{u,\text{req}}\gamma_i^{\text{req}} g_{i,i}(g_{i_1,B} + g_{i_2,B})} \tag{16}$$

$$p_i^{Z_0} = \frac{\gamma_j^{u,\text{req}} N_0 (g_{i,i} - \gamma_i^{\text{req}}\eta) + \gamma_j^{u,\text{req}}\gamma_i^{\text{req}} N_0 (g_{i_1,B} + g_{i_2,B})}{g_{j,B}(g_{i,i} - \gamma_i^{\text{req}}\eta) - \gamma_j^{u,\text{req}}\gamma_i^{\text{req}} g_{i,i}(g_{i_1,B} + g_{i_2,B})} \times \frac{\gamma_i^{\text{req}} g_{i,i}}{g_{i,i} - \gamma_i^{\text{req}}\eta} + \frac{\gamma_i N_0}{g_{i,i} - \gamma_i^{\text{req}}\eta} \tag{17}$$

$$p_j^{Z_1} = \frac{\gamma_j^{u,\text{req}} [P_i^{\max}(g_{i_1,B} + g_{i_2,B}) + N_0]}{g_{j,B}} \tag{18}$$

$$p_i^{Z_3} = \frac{P_j^{\max} g_{j,B} - \gamma_j^{u,\text{req}} N_0}{g_{i,i} - \gamma_i^{\text{req}}\eta} \tag{19}$$

$$p_i^{Z_4} = \frac{P_j^{\max} g_{j,B} - \gamma_j^{u,\text{req}} N_0}{\gamma_j^{u,\text{req}} g_{i,B}} \tag{20}$$

$$p_j^{Z_5} = \frac{P_i^{\max}(g_{i,i} - \gamma_i^{\text{req}}\eta) - \gamma_i^{\text{req}} N_0}{\gamma_j^{u,\text{req}} g_{i,i}} \tag{21}$$

Based on the above, we obtain a finite set $\{Z_1, Z_2, Z_3, Z_4, Z_5\}$, which contains the optimal solution, so that it can be searched and compared for all elements to obtain the maximum $R_{i,j}^u$. Thus, the power allocation in the DUi-CUj pair for reusing the uplink subcarrier is solved. Similarly, for the downlink, the power allocation for the maximum $R_{i,j}^d$ can be solved by the same algorithm.

3.2. User Pairing

We proposed the most favorable power allocation algorithm for each DU-CU pair and obtained the maximal rate $R_{i,j}^u$. However, not every CU has a shared DU. For each unpaired CUj (uplink, for instance), the maximum achieved rate is

$$R_j^{u,\max} = \log_2(1 + \frac{P_j^{\max} g_{j,B}}{N_0}) \tag{22}$$

When an unpaired CUj shares its uplink subcarrier with DUi, the sum rate will vary. To express the rate variety, we define the cell's capacity gain for uplink as

$$\Delta R_{i,j}^u = R_{i,j}^u - R_j^{u,\max} \tag{23}$$

Similarly, the cell's capacity gain for the downlink can be defined as $\Delta R_{i,j}^d = R_{i,j}^d - R_j^{d,\max}$. Obviously, the optimal user pairing problem becomes a bipartite matching problem for reaching the maximum weight. $\mathcal{P}3$ can be formulated as

$$\mathcal{P}3: \max_{\rho_{i,j}} \sum_{j=1}^{P}\sum_{i=1}^{Q} (\rho_{i,j}^u \Delta R_{i,j}^u + \rho_{i,j}^d \Delta R_{i,j}^d) \tag{24}$$

$$\text{s.t.} \quad \sum_{j=1}^{P} \rho_{i,j}^d + \rho_{i,j}^u \le 1, \quad \forall i \in \mathcal{D} \tag{24a}$$

$$\sum_{i=1}^{Q} \rho_{i,j}^d + \rho_{i,j}^u \le 1, \quad \forall j \in \mathcal{C} \tag{24b}$$

$$\rho_{i,j}^u, \rho_{i,j}^d \in \{0,1\}, \quad \forall i \in \mathcal{D}, \ \forall j \in \mathcal{C} \tag{24c}$$

To solve $\mathcal{P}3$ through bipartite graph matching, we establish two sets of vertices; one is the set of DUs, andthe other is the set of CUs with subcarriers including the uplink and downlink. And then, we compute the weight of the edge between the two vertices with $\Delta R^{u}_{i,j}$ or $\Delta R^{d}_{i,j}$, which depends on the transmission direction of the CU. This problem is solved by Kuhn–Munkres algorithm. The specific algorithm flow for user pairing is detailed in Algorithm 1.

Algorithm 1 The optimal user pairing algorithm of HA

```
Initialize the cell's sum rate variation matrix {ΔR_{i,j}}_{Q×P}, and the pairing indicator
  matrix {ρ_{i,j}}_{Q×P}.
for j = 1 : Q do
  for i = 1 : P do
    Determine the optimal power solution (p_i^{op}, p_j^{op}) for the single pair CUj-DUi by
    applying the power control algorithm described in Section 3.1.
    Substitute (p_i^{op}, p_j^{op}) in Equations (2)–(10), (22) and (23) to obtain ΔR_{i,j}, which
    includes both uplink and downlink rates.
    Set ρ_{i,j} = 1.
    if ΔR_{i,j} < 0 then
      Under these conditions, we assume that the pairing attempt between CUj and
      DUi fails, FD-D2D access to the cell is prohibited, and CUj maintains its original
      connection, that is, set
      ΔR_{i,j} = 0
      R^C_{i,j} = R_j^{unp}
      R^D_{i,j} = 0
      ρ_{i,j} = 0
    end if
  end for
end for
Use the Kuhn–Munkres algorithm for maximum weight to determine the most favor-
  able pattern {ρ_{i,j}}_{Q×P} of {ΔR_{i,j}}_{Q×P}.
Return the optimal user pairing pattern {ρ_{i,j}}_{Q×P} and sum of the corresponding se-
  lected elements in ΔR_{i,j}.
```

The computational complexity of our approach is polynomial and depends on the number of vertices and edges. Specifically, the most favorable power solution for a single CU-DU pair is searched in a limited set through one-dimensional searching, in which the complexity is $\mathcal{O}(1)$. This leads to a total complexity of $\mathcal{O}(PQ)$ for the power control algorithm applied to all CU-DU pairs. Additionally, since our assumption is that the quantity of CUs is greater than or equal to the quantity of DUs, i.e., $P \geq Q$, the Kuhn–Munkres algorithm for resource allocation addresses user pairing in the complexity of $\mathcal{O}(P^3)$. Thus, the total complexity of MaxCU-OPOP is $\mathcal{O}(PQ + P^3)$, which is a significant reduction compared to the complexity recorded in refs. [23–25].

4. Numerical Result

In this section, the numerical result is presented to verify the proposed FD-MaxSumCell-HA scheme. We consider a circular cell with the BS located in the center, where the FD-DUs and CUs are distributed randomly. The FD-MaxSumCell-HA scheme is implemented using Monte Carlo methods over 10,000 times to smooth the randomness in the simulation. The relevant parameters in our simulation are shown in Table 2. The fading, path loss, and N_0 are in a general configuration, and the cell radius and power depend on the experience of operator. The setting of SIS is based on the current level of self-interference suppression technology, designed to be an easy-to-achieve value.

Table 2. The parameter values used in the simulation

Parameter	Value
Number of CUs (P)	20
Number of DUs (Q)	0 to 20
Cell radius	500 m
Users distribution	Uniform
Fast fading	Mean = 1
Slow fading	Standard deviation = 8 dB
Noise spectral density (N_0)	−174 dBm/Hz
$P_j^{\max}, P_i^{\max}$	24 dBm
$P_{BS}^{\max}$	46 dBm
Exponent coefficients of path loss (α)	3
Constant coefficients of path loss (G)	10^{-2}
D2D distance (d)	10 m
UAV hover height	80 m
Bandwidth	10 MHz
Self-interference suppression	110 dB
Number of subcarriers (L)	20
$\gamma_j^{d,\mathrm{req}}, \gamma_j^{u,\mathrm{req}}, \gamma_i^{\mathrm{req}}$	10 dB

We assume that one CU is assigned with one subcarrier, and the transmit power of the BS is uniformly distributed in frequency; hence, the transmit power from the BS to CUj is $P_{B,j} = P_{BS}^{\max}/L$. It is worth mentioning that most of the weight of the three-tier SIS architecture comes from the components required to cancel nonlinear SI in the RF chain. Considering the payload limitations of UAVs, for the communication transceivers mounted on UAVs, we only consider using chips for baseband interference cancellation and employing antenna isolation and air interface SIS techniques. Spatial SI can achieve 50–60 dB suppression through simple antenna isolation techniques and spatial self-interference cancellation algorithms [17,18], and the base band can use deep learning chips to predict and reconstruct the transmitted signal for interference cancellation, achieving 40–50 dB cancellation depending on the chip's computational capability [29]. Therefore, we chose to examine the simulation results with a SIS capability of 110 dB.

Two metrics are used to evaluate the performance of the scheme; one is spectral efficiency, i.e., the sum rate, of the cell, and the other is D2D's access rate, which is defined as the ratio of accessed DUs to the total DUs. To verify the superiority of the FD-MaxSumCell-HA scheme, we compare it with traditional half-duplex D2D underlaying networks. Moreover, we consider three scenarios of cellular users for each implementation: (1) There are only uplink CUs in the cell. (2) There are only downlink CUs in the cell. (3) There are joint uplink CUs and downlink CUs (JUAD) in the cell. This is carried out to eliminate the randomness of the user's transmit direction

As shown in Figure 3a, whether using FD or traditional HD, D2D underlaying cellular networks can greatly increase the sum rate of the cell compared with networks that only have CUs, and the FD-MaxSumCell-HA scheme further improves the sum rate compared with the HD-D2D scheme. In particular, when there are 20 DUs in the cell, the sum rate of FD-MaxSumCell-HA shows a notable improvement of 43% compared to the HD-D2D scheme. Specifically, in the JUAD scenario, the sum rate of FD-MaxSumCell-HA is 1129.86 bps/Hz, surpassing the conventional HD scheme, which achieves a sum rate of 792.48 bps/Hz. The reason is that the sum rate of DUs improved nearly twofold because of the co-frequency co-time full-duplex adopted in D2D. Although, due to the residual SI and other interference introduced by dual-direction transmission, the improvement never reached twofold, the performance of the overall cell improved greatly. As for the access rate depicted in Figure 3b, as the number of DUs increases, the access rate of DUs for the two schemes monotonically decreases. This is because the more reuse occurs in the same subcarrier, the more interference is introduced, which will cause the DUs to not satisfy the requested QoS and exhibit access failure. However, the FD-MaxSumCell-HA scheme decreases slowly compared with the traditional HD-D2D scheme. This is because FD improves the spectral efficiency of D2D and makes it easier for DU to meet the QoS requirement. Therefore, both metrics are improved when the system adopts the FD-MaxSumCell-HA scheme.

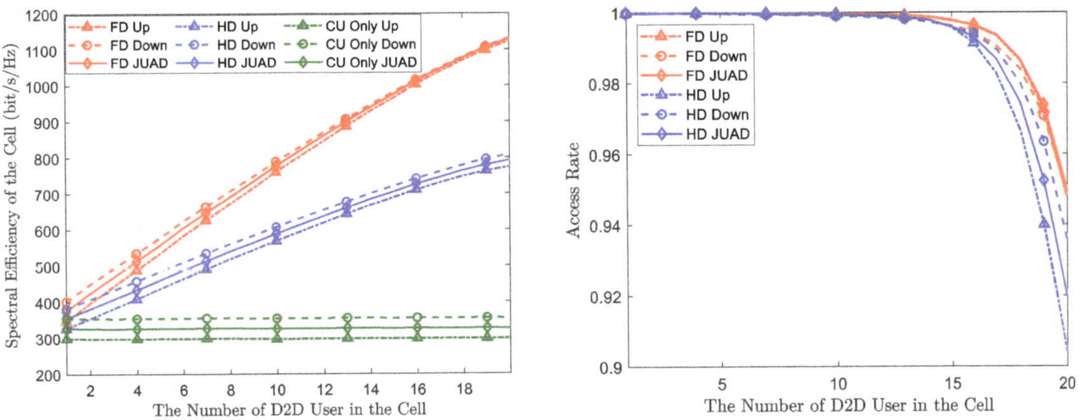

(**a**) The comparison for sum rate (**b**) The comparison for access rate

Figure 3. Performance comparison of FD-MaxSumCell-HA versus traditional HD-D2D networks with varying numbers of DUs from 0 to 20.

To verify the effectiveness of HA proposed in this paper, we set the scheme in which CUs and DUs are randomly paired as the benchmark for comparison. And we only consider the JUAD scenario in this comparison. As illustrated in Figure 4a, both FD-D2D adopting HA and HD-D2D adopting HA perform better than them adopting random pairing in the sum rate comparison. This is because there is more severe interference when the CU is close to the DU in the same pair, and random pairing increases the chance of this. In particular, HD-D2D adopting HA is even better than FD-D2D with random pairing. This means that the gain brought by an excellent pairing algorithm is superior to the enhancement of the duplex mode. Figure 4b depicts the access rate comparison, where the HA scheme remains superior to the random pairing scheme. The access rate of FD and HD adopting the random scheme is even less than 50%.

Figure 5 shows the system performance comparison between the FD-MaxSumCell-HA and HD-D2D underlaying networks and the SIS of FD-D2D. The sum rate of the FD-MaxSumCell-HA scheme monotonically increase as SIS increases. FD-MaxSumCell-HA performs better even when SIS is low, which is easy to implement via antenna isolation. The access rate of FD-MaxSumCell-HA remains superior to the HD-D2D scheme when SIS is from 70 dB to 125 dB. However, when the access rate reaches 95%, it no longer improves with an increase in SIS. This is because mutual interference incurred by CU and DU reuse replaces RSI as a main factor, which depends on the resource coordination scheme.

Figures 3–5 illustrate that our designed algorithm is highly robust. Compared to random allocation and traditional HD transmission, the combination of FD and the HA algorithm provides significant performance gains for the proposed network model. Therefore, even if the CSI reporting period is too long, causing some channel gain estimates to be inaccurate, the proposed model and algorithm can still enhance the cell's spectral efficiency in most cases.

The reason for the performance enhancement of the FD-D2D underlaying network is that FD-D2D devices can improve the SE of the cell nearly twofold compared to traditional HD-D2D devices. As can be seen in Figure 6, in our scheme simulation, the sum rate of the

FD-D2D pairs is approximately 1.73 times than that of HD-D2D pairs when DUs full load. This phenomenon leads to the BS being more inclined to allocate resource to DUs. The proposed scheme tends to be unfair for CUs, which results in more severe degradation of the performance of CUs. As demonstrated in Figure 7, the SE of CUs in the FD-MaxSumCell-HA scheme declines more sharply than that in the HD-MaxSumCell-HA scheme, and it is only 60% of the HD-MaxSumCell-HA scheme when DUs are equal to 20 in the joint uplink and downlink user scenario. But from another perspective, the system may seek to shift more traffic from CUs to DUs in certain scenarios; hence, this phenomenon is not always detrimental to wireless systems.

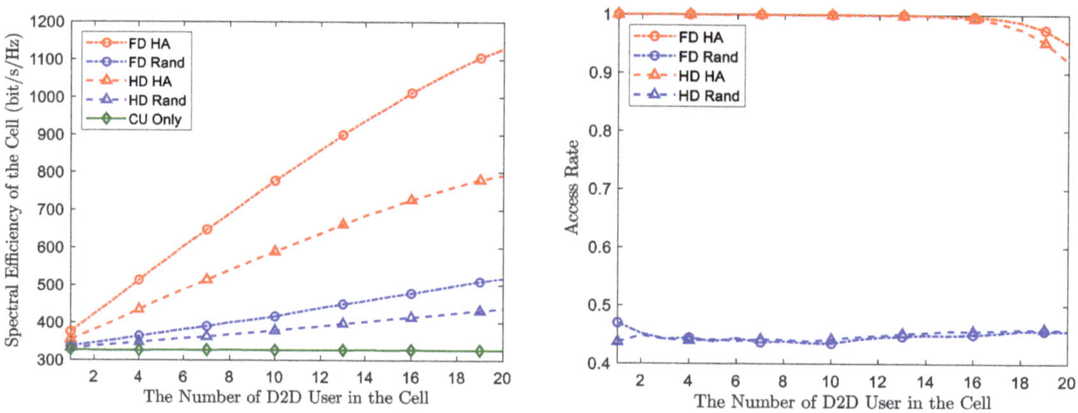

(**a**) The comparison for sum rate (**b**) The comparison for access rate

Figure 4. The performance comparison between HA and random pairing with respect to the number of DUs, which ranges from 0 to 20.

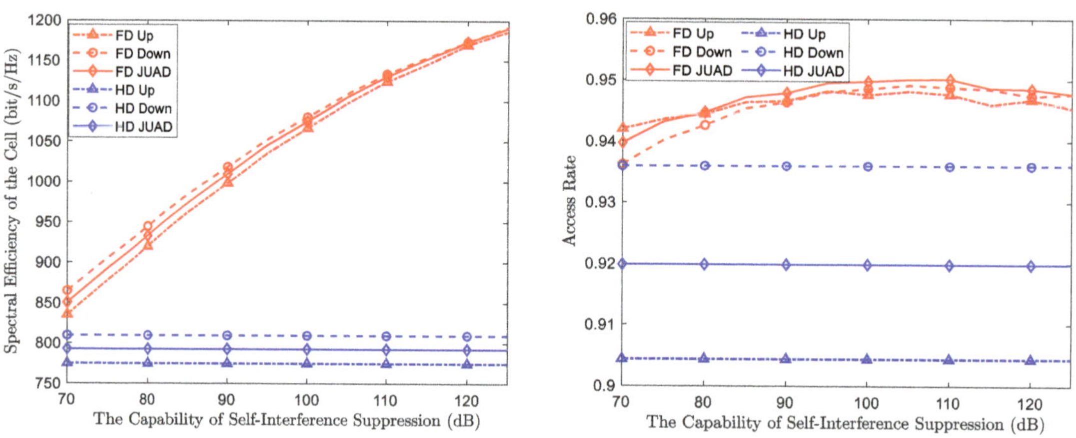

(**a**) The comparison for sum rate (**b**) The comparison for access rate

Figure 5. The performance comparison between FD-MaxSumCell-HA and traditional HD-D2D networks with respect to SIS, which ranges from 70 dB to 125 dB.

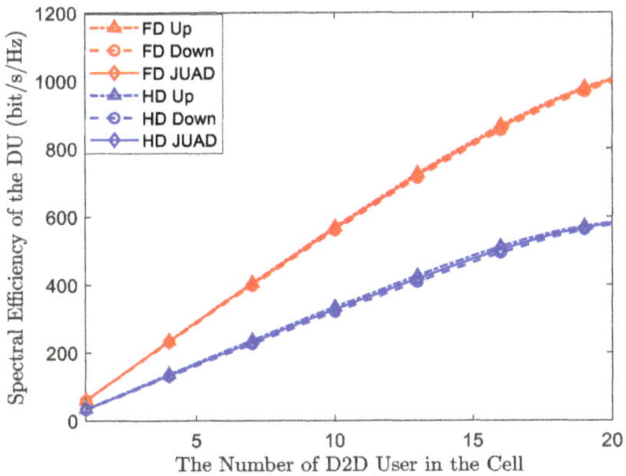

Figure 6. The SE of DUs after employing the user pairing algorithm.

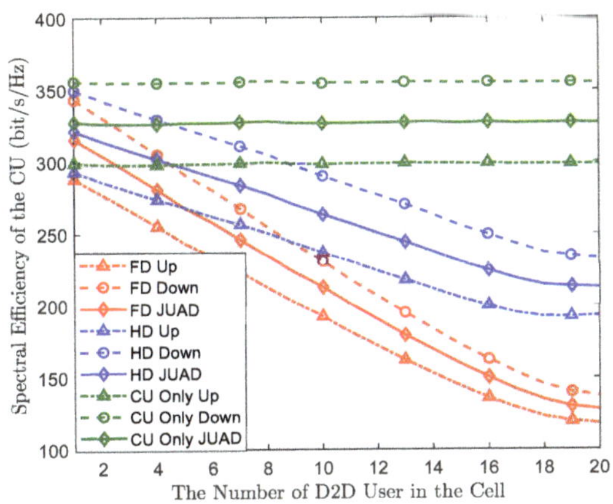

Figure 7. The SE of CUs after employing the user pairing algorithm.

5. Conclusions

In this paper, which aims to further improve spectral efficiency, flexibility, and speed, we propose a novel FD-UAV-aided D2D network model and develop an FD-MaxSumCell-HA scheme, which adopts FD technology in UAV linking, to maximize the sum rate of the overall system. The optimization problem is MINLP, which is NP-hard and mathematically intractable. Thus, we decompose the problem into two subproblems, i.e., power allocation and user pairing, to solve it. The numerical results demonstrate that our proposed FD-MaxSumCell-HA scheme is superior to traditional HD-D2D underlaying cellular networks in both the system sum rate and access rate of D2D. In particular, when there are 20 CUs and 20 DUs in the cell, the sum rate of the FD-MaxSumCell-HA scheme improves by 43% against the traditional scheme. Moreover, the proposed scheme is better than traditional ones even when SIS is only 70 dB, which is easy to implement. Therefore, FD-MaxSumCell-HA has good application prospects in actual networks. However, in this paper, we do not consider the channel uncertainty caused by UAV mobility and perturbation, which is a problem to be solved in future research.

Author Contributions: Conceptualization, Y.L.; methodology, Y.Z. and Y.L.; software, Y.Z.; validation, Y.Z.; writing—original draft preparation, Y.Z.; writing—review and editing, Y.Z.; supervision, Y.L. All authors have read and agreed to the published version of the manuscript.

Funding: This work was supported by the low-altitude economy project of the China Telecom Research Institute.

Data Availability Statement: Data are contained within the article.

Acknowledgments: We would like to thank Shihai Shao and his team from the National Key Laboratory of Science and Technology on Communications of the University of Electronic Science and Technology of China for their technical guidance.

Conflicts of Interest: The authors declare no conflicts of interest.

Abbreviations

The following abbreviations are used in this manuscript:

D2D	Device-to-device
FD	Full-duplex
HD	Half-duplex
UAV	Unmanned aerial vehicle
DU	D2D user
CU	Cellular user
HA	Heuristic algorithm
BS	Base station
SE	Spectral efficiency
EE	Energy efficiency
JUAD	Joint uplink and downlink
SI	Self-interference
RSI	Residual self-interference
MaxSumCell	Maximizing sum rate of cell
SIS	Self-interference suppression
QoS	Quality of service

References

1. Islam, T.; Kwon, C. Survey on the state-of-the-art in device-to-device communication: A resource allocation perspective. *Ad. Hoc. Netw.* **2022**, *136*, 102978. [CrossRef]
2. Feng, D.; Lu, L.; Wu, Y.Y.; Li, G.Y.; Feng, G.; Li, S. Device-toDevice Communications Underlaying Cellular Networks. *IEEE Trans. Commun.* **2013**, *61*, 3541–3551. [CrossRef]
3. Li, X.; Shankaran, R.; Orgun, M.; Fang, G.; Xu, Y. Resource Allocation for Underlay D2D Communication with Proportional Fairness. *IEEE Trans. Veh. Technol.* **2018**, *67*, 6244–6258. [CrossRef]
4. Kai, C.; Li, H.; Xu, L.; Li, Y.; Jiang, T. Energy-Efficient Device-to-Device Communications for Green Smart Cities. *IEEE Trans. Industrial Inform.* **2018**, *14*, 1542–1551. [CrossRef]
5. Ni, M.; Pan, J. Throughput Analysis for Downlink Resource Reusing D2D Communications in Cellular Networks. In Proceedings of the IEEE Global Communications Conference (GLOBECOM), Singapore, 4–8 December 2017; pp. 1–7.
6. Idris, F.; Tang, J.; So, D.K.C. Resource and energy efficient device to device communications in downlink cellular system. In Proceedings of the 2018 IEEE Wireless Communications and Networking Conference (WCNC), Barcelona, Spain, 15–18 April 2018; pp. 1–6.
7. Kai, C.; Xu, L.; Zhang, J.; Peng, M. Joint Uplink and Downlink Resource Allocation for D2D Communication Underlying Cellular Networks. In Proceedings of the 2018 10th International Conference on Wireless Communications and Signal Processing (WCSP), Hangzhou, China, 18–20 October 2018; pp. 1–6.
8. Kai, C.; Wu, Y.; Peng, M.; Huang, W. Joint Uplink and Downlink Resource Allocation for NOMA-Enabled D2D Communications. *IEEE Wirel. Commun. Lett.* **2021**, *10*, 1247–1251. [CrossRef]
9. Kai, C.; Li, H.; Xu, L.; Li, Y.; Jiang, T. Joint Subcarrier Assignment with Power Allocation for Sum Rate Maximization of D2D Communications in Wireless Cellular Networks. *IEEE Trans. Veh. Technol.* **2019**, *68*, 4748–4759. [CrossRef]
10. Li, Y.; Aghvami, A.H.; Dong, D. Path Planning for Cellular-Connected UAV: A DRL Solution with Quantum-Inspired Experience Replay. *IEEE Trans. Wirel. Commun.* **2022**, *21*, 7897–7912. [CrossRef]
11. Li, Y.; Aghvami, A.H. Radio Resource Management for Cellular-Connected UAV: A Learning Approach. *IEEE Trans. Commun.* **2023**, *71*, 2784–2800. [CrossRef]
12. Zeng, Y.; Zhang, R.; Lim, T.J. Wireless communications with unmanned aerial vehicles: Opportunities and challenges. *IEEE Commun. Mag.* **2016**, *54*, 36–42. [CrossRef]

13. Miao, J.; Liao, Q.; Zhao, Z. Joint Rate and Coverage Design for UAV-Enabled Wireless Networks with Underlaid D2D Communications. In Proceedings of the 2020 IEEE 6th International Conference on Computer and Communications (ICCC), Chengdu, China, 11–14 December 2020; pp. 815–819.
14. Huang, W.; Yang, Z.; Pan, C.; Pei, L.; Chen, M.; Shikh-Bahaei, M.; Elkashlan, M.; Nallanathan, A. Joint Power, Altitude, Location and Bandwidth Optimization for UAV with Underlaid D2D Communications. *IEEE Wirel. Commun. Lett.* **2019**, *8*, 524–527. [CrossRef]
15. Yin, C.; Yang, H.; Xiao, P.; Chu, Z.; Garcia-Palacios, E. Resource Allocation for UAV-Assisted Wireless Powered D2D Networks with Flying and Ground Eavesdropping. *IEEE Commun. Lett.* **2023**, *27*, 2103–2107. [CrossRef]
16. Lea, B.; Shome, D.; Waqar, O.; Tomal, J. Sum rate maximization of D2D networks with energy constrained UAVs through deep unsupervised learning. In Proceedings of the 2021 IEEE 12th Annual Ubiquitous Computing, Electronics & Mobile Communication Conference (UEMCON), New York, NY, USA, 1–4 December 2021; pp. 453–459.
17. Shi, C.; Pan, W.; Shao, S. RF Wideband Self-Interference Cancellation for Full Duplex Phased Array Communication Systems. In Proceedings of the ICC 2022—IEEE International Conference on Communications, Seoul, Republic of Korea, 16–20 May 2022; pp. 1094–1099.
18. Shi, C.; Pan, W.; Shen, Y.; Shao, S. Robust Transmit Beamforming for Self-Interference Cancellation in STAR Phased Array Systems. *IEEE Signal Process. Lett.* **2022**, *29*, 2622–2626. [CrossRef]
19. He, Y.; Zhao, H.; Guo, W.; Shao, S.; Tang, Y. Frequency-Domain Successive Cancellation of Nonlinear Self-Interference with Reduced Complexity for Full-Duplex Radios. *IEEE Trans. Commun.* **2022**, *70*, 2678–2690. [CrossRef]
20. Yang, T.; Zhang, R.; Cheng, X.; Yang, L. Graph Coloring Based Resource Sharing (GCRS) Scheme for D2D Communications Underlaying Full-Duplex Cellular Networks. *IEEE Trans. Veh.* **2017**, *66*, 7506–7517. [CrossRef]
21. Hemachandra, K.T.; Rajatheva, N.; Latva-Aho, M. Sum-rate analysis for full-duplex underlay device-to-device networks. In Proceedings of the 2014 IEEE Wireless Communications and Networking Conference, Istanbul, Turkey, 6–9 April 2014; pp. 514–519.
22. Cheng, W.; Zhang, X.; Zhang, H. Optimal power allocation for full-duplex D2D communications over wireless cellular networks. In Proceedings of the 2014 IEEE Global Communications Conference, Austin, TX, USA, 8–12 December 2014; pp. 4764–4769.
23. Li, S.; Ni, Q.; Sun, Y.; Min, G. Resource allocation for weighted sumrate maximization in multi-user full-duplex device-to-device communications: Approaches for perfect and statistical CSIs. *IEEE Access* **2017**, *5*, 27229–27241. [CrossRef]
24. Liu, F.; Hou, X.; Liu, Y. Capacity improvement for full duplex deviceto-device communications underlaying cellular network. *IEEE Access* **2018**, *6*, 68373–68383. [CrossRef]
25. Vu, H.V.; Tran, N.H.; Le-Ngoc, T. Full-Duplex Device-to-Device Cellular Networks: Power Control and Performance Analysis. *IEEE Trans. Veh. Technol.* **2019**, *68*, 3952–3966. [CrossRef]
26. Chung, M.; Sim, M.S.; Kim, D.K.; Chae, C. Compact full-duplex MIMO radios in D2D underlaid cellular networks: From system design to prototype results. *IEEE Access* **2017**, *5*, 16601–16617. [CrossRef]
27. Khandaker, M.R.A.; Masouros, C.; Wong, K. Secure full-duplex device-to-device communication. In Proceedings of the 2017 IEEE Globecom Workshops, Singapore, 4–8 December 2017; pp. 1–6.
28. Lee, N.; Lin, X.; Andrews, J.G.; Heath, R.W., Jr. Power control for D2D underlaid cellular networks: Modeling, algorithms, and analysis. *IEEE J. Sel. Areas Commun.* **2015**, *33*, 1–13. [CrossRef]
29. Wang, X.; Zhao, H.; He, Y.; Hu, P.; Shao, S. A Simple Neural Network for Nonlinear Self-Interference Cancellation in Full-Duplex Radios. In *IEEE Transactions on Vehicular Technology*; IEEE: Piscataway, NJ, USA, 2024. [CrossRef]

electronics

MDPI

Article

An Improved Lightweight Deep Learning Model and Implementation for Track Fastener Defect Detection with Unmanned Aerial Vehicles

Qi Yu, Ao Liu *, Xinxin Yang * and Weimin Diao

School of Electronic Information Engineering, Beihang University, Beijing 100191, China; 16231012@buaa.edu.cn (Q.Y.); diaoweimin@buaa.edu.cn (W.D.)
* Correspondence: buaaliuao@buaa.edu.cn (A.L.); yangxx@buaa.edu.cn (X.Y.)

Abstract: Track fastener defect detection is an essential component in ensuring railway safety operations. Traditional manual inspection methods no longer meet the requirements of modern railways. The use of deep learning image processing techniques for classifying and recognizing abnormal fasteners is faster, more accurate, and more intelligent. With the widespread use of unmanned aerial vehicles (UAVs), conducting railway inspections using lightweight, low-power devices carried by UAVs has become a future trend. In this paper, we address the characteristics of track fastener detection tasks by improving the YOLOv4-tiny object detection model. We improved the model to output single-scale features and used the K-means++ algorithm to cluster the dataset, obtaining anchor boxes that were better suited to the dataset. Finally, we developed the FPGA platform and deployed the transformed model on this platform. The experimental results demonstrated that the improved model achieved an mAP of 95.1% and a speed of 295.9 FPS on the FPGA, surpassing the performance of existing object detection models. Moreover, the lightweight and low-powered FPGA platform meets the requirements for UAV deployment.

Keywords: track; fastener defect detection; model improvement; FPGA; UAV

1. Introduction

Track fasteners are essential components that connect the rails to the sleepers and used to secure the rails and prevent lateral and longitudinal displacement [1]. Due to factors such as wear and tear on train wheels and the irregular deformation of the tracks over prolonged periods of train operation, trains are prone to vibrations during high-speed travel. These vibrations not only affect the trains themselves but are also transmitted to the track fasteners. Coupled with the impact of train loads, this can lead to the fracture and damage of track fasteners, thereby affecting the safe operation of trains. Common abnormalities in track fasteners include fracture, displacement, and dislodgement [2].

The speed and mileage of high-speed trains are gradually increasing, and urban rail transit is also developing gradually. Therefore, the efficient detection of track fastener defects is crucial. Initially, track fastener defect detection relied mainly on manual visual inspection. This method is inefficient, costly in terms of labor, and has unreliable accuracy, making it incapable of meeting modern requirements. This has also been confirmed in railway bridge inspection [3]. In order to improve detection efficiency, researchers have developed non-destructive testing methods, such as detection based on vibration signals [4,5], ultrasonic detection [6], laser detection [7], and machine vision detection [8]. With the rapid development of artificial intelligence, machine vision-based detection methods have emerged in various scenarios, including track fastener defect detection. Currently, machine vision-based detection methods can be categorized into two main types: those based on traditional image processing techniques and those based on deep learning approaches.

Detection methods based on image processing rely on manually designed features. After extracting features, a trained classifier is used for detection and classification. This results in the detection performance being influenced by manually designed features. Therefore, these algorithms often have lower detection accuracy and poor adaptability to variations in factors such as lighting and noise in real-world engineering scenarios, leading to low robustness. Khan et al. [9] utilized Harris–Stephens and Shi–Tomasi feature detectors to extract feature points and feature vectors from images. Subsequently, they matched the features of input images with those of training images to detect track fasteners. Feng et al. [10] proposed a probabilistic structural subject model (STM) to model the fastener. This model can detect the wear state of the fastener and is robust to changes in lighting conditions. Gibert et al. [11,12] proposed a fastener detection algorithm based on a multi-task learning framework. The algorithm uses image-oriented gradient histograms (HOGs) to extract fastener features and uses support vector machine (SVM) classifiers to classify and recognize damaged and missing fasteners, improving detection accuracy. Wang et al. [13] proposed an automated method for detecting defects in track fasteners. Initially, they located track fasteners precisely using the background difference method. Then, they extracted linear features from images based on an improved Canny operator and Hough transform. Subsequently, they extracted feature vectors for track fastener defects by combining local binary patterns (LBP) and HOGs. Finally, they employed an SVM to classify the feature vectors. This method demonstrated higher real-time performance and accuracy. Although the aforementioned image processing-based detection methods have improved detection accuracy to some extent, their complex image-processing and feature extraction processes still cannot improve the efficiency of fastener detection.

Detection methods based on deep learning primarily utilize convolutional neural networks (CNNs) to learn features from images. Compared to image processing-based detection methods, they do not require manual feature design, thus offering better robustness. These algorithms can be classified into two major categories: two-stage detection algorithms based on candidate regions and one-stage detection algorithms based on end-to-end learning. The main representatives of two-stage algorithms include R-CNN [14], Fast R-CNN [15], and Faster R-CNN [16]. Wei et al. [2] applied Faster R-CNN to track fastener detection. Despite the improvement in detection accuracy, the issue of slow detection speed persists. The one-stage algorithms are mainly represented by SSD [17] and the YOLO [18–22] series. Compared to other algorithms, the YOLO series algorithms have significant advantages in both detection speed and accuracy. Therefore, they are widely used in track fastener defect detection. Qi et al. [23] proposed an improved MYOLOv3-Tiny network based on YOLOv3. Depth-wise and pointwise convolution were used, and the backbone network was redesigned. The experiments showed that the network achieved higher detection precision and faster detection speed compared to R-CNN. Fu et al. [24] proposed a MobileNet-YOLOv4 algorithm for track fastener detection. This algorithm replaces the CSPDarknet53 feature extraction network in the YOLOv4 algorithm with MobileNet, which enables the extraction of subtle features of track fasteners while reducing the number of parameters and computational complexity, thus improving detection speed. Li et al. [25] proposed an improved track fastener defect detection model based on YOLOv5s. In this model, a convolutional block attention module (CBAM) is added to the Neck network of YOLOv5s to enhance the extraction of key features and suppress irrelevant features. Additionally, a weighted bi-directional feature pyramid network (BiFPN) is introduced to achieve multi-scale feature fusion. The experimental results demonstrate that the improved model enhances both accuracy and detection speed. Wang et al. [26] introduced the CBAM attention mechanism into the backbone network of YOLOv5, replaced the standard convolution blocks in the neck network with GSConv convolution modules, and integrated BiFPN. Finally, they designed a lightweight decoupled head structure to improve detection accuracy and enhance the robustness of the model. The experimental findings testify to the YOLOv5-CGBD model's ability to conduct real-time detection, with mAP0.5 scores of 0.971 and 0.747 for mAP0.5:0.95, surpassing those of the original YOLOv5 model by

2.2% and 4.1%, respectively. Although the above methods can accurately detect fastener defects, there is still room for improvement in terms of false detection rates. Additionally, the detection speed of the models is relatively slow, making it challenging to apply them in engineering practice.

Due to its low cost, high flexibility, and ease of control, UAV-based detection is widely employed across various fields. For instance, in agriculture, it is utilized for tree detection [27,28]; in transportation, it is employed for vehicle tracking [29,30]; in environmental conservation, it is used for inspections [31]; in industry, it is applied for power facility inspections [32]; and in infrastructure, it is employed for bridge crack inspections [33]. In the field of railway inspection, utilizing UAVs can reduce labor costs, improve efficiency, and enhance safety. Wu et al. [34] proposed the use of UAV vision for detecting surface defects on railway tracks. Similarly, Milan et al. [35] suggested the use of UAVs for inspecting railway infrastructure. The development of autonomous UAVs for analyzing data in real time is an emerging trend in UAV data processing [36]. However, current track fastener defect detection models rely on Nvidia graphics cards, which cannot meet the engineering requirements for lightweight, low-power, and real-time devices.

To address the aforementioned issues, the main contributions of this article are as follows:

1. We converted the YOLOv4-tiny model to output single-scale features, which resulted in improved detection speed. Furthermore, we utilized the K-means++ algorithm to re-cluster anchor boxes, thereby improving the model's detection accuracy.
2. We developed the model using an FPGA development platform and deployed the model on the FPGA platform after transformation [37,38], achieving the lightweight, low-power, and real-time requirements of the track fastener defect detection device.

2. Materials and Methods

2.1. YOLOv4-Tiny Algorithm

YOLO is an end-to-end object detection algorithm. It takes the entire image as input, and after processing through a CNN, it yields the localization and classification results of objects. The core of the YOLO detection algorithm involves segmenting the neural network's input image into an $n * n$ grid, where each grid cell has S predefined anchor boxes. Detection results are obtained by applying non-maximum suppression to remove duplicate and ineffective anchor boxes. Additionally, techniques such as residual network structures, feature fusion, and multi-scale output are employed to improve detection capabilities across various scenarios. The loss function of YOLO is represented as Equation (1).

$$LOSS = loss_{loc} + loss_{obj} + loss_{cls} \tag{1}$$

$loss_{loc}$, $loss_{obj}$, and $loss_{cls}$ represent the position regression loss function, the object confidence loss function, and the target classification loss function, respectively.

YOLOv4-tiny is a lightweight version of YOLOv4 proposed by Bochkovskiy et al. In comparison to YOLOv4, YOLOv4-tiny employs a lighter architecture, enabling it to achieve efficient detection speeds even in resource-constrained environments. Therefore, YOLOv4-tiny is better suited for running on embedded devices. The structure of YOLOv4-tiny is shown in Figure 1.

From Figure 1, it can be seen that the backbone network of YOLOv4-tiny consists of Resblocks. The structure of the Resblock is shown in Figure 2. The backbone network outputs multi-scale features, which are then utilized by the YOLO head for detection.

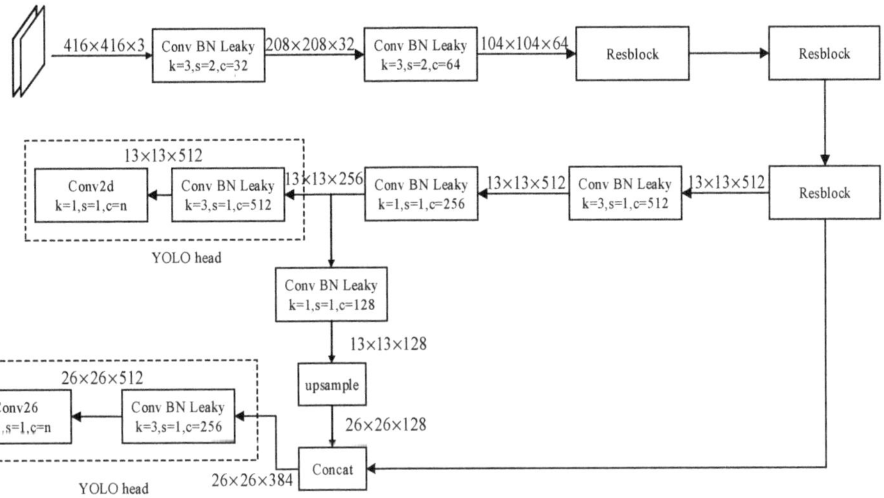

Figure 1. Structure of YOLOv4-tiny.

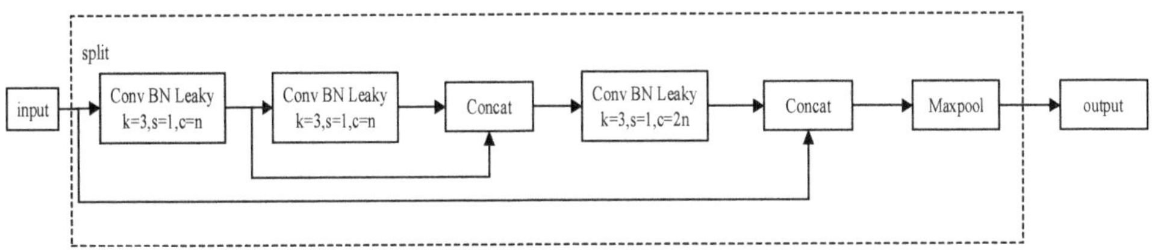

Figure 2. Structure of the Resblock.

In ConvBNLeaky, k represents the size of the convolutional kernel, s represents the stride, and c represents the number of channels. ConvBNLeaky consists of a convolutional layer, a batch normalization layer (BN), and a Leaky activation function. The Leaky function is represented as Equation (2). Compared to the ReLU activation function, during the backpropagation process in deep learning training, the Leaky activation function can still compute gradients for the parts of the input that are less than zero.

$$Leaky(x_i) = \begin{cases} x_i & x_i \geq 0 \\ ax_i & x_i < 0 \end{cases} \quad (2)$$

2.2. *YOLOv4-Tiny Improvement*

2.2.1. Single-Scale Feature Output

The original YOLOv4-tiny model has two-scale feature outputs. By detecting objects at two scales, YOLOv4-tiny can obtain a more comprehensive understanding of target information and can handle complex scenes more effectively. Compared to other detection tasks such as face detection and vehicle detection, track fastener defect detection tasks typically demonstrate relatively fixed sizes of objects in the image. An image displaying anomalous track fasteners is shown in Figure 3.

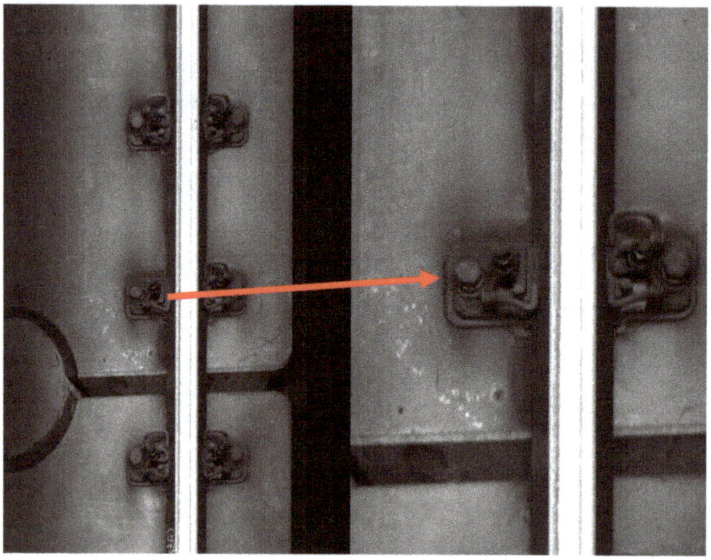

Figure 3. Captured images and abnormal fasteners.

Due to the fixed perspective of the camera and the consistent size of the track fasteners, the size of the detection targets remains fixed relative to the image. To improve the detection speed and reduce computational complexity, we modified YOLOv4-tiny to output features at a single scale. From Figure 3, it can be observed that the track fasteners belong to medium-sized objects. Therefore, we retained features at the scale of (26, 26) while removing features at the scale of (13, 13). The improved model structure is shown in Figure 4.

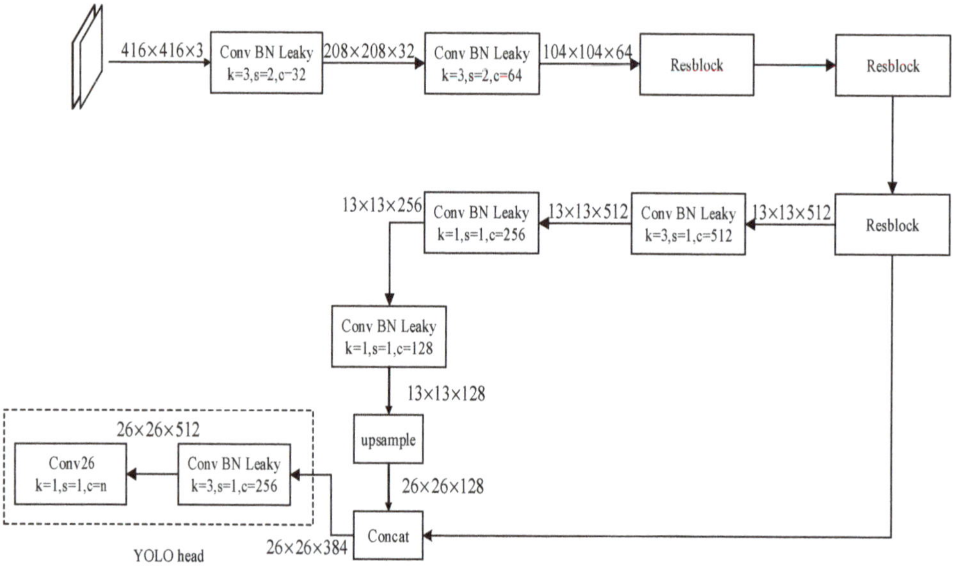

Figure 4. Improved YOLOv4-tiny network structure.

Experiments will be used to validate the hypothesis that the size of the detection targets remains fixed relative to the image.

2.2.2. Anchor Box Optimization

The original YOLOv4-tiny model has problems such as inaccurate localization in track fastener defect detection tasks due to its utilization of default anchor boxes. The default anchor boxes in YOLOv4-tiny are generated through clustering analysis conducted on the COCO dataset, which predominantly consists of object categories commonly encountered in everyday scenarios. Consequently, the anchor boxes obtained from this process may not be optimally tailored for the track fasteners, leading to issues such as inaccurate localization in detection tasks.

To improve the accuracy of the model in detecting track fasteners, this study obtained new anchor box parameters from proprietary datasets. We employed the K-means++ algorithm to conduct clustering analysis on the fastener dataset to obtain new anchor box parameters. Compared to the K-means algorithm, the K-means++ algorithm optimizes the selection of initial cluster centers by maximizing the distance between K initial cluster centers as much as possible, effectively improving clustering efficiency. The steps of the K-means++ algorithm are as follows:

Step 1: Randomly select a sample from dataset N as the first cluster center.

Step 2: Compute the distance $D(x)$ from each sample x to the nearest existing cluster center and calculate the probability $P(x)$ of each sample being identified as the next cluster center using the following formula:

$$IoU = \frac{A \cap B}{A \cup B} \quad (3)$$

$$D(x) = 1 - IoU \quad (4)$$

$$P(x) = \frac{D(x)^2}{\sum_{x \in N} D(x)^2} \quad (5)$$

where IoU denotes the degree of matching between the anchor box and the labeled box. Select the sample with the maximum value of $P(x)$ as the next cluster center.

Step 3: Repeat step 2 until k cluster centers have been selected.

Step 4: Utilize the K-means algorithm to obtain new anchor box parameters.

The original and the new parameters of the anchor boxes are shown in Table 1.

Table 1. The original and the new parameters of the anchor boxes.

Algorithm	Anchor Box
YOLOv4-tiny	[(10, 14) (23, 27) (37, 58)] [(81, 82) (135, 169) (344, 319)]
K-means++	[(25, 27) (34, 48) (55, 73)]

2.3. *Hardware Platforms*

2.3.1. Comparison of Hardware Platforms

Currently, almost all deep learning algorithms run on GPUs. This is because GPUs offer powerful computational capabilities, and frameworks like PyTorch provide convenience for researchers in their studies. However, the powerful computational capabilities of GPUs also come with drawbacks such as large size and high power consumption. As mentioned earlier, we plan to utilize UAVs for track fastener defect detection. Therefore, we require a lightweight, low-power, high-performance real-time computing platform.

We have noticed that an increasing number of researchers are choosing field-programmable gate arrays (FPGAs) as deployment platforms for deep learning models. Compared to GPUs, FPGAs offer advantages such as programmability, flexibility, and low power consumption. With Xilinx's introduction of the deep learning processing unit (DPU), FPGAs can also provide high-performance inference for deep learning models.

In conclusion, FPGAs were chosen as the hardware platform for our algorithm.

2.3.2. The ZCU104 Development Platform

The hardware development platform used in this paper is the Zynq Ultrascale+ MPSoC ZCU104 development platform from Xilinx. The ZCU104 development board is shown in Figure 5. The ZCU104 is a high-performance development platform suitable for various embedded systems and application scenarios, such as artificial intelligence, video processing, network communication, and industrial control. The ZCU104 platform employs the ZU7EV chip, which includes a quad-core ARM Cortex™-A53 processor and a dual-core Cortex-R5 processor, with a CPU frequency of 1200 MHz.

Figure 5. The ZCU104 development board.

The hardware development platform resources also include 312 Block RAMs (BRAMs) for data storage, 1728 digital signal processors (DSPs) for digital signal processing and algorithm acceleration, 230,400 look-up tables (LUTs) for executing logic operations, and 460,800 flip-flops (FFs) for storing state information.

2.3.3. Hardware Platform Development

The development process on the ZCU104 platform is shown in Figure 6.

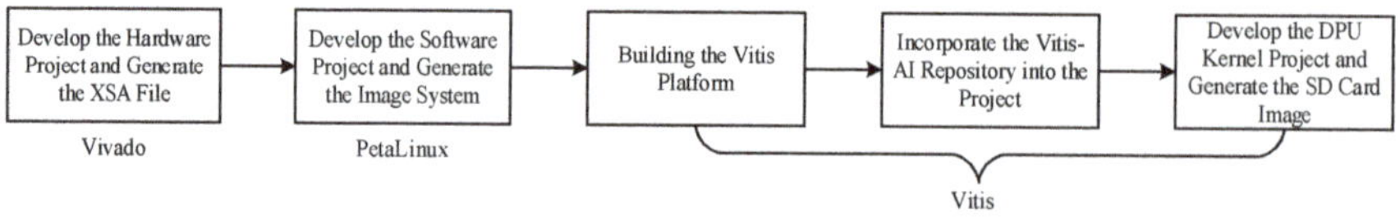

Figure 6. The development process on the ZCU104 platform.

The hardware project was developed on the Vivado 2021.1 platform. We utilized the Zynq UltraScale + MPSoC IP module from the Zynq series, alongside the board preset for ZCU104. This IP module is shown in Figure 7. After configuring all of the ports, an XSA file was generated. The XSA file contained all of the hardware information.

Figure 7. ZCU104 IP module.

PetaLinux is a specialized development platform designed for embedded Linux system development, introduced by Xilinx. This platform enables the configuration of the Linux kernel, device tree, and root file system (rootfs). We utilized PetaLinux 2021.2 and the XSA file to generate a Linux image system that incorporates the required dependency library files. Subsequent development will be based on this customized Linux system.

Vitis is a software development platform introduced by Xilinx, designed to simplify the software development process on FPGAs. It offers a unified software development environment. After building the Vitis platform and incorporating the Vitis-AI repository, we developed the DPU kernel project. The DPU is a hardware accelerator dedicated to deep learning inference tasks, introduced by Xilinx. Its primary objective is to expedite the inference computations of deep learning models, including convolutional neural networks (CNNs). The top-level architecture of the DPU is shown in Figure 8.

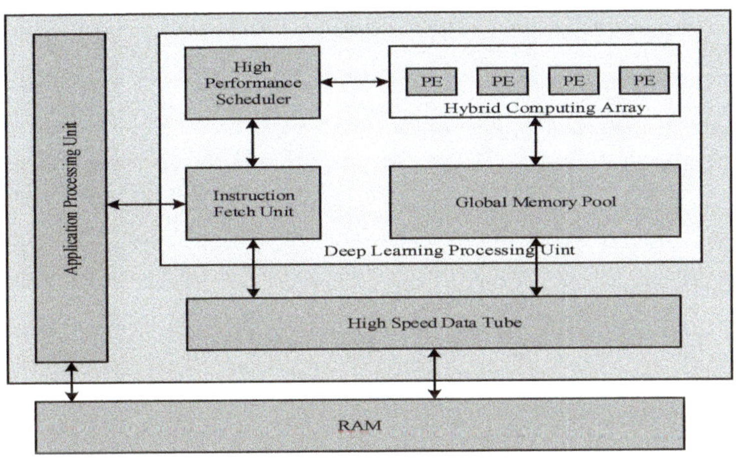

Figure 8. The top-level architecture of the DPU.

A DPU module with model number B4096 was utilized in this paper. With UltraRAM enabled, the ZCU104 platform supports a maximum of two B4096 modules.

Finally, we packaged all of the files into an SD card image.

2.4. Model Transformation

After completing hardware platform development, it is necessary to transform the trained network model to enable forward inference on the hardware platform. The process of model transformation is shown in Figure 9.

Vitis-AI is a development platform aimed at AI acceleration, introduced by Xilinx. It offers a comprehensive set of tools and libraries to assist developers in converting various deep learning models into formats suitable for FPGA deployment, while also accelerating deep learning inference tasks. Following the process shown in Figure 9, we utilized the Vitis-AI 1.4 platform to quantize and compile our model, transforming it into an Xmodel file executable on the hardware platform.

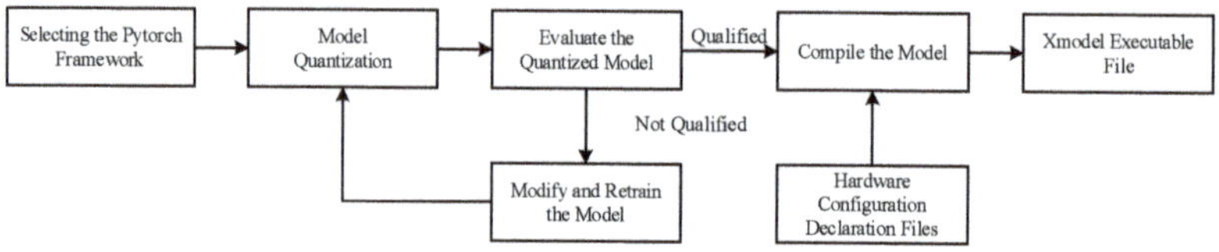

Figure 9. The process of model transformation.

3. Experimental Results

3.1. Dataset

The dataset used in this paper was collected using a line laser camera, comprising a total of 2000 images with a resolution of 800 × 1261 pixels. After removing distorted and blurry images, 1100 images were obtained. Each image contained approximately 6 to 12 fasteners, with a total of approximately 8000 fasteners. Approximately 200 images contained abnormal fasteners. The dataset comprises two distinct categories of fasteners, denoted Class A and Class B, alongside their respective abnormal counterparts, labeled Class A–F and Class B–F.

3.2. Experimental Setting

The experimental environment was configured with Windows 10 as the operating system, NVIDIA GeForce RTX 3070 as the GPU model with 8 G of video memory, Python 3.8 as the compilation language, Pytorch 1.8.0 as the deep learning framework, CUDA 10.2 as the CUDA version, and ZCU104 development platform as the hardware platform. The training parameters were set as follows: the initial learning rate was 0.001, the momentum parameter was 0.9, the weight decay factor was 0.0005, the input image size was 416 × 416, and the Batch Size was 16. A total of 200 epochs were trained using stochastic gradient descent (SGD) for the whole training process.

Figure 10 shows the comparison of loss curves, where the red curve represents the loss curve of the YOLOv4-tiny algorithm, and the blue curve represents the loss curve of the Improved YOLOv4-tiny algorithm. Lower loss values during training indicate better training results. From Figure 10, it can be observed that the loss value of the Improved YOLOv4-tiny algorithm is lower than that of the YOLOv4-tiny algorithm after 75 epochs.

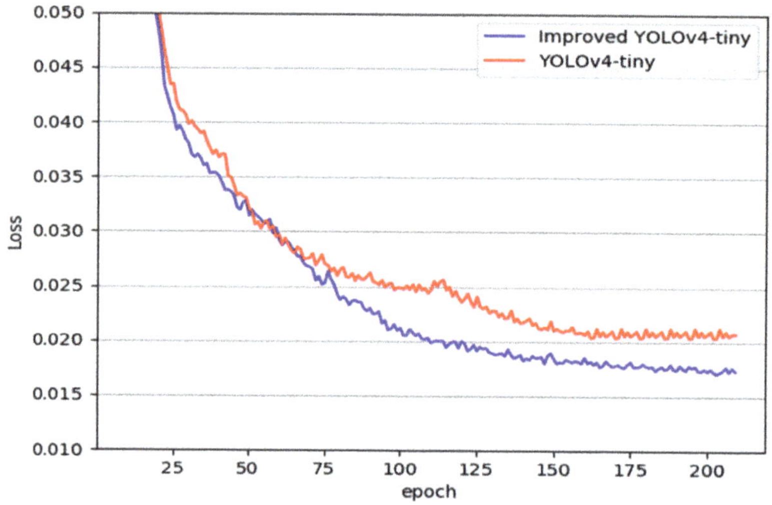

Figure 10. Comparison of loss curves.

3.3. Evaluation Indicators

In this paper, we evaluated the performance of the algorithms according to two aspects, detection accuracy and detection speed, using evaluation methods commonly employed for target detection algorithms.

Detection accuracy evaluation metrics comprise recall, false detection, and mean average precision (mAP).

In the field of object detection, TP denotes the number of positive samples detected correctly, FP denotes the number of positive samples detected incorrectly, TN denotes the number of negative samples detected correctly, and FN denotes the number of negative samples detected incorrectly. All of the metrics are calculated when $IoU = 0.5$.

Recall, denoted by R, is the probability that the model correctly identifies a positive sample in a single category. It is defined as follows:

$$R = \frac{TP}{TP + FN} \tag{6}$$

False detection, denoted by FPR, is the probability that the model incorrectly identifies a negative sample as a positive sample in a single category. It is defined as follows:

$$FPR = \frac{FP}{FP + TN} \tag{7}$$

High R and low FPR are required for the task of track fastener defect detection.

The mAP is the area enclosed by the precision and recall curves. It is an overall network performance evaluation metric considering precision and recall [39]. Therefore, mAP is a more authoritative metric in model performance evaluation, and a larger mAP value represents higher detection precision. It is defined as follows:

$$AP = \int_0^1 P{\cdot}RdR \tag{8}$$

$$mAP = \frac{1}{N}\sum_{i=1}^{N} AP_i \tag{9}$$

where N is the number of categories in the dataset and P is precision, which denotes the probability that the model detects correctly in a single category. It is defined as follows:

$$P = \frac{TP}{TP + FP} \tag{10}$$

The detection speed is evaluated in terms of frames per second (FPS), the number of frames per second that the model processes for the image.

3.4. Experiments on the GPU

3.4.1. Ablation Experiments

We conducted ablation experiments for the two improvements proposed in this paper. We modified YOLOv4-tiny to output single-scale feature maps and then replaced the original anchor boxes with anchor boxes optimized using the K-means++ algorithm. The final results are shown in Table 2.

The experimental results indicate that single-scale feature output can significantly improve detection speed, increasing from 316.3 FPS to 521.9 FPS. However, there was a decrease in mAP by 1.8%, and the FPR for each class of fasteners also increased.

Table 2. Comparison of the results of the ablation experiments.

Network Model	Class	R/%	FPR/%	mAP/%	FPS
YOLOv4-tiny	A	75.0	12.9	90.5	336.3
	B	91.7	0		
YOLOv4-tiny + Single-Scale Feature Output	A	72.6	13.3	88.7	554.9
	B	89.8	0.9		
YOLOv4-tiny + Single-Scale Feature Output + Anchor Box Optimization (Improved YOLOv4-tiny)	A	86.1	3.1	95.8	554.9
	B	100	0		

The experimental results also indicate that optimizing the anchor boxes significantly improves detection performance. The Improved YOLOv4-tiny model achieved a 5.3% increase in mAP compared to YOLOv4-tiny. This validates our previous hypothesis that the relative size of detected objects remains consistent with respect to the image.

3.4.2. Comparison Experiments

To further validate the detection performance of the improved model, the model in this paper was compared with the existing mainstream target detection algorithms Faster R-CNN and SSD. The experiments were conducted in the same hardware and software environment, as well as with identical training and testing parameters. The experimental results are shown in Table 3.

Table 3. Performance comparison of various target detection algorithms.

Network Model	Class	R/%	FPR/%	mAP/%	FPS
Faster R-CNN	A	77.5	13.6	90.6	10.7
	B	88.3	0		
SSD	A	82.0	5.8	93.4	30.3
	B	99.5	0		
YOLOv4-tiny	A	75.0	12.9	90.5	336.3
	B	91.7	0		
Improved YOLOv4-tiny	A	86.1	3.1	95.8	554.9
	B	100	0		

This can be seen based on the data in Table 3. In terms of the mAP metric, Improved YOLOv4-tiny achieved the best performance, reaching 95.8%. Compared to Faster R-CNN, SSD, and YOLOv4-tiny, the improved model's mAP increased by 5.2%, 2.4%, and 5.3%, respectively. In terms of the false positive rate (FPR) metric, Improved YOLOv4-tiny also achieved the best performance, with a rate of 3.1% for Class A fasteners. This is lower than the rates achieved by Faster R-CNN, SSD, and YOLOv4-tiny, which were 13.6%, 5.8%, and 12.9%, respectively. In terms of detection speed, Improved YOLOv4-tiny also achieved the best performance, reaching 554.9 FPS. Compared to Faster R-CNN, SSD, and YOLOv4-tiny, the improved model's speed increased by 544.2 FPS, 524.6 FPS, and 218.6 FPS, respectively. In summary, compared to other target detection models, the Improved YOLOv4-tiny model in this paper outperformed in terms of detection accuracy, detection error rate, and detection speed.

3.5. Experiments on the FPGA

To validate the detection performance of our algorithm on the ZCU104 development platform, we compared both the improved model and the original model after transformation. In the experiment, we utilized two DPU modules with the model number B4096 and set their frequency to 300 MHz. Furthermore, we attempted to improve the detection speed by employing parallel processing techniques. The experimental results are shown in Table 4.

Table 4. Performance comparison of algorithms on the FPGA.

Network Model	Class	R/%	FPR/%	mAP/%	Thread	FPS
YOLOv4-tiny	A	75.0	6.9	89.5	1	70.9
	B	87.5	0		8	179.6
Improved YOLOv4-tiny	A	83.3	3.23	95.1	1	84.2
	B	100	0		8	295.9

This can be seen based on the data in Table 4. In terms of the mAP metric, the Improved YOLOv4-tiny achieved 95.1% on the FPGA, which was 5.6% higher than the original YOLOv4-tiny. In terms of detection speed, the Improved YOLOv4-tiny achieved 295.9 FPS on the FPGA, which was 116.3 FPS higher than the original YOLOv4-tiny. Additionally, parallel processing significantly improved detection efficiency compared to single-thread processing.

3.6. Experimental Comparison of Different Platforms

To validate the FPGA platform as more suitable for practical engineering, we compared the results across the two hardware platforms. The experimental results are shown in Table 5.

Table 5. Performance comparison of the algorithm on the GPU and FPGA.

Network Model	Hardware Platform	mAP/%	FPS	Power Consumption/W
Improved YOLOv4-tiny	GeForce RTX 3070	95.8	554.9	235
Improved YOLOv4-tiny	ZCU104	95.1	295.9	20

This can be seen based on the data in Table 5. In terms of the mAP metric, the performance of the improved model on the FPGA was 0.7% lower than on the GPU. This is attributed to the quantization of model parameters during the model transformation process, resulting in slight precision loss. However, an mAP of 95.1% still meets engineering requirements. In terms of detection speed, the improved model achieved 295.9 FPS on the FPGA, which was lower than the 554.9 FPS achieved on the GPU. However, it still met the real-time requirements in practical engineering applications. In terms of power consumption, the improved model's power consumption on the FPGA was 25 W, significantly lower than the 235 W on the GPU.

In summary, the improved model achieved sufficiently good detection accuracy and speed on the FPGA with very low power consumption. Compared to the GPU platform, the FPGA platform is more suitable for meeting the requirements of track fastener defect detection tasks.

3.7. Visualization of Detection Results

The visualization of detection results is important in practical applications. Figure 11 shows the detection results of the improved model. It can be observed from Figure 11 that the algorithm exhibits excellent recognition performance for both types of fasteners, with the bounding boxes' positions and sizes matching the actual objects. Additionally, the confidence scores for both positive and negative samples are very high, meeting the requirements of practical detection.

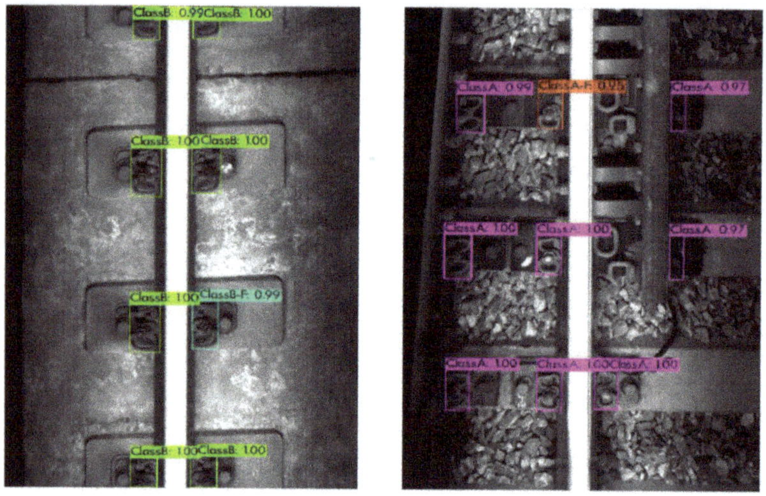

Figure 11. Visualization of detection results.

4. Conclusions

This paper addresses the issues of low efficiency in current track fastener detection algorithms and the lack of lightweight and low-power hardware platforms suitable for practical engineering applications. We constructed our own dataset of track fasteners, proposed an improved model based on YOLOv4-tiny, and deployed the transformed model on an FPGA hardware platform. Considering the dataset characteristics, the model was improved to achieve single-scale feature output, significantly enhancing detection speed. Additionally, to improve detection accuracy, we employed the K-means++ algorithm to cluster the dataset and obtain more suitable anchor boxes. Finally, we developed and deployed the model on the FPGA platform. The experimental results demonstrate that the improved model achieves an mAP of 95.1% and a speed of 295.9 FPS on the FPGA, surpassing the performance of the original YOLOv4-tiny. Moreover, the power consumption of the FPGA platform is 20 W, much lower than that of the GPU platform, meeting the requirements for UAVs carrying detection equipment.

Our improved model has been specifically designed for the fastener types in this dataset and may not be suitable for recognizing other types of fasteners. Additionally, considering the support provided by the Vitis development tools for YOLOv4 series algorithms on the ZCU104 platform, we chose to improve YOLOv4-tiny instead of applying the latest YOLO versions. In the future, we plan to expand the dataset scope and explore the application potential of the latest algorithms on FPGA platforms to optimize and extend our model, making it adaptable to a wider range of fastener types and detection environments.

Author Contributions: Conceptualization, Q.Y. and A.L.; methodology, Q.Y.; investigation, Q.Y. and A.L.; writing—original draft, Q.Y.; writing—review and editing, X.Y. and W.D.; supervision, X.Y. and W.D.; project administration, Q.Y., A.L., X.Y. and W.D. All authors have read and agreed to the published version of the manuscript.

Funding: This research received no external funding.

Data Availability Statement: You can use this link to download the dataset: https://github.com/Yuqi1998/FastenerDataset (accessed on 26 April 2024).

Conflicts of Interest: The authors declare no conflicts of interest.

References

1. Xiang, J.; Yuan, C.; Yu, C.; Lin, S.; Yang, H. Analysis of Elastic Bar Fracture Causes of Fasteners in Ballastless Track of High-Speed Railway. *J. Rail Way Sci. Eng.* **2019**, *16*, 1605–1613.
2. Wei, X.; Yang, Z.; Liu, Y.; Wei, D.; Jia, L.; Li, Y. Railway Track Fastener Defect Detection Based on Image Processing and Deep Learning Techniques: A Comparative Study. *Eng. Appl. Artif. Intell.* **2019**, *80*, 66–81. [CrossRef]
3. Bono, F.M.; Radicioni, L.; Cinquemani, S.; Benedetti, L.; Cazzulani, G.; Somaschini, C.; Belloli, M. A Deep Learning Approach to Detect Failures in Bridges Based on the Coherence of Signals. *Future Internet* **2023**, *15*, 119. [CrossRef]
4. Chellaswamy, C.; Krishnasamy, M.; Balaji, L.; Dhanalakshmi, A.; Ramesh, R. Optimized Railway Track Health Monitoring System Based on Dynamic Differential Evolution Algorithm. *Measurement* **2020**, *152*, 107332. [CrossRef]
5. Zhan, Z.; Sun, H.; Yu, X.; Yu, J.; Zhao, Y.; Sha, X.; Chen, Y.; Huang, Q.; Li, W.J. Wireless Rail Fastener Looseness Detection Based on MEMS Accelerometer and Vibration Entropy. *IEEE Sens. J.* **2020**, *20*, 3226–3234. [CrossRef]
6. Mao, Q.; Cui, H.; Hu, Q.; Ren, X. A Rigorous Fastener Inspection Approach for High-Speed Railway from Structured Light Sensors. *ISPRS J. Photogramm. Remote Sens.* **2018**, *143*, 249–267. [CrossRef]
7. Damljanović, V.; Weaver, R.L. Laser Vibrometry Technique for Measurement of Contained Stress in Railroad Rail. *J. Sound Vib.* **2005**, *282*, 341–366. [CrossRef]
8. Guerrieri, M.; Parla, G.; Celauro, C. Digital Image Analysis Technique for Measuring Railway Track Defects and Ballast Gradation. *Measurement* **2018**, *113*, 137–147. [CrossRef]
9. Khan, R.A.; Islam, S.; Biswas, R. Automatic Detection of Defective Rail Anchors. In Proceedings of the 17th International IEEE Conference on Intelligent Transportation Systems (ITSC), Qingdao, China, 8–11 October 2014; pp. 1583–1588.
10. Feng, H.; Jiang, Z.; Xie, F.; Yang, P.; Shi, J.; Chen, L. Automatic Fastener Classification and Defect Detection in Vision-Based Railway Inspection Systems. *IEEE Trans. Instrum. Meas.* **2014**, *63*, 877–888. [CrossRef]
11. Gibert, X.; Patel, V.M.; Chellappa, R. Sequential Score Adaptation with Extreme Value Theory for Robust Railway Track Inspection. *arXiv* **2015**, arXiv:1510.05822.
12. Gibert, X.; Patel, V.M.; Chellappa, R. Deep Multitask Learning for Railway Track Inspection. *IEEE Trans. Intell. Transp. Syst.* **2017**, *18*, 153–164. [CrossRef]
13. Wang, Z.; Wang, S. *Research of Method for Detection of Rail Fastener Defects Based on Machine Vision*; Atlantis Press: Amstelkade, The Netherland, 2015.
14. Girshick, R.; Donahue, J.; Darrell, T.; Malik, J. Rich Feature Hierarchies for Accurate Object Detection and Semantic Segmentation. *arXiv* **2014**, arXiv:1311.2524.
15. Girshick, R. Fast R-CNN. *arXiv* **2015**, arXiv:1504.08083.
16. Ren, S.; He, K.; Girshick, R.; Sun, J. Faster R-CNN: Towards Real-Time Object Detection with Region Proposal Networks. *IEEE Trans. Pattern Anal. Mach. Intell.* **2017**, *39*, 1137–1149. [CrossRef] [PubMed]
17. Liu, W.; Anguelov, D.; Erhan, D.; Szegedy, C.; Reed, S.; Fu, C.-Y.; Berg, A.C. SSD: Single Shot MultiBox Detector. In *Proceedings of the Computer Vision—ECCV 2016, Amsterdam, The Netherlands, 11–14 October 2016*; Leibe, B., Matas, J., Sebe, N., Welling, M., Eds.; Springer International Publishing: Cham, Switzerland, 2016; pp. 21–37.
18. Redmon, J.; Divvala, S.; Girshick, R.; Farhadi, A. You Only Look Once: Unified, Real-Time Object Detection. *arXiv* **2016**, arXiv:1506.02640.
19. Redmon, J.; Farhadi, A. YOLO9000: Better, Faster, Stronger. In Proceedings of the 2017 IEEE Conference on Computer Vision and Pattern Recognition (CVPR), Honolulu, HI, USA, 21–26 July 2017; pp. 7263–7271.
20. Redmon, J.; Farhadi, A. YOLOv3: An Incremental Improvement. *arXiv* **2018**, arXiv:1804.02767.
21. Bochkovskiy, A.; Wang, C. Y.; Liao, H.-Y.M. YOLOv4: Optimal Speed and Accuracy of Object Detection. *arXiv* **2020**, arXiv:2004.10934.
22. Wang, C.-Y.; Bochkovskiy, A.; Liao, H.-Y.M. YOLOv7: Trainable Bag-of-Freebies Sets New State-of-the-Art for Real-Time Object Detectors. *arXiv* **2023**, arXiv:2207.02696.
23. Qi, H.; Xu, T.; Wang, G.; Cheng, Y.; Chen, C. MYOLOv3-Tiny: A New Convolutional Neural Network Architecture for Real-Time Detection of Track Fasteners. *Comput. Ind.* **2020**, *123*, 103303. [CrossRef]
24. Fu, J.; Chen, X.; Lv, Z. Rail Fastener Status Detection Based on MobileNet-YOLOv4. *Electronics* **2022**, *11*, 3677. [CrossRef]
25. Li, X.; Wang, Q.; Yang, X.; Wang, K.; Zhang, H. Track Fastener Defect Detection Model Based on Improved YOLOv5s. *Sensors* **2023**, *23*, 6457. [CrossRef] [PubMed]
26. Wang, L.; Zang, Q.; Zhang, K.; Wu, L. A Rail Fastener Defect Detection Algorithm Based on Improved YOLOv5. *Proc. Inst. Mech. Eng. Part F J. Rail Rapid Transit* **2024**, 09544097241234380. [CrossRef]
27. Qin, Z.; Wang, W.; Dammer, K.-H.; Guo, L.; Cao, Z. Ag-YOLO: A Real-Time Low-Cost Detector for Precise Spraying with Case Study of Palms. *Front. Plant Sci.* **2021**, *12*, 753603. [CrossRef] [PubMed]
28. Han, P.; Ma, C.; Chen, J.; Chen, L.; Bu, S.; Xu, S.; Zhao, Y.; Zhang, C.; Hagino, T. Fast Tree Detection and Counting on UAVs for Sequential Aerial Images with Generating Orthophoto Mosaicing. *Remote Sens.* **2022**, *14*, 4113. [CrossRef]
29. Tilon, S.; Nex, F.; Vosselman, G.; Sevilla de la Llave, I.; Kerle, N. Towards Improved Unmanned Aerial Vehicle Edge Intelligence: A Road Infrastructure Monitoring Case Study. *Remote Sens.* **2022**, *14*, 4008. [CrossRef]
30. Balamuralidhar, N.; Tilon, S.; Nex, F. MultEYE: Monitoring System for Real-Time Vehicle Detection, Tracking and Speed Estimation from UAV Imagery on Edge-Computing Platforms. *Remote Sens.* **2021**, *13*, 573. [CrossRef]

31. Luo, W.; Han, W.; Fu, P.; Wang, H.; Zhao, Y.; Liu, K.; Liu, Y.; Zhao, Z.; Zhu, M.; Xu, R.; et al. A Water Surface Contaminants Monitoring Method Based on Airborne Depth Reasoning. *Processes* **2022**, *10*, 131. [CrossRef]
32. Liu, C.; Liu, Y.; Wu, H.; Dong, R. A Safe Flight Approach of the UAV in the Electrical Line Inspection. *Int. J. Emerg. Electr. Power Syst.* **2015**, *16*, 503–515. [CrossRef]
33. Rau, J.Y.; Hsiao, K.W.; Jhan, J.P.; Wang, S.H.; Fang, W.C.; Wang, J.L. Bridge Crack Detection Using Multi-Rotary UAV and Object-Base Image Analysis. *Int. Arch. Photogramm. Remote Sens. Spat. Inf. Sci.* **2017**, *XLII-2-W6*, 311–318. [CrossRef]
34. Wu, Y.; Qin, Y.; Wang, Z.; Jia, L. A UAV-Based Visual Inspection Method for Rail Surface Defects. *Appl. Sci.* **2018**, *8*, 1028. [CrossRef]
35. Banić, M.; Miltenović, A.; Pavlović, M.; Ćirić, I. Intelligent Machine Vision Based Railway Infrastructure Inspection and Monitoring Using UAV. *Facta Univ. Ser. Mech. Eng.* **2019**, *17*, 357–364. [CrossRef]
36. Nex, F.; Armenakis, C.; Cramer, M.; Cucci, D.A.; Gerke, M.; Honkavaara, E.; Kukko, A.; Persello, C.; Skaloud, J. UAV in the Advent of the Twenties: Where We Stand and What Is Next. *ISPRS J. Photogramm. Remote Sens.* **2022**, *184*, 215–242. [CrossRef]
37. Zhu, J.; Wang, L.; Liu, H.; Tian, S.; Deng, Q.; Li, J. An Efficient Task Assignment Framework to Accelerate DPU-Based Convolutional Neural Network Inference on FPGAs. *IEEE Access* **2020**, *8*, 83224–83237. [CrossRef]
38. Dobai, R.; Sekanina, L. Towards Evolvable Systems Based on the Xilinx Zynq Platform. In Proceedings of the 2013 IEEE International Conference on Evolvable Systems (ICES), Singapore, 16–19 April 2013; pp. 89–95.
39. Padilla, R.; Netto, S.L.; da Silva, E.A.B. A Survey on Performance Metrics for Object-Detection Algorithms. In Proceedings of the 2020 International Conference on Systems, Signals and Image Processing (IWSSIP), Niteroi, Brazil, 1–3 July 2020; pp. 237–242.

MDPI AG
Grosspeteranlage 5
4052 Basel
Switzerland
Tel.: +41 61 683 77 34

Electronics Editorial Office
E-mail: electronics@mdpi.com
www.mdpi.com/journal/electronics

www.ingramcontent.com/pod-product-compliance
Lightning Source LLC
Chambersburg PA
CBHW061454210926
51850CB00008B/1711